Micro-institutional Foundations of Capitalism

What is the relationship between internal development and integration into the global economy in developing countries? How and why do state–market relations differ? And do these differences matter in the post-cold war era of global conflict and cooperation? Drawing on research in China, India, and Russia and examining sectors from textiles to telecommunications, *Micro-institutional Foundations of Capitalism* introduces a new theory of sectoral pathways to globalization and development. Adopting a historical and comparative approach, the book's Strategic Value Framework shows how state elites perceive the strategic value of sectors in response to internal and external pressures. Sectoral structures and organization of institutions further determine the role of the state in market coordination and property rights arrangements. The resultant dominant patterns of market governance vary by country and sector within country. These national configurations of sectoral models are the micro-institutional foundations of capitalism, which mediate globalization and development.

ROSELYN HSUEH is an associate professor of political science at Temple University. She is the author of *China's Regulatory State: A New Strategy for Globalization* (Cornell University Press, 2011) and scholarly articles and book chapters on states and markets, comparative regulation and governance, international political economy, and political economy of development. She is the recipient of the Fulbright Global Scholar Award and other prestigious fellowships for international fieldwork. She is a frequent commentator on politics, finance and trade, and economic development in China and beyond. The BBC World News, *The Economist*, *Foreign Affairs*, *Foreign Policy*, National Public Radio, and *The Washington Post*, among other media outlets, have featured her research.

T0381662

Micro-institutional Foundations of Capitalism

Sectoral Pathways to Globalization in China, India, and Russia

ROSELYN HSUEH

Temple University

CAMBRIDGE
UNIVERSITY PRESS

University Printing House, Cambridge CB2 8BS, United Kingdom

One Liberty Plaza, 20th Floor, New York, NY 10006, USA

477 Williamstown Road, Port Melbourne, VIC 3207, Australia

314–321, 3rd Floor, Plot 3, Splendor Forum, Jasola District Centre,
New Delhi – 110025, India

103 Penang Road, #05-06/07, Visioncrest Commercial, Singapore 238467

Cambridge University Press is part of the University of Cambridge.

It furthers the University's mission by disseminating knowledge in the pursuit of
education, learning, and research at the highest international levels of excellence.

www.cambridge.org
Information on this title: www.cambridge.org/9781108472135
DOI: 10.1017/9781108593441

First published 2022

A catalogue record for this publication is available from the British Library.

Library of Congress Cataloging-in-Publication Data
NAMES: Hsueh, Roselyn, 1977- author.
TITLE: Micro-institutional foundations of capitalism : sectoral pathways to globalization in
China, India, and Russia / Roselyn Hsueh, Temple University, Philadelphia/
DESCRIPTION: Cambridge, United Kingdom ; New York, NY : Cambridge University Press,
2022. | Includes bibliographical references and index.
IDENTIFIERS: LCCN 2021044774 (print) | LCCN 2021044775 (ebook) |
ISBN 9781108472135 (hardback) | ISBN 9781108459037 (paperback) |
ISBN 9781108593441 (epub)
SUBJECTS: LCSH: Capitalism–Political aspects–China. | Capitalism–Political aspects–India. |
Capitalism–Political aspects–Russia (Federation) | Globalization–Economic aspects–China. |
Globalization–Economic aspects–India. | Globalization–Economic aspects–Russia
(Federation) | Post-communism–Economic aspects.
CLASSIFICATION: LCC HC427.95 .H78 2022 (print) | LCC HC427.95 (ebook) |
DDC 338.9/0091724–dc23/eng/20211119

LC record available at https://lccn.loc.gov/2021044774
LC ebook record available at https://lccn.loc.gov/2021044775

ISBN 978-1-108-47213-5 Hardback
ISBN 978-1-108-45903-7 Paperback

To my wonderful family, without you none of this would be worth it.

Contents

Figures

Tables

Acknowledgments

This book was completed during the COVID-19 global pandemic, which has disrupted the countries, economies, and peoples examined in it. *Micro-institutional Foundations of Capitalism*'s longitudinal and comparative sectoral approach empowers the conclusion that the *national configurations of sectoral models* identified in the book will witness incremental change. The pandemic reinforces the complex interdependence of the dominant patterns of market governance at the sectoral level, revealing the intersubjectivity of our values and organization of institutions.

In the protracted journey of writing *Micro-institutional Foundations of Capitalism*, I am indebted to many colleagues and friends, who inspired me, took the time to talk with me, and engaged my ideas even when they disagreed. Importantly, I am grateful to informants in the field whose insights about their positions and their contexts helped to hone my understanding. Moreover, several academic institutions provided the resources undergirding this ambitious project. I claim full responsibility for any of the mistakes. Below I name some of the peoples and institutions, who aided in the germination, research, analysis, and writing of the book.

I first became interested in the questions probed in *Micro-institutional Foundations of Capitalism* during my first semester of graduate school at the University of California, Berkeley. In the late Kiren Chaudhry's doctoral seminar Political Economy of Development and Underdevelopment, we debated the seeming contradictions of internal state-society relations, the timing and scope of insertion into the global economy, and the state's capacity in late development. Investigating the how, the why, and the implications of China's global economic integration in the context of authoritarian rule felt urgent. Thus was born my first book *China's Regulatory State: A New Strategy for Globalization*, on which this book builds and extends. *China's Regulatory State* was the first to identify China's strategic use of economic liberalization and reregulation to enhance state control of markets.

During my fieldwork for *China's Regulatory State*, I flew to Delhi from Beijing with several friends to travel across India. The stark differences between the capitals of the world's most populated countries, although internally logical with value-bounded rationality I contend in *Micro-institutional Foundations of Capitalism*, left a strong impression. It wasn't just the sparkling clean and manicured ring roads of Beijing, a few decades of globalization and development in the making; and the cacophony of cycle rickshaws in Delhi's narrow alleyways in the largest democracy on the globe. The foreboding concrete buildings on Yanan Road housing State Council ministries and the buzzing meetings between foreign investors, Chinese manufacturers, and sector associations at trade fairs had struck a sharp contrast back in Beijing. Now, so did the Public Tele Info Centers (PTICs) run by enterprising private entrepreneurs selling the mobile subscriptions of foreign-invested and domestic telecommunications carriers; and the textile wallas lining the streets of Gurgaon. During that first trip, Lilli-Anne Suzuki endured my nightly musings, including comparing the handlooms and power looms in Rajasthan to the textile combines and garment factories producing high-tech Uniqlo apparel in Suzhou. I also remember placing a phone call near Agra to Jennifer Bussell at a kiosk in one of those PTICs.

After the publication of *China's Regulatory State*, I began to earnestly conduct the research necessary for this book. I am grateful to Ashok Bardhan and Pranab Bardhan for initial introductions to academics and key informants in India. I benefited from the insights of Pradip Baijal, Rajat Kathuria, and S.D. Saxena, among others. Many thanks to the generosity of the Ahuja and Arora families, Vasundhara Sirnate, Suchi Sengupta, and Adnan Farooqui. Steve Fish, Theo Grigoriadis, and Susanne Wengle provided initial introductions for fieldwork in Russia. I very much appreciated the insights of Fuad Aleskerov, Olga Bychkova, Oleg Kharkhordin, and Andrei Yakovlev. Many others who shall remain anonymous also facilitated my research trips. My institutional hosts were, in Beijing, the Institute of World Economics and Politics, Chinese Academy of Social Sciences; in Delhi, the Center for Policy Research, and in Moscow, the Higher School of Economics.

Fellowships and grants from Temple University, the University of California, Berkeley, the University of Pennsylvania, and the Fulbright Foundation supported research and writing. I am grateful to the following academic institutions, which hosted conferences, presentations, talks, and workshops, where I received critical and helpful feedback. I presented at the annual meetings and conferences of the American Political Science Association, Association of Asian Studies, International Studies Association, and Law and Society Association. I shared research findings at Academia Sinica, American University, Brown University, Cornell University, Georgetown University, George Washington University, Harvard University, Johns Hopkins University, National Taiwan University, Tecnológico de Monterrey, Tsinghua University School of Public Policy and Management, the University of British Columbia, the University of California, Berkeley, the University of Michigan, the University of Pennsylvania, the University of Southern California, and the University of Texas, Austin. Special thanks to the Perry World House at Penn for the visiting fellowship, which granted me the time and space to begin the book writing process of this ambitious project.

At different stages of research and analysis, I received helpful advice and feedback from the following individuals, who are exonerated from any responsibility pertaining to the book's contents: Caroline Arnold, Celeste Arrington, Harley Balzer, Ashok Bardhan, Pranab Bardhan, Boris Barkanov, Jeb Barnes, Phil Cerny, Sanjoy Chakravorty, Jonathan Chu, Ruth Collier, Mark Dallas, Rich Deeg, Jacques deLisle, Martin Dimitrov, Rick Doner, Navorz Dubash, Henry Farrell, Adnan Farooqui, Orfeo Fioretos, Steve Fish, Mark Frazier, Mary Gallagher, Jane Gingrich, Avery Goldstein, Yoram Haftel, Emily Hannum, Justin Hastings, Kathy Hochstetler, Yue Hou, Mike Horowitz, Lily Hsueh, Bill Hurst, Nathan Jensen, Stephen Kaplan, Adrienne LeBas, Devesh Kapur, Peter Katzenstein, Moonhawk Kim, Atul Kohli, Genia Kostka, Jonathan Koppell, Paul Lagunes, Julie Lynch, Lauren MacLean, Andy Mertha, Sebastian Mazzuca, Rahul Mukherji, Mike Nelson, Abe Newman, Kevin O'Brien, Mitchell Orenstein, Louis Pauly, Tony Porter, Tom Remington, Maria Repnikova, Peter Rutland, Ryan Saylor, Suchi Sengupta, Ken Shadlen, Rudy Sil, Aseema Sinha, Dorie Solinger, Sandra Suarez, Adam Segal, Manny Teitelbaum, Eric Thun, Yves Tiberghien, Peter Trubowitz, Dali Yang, Steve Vogel, Yuval Weber, Yuhua Wang, Susanne Wengle, Tyrene White, Carol Wise, Yu-Shan Wu, Min Ye, Minyuan Zhao, and Yu Zheng.

Special thanks to Pranab Bardhan, Orfeo Fioretos, Rich Deeg, Rick Doner, Devesh Kapur, Peter Katzenstein, Kevin O'Brien, Rudy Sil, Dorie

Solinger, Steve Fish, Andy Mertha, and Steve Vogel for their inspiration, support and encouragement over the years. Terri Givens, the late Francis Rosenbluth, and Evelyn Simien also provided support and encouragement at crucial junctures. At Cambridge University Press, Robert Dreesen inquired early on if I had a book that CUP could publish. Rachel Blaifeder, Jadyn Fauconier-Herry, and Mark Fox shepherded the production process at CUP. Thank you to my research assistants: my doctoral students James Frick, Stephanie Kasparek, Felix Puemape, and Alyona Sokolova, and undergraduates Ismael Mahamane Bamba, Ben Dunbar, Rebecca Johnson, and Rachel Shifman.

At Temple University and in greater Philadelphia, these colleagues imparted academic camaraderie: Vin Arceneaux, Bill Burke-White, Sanjoy Chakravorty, Cary Coglianese, Hai-Lung Dai, Heath Davis, Rich Deeg, Jacques deLisle, Jennifer Dixon, Eileen Doherty-Sil, Tulia Falleti, Orfeo Fioretos, Avery Goldstein, Mauro Guillen, Alexandra Guisinger, Emily Hannum, Mike Horowitz, Devesh Kapur, Robin Kolodny, LaShawn Jefferson, Julie Lynch, Neysun Mahboubi, David Nickerson, Mitchell Orenstein, Mark Pollack, Toby Schulze-Cleven, Deb Seligsohn, Rudy Sil, Hillel Soifer, Sandra Suarez, Lynn White, Sean Yom, and Adam Zeigfeld. Thank you to Liz Spiegler and Intervarsity's Temple University faculty and staff fellowship for weekly virtual meetings during the pandemic.

My family and I are forever grateful to our "Philadelphia family," whose love and support sustained us. They are the Agran family, Delores Brisbon, Heewon Chang, the Daly's, David and Lisa Eckmann, Arthur and Joanne Frank, Linda Hanlon and Chris Lines, Jeffrey Halili and Jennifer Hsiung, Drew Harrison, Mindy Huffstetler, Mijin Kang, Dorothy and John Kwock, Nimisha Ladva, the Malaeb's, the St. Germain's, Debbie Tannebaum, Gina Thomas, and Jen Wang. Green Engine (and its cheerful staff) in Bryn Mawr fueled me with coffee and deliciousness. I also benefited from the encouragement and prayers of Aleatha Allen, Bob Cole, and Elaine Jones in the Bible class led by Delores Brisbon on Tuesdays in Old City; our GCC Family Group; and the late Mary and George Schneider of the First Presbyterian Church of Philadelphia. I coveted Dorothy Kwock's daily prayers and her gifts of Sweet Ashley's chocolate. A special shoutout to Regine St. Germain, my prayer partner through the years.

My husband Robbie Romano's love and commitment and our children's silliness and laughter incubated the writing of this book. Thank you to my identical twin sister Lily, a fellow academic, and her husband

Joseph for walking alongside Robbie and me. Dear friends from afar were Bonnie Henson, Jocelyn Kiley, Nonna Gorilovskaya, the late Linda McFatridge, Robin Turner, Rachel Van Sickle-Ward, and Peggy Sue Wright. From Berkeley, Bonnie Ho, Martha Kelley, and Susan Phillips provided counsel, prayers, and spiritual direction. During the pandemic we joined the virtual Sunday services of Doug Bunnell and his team at the Presbyterian Church of Bellingham.

The book's completion during the pandemic was punctuated with the most memorable family road trip across the country. The final push toward publication would not have been possible without the homecoming and sense of belonging that I experienced at the final destination during a tumultuous time for the country and the world. There, along with my parents, we weathered the pandemic with my brother Peter and his wife Robin and my sister-in-law Raquel and her husband Chuy and their families. I dedicate this book to Robbie and our children, and to my parents Pauline and Shay, whose love and sacrifice made all this possible.

PART I

POLITICS OF MARKET GOVERNANCE

Understanding Varieties of Market Governance in the Age of Globalization

Since the end of the Cold War in 1991, three decades of market reform and greater exposure to the international economy have introduced liberal economic tools in the largest emerging economies in the developing world. China, the world's largest autocracy, Communist by name and one-party authoritarian regime in practice, has liberalized its economy on the macro level and draws in more foreign direct investment (FDI) than any country in the world except the United States. India, the world's most populous multi-party democracy, following decades of economic socialist institutions in the post-Independence period, has also liberalized its macro-economy. Russia, after the breakdown of the Soviet Union, underwent massive economic liberalization, dismantling Communist institutions and launching democratic reforms.

Dominant theories in political science suggest that globalization and attendant economic liberalization positively affect growth and development and vary by regime type.[1] Furthermore, studies in comparative political economy debate liberal versus developmental state models of development.[2] Indeed, since the end of the Cold War in 1991, and even before that, these countries extensively enacted market reforms and exposed internal markets to the international economy during the height of neoliberalism. Moreover, China's, India's, and Russia's participation

---

[1] See Chapter 2 on the internal and external pressures faced by developing countries during global economic integration. Also refer Lake (2009b) on the various threads of the Open Economy paradigm and Przeworski et al. (2000) on the relationship between regime type and development.

[2] Section 1.1 of this chapter situates this study in these debates.

in global trade agreements, standards-setting bodies, and other international organizations have been touted as the beginning of these economic juggernauts playing by the rules of the global community.[3] They have maintained steady GDP growth and today boast some of the most competitive industries and companies in the developing world.

Beyond macro-economic indicators and simple observations that these are large and diverse developing countries shedding socialist economies, however, what is often overlooked is that these countries' developmental trajectories are nationally distinct *and* sectorally variegated. In 1978, the Open Door Policy unleashed China's integration into the international economy. Deng Xiaoping, in his famous "Southern Tour" in 1992, welcomed foreign investment and shortly thereafter dismantled many state institutions, which centrally managed industries. In today's globalized China, which leads the world in exports and ranks third in imports, a centralized sector-specific ministry directs fifth-generation technology standard (5G) telecommunications networks and semiconductor fabrication through state-controlled corporate shareholding and government-coordinated research and development (R&D). Yet local governments exercise discretion in regulating overexpansion in predominantly privately held and globally competitive technical textiles and apparel and clothing.

India began to liberalize its internal economy in the 1980s and, in 1991, the Congress Party (under the leadership of Narasimha Rao) launched India's global economic integration with Big Bang liberalization. Macro-liberalization introduced foreign-invested competition in telecommunications and boosted textile exports. Today, the Indian government monitors hypercompetitive value-added and mobile service providers with an independent regulator, and the judiciary arbitrates regulatory disputes. The actual amount and scope of FDI notwithstanding, telecommunications services and manufacturing are almost completely liberalized. In contrast, the Ministry of Textiles devotes resources to shelter rural, small-scale handlooms and power looms from liberalized trade and export-oriented industrialization, even while actual market coordination in the informal, unorganized sector remains decentralized and outside of central-level regulation.

Russia, today, has also experienced macro-level economic liberalization, followed by sectoral-level reregulation. Perestroika reforms, in the 1980s, introduced competition in light industries, including textiles.

---

[3] For example, see Steinfeld (2010).

Fast forward several decades, after the collapse of the Soviet Union and the post-1998 political centralization efforts pursued by Vladimir Putin, the textile industry, which was decentralized and deregulated during the Gorbachev era, has witnessed regulatory centralization, particularly in technical sectors. State-owned regional telecommunications landlines, which the government never privatized, became centralized into one corporate entity. However, amidst encroaching information control by the Russian government, privately-owned mobile and value-added services operate in fiercely competitive markets.

In the neoliberal era and beyond, these countries have experienced radically different industrial outcomes, trade composition, and contribution to output of labor and physical capital.[4] What is more, all three countries, differences in regime type notwithstanding, have witnessed political centralization and economic retrenchment, which vary by sector, before and after economic crises, such as the 2008 Global Financial Crisis. Where the International Monetary Fund (IMF), the World Bank, and the European Union debate the extent and scope of austerity measures and advocate some form of state intervention, China, India, Russia, and their internal industrial and subnational regional variations question conventional wisdom on the relationship between economic liberalization, the nature of state and market institutions, and the effects on political and economic development. Existing scholarship shows that advanced industrialized and developing countries alike have liberalized and reregulated as they responded to the global economy in the context of neoliberalism.[5] These perspectives debate uniform and linear liberalization trajectories and the specific modes of state intervention, which achieve corresponding types of developmental outcomes.

This book unravels the empirical and theoretical puzzles about the varying role of the state in market governance and sectoral-level patterns and developmental outcomes in the context of global economic integration. What explains intranational sectoral variation in the context of globalization? How do state goals and methods in market governance vary?

---

[4] Figures in this chapter and the rest of the book show national and sectoral variation in science and technology patents (1980–2015); patent publications in telecommunications and other information communications technology sectors (1992–2013); technology intensity of exports and imports (1990–2014); and other indicators of industrial development.

[5] Studies on developed countries include Vogel (1996, 2006) and Rodrik (1998); and on less developed countries include Rodrik (1999), Kurtz and Brooks (2008), Hsueh (2011), and Nooruddin and Rudra (2014).

How do we both examine the agency and capacity of the state and disaggregate it to identify the various actors and multidimensional motives and effects? To answer these questions, the book advances existing literature with three novel claims, which make general propositions demonstrated through case-specific findings. First, mediating the impacts of economic liberalization on industrialization are dominant national sector-specific patterns of market governance. Market governance structures comprise two dimensions: *Level and scope of the state in market coordination* and *dominant distribution of property rights arrangements*. Introduced in detail later in Chapter 1, the holistic typology developed in this book recognizes the various state and market authorities in coordination mechanisms and broadens measures of institutional quality beyond de jure private property rights and credible commitment.

Second, the Strategic Value Framework, elaborated in Chapter 2, contends that the values and identities of state elites, as they respond to objective internal and external pressures that are political and economic in nature, interact with micro-level sectoral structures and sectoral organization of institutions and shape dominant national sector-specific patterns of market governance. The unified theoretical framework, which builds on and extends my earlier scholarship, bridges materialist arguments with constructivism and historical institutionalism to show how market institutions, which vary by sector, are a result of *intersubjective* responses to *objective* material circumstances.[6] It theorizes that objective measures of what is strategic to state elite decision-makers as they define, make claims upon, and contest contemporary internal and external pressures associated with industrial development are interpreted intersubjectively.

Values and identities rooted in prior episodes of national consolidation shape and reshape *perceived strategic value*. Stable and dynamic overtime, these national narratives of how sectors are appraised differently shape state imperatives, and interact with *sectoral structures and organization of institutions*. The interactive effects of strategic value and sectoral logics determine the patterns and details of market governance. In the first step, in the context of internal and external economic and political pressures, the higher the perceived strategic value of a sector, the more likely the state will enhance its control, centralize bureaucratic coordination, and regulate market entry and business scope. The lower the perceived strategic value of a sector, the more likely the state will

---

[6] Hsueh (2011, 2012, 2016).

relinquish its control, decentralize bureaucratic coordination, and deregulate market entry and business scope.

In the second step, the Strategic Value Framework theorizes that the state is more likely to impart deliberate market coordination and enhance its authority when a service or product entails complex technology, when the drivers of producer-driven commodity chains are industrial capital, when R&D and production are core competencies, and when key network links are investment based. In contrast, decentralized or dispersed market coordination is more likely for products or services comprising linear technology, when the drivers of buyer-driven commodity chains are commercial capital, when core competencies are design and marketing, and when key network links are trade based. The domestic sector's global competitiveness and position in the global commodity chain also have effects.

Importantly, country-specific sectoral organization of institutions also shapes the political and economic resources available to economic actors during critical political episodes of domestic and global economic engagement. Institutional arrangements in specific moments in time (which have remained intact over time) influence the level and scope of the state in market coordination and ownership structures. The stakeholders of these institutional arrangements will need to be accommodated even if objective and perceived pressures dictate the radical transformation of market coordination and ownership structures.

The resultant *national configurations of sectoral models*, the third claim of the book, negotiate global economic integration with impacts on actual developmental outcomes. The national sector-specific pathways to globalization and development, presented in their full complexity in Chapters 3–11, uncover that the "global liberal order" of the post-Cold War era is as much a normative imagination as it is a reality with uneven implementation and developmental implications, which vary by country and sectorally (within country). To substantiate these arguments, building on my prior work's emphasis on the nation-state as an important unit of analysis and the industrial sector as another, this book adopts a multilevel comparative case research design.[7] Comparative case analysis at the national and intranational sectoral and subsector levels facilitates the identification of the macro-national and micro-sectoral agential, structural, and institutional factors shaping dominant national sector-specific

---

[7] Hsueh (2012, 2015).

patterns of market governance and their mediation in developmental outcomes. Illustrative company cases further demonstrate sector-specific patterns within a country.

Case-specific findings validate the *national configurations of sectoral models,* which depart from existing models of development and capitalism. Empirically, the book traces and compares (from sectoral origins) the developmental trajectories (historical and 1980–present, including the COVID-19 global pandemic) of capital-intensive telecommunications and labor-intensive textiles in China, India, and Russia, which are countries of comparable size and scale, federal structures, existing industrial bases, and geopolitical significance. Telecommunications and textiles and their subsectors are selected because of their different institutional legacies and structural attributes – the former a technologically advanced and knowledge-intensive industry with new political stakeholders and the latter a labor-intensive and politically and developmentally established industry.

The analytical approach and empirical strategy show that the conventional wisdom of national models (commonly justified by single-sector or single-country studies) in the open economy, developmental state, regime type, and policy sequencing perspectives falls short in identifying the factors, which shape diverging national sector-specific trajectories of simultaneous state- and market-building. Analysis at the subsectoral level (telecommunications services versus telecommunications equipment and apparel and clothing versus technical textiles) further substantiates the Strategic Value Framework. The multilevel comparative case studies incorporate in-depth, semi-structured interviews with key government and market stakeholders, qualitative and quantitative data, and primary and secondary historical documents conducted and collected, respectively, during iterations of in-depth international fieldwork.

Section 1.1 of this chapter situates the *national configurations of sectoral models* in existing debates on states and markets and their impacts on development. The discussion considers the analytical utility and theoretical contributions of disaggregating to the sectoral level, deliberated in further detail in Chapter 2. The sectoral level of analysis challenges the conventional wisdom of the neoliberal and developmental state models of development in the context of complex interdependence. Section 1.2 introduces an original conceptualization of market governance, comprising of market coordination and distribution of ownership dimensions, developed based on research findings. Section 1.3 characterizes the typology of market governance and codes the empirical cases. Section 1.4 provides the book's roadmap.

1.1 NATIONAL SECTOR-SPECIFIC VARIATION
IN GLOBALIZATION AND DEVELOPMENT

Scholars have long debated the role of the state in confronting economic internationalization. Among scholars, some depict the retreat of the state; others argue the state has retained its capacity to make policy.[8] Yet other scholars have found cross-national variation in the state's responses to globalization and most agree governments today must contend with some form of global economic integration.[9] Existing models of development shed some light on the responses to and impacts of globalization.[10] The BRICS nations have departed from the developmental states of East Asia, which strictly regulated FDI in the post-World War II period during the Cold War.[11] These countries have also eschewed the historical experience of Latin American countries during a similar stage of development, whereby economic liberalization facilitated coalitions of FDI and local business interests, which exploited physical and natural resources.[12]

In 1980, shortly before initial economic liberalization, in our case countries (China, India, and Russia), with macro-level restrictions on foreign direct investment in place, FDI as a percentage of GDP was negligible and lower or comparable to the newly industrialized countries (NICs) of East Asia (Figure 1.1). Brazil, in comparison, experienced a higher influx of foreign investment. By 2005, a few decades into neoliberalism, China, India, and Russia have exceeded the East Asian NICs

---

[8] See Strange (1996), Rodrik (1999), and Grande and Pauly (2005) on the former. On the latter, see Gourevitch (1978, 1986), Katzenstein (1978), Garrett and Lange (1995), Keohane and Milner (1996), Weiss (2003), Kahler and Lake (2003), Paul, Ikenberry, and Hall (2003), S. K. Vogel (1996, 2006), and Levy (2006).

[9] See Zysman (1983), Kitschelt (1991), S. K. Vogel (1996, 2006), Hall and Soskice (2001), Guillen (2001), and Wilensky (2002).

[10] On lessons drawn and departures from the developmental state and Latin American experiences, see Hsueh (2011) on China, Sinha (2005) on India, and Wengle (2015) on Russia.

[11] First referred together by Goldman Sachs in 2001, the BRICS nations are Brazil, India, Russia, and China, with South Africa added to the group in 2010. Together they represent about 42 percent of the global population, 23 percent of GDP, 30 percent of the territory and 18 percent of the global trade, and were predicted to dominate the world economy by 2050 and potentially act as a political bloc. On the developmental state, representative studies include Johnson (1982, 1987), Haggard (1990, 2018), and Woo-Cumings (1999). See Hsueh (2011) on how China pursued a bifurcated strategy markedly different from the developmental state model.

[12] On business politics and the state in Latin America's development trajectory during the post-WWII Cold War era, see Evans (1987, 1995), Schneider (2004, 2013), and Kurtz and Brooks (2008), among others.

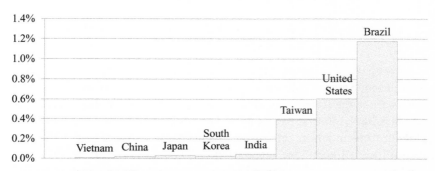

FIGURE I.I. Foreign direct investment as % of GDP, various countries (1980)
Source: United Nations Conference on Trade and Development (2009); International Monetary Fund (2010).

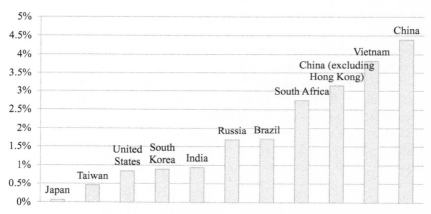

FIGURE I.2. Foreign direct investment as % of GDP, various countries (2005)
Source: UN Conference on Trade and Development (2009); IMF (2010).

and the United States in FDI as a percentage of GDP (Figure 1.2). A longitudinal view (1990–2019) also shows our case countries have drawn significant FDI in the last several decades, converging to similar proportions as a percentage of their respective GDPs (Figure 1.3). Moreover, all three countries have extensively globalized in terms of trade flows. With the exception of the 1990s, shortly after the collapse of the Soviet Union opened Russia to the outside world, the three countries' proportion of trade to GDP has been at comparable levels (Figures 1.4 and 1.5).

Marco-level FDI and trade flows, however, belie the *intersecting* reality of macro-level liberalization in response to global market pressures and ideological norms, and micro-sectoral-level variations in market governance and developmental outcomes, in the aforementioned large developing countries with existing industrial bases and complex internal

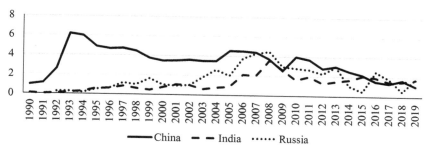

FIGURE 1.3. Foreign direct investment as % of GDP, China, India, and Russia (1990–2019)
Source: The World Bank (2021).

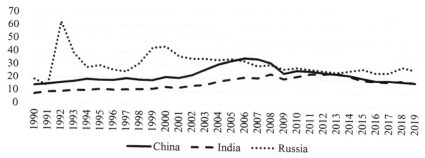

FIGURE 1.4. Exports of goods and services as % of GDP, China, India, and Russia (1990–2019)
Source: The World Bank (2021).

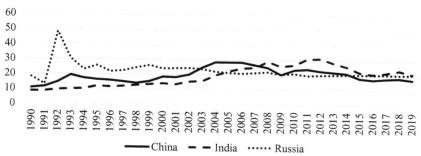

FIGURE 1.5. Imports of goods and services as % of GDP, China, India, and Russia (1990–2019)
Source: The World Bank (2021).

diversity. If we take quantity of science and technology patents as an indicator of developmental outcomes, we might draw the conclusion that China has far exceeded India and Russia in terms of technological advancement (Figure 1.6). Yet, when we disaggregate this measure, and

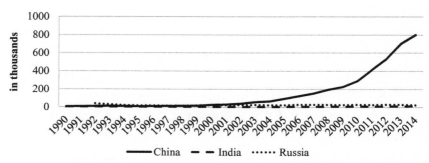

FIGURE 1.6. Science and technology patents, China, India, and Russia (1990–2014)
Source: World Bank (2015).

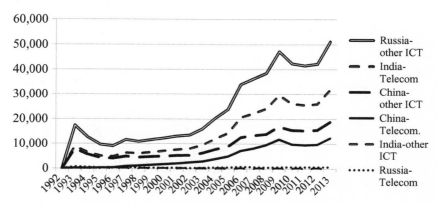

FIGURE 1.7. Patents: Telecommunication and other Information
communications technology, China, India, and Russia (1992–2013)
Source: World Intellectual Property Organization (2015).

zero in on information and communications technology (ICT) and telecommunications, among the book's main sector case studies, the picture
becomes much more complicated (Figure 1.7). For example, Russia leads
in ICT patents but lags behind in telecommunications patents.

How do we explain intracountry sectoral variation, which appears to
contradict our understanding about the relationship between economic
openness and developmental outcomes in addition to conventional
wisdom about national-level differences? The Open Door Policy launched
in 1978 inserted China into the international economy at the height of
neoliberalism and global market pressures. Macro-liberalization picked
up in the 1990s, and Deng Xiaoping during his "Southern Tour"
announced free trade zones and the liberalization of FDI. The Chinese
government dismantled the Ministry of Textile Industry and ended the

telecommunications monopoly in 1993. China joined the World Trade Organization (WTO) in 2001. Today, China is more open to FDI than the developmental states of East Asia (Taiwan, South Korea, and Japan) during a comparable stage of economic development.[13] Also, China has attracted higher levels of FDI as a percentage of GDP than its East Asian neighbors and other developed and developing countries of comparable size.

In 2020, however, despite liberalization commitments made in China's WTO Accession Protocols two decades earlier, state-owned carriers operate basic telecommunications services. Moreover, a centralized supraministry manages telecommunications infrastructural development and market access, but rather differently across services and equipment subsectors, including downstream digital retail, such as financial technology, and upstream semi-conductors, respectively. Conventional wisdom focuses on the political centralization efforts of Chinese Communist Party General Secretary and President Xi Jinping for personal gain and authoritarian control since taking the helm in 2012; yet this explanation captures only half the story.

Chapters 3–5 reveal the reinforcement of the central state's role in strategic sectors, which contribute to the national technology base and have applications for national security, predates the rise of Xi. A former R&D executive of Motorola China explained, "The actual content of restructuring [in 2008] was rational. Integrated carriers address technological convergence issues."[14] "There are lots of reasons for controlling market entry in telecommunications, some technical speed issues, but mostly security, social stability, and state secrets," explained a former official of the Ministry of Post & Telecommunications.[15] Importantly, despite post-Xi political centralization, subnational governments and private regulation, including nongovernmental sector associations, govern market activities in textiles and other less value-added, labor-intensive sectors. "China Nonwovens & Industrial Textiles Association does not have a role in policymaking," explained Li Lingshen, chairman of the nongovernmental business association, the only textile organization designated a national-level association.[16]

---

[13] Lardy (2002), Guthrie (1999), Zweig (2002), Huang (2003), Steinfeld (2004), and Gallagher (2005). On the characteristics of the developmental state model, see Johnson (1982), Amsden (1989), Haggard (1990), Wade (1990), E. Vogel (1991), Evans (1995), and Woo-Cummings (1999).

[14] Interview on September 29, 2008 in Beijing.

[15] Interview on September 23, 2008 in Beijing.

[16] Interview on March 12, 2013 in Beijing.

After decades of pursuing insular economic policies, the Indian government began to relax its restrictive trade and FDI regime, in the 1980s, and unleashed economy-wide liberalization, in 1991.[17] The Gulf War and the Balance of Payment Crisis were the approximate causes of initial openness to the global economy following a decade of the introduction of internal market competition. Capital- and knowledge-intensive, value-added industries, such as telecommunications, represent the apex of economic liberalization and modernization in India. Today the Indian government haltingly monitors hypercompetitive value-added and mobile service providers with an independent regulator, detailed in Chapter 7. "The bidding process [for telecommunications spectrum] was not transparent and was ridden with controversy. Bidders bid high amounts because they thought they could negotiate with the Indian state later – a prisoner's dilemma. These new entrants thought they could manipulate the process, that they would be too big to fail later – so they thought."[18] Dominant perspectives examine sources of liberalization and debate the agents and contents of neoliberal reforms, including the Bharatiya Janata Party of which the current prime minister Narendra Modi (who is a right-wing nationalist) is a member. These explanations, however, overlook that in labor-intensive, predominantly rural and small-scale industries, such as apparel and clothing and technical textiles, India is neither very globalized nor industrialized, as shown in Chapter 8. The Ministry of Textiles and subnational authorities allocate resources to buffer privately held rural, small-scale handlooms and power looms from liberalized markets. "We do not want big brands entering India to displace existing traditional shops and retailers," explained a textile merchant.[19] Based in Rajasthan, the textile merchant's family has sold textiles since India's pre-independence times. The country's independence was founded on rural and agrarian interests and cotton nationalism championed by Mahatma Gandhi. Tracing from sectoral origins, Chapter 6 shows that their role in the Indian nationalist imagination contributes to the high perceived strategic value of small-scale rural sectors for national development; whereas transnational elites shape knowledge intensive and globally integrated sectors.

---

[17] WTO reports show in 1990, 355 percent represented the top tariff rate in India. The average fell to 40 percent in 2000, 12 percent in 2007, and just over 7 percent in 2014.

[18] Interview on February 21, 2013 in New Delhi with Rajat Kathuria, chair of the Indian Council for Research on International Economic Relations.

[19] Conversation with a small-scale cloth maker and merchant on January 24, 2006 in Jaisalmer, India.

The collapse of the Soviet Union in 1991 paralleled the newly formed Russian Federation's adoption of a program of "shock therapy," which entailed privatization, liberalization, and stabilization advocated by the Washington Consensus of the United States, the IMF, and the World Bank.[20] The prevailing view contends that new owners emerged overnight to helm state-owned companies where they previously served as state managers and workers. Simultaneous liberalization and privatization unleashed new and old political actors and ushered in foreign participation of all stripes (multilateral and nongovernmental organizations, Western governments, multinationals, and direct and portfolio investment).

This, however, characterizes the bird's-eye view. The Russia chapters, presented in Chapters 9–11, disclose how existing sectoral organization of institutions interacts with perceived strategic value and shapes sectoral variation in market governance in the post-liberalization era. "When the Berlin Wall fell, apparel and clothing had already experienced nearly a decade of deregulation under *perestroika*. With the supply chain during the Soviet era scattered across the union, raw materials were difficult to set up," exclaimed a global textile trader, who searched for T-shirt producers in the Russian countryside shortly after the collapse of the Soviet Union. "It costs a lot more to set up textile factories than to set up shop to sell telecoms equipment and services. The Russian textile industry never recovered."[21]

In contrast, "Russia kept the landline in the state's hands. Telecoms is a military sector. You can't just privatize fixed-line. But there isn't a connection between military and mobile. This is why there is so much market development and almost anyone can enter mobile, leading to the market behavior of operations witnessed today," explained a telecoms engineer.[22] In the Putin period and beyond, "[mobile and value-added service providers] must contend with the rules and regulations of the national security laws on data collection and storage." Since the early 2000s, Russia outranks China and India by mobile subscriptions per 100 inhabitants (Figure 1.8). In contrast, Russia's landline subscriptions are closer to China's numbers despite having a much more extensive cross-country fixed-line networks under the Soviet Union (see Figure 1.9). Nevertheless, Russia witnessed growth in fixed-line networks after the Communications Law of 2004 (enacted during the Putin era) further centralized the role of the state in market coordination. The law

---

[20] Aslund (1995), Stiglitz, (2001), and Sachs (2005).
[21] Interview with Guy Carpenter on May 27, 2015.
[22] Interview on June 10, 2015 with Alexander Akhmataev, Project Director, Rostelecom.

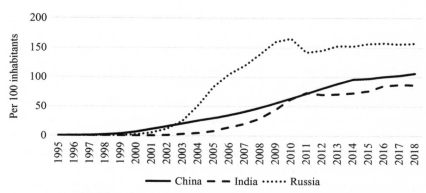

FIGURE 1.8. Mobile subscriptions per 100 inhabitants, China, India, and Russia (1995–2018)
Source: International Telecommunication Union (ITU) Statistics, 2020.

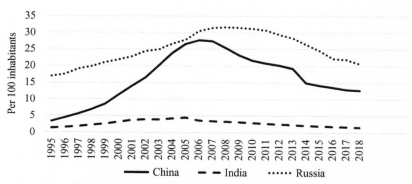

FIGURE 1.9. Fixed-line subscriptions per 100 inhabitants, China, India, and Russia (1995–2018)
Source: International Telecommunication Union (ITU) Statistics, 2020.

maintained state-owned Rostelecom's monopoly position and control of Internet Service Providers (ISPs).

1.1.1 Disaggregating to the Sector: Challenges to the Neoliberal and Developmental State Models

The decline of the modified gold standard in 1973, which upended the Bretton Woods system of monetary management, and the exogenous shocks and debt regimes of the developing world in 1979, became the pretext for the rise of market ideologies in the advanced industrialized world and their enforcement via loan and aid conditionality to developing countries by the IMF and World Bank.[23] Even in the context of successful development, none of the developmental states of East Asia or Latin America, for that matter, established regulatory institutions that resembled the independent administrative agencies tasked with ensuring a competitive equal playing field witnessed in the wealthy western democracies.[24] Economic nationalism, a "soft authoritarian" political system, and auspicious Cold War politics – which provided a context for foreign capital flows absent of conditionality – characterized "state-directed development" of East Asia.[25]

Elsewhere in the developing world, Peter Evans has shown, countries were unable to calibrate the "triple alliance" relationship between the state, local capital, and foreign capital in ways that contributed to local development, and the autonomous state "embedded" in society never emerged to engage the global economy to achieve state goals in quite the same way.[26] Rather, in response to domestic and global conditions and neoliberal ascendence, the state, in Latin America in varying ways and degrees, incorporated the demands by activist labor movements and industrial elites nurtured by import substitution industrialization (ISI) policies, with social welfare and export-oriented economic and trade policies, respectively. Thus, emerged what Sarah Brooks and Marcus Kurtz termed "embedded neoliberalism."[27] Still, analysts blamed the lack of regulatory institutions for the sufferings endured by East and Southeast Asia in light of the 1998 financial crisis, even as such scholars as Robert Wade argued that "deeper causes of the Asian crisis lie in the core economies and their governments, especially that of the U.S., and in the kind of international financial system they have created."[28]

The diverse economic and industrial outcomes, which vary by country and by sector within country, challenge the Keynesian notion that the state has the will and capacity and can be good for industrial planning purposes, personified by the phenomenal growth of the developmental

---

[23] Stiglitz (2001).

[24] Vogel (1996) finds that even among advanced industrialized countries, the actual nature and scope of market regulation varies remarkably due to existing ideas, institutions, and interests.

[25] Johnson (1982), Cheng and Haggard (1987), Amsden (1989), Wade (1990), Woo-Cumings (1991, 1999), Evans (1995), and Kohli (2004).

[26] See Evans (1979 and 1995).

[27] See Kurtz and Brooks (2008). Also, see Murillo (2009) on the partisan origins of this new politics, and Etchemendy (2011) on the role of policymaking styles and the compensatory measures that explain cross-national variation across Iberian and Latin American countries.

[28] See Wade (2000).

state in the 1960s and 1970s and conventional wisdom about China in the 1990s and beyond. At the same time, they also defy the neoliberal view that interventionism produces inefficiencies and inefficacies, which adherents claimed was shown by the apparent cronyism and feeble responses of some of the NICs to the Asian Financial Crisis in the 1990s, and India under Nehruvian socialism. Furthermore, China's pursuit of industrialization of the entire economy by liberalizing FDI rather than focusing singularly on foreign aid and protectionism calls into question the dependency paradigm that FDI is necessarily exploitative and leads to dependent development and that only aid can get societies out of the cycle of poverty when savings cannot.

Through FDI and exposure to technology and knowledge transfers in exchange for market access, China has developed high-tech, high-value-added products, such as semiconductors and manmade nonwoven fabric. Yet China's continued strength in low-value-added production, such as those in undergarments and other apparel, forces a re-examination of the idea that countries should emphasize competition in the production of higher value goods by producing better and more efficient ones. In fact, China's FDI-cum-import-substitution strategy, shown in Chapters 3–5, to govern markets questions the neoclassical view that countries should focus on absolute strength (which is after all, context specific and time dependent) to obtain optimal efficiency. China's pursuit of both comparative and competitive advantage shatters the notion that countries should focus energies and resources only on leading sectors because growth is significantly faster in some segments of the economy. And that pursuit appears to resolve, along with a strictly regulated currency regime, the gap between imports and exports, which plagues many developing countries.

The global structural contexts in which the Chinese model has defied conventional wisdom on the promises and pitfalls of both state intervention and deregulation cannot be disconnected from China's recent economic development. China opened its door to the world as the Cold War came to an end. The country integrated into the international economy during neoliberal ascendance, which replaced Cold War politics when the Soviet Union and its satellites collapsed. During this period of transnational rule-making by multilateral organizations, such as the WTO, and global sectoral alliances, such as the International Telecommunications Union, China joined the game and adopted the prevailing norms rather than turn the other way. In this effort, China has welcomed foreign influences and joined regional and transnational forums, even while maintaining control of its economy through a bifurcated strategy of market liberalization and reregulation, which varies by sector.[29]

Yet what then does China's development model imply for developing countries seeking to fast-track industrialization even while opening up to the outside world? Can these countries succeed if they pursue a bifurcated strategy of growth and development, or, at the very least, get policies just right?[30] The mixed industrial and economic effects witnessed in China's strategic and less strategic industries as shown in the book's case studies oblige us to move away from simplistic ideas of the mutual benefits of liberal markets and trade and the macro-level economic indicators that measure them. Sequencing or combining strategies of import-substitution and export-orientation, or specifying the optimal relationship between government and business might not do the trick either. Russia's market-based import-substitution strategy in previously decentralized and deregulated sectors, as shown in Chapter 11 on Russian textiles, have witnessed limited success.

The internal and global contexts in which states balance sectoral attributes and country-specific sectoral institutional characteristics with state imperatives deserve critical consideration. Many developing countries have experienced less-than-desirable side effects from the internationalization of finance and neoliberal policies. The BRICS nations have globalized in the context of the adoption of neoliberal policies advocated by the Washington Consensus, the influence of economic groups vis-à-vis the state during the rapid disintegration of the Soviet Union and related dismantling of the Communist state, and relatively high growth rates in China and India. Recent studies in the political economy of development highlight the role of state capacity, policies to upgrade human capital and innovation, coalitional dynamics, and resource endowments.[31] In their emphases on state agency, pluralistic dynamics, or structural constraints, these studies pay less attention to the constellation of path-dependent values and institutions negotiated by political economic elites during significant moments in developing

---

[29] Hsueh (2011).

[30] To maximize the benefits of economic globalization, Rodrik (2007) suggests solutions to get out of poverty "usually requires following policies that are tailored to local economic and political realities" and Harrison and Rodríguez-Clare (2010) call for a soft industrial policy, "whereby government, industry and cluster-level private organizations can collaborate on interventions to increase productivity."

[31] For example, Doner and Schneider (2016), Smith (2007), and Dunning (2008), respectively.

countries' attempts at national consolidation. They are also less informative in explicating the extent and scope of market governance (and
attendant socioeconomic development).

Development is not as simple as adopting best practices or creating
robust conditions, such as state capacity and social network institutions,
to increase trust, incentives, satisfaction, accountability, quality, and
citizen engagement.[32] The dominant patterns of market governance identified in this book shed light on the complexity of development trajectories, which vary by country and sector. They expose development as
complex and non-linear and varies by country and sectors within country.
In doing so, the book's findings extend beyond existing works, which
have characterized institutional adaptation and the coevolutionary process of markets and governments.[33] These studies examine micro-
institutional foundations and identify important subnational variations
and explicate the complexity of institutional change. Without explicitly
linking micro-institutional change to macro-level processes, however,
they do not capture the full story of change and continuity. Moreover,
while adaptive institutional and coevolutionary accounts have examined
subnational geographical variation, they pay less attention to the impacts
of *sectoral structures and organization of institutions*.

In the context of neoliberal ascendance and open economy politics, it is
at the industrial sector that countries today are exposed to the global
economy. Sectors, defined as structural technological attributes, sites of
global division of labor and global value chains, and nation-specific forms
of industrial organization, and their impacts hypothesized in Chapter 2,
therefore, play an important role in shaping market governance. This
book's historical process-tracing from sectoral origins in Chapters 3, 6,
and 9 (China, India, and Russia, respectively) shows that political dynamics during the founding of national and sectoral institutions develop
identities and values, which affect economic decision-making in subsequent exposures to the global economy and rounds of market reform.
They have lasting effects in the context of interacting endogenous and
exogenous forces. Regardless of the extent and scope of state control and
deregulation and reregulation of economies, all markets are embedded in
complex national configurations deeply intertwined with *perceived strategic value,* which interacts with *sectoral structures and organization of
institutions* and shapes the political logic of market institutions.

---

[32] Khemani et al. (2016) and Andrews, Pritchett, and Woolcock (2017).
[33] Tsai (2006, 2016), Dimitrov (2013), Naughton and Tsai (2015), and Ang (2016).

The sector-specific chapters show that the impacts of the *national configurations of sectoral models* on actual developmental outcomes are as multifaceted as the contributions and limits of neoliberalism.[34] For example, deregulation in China (in what are perceived as less strategic sectors for national security and the national technology base) in the aftermath of the Tiananmen Square Incident in 1989 empowered private market actors to engage in economic activities, which modernized the mass production of advanced textiles. Yet, it also led to market over-expansion and environmental degradation. Likewise, the Chinese state's coordination and investment in R&D and courting of FDI facili-tated the modernization of the telecommunications infrastructure to wire the nation. In doing so, the authoritarian state also acquired the technology and knowhow to build the Great Firewall of China and engage in cross-border cyberwarfare.

The book calls into question the lessons of cookie cutter development models that could be lifted as blueprints. Without understanding the interacting perceived strategic value and sectoral structural and institu-tional logics driving state goals and state methods, we may simply believe there are portable developmental models that all countries undergoing development can easily emulate without consequence. The national and sectoral case studies show how and with what methods, and to what effects global ideas and economic reverberations (be they neoliberalism, the 1990s economic crises, the 2008 global financial crisis, or the 2020 COVID-19 global pandemic) are reflected and refracted. Different types of market coordination and property rights arrangements as a function of strategic value and sectoral logics have shaped country and sector-specific infrastructural development and technological innovation and their varied consequences associated with different stages of industrial upgrad-ing.[35] Simply put, whether a country can resolve "the trilemma" identi-fied by Dani Rodrik and simultaneously enjoy an open economy, attune to national imperatives, and respond to mass politics, will vary by nation because of sectoral variation within a country.[36]

---

[34] For neoliberalism, these are individual freedom and market competition, on the one hand, and limits on state power and institutional void, on the other hand (Deane 1978, Hall 1989, Vail 2018).

[35] Cammett (2007).

[36] Rodrik (2007) characterizes the "trilemma" as the inability of countries to simultaneously maintain independent monetary policies, fixed exchange rates, and an open capital account.

1.2 DIMENSIONS OF MARKET GOVERNANCE: MARKET COORDINATION AND PROPERTY RIGHTS

Amartya Sen has characterized development as an "integrative process of expansion of substantive freedoms that connect with one another."[37] Sen further contends that recognizing development as a process requires an investigation of the role markets play in contributing to economic growth and progress. The market, in an economistic understanding, is the arena in which exchanges of goods and services, based on demand and supply, between buyers and sellers take place. Markets, however, do not only always operate to facilitate the freedom of exchange and transaction in the Adam Smith ideal, nor are they neutral and natural institutions operating freely on their own.

Rather, in his classic work, Karl Polanyi contends that an institutionalist understanding of markets reveals the complexity of how markets actually operate and the role the state plays in that fact.[38] Moreover, Pranab Bardhan and other scholars have shown that across the developing world, the complex interaction of markets with agential and structural forces, positive or negative, departs from the economic orthodoxy of neoliberalism and the developmental state.[39] The state does not always play a positive role in promoting growth and equity, but it is central in the politics of the economic organization of markets.

In order to examine the true impacts of the global movement to liberalize, and other internal and external pressures, including the various political backlashes against neoliberalism, this study understands markets in the context of the state and its existing power structures, and how those power structures are multidimensional and manifest in many guises.[40] The book, thus, conceptualizes and operationalizes, based on research findings, market governance structures as having the following two dimensions, first distinguished and combined in this conceptualization in Hsueh (2016). The study identifies the *role of the state in market coordination* and the *dominant distribution of property rights arrangements* as separate but equally important dimensions of market governance.

[37] Sen (1999), 8.   [38] Polanyi (1944).
[39] Chaudhry (1993), Bardhan (2010), and Hsueh (2011).
[40] The focus on the state builds on the existing scholarship on market reform in developed and developing countries by S. K. Vogel (1996, 2018) and Chaudhry (1993, 1997) and Hsueh (2011, 2016), respectively.

This holistic and multidimensional understanding of market govern-ance identifies the various state and private authorities in coordination mechanisms and broadens measures of institutional quality beyond de jure private property rights and credible commitment. These dimensions identify what Janos Kornai calls "system-specific attributes ... [and] observable traits" and "not [taking] a normative approach ... [to] char-acterize [political economic] systems."[41] This approach allows for under-standing, through comparative analysis, the actual and various imperfect market governance structures as they occur in practice, what explains them, and their mediating impacts on development.

Distinguishing the distribution of property rights arrangements, in addition to the role that the state plays in the rules of the game, whether it pertains to market entry and exit, competition, or production and service processes, facilitates the understanding of whether the state or the market is undermined or enhanced, how, and why in the context of global economic integration. Steven K. Vogel has found that explicit actions taken by the state to liberalize markets sometimes undermine the role of the state and enhance markets.[42] Other times, explicit actions taken by the state to introduce competition involve reregulation – the reformulation of old rules and the creation of new ones – to enhance state control.

1.2.1 Role of the State in Market Coordination: Extent and Scope of State Control

The study first distinguishes the role of the state in coordination mechan-isms to delineate the complexity of who possesses economic and political authority, concerning which issue areas, and with what mechanisms in the coordination of entry and exit, demand and supply of production and services, and related effects. Identifying the role of the state in market coordination provides critical information about the state capacity and authority required to govern markets, which developing countries, demo-cratic or authoritarian, often lack.[43]

Kiren Aziz Chaudhry has emphasized that creating and regulating markets requires the state capacity to sustain myriad financial, legal, and civil institutions engaged in stable and long-term commitments to regulate the action of producers, importers, and labor; enforce contracts;

---

[41] Kornai (2000).   [42] S. K. Vogel (1996, 2018).   [43] Chaudhry (1993), 252.

and ensure the free exchange of information among economic groups. The state must also maintain a primary repository of information on the private sector in order to tax, regulate, and provide information to reduce transaction costs and ensure confidence and trust in investment decisions. To do so, political authorities require the tools to provide incentives and disincentives for economic actors in concert with collective social goals.

Thus, this conceptualization identifies *extent and scope of the state in market coordination*. On the one hand, *high extent and scope of state control* in market coordination captures the different empirical manifestations of state control. These include direct and indirect nature, formal and informal nature, and level of government, as shown in Table 1.1. On the other hand, *low extent and scope of state control* captures decentralized state, public–private coordination, and private–private coordination. Indicators are the various mechanisms employed by the state in market coordination: Rules and regulations, such as registration, licensure, permits, standards, corporate governance, labor laws, and environmental laws, on market entry, business scope, and investment level.

The actual match between the operationalized role of the state and the sector in question sheds light on whether the state has the administrative capacity to accomplish specific tasks required due to sectoral specificities and particularities. Findings of this book show that not all states possess the necessary administrative capacity; and if and when such administrative capacity exists, it is unevenly exercised and distributed across industrial sectors. The questions become, first, given finite resources in developing countries, even if the political will exists, what explains when and why the state exercises administrative capacity? Second, in which sectors and issue areas is such administrative capacity exercised? Thirdly, how does the state obtain its sources of political legitimacy? The Strategic Value Framework in Chapter 2 introduces a unified theoretical model to answer these questions.

1.2.2 Property Rights: Public/State Stakeholders and Private Stakeholders

Identifying the distribution of ownership arrangements further uncovers the extent and scope of the state's power *and* the role of other market actors in the process of development. As defined by Charles Lindblom, property is a set of rights to control tangible or intangible assets – to refuse use of them to others, to hold them intact, or to use them up – and are grants of authority made to persons and organizations, both public

TABLE 1.1. *Dimensions of market governance: Conceptual and operational definitions*

Role of the State in Market Coordination	Property Rights Arrangements
• *Conceptual Definition:* Extent and scope of the state (who, how, and with what mechanisms) in the coordination of entry and exit, demand and supply, and effects • *Operational Definition:* High state control, low state control • *Who:* Central-level or decentralized or mixed government authorities: Bureaucracy, regulator, government sponsored or nonstate bodies • *How:* Regulate, buy, sell, produce, or provide services or influence decisions on purchase, sales, and production • *What mechanisms:* Rules and regulations, such as registration, licensure, permits, standards, corporate governance, labor laws, and environmental laws, on entry, business scope, and investment level • Actual match between operational definition and sector in question conveys information about *state capacity*	• *Conceptual Definition:* Type of market actors with the rights to control tangible or intangible assets (any level of government and/or those who represent nonstate economic actors) • *Operational Definition:* Public/state stakeholders, private stakeholders • *Who:* Controlling interests (government or private stakeholders or mixed ownership) in any given sector, subsector, market segment, or firm • *How:* Grants of authority, made to persons and organizations, both public and private, and acknowledged by other persons and organizations, of property use and control rights and responsibilities • *What mechanisms:* De jure or legally conferred, or de facto, i.e., what happens in practice, set of rights to control assets: To refuse use of them to others, to hold them intact, or to use them up

and private, and acknowledged by other persons and organizations.[44] Property rights can be de jure or legally conferred, but it can also be de facto, i.e., what happens in practice. The type of actors with the rights to control assets can be any given level of government and those who represent private economic actors in the market. The operational definition captures the dominant controlling interest (government or private) in any given sector, subsector, or market segment, and the measure indicators can be more precise and capture actual percentage of shareholding.

[44] Lindblom (1977).

Public/state stakeholders range from wholly state-owned companies to companies with state-shareholding in mixed ownership types. *Private stakeholders* are wholly privately owned producers and service providers and other nonstate shareholders, including foreign investors. *Mixed ownership* types are independently incorporated joint ventures with shareholding arrangements involving state-owned or state-shareholding enterprises and privately owned enterprises or individuals. In which category an ownership arrangement falls depends on whether the state or the private sector is the controlling interest.

Understanding the different types *and* the political significance of property rights holders are important because they constitute the contextual circumstances, which influence firm-level behavior and developmental outcomes. The book asserts that the dominant distribution of property rights arrangements in concert with the role of the state in market coordination are the micro-institutional foundations of capitalism. They vary by country and sector within country and are shaped by historically rooted values and path dependent sectoral organization of institutions that structure the state elites' responses to internal and external pressures associated with global economic integration. Table 1.1 shows the analytical conditions of the two dimensions of market governance (*role of the state in market coordination* and *dominant distribution of property rights arrangements*).

1.3 TOWARD A TYPOLOGY OF MARKET GOVERNANCE

The multiplicity of property rights arrangements and their meaning for the political economy must be understood in the context of the role of the state in market coordination and vice versa. These dimensions of market governance reveal the myriad ways in which the state can direct the development of an industry and markets with or without prohibiting private ownership and market entry as a growing law literature has also noted.[45] They further acknowledge the reality that the state's various and multidimensional roles in the market include acting as a regulator, operating as a controlling interest, and engaging in actual production or service and market creation.[46]

---

[45] Milhaupt and Zheng (2015) makes a similar argument about the role of the state beyond ownership.

[46] Zheng (2017) identifies in American constitutional law, anti-trust, and international law where these roles have become tests for demarcating the market-versus-state divide.

On the one hand, the state can introduce competition, yet maintain control of physical resources and infrastructure by retaining state owner-ship or restricting market entry in key market segments. A low degree of state control in market coordination does not necessarily translate into private ownership. On the other hand, private ownership and market entry can go hand in hand with centralized control of other issue areas, including business scope and capital investment, to direct the develop-ment of an industry. A high degree of government coordination in indus-trial development does not necessarily translate into state ownership or controlling interest of infrastructure and resources.

The two dimensions analyzed together establish a typology, which captures the empirical reality of varieties of market coordination and mixed ownership in developing countries across regime type and political economic system (including the book's case countries and sectors) and their various meanings.[47] As shown in Table 1.2, variation along these dimensions creates the following types of market governance structures. Also shown, the typology differentiates and identifies the country and main sector cases, including across time, examined in the rest of the book.

Centralized governance involves sector-specific regulation and high degree of state coordination, with the state acting as an important prop-erty stakeholder. This type of market governance, whereby the scope and content of market regulation to achieve state goals is just as important as the government's ownership of tangible assets, manages basic telecommu-nications services owned by the state in China and state-owned fixed-line networks in Russia. The Chinese government's intervention in the cor-porate governance of privately owned, state-funded companies in semi-conductors to build indigenous technological capacity also exemplifies this type of market governance. The creation of the Ministry of Textiles in India has introduced competition and deliberately intervened in market developments, such as the state-owned National Textile Corporation's periodic undertakings of failing large-scale textile mills and protectionist policies for the predominantly privately owned small-scale, labor-inten-sive textile sectors.

Regulated governance comprises regulation and a moderate degree of state coordination with predominantly private stakeholders. This is an

---

[47] See Whiting (1999), Clarke, Murrell, and Whiting (2006), and Hou (2019) on the variety of property rights in China; and Hsueh (2011, 2012) on the relationship between state goals and rules and regulations with effects on property rights as the means to those ends in China and India.

TABLE 1.2. *Typology of market governance and empirical cases*

Dominant Property Rights Arrangements	**Public/State Stakeholders** • Public/State Ownership • State Shareholding • State Sponsorship	**Private Stakeholders** • Private Ownership • Holding Company/ Business Group
Extent and Scope of State Coordination		
High State Control • Centralized State • Direct or Indirect • Formal or Informal	**Centralized Governance** Telecoms in China Telecoms in Russia Textiles in India *Next Generation Technology in China	**Regulated Governance** Telecoms in India *Non-Defense Telecoms Equipment in Russia *IT/Software Services in Russia
Low State Control • Decentralized State • Public–Private • Private–Private	**Decentralized Governance** Textiles in China *Technical Textiles in India *Technical Textiles in Russia	**Private Governance** Textiles in Russia *Apparel and Clothing in China

*Denotes subsector variation.

institutional environment whereby state goals of market competitiveness are paramount and the government serves as a minority stakeholder of property. This type of market governance is represented by the regulation of central-level bureaucracies of state-owned landlines and the predominantly private enterprises in India's mobile and value-added telecommunications services. Regulated governance also administers nondefense telecommunications equipment in Russia, which separately manages service provision with greater state scrutiny and oversight. The actual degree of regulatory independence from political forces varies by perceived strategic value and regime type.

Decentralized governance characterizes a mix of sector- and nonsector-specific regulation and low to moderate degree of state coordination with the state involved in some capacity as a property stakeholder. Empirically this is a mix of market coordination by state and subnational government bureaucracies or public–private coordination arrangements at varying levels of state capacity. In India, subnational governmental promotion of predominantly privately owned small-scale technical textiles, which facilitates trade and market liberalization, falls within this type. Decentralized governance also characterizes the central state and subnational government sponsorships of technical textiles in China and their counterparts involving oil and gas assets and petrochemicals in Russia.

Private governance comprises non-sector-specific regulation and low degree of state coordination with predominantly private stakeholders. This is characterized by incidental supervision and management by subnational government authorities and nonstate economic actors with limited state intervention of a predominantly privately owned market. Market coordination by predominantly privately owned enterprises, in apparel and clothing in China and Russia, represents private governance. This does not necessarily mean, however, that there is no role for the state or that it is not in the state's strategic interests to decentralize. The central state in China has decentralized state control to local governments and nonstate actors in order that textiles can benefit from global economic integration. Such state actions, as the study shows, have context-dependent political and economic consequences.

1.4 ROADMAP FOR THE REST OF THE BOOK

The two chapters in Part I of the book establish the groundwork for understanding the politics of national sector-specific market governance in global development. The first chapter has articulated the empirical and theoretical puzzles and situated the study in research on globalization and development models. It has also previewed the multilevel comparative sectoral analysis adopted by the book as well as conceptualized and operationalized the market coordination and property rights dimensions of market governance and the different ideal types of market governance structures based on research findings.

Chapter 2 presents the Strategic Value Framework, which identifies the interacting impacts of the *perceived strategic value* of state elites and *sectoral structures and organization of institutions* during critical moments of exposures to the global economy. These are the factors which explain why developing countries facing internal and external pressures, which apply to all sectors within individual countries, adopt national sector-specific patterns of market governance structures. They extend and build on my previous scholarship on China's regulatory state, Chinese style capitalism, and comparison of China and India at the sectoral level of analysis. The book's research design tests and refines the theoretical model and market governance conceptualization and typology.

Part II of the book presents the systematic overtime comparisons of the main case countries of different regime types (China, India, Russia) and sectors (services and manufacturing of telecommunications and textiles at varying levels of capital, knowledge, and labor-intensity). The multilevel comparative case studies, which include illustrative company case studies, disaggregate the national and investigate the sector and subsector to show how the identified sectoral variations shape political and economic development. On the one hand, by comparing countries and sectors, the book shows when and how national factors have held constant in spite of differences in sectoral structures and organization of institutions. On the other hand, cross-time process-tracing at different levels of analysis shows the precise nature of macronational and microsectoral interactions and the when and how of change and continuity.

The historical process-tracing of the origins and evolution of perceived strategic value and sectoral structures and organization of institutions presented in the first chapter of each set of country and sector case studies establishes how state elites respond intersubjectively to objective internal and external pressures during critical moments of national consolidation. Each country's next two chapters process trace from 1980 to 2020, including initial responses to the COVID-19 pandemic, the dominant intranational sectoral patterns of market governance, which vary by perceived strategic value and sectoral characteristics.

Part III of the book contends national sector-specific patterns of market governance shed light on understanding global reregulation in postneoliberalism, with the rise of reactionary politics globally. Chapter 12 also assesses developmental outcomes and emergent capitalisms in light of the *national configurations of sectoral models*. It analyzes how the Strategic Value Framework and the micro-institutional foundations of capitalism in China, India, and Russia uncover the ways in which these countries have responded to pressing global issues, such as the U.S.-China trade war, cross-border cyberwarfare, and COVID-19 pandemic, and implications for the future of global conflict and cooperation.

2

Perceived Strategic Value and Sectoral Structures and Organization of Institutions

Developing countries, today, are more intimately integrated with the rest of the world than ever before. In this context of interconnectedness, indigenous market governance institutions that may or may not resemble those of wealthy western democracies or other countries of the developing world have emerged to confront new and old interests of the state and society. Scholars of the political economy of development, studying early and late development, have pointed to the difficulties inherent in the relationship between state- and market-building as countries become exposed to the international economy.[1] In less-developed countries, throughout history, these are simultaneous processes. This book contends that, rather than an existing regulatory model, the starting point for understanding diverging sectoral patterns of market governance in developing nations is the unified theoretical framework introduced in this chapter and the empirical market governance typology presented in Chapter 1. This analytical tool kit empowers investigation at the sectoral level of analysis reinforced by the complex interdependence of state- and market-building in the neoliberal era.

The Strategic Value Framework offers a unified explanation, linking macronational and microsectoral-level changes and continuities of what appear to be contradictory and irreconcilable forces at work within globalizing countries to combine the use of markets with calibrated state intervention. The theoretical model identifies the effects of *perceived strategic value*, *objective* and *intersubjective* in nature, which is rooted

---

[1] See Gerschenkron (1962) and Chaudhry (1993, 1997).

in state elite responses to internal and external pressures experienced during significant moments of national consolidation; and interactions with the *sectoral structures and nation-specific organization of institutions*. Interacting strategic value and sectoral logics shape national and intranational sectoral patterns of market governance in the context of the relative impacts of an open economy, global norms and international organizations, resource and factor endowments, regime type and political institutions, and national characteristics and domestic structures.

In this chapter, Section 2.1 discusses the internal and external pressures that existing scholarly perspectives debate as causal forces of change, which are experienced by countries and sectors during significant exposures to the global economy. It develops the argument that these factors fall short of explicating the national and intranational sectoral variations uncovered in their full complexity in the book's case studies (Chapters 3–11). The conceptualization and operationalization of the two-step Strategic Value Framework are presented in Section 2.2. Section 2.3 introduces the study's multilevel comparative case research design (time, country, sector, subsector, and firm). The empirical strategy evaluates the relative causal force of open economy politics, regime type, resource endowments, and national and subnational political institutions; and validates the book's arguments featuring the industrial sector as a critical unit of analysis. The study's longitudinal national and sector case studies leverage extensive fieldwork, semi-structured in-depth interviews, qualitative and quantitative data, and secondary and primary historical data. Section 2.4 summarizes the case-specific findings, which substantiate the *national configurations of sectoral models* identified by the Strategic Value Framework.

2.1 STRATEGIC VALUE FRAMEWORK AND INTERNAL AND EXTERNAL PRESSURES

The "exogenous easing of international exchange," which means "processes generated by underlying shifts in transaction costs marked by the multi-nationalization of production that produce observable [increased] flows of goods, services, and capital," characterizes the economic dimension of globalization.[2] Studying the domestic level market governance of these economic flows, this study recognizes that globalization is a much

---

[2] See Keohane and Milner (1996).

larger phenomenon that is marked by increasing levels of transboundary movements and their associated effects, and involves changes in psychological, social and political boundaries.[3] Indeed findings show that the commonality of market liberalization and reregulation in the neoliberal era in the context of the end of the Cold War and economic crises has translated into diverse market governance structures, revealing stark differences in micro-institutional foundations, which vary by sector. Dominant perspectives on the causal forces of global markets and norms and international organizations, factor and resource endowments, regime type and political institutions, and national characteristics and domestic structures in the context of global economic integration shed light on but are insufficient in explicating national and intranational sectoral variations.

2.1.1 Global Markets and Norms and International Organizations

International political economy scholars debate whether the agents of change are global economic competition, policy diffusion by sociocultural peers, or markets and interest groups in their manipulation and internalization of global trends. Open Economy Politics (OEP)-based explanations centered on material conditions, production profile, and position in the international economy have rested on macroeconomic and pluralist models of preference formation to explain the impacts of global economic integration. Liberal pluralists and institutionalists examine their impacts on electoral reform and coalitional change.[4] They also debate the relative importance of sectors versus factors and the impact of sectoral interests and coalitions.[5]

Recent OEP studies call for understanding economically suboptimal but politically motivated policies and variation in the returns to economies of scale due to domestic and global politics.[6] Other scholarship has found the state employs specific governance mechanisms to control economic and political actors in an effort to contravene global ideological

---

[3] See Katzenstein, Keohane, and Krasner (1998) and Held et al. (1999).
[4] See Rosenbluth and Thies (2010).
[5] For pluralist models, see Magee (1980), Frieden (1991), Midford (1994), Frieden and Rogowski (1996), and Hiscox (2001). For related work on strategic choice in which OEP is a subset, see Lake and Powell (1999).
[6] See Lake (2009a). See Mosley (2003) on effects of the relative costs and benefits of information provided by financial institutions on policymaking in developed countries.

and market pressures.[7] The process-tracing of labor and capital-intensive sectors in the three case countries show that the state has followed the economywide introduction of competition with sectoral level reregulation.[8] The critical questions become why, how, and with what governance mechanisms and their effects?

Another set of perspectives focus on the cognitive consensus on principles and norms as mediated by international organizations at the national level, which play a crucial role in issue- or sector-specific regulatory reform.[9] Indeed bureaucrats of the Indian Administrative Service received training in the United Kingdom on divestment during the hey days of Thatcherism, as discussed in the India Chapters 6–8. Other scholarship characterizes global pressures of coercion, normative emulation, and competitive mimicry on the adoption of market reforms.[10] Research identifies the ebbs and flows of the dynamic interventions of the Bretton Woods institutions and effects on and responses by developing countries.[11] International institutions, states, and private corporate actors interact to create transnational governance and private governance regimes around issues such as global finance and climate change.[12]

Financial openness in the developing world and the new form and organization of the international economy under neoliberalism became subject to financial crises in early 1994 in Mexico, Turkey, and Latin America, and in 1997–1998 in Asia and Russia. The Tech Bust of 2001 and the banking crisis of 2008 also had wide-reaching global effects, including on China, India, and Russia. Identifying the role of subnational actors in affecting decision-making in foreign jurisdictions in the period following the post-2008 financial crisis, International Relations scholars contend a "new interdependence" has emerged and "it will be ever more difficult to examine national trajectories of institutional change in isolation from each other."[13] At the same time, "it will be difficult to understand international institutions without paying attention to the

---

[7] See Chaudhry (1993) on the counter-reaction of the state during global economic integration, Stoner-Weiss (2006) on state intrusiveness, and Carney (2015) on state capacity.

[8] Hsueh (2011, 2012) characterizes this macro-micro interaction as "liberalization two-step."

[9] See Aggarwal (1985), Weyland (2007), Katada and Solis (2008), and Sinha (2016).

[10] See Henisz, Zelner, and Guillén (2005). See Kentikelenis and Babb (2019) on the United State's purposive role in engineering neoliberalism.

[11] See Simmons and Elkins (2004) and Soederberg, Menz, and Cerny (2005). Also, see Ban and Blyth (2013)'s special issue, including Babb (2013).

[12] See Gourevitch and Shinn (2005), Deeg and Sullivan (2009), and L. Hsueh (2019).

[13] See Farrell and Newman (2014).

ways in which they both transform and are transformed by domestic institutional politics."

The book's longitudinal country- and sector-specific case studies show China, India, and Russia liberalized their economies at roughly the same time during several critical junctures of global economic integration and thus serve as "critical cases where we can examine the domestic dynamics of Washington Consensus support and contestation" before and after macro-level liberalization.[14] For example, liberalization, privatization, and stabilization in some form affected all sectors in the immediate aftermath of the Soviet collapse; what drives sectoral variation from the very beginning in their degree and scope and their impacts have received less attention (see Chapters 9–11).

Less than subtle sectoral variation in China also serves as critical cases of inquiry. In 1978, the Open Door Policy unleashed China's integration into the international economy. Deng Xiaoping, in his famous "Southern Tour" in 1992, welcomed foreign investment and shortly thereafter dismantled many state institutions, which centrally managed industries. Two decades after the World Trade Organization (WTO) accession, today's globalized China directs next-generation 5G telecommunications networks and semiconductor chip fabrication through state-controlled corporate shareholding and government-coordinated research and development (R&D) with a centralized sector-specific ministry (Chapter 4). Yet, local governments exercise discretion in regulating overexpansion in predominantly privately held and globally competitive technical textiles and apparel and clothing whereby sector associations exercise private regulation (Chapter 5). Sectoral variation in the role of the state in market coordination and property rights arrangements is also reflected in in the global activities of indigenous Chinese industry.

2.1.2 Factor and Resource Endowments

Global markets and norms notwithstanding, countries' natural resource endowments shape how they are governed and affect their developmental outcomes. Specific resource endowments located in key geographies alleviate resource constraints, and combined with coercive

---

[14] See Ban and Blyth (2013). This book follows Collier and Collier (1991) to define critical junctures as "periods of fundamental political reorientation in which new institutions are founded setting distinct trajectories of change."

colonization – which had provided sources for inputs and markets for goods – determine divergence between regions and differentiation within particular regions in development.[15] A "political resource curse" makes authoritarian regimes more durable, increases certain types of corruption, and helps trigger violent conflict in low- and middle-income countries.[16]

How natural resources are expropriated, handled, and exchanged by state and society stakeholders becomes key to understanding state capacity.[17] The nature of existing institutions shapes how resource endowments are contested and distributed.[18] Variation in economic and human capital launches development trajectories, and the rule of law and property rights create the incentive structures for contestation and distribution.[19] The timing of a resource boom and a country's level of inequality and economic diversification determine the relationship between resource endowments and democratic and authoritarian stability.[20]

In the Strategic Value Framework, existing resource endowments or the lack thereof are the objective indicators of application for national security and contribution to the national technology base, which state actors take into account. Such indicators also include the factor/asset flexibility of existing sectoral structures and organization of institutions. Resource and factor endowments as indicators of strategic value and sectoral attributes shape the role of the state in market coordination and therefore development prospects. Corporate governance interventions in Russia's oil sectors under Putin affect not only the subsectors in question but also the entire supply and commodity chain, as shown in the case study on Russian technical textiles (Chapter 11). Abundant rural labor in India is a key factor endowment; thus, labor-intensive and less value-added sectors, such as textiles, are perceived strategically by political elites proffering economic policies, which cater to rural constituencies (Chapter 8).

2.1.3 Regime Type and Political Institutions

Conventional wisdom suggests the importance of democracy versus authoritarianism on variation in economic policies and development

---

[15] See Pomeranz (2000).   [16] See Ross (2015).
[17] See Saylor (2014) and Kinzley (2018).   [18] See Menaldo (2016).
[19] See Jones (1981) and Acemoglu and Robinson (2012), respectively.
[20] See Smith (2007) and Dunning (2008), respectively.

outcomes. On the one hand, existing research shows the correlation between economic growth and democracy, and democracies are much more likely to survive in wealthy countries.[21] In contrast, some income inequality is more likely to promote democratization.[22] On the other hand, multiple studies show a relationship between autocracies and development outcomes. Yet, they also show that variations in growth is higher among autocracies and that the fastest-growing countries tend to be autocracies because they are later developers.[23] In other words, it is a historical coincidence that developing countries on growth trajectories are autocracies.

Conflicting evidence suggests that the relationship between regime type and development is complex and that while political institutions matter for development, analysis in terms of regime type alone may not capture the relevant differences.[24] Scholars debate the intervening factors or causal mechanisms that link regime type and development outcomes. The rich literature on corruption shows differences in quantity versus quality and types of corruption, variation in political access to rents, and impacts on timing and scope of governance reform and growth.[25] Another thread of literature shows it is about the scope and strength of political institutions that represent interests. Democracies affect growth by enhancing human capital and strengthening the protection of property rights.[26]

Relatedly, governance effectiveness is correlated with levels of generalized trust, and such levels vary by extent of democracy rather than their presence.[27] Accountability institutions are key; without them, authoritarianism can distort development while severe accountability failures mar democratic governance.[28] Moreover, scholars have found among autocracies, single-party autocracies have higher growth than personalist

---

[21] See Przeworski et al. (2000) and Boix (2003).

[22] See Acemoglu and Robinson (2006) and Ansell and Samuels (2010).

[23] See Knutsen and Rasmussen (2018a) and Luo and Przeworski (2019), respectively.

[24] See Przeworski and Limongi (1993).

[25] See Wedeman (2012, 2018) and Ang (2020), respectively; Bussell (2012); and Lorentzen and Lu (2018).

[26] See Baum and Lake (2003), Tavares and Wacziarg (2001), and Doucouliagos and Ulubasoglu (2008) on human capital and Clague et al. (1996) and Knutsen, Rygh, and Hveem(2011) on property rights protection. See Doner and Schneider (2016) on upgrading coalitions and institutions in development.

[27] See Jamal and Nooruddin (2010).

[28] See Bardhan (2010). Also see Tsai (2007), Khemani et al. (2016), Lagunes and Pocasangre (2019), and Ho (2019).

regimes and monarchies, and that stronger parties and stable governments can compensate for weaker development coalitions regardless of regime type.[29] It is no surprise then that to the Chinese government political stability and Communist Party legitimacy are part and parcel of the perceived strategic value of national security and the national technology base, as shown in Chapters 3–5.

The book's research design incorporates various regime types (authoritarian China, democratic India, and semi-authoritarian Russia) to demonstrate their important but not always primary effects on market governance structures at the national and sectoral levels.[30] Holding country characteristics constant and comparing sectors within countries, the multilevel case studies indicate that regime type does not necessarily map with how countries have departed across industrial sectors from economic orthodoxy of either neoliberalism or the developmental state in pursuing industrial development. Moreover, sector-specific patterns of market governance, which have held across time and regime turnovers within a country, demonstrate that sectoral market governance structures are the dominant causal mechanisms that link globalization and development outcomes.

Nevertheless, the process-tracing of sectors shows how differences in regime type affect the ways in which historically rooted values and institutions replicate, reinforce, and transform overtime. Regime type effects are prevalent in the Russia sector cases: Putin-era authoritarianism centralized the governance of industrial sectors perceived strategic for national security and resource management, such as oil and gas and telecommunications, when they were first decentralized if not completely privatized after the fall of the Soviet Union (Chapter 9–11). The study's research design also exposes how electoral politics in India have reenforced *perceived strategic value* and *nation-specific sectoral organization of institutions* (Chapters 6–8).

With the support of political parties of various stripes whose electoral prospects profit from national narratives of cotton nationalism and the political support of the predominately small-scale rural enterprises of labor-intensive and less-valued added sectors, the Ministry of Textiles in

---

[29] See Knutsen and Rasmussen (2018b) and Bizzarro et al. (2018), and Doner and Schneider (2016), respectively. Also, see Huntington (1968) on the role of political order and party institutionalization.

[30] The book classifies Russia as a semi-authoritarian/hybrid regime because the Russia sector and subsector case studies examine the twenty plus years of the Putin period, which have contained elements of both democratic and authoritarian governance.

India devotes considerable resources to shelter rural, small-scale handlooms and power looms from liberalized trade and export-oriented industrial upgrading promoted by the Indian government (Chapter 8). In contrast, in post-Big Bang Liberalization, the Indian government monitors hypercompetitive value-added and mobile service providers with an independent regulator, and the judiciary arbitrates regulatory disputes though the amount and scope of foreign direct investment (FDI) varies across telecommunications subsectors (Chapter 7).

2.1.4 National Characteristics and Domestic Political Structures

In the study of comparative political economy, a rich tradition builds on Alexander Gerschenkron and Karl Polanyi to investigate the role of domestic political structures and national characteristics in shaping varying levels of state control as countries are exposed to the global economy.[31] The next generations of scholars employ "varieties of capitalism" approaches, which stress eclectic mixtures of policies based on historical legacies and institutions, and on resources, opportunities, and costs of global integration.[32] Some studies show how differences in capitalist arrangements, paths to development, and national identities influence how countries respond to different types of capital flows, trade, and other forces of globalization.

Others contend that developmental paths are not inevitable but may be forged through purposive state action and that state institutional structures affect how the private sector interacts with the state and the structure of the private sector itself. In the face of globalizing changes, state activism in the developed world has shifted rather than fallen away; state officials have changed their goals and instruments, but they have by no means curbed their ambitions.[33] The state in the developing world often intervenes in the face of mobile global capital because of weak regulatory institutions, and not because it eschews global pressures to liberalize.[34]

---

[31] See Shonfield (1969) and Zysman (1983).

[32] Representative studies, which investigate national institutional structures to understand cross-national variation in the state's response to globalization include Reich (1989), Kitschelt (1991), Zysman (1994), Kitschelt et al. (1999), Hall and Soskice (2001), Guillen (2001), Wilensky (2002), and more recently, S. K. Vogel (2006), Schneider (2013), and Thelen (2014).

[33] See Levy (2006), Gingrich (2011), and Vail (2018) on how the state actively moves toward the market to achieve state goals.

[34] See Chaudhry (1993, 1997).

In this understanding, the global reregulation witnessed after economic and financial crises should not come as a surprise.

More recent scholarship on the Global South has examined subnational characteristics, be it region, city, sector, or firm. Country-specific studies examine the impacts of local and regional institutions and historical legacies.[35] Sectoral analyses have argued that development prospects are a function of sectors defined as forms of industrial organization, sites of global division of labor, and global value chains.[36] Yet, other studies identify firm-level characteristics as instrumental for understanding policy outcomes.[37] What becomes apparent is that uniform and linear liberalization trajectories simply do not exist as globalizing countries experience the relative impacts of an open economy, global norms and international organizations, resource and factor endowments, regime type and political institutions, and domestic structures. While existing state structures and organization of institutions shape market governance, it is not sufficient to explicate national and intranational sectoral variation. The question becomes how reregulation takes place and why it takes the forms that it does.

The book's multilevel research design provides leverage to examine the internal and external pressures identified by the dominant perspectives. It shows the sectoral level of analysis reveals *perceived strategic value* interacts with *sectoral structures and existing organization of institutions.* How objective conditions – sectors, macroeconomic tools, and economic crises – are perceived *intersubjectively* by state and market actors affects the content and the enforcement of economic policies whether intentionally and purposefully constructed by the state to detrimental societal effects or to the facilitation of economic development. During the 1997 East Asian financial crisis, the Chinese government forced the cutting of spindles and mergers and acquisitions in technical textiles with applications for national security and the national technology base, but

---

[35] See Tsai (2002), Thun (2006), Hurst (2009), Donaldson (2011), and Ong (2012) on China; Sinha (2005) on India; Montero (2002) on Brazil; Snyder (2001) on Mexico; and Stoner-Weiss (2006) and Wengle (2015) on Russia. Also, see Post (2014) on Argentina.

[36] Sectoral studies of the advanced industrialized world include Campbell, Hollingsworth, and Lindberg (1991), Kitschelt (1991), Hollingsworth, Schmitter, and Streeck (1994), S. K. Vogel (1996, 2006). Studies that have examined sectors in the developing world include Kurth (1979), Doner (1991, 2009), Shafer (1994), Segal and Thun (2001), Gereffi, Humphrey, and Sturgeon (2005), Cammett (2007), Dallas (2014), Wengle (2015), Hsueh (2011, 2015, 2016), Sinha (2016), and Shadlen (2017).

[37] See Naseemullah (2017) on India and Addis (1999) on Brazil, among others.

imparted few resources to rescue textile apparel and clothing, which struggled in parallel (Chapter 5). Measured in value-bounded terms, what may appear irrational becomes very rational.

The country-sector case studies also show the Indian government introduced macroliberalization in response to political and economic crises in the late 1970s and 1980s; however, the establishment of the Ministry of Textiles centralized market coordination in an industry closely associated with India's independence and selectively retained state control in some subsectors and introduced competition in others (Chapter 8). Moreover, the Russian textile industry, which was decentralized and deregulated during the Gorbachev era, has witnessed regulatory centralization, particularly in chemical fiber-processing and nonwoven textiles, which employ inputs from nationalized oil sectors perceived critical for national security and resource management (Chapter 11).

2.2 STRATEGIC VALUE FRAMEWORK: PERCEIVED STRATEGIC VALUE AND SECTORAL CHARACTERISTICS

The Strategic Value Framework is a unified theoretical model, which identifies the key drivers of national and intranational sectoral variation in market governance. The two-step framework bridges materialism, constructivism, and historical institutionalism in its recognition of *objective* and *intersubjective* conditions faced by state and market actors at the national and sectoral levels. The Strategic Value Framework, in the first step, conceptualizes economic and political dimensions, which constitute the scope of strategic value and combine to produce an approximate score on the degree of strategic value. It then argues that objective political and economic conditions are interpreted *intersubjectively* by state and market actors as a function of the process of cognition concerning historical experience, institutional context, and local interpretation.[38]

Thus measured objectively and intersubjectively, *perceived strategic value* determines the dominant sectoral patterns of market governance. From there, in the second step, the theoretical model posits that the actual methods employed in market coordination and property rights arrangements are shaped by *sectoral structural attributes*, which are the

---

[38] See Katzenstein (1996, 1998), Abdelal (2001), and Herrera (2004, 2010).

Global Markets and Norms and International Organizations	Factor and Resource Endowments	Regime Type and Political Institutions	Domestic Structures and Subnational Characteristics
• Exert pressure to respond • Apply immediately before and after macro-liberalization • Apply to all sectors (some more than others)	• Exert pressure to respond • Apply across time after discovery • Apply to all sectors (some more than others)	• Exert pressure to respond • Apply across time after founding • Apply to all sectors (some more than others)	• Exert pressure to respond • Apply across time • Apply to all sectors (some more than others)

Strategic Value Logic
(*Intersubjective* Interpretations of *Objective* Political and Economic Pressures) shapes
• How the state formulates goals and methods
• Who controls industrial policy
• What kinds of measures are employed

Sectoral Logic
(Sectoral Structural Attributes and Existing Organization of Institutions) shapes
• How government goals are implemented
• What kinds of measures are employed

Dominant Sectoral Patterns of Market Governance Structures
• Degree and scope of the State's Role in Market Coordination
• Distribution of Property Rights Arrangements

FIGURE 2.1. Basic argument: Internal and external pressures and strategic value and sectoral logics

same everywhere, *and sectoral organization of institutions*, which are nation-specific and path dependent. Taken together, the two-part theoretical framework represents the pragmatic bridge of different theoretical constructs encouraged by Rudra Sil and Peter Katzenstein.[39]

Elaborated in the rest of Section 2.2, Figure 2.1 illustrates the basic argument about the interactive strategic value and sectoral logics and how they shape and refract internal and external pressures during global economic integration.

[39] See Sil and Katzenstein (2010).

2.2.1 Perceived Strategic Value: Economic and Political Dimensions and Intersubjectivity

The Strategic Value Framework's identification of political and economic dimensions of strategic value and the *intersubjectivity* in which *objective* measures are interpreted by state elites are grounded in scholarship at the intersection of international and comparative political economy, which has documented the strong relationship between economic and political pressures from within and without, state responses, and national development. Kiren Chaudhry on oil economies in the post-second world war (WWII) period has found, too often, that a less-than-coherent state apparatus and a society agitated by the complexities and changes that go hand in hand with globalization must grapple with achieving economic and political development at the same time.[40] The state needs to have political legitimacy and administrative capacity or proxies, whether an all-powerful external patron, sustainable sources of capital infusion, and/or intrusive state intervention.

Political legitimacy and administrative capacity, however, are not easily attainable in the developing world undergoing significant political consolidations, be it war or internal conflict or external intervention in the form of global markets or colonialism or both. State formation in the post-WWII period confronted a litany of constraining political economic factors, from colonial legacy and Cold War dynamics as identified by Atul Kohli to neoliberal ascendance and the global economic system, which influenced the type of elite coalitions that arise to undergird any attempts at creating regulatory institutions.[41] Geopolitical insecurity and severe resource constraints influence institutional capacities of the state as shown in the works of Richard Doner.[42] Moreover, Richard Stubbs and Mark Zachary Taylor, respectively, contend that geopolitics and war, including the threat of and eruption of domestic tensions and conflicts, have lasting impacts on internal reforms and development outcomes.[43] Thus, the Strategic Value Framework contends, on the *political dimension*, *applications for national security* broadly defined, including *internal social and political stability*, *regime legitimacy*, and *external security and foreign relations*, are the objective considerations motivating state elites (Table 2.1).

---

[40] See Chaudhry (1993, 1997).   [41] See Kohli (2004 and 2020).
[42] See Doner, Ritchie, and Slater (2005) and Doner (2009). Also refer to Johnson (1962) on the critical role of internal and external pressures shaping political mobilization.
[43] See Stubbs (1999, 2005), Taylor (2012, 2016), and Gunitsky (2017).

TABLE 2.1. *Strategic value conceptualized: Objective and intersubjective*

Objective internal and external political and economic pressures:

- Political: Internal security/social and political stability, regime legitimacy, and external security and geopolitics
- Economic: National technology base; economic growth and development of the rest of the economy, and global competitiveness of domestic industry

Intersubjective interpretation of objective pressures:

- Bounded rationality and aspiration-based adaptation of values
- Values as reflection of constitutive power of institutions and interpretations of economic conditions, state-society relations, and coalitional dynamics

Shapes:

- How the state formulates goals and methods
- Who controls industrial policy
- What kinds of measures are employed

Recent scholarship has sought to understand why and how some countries have responded to sectoral and global economic changes to achieve development and escape the potentially devastating effects of global financial integration in 2008 and beyond.[44] Comparative studies by Dorothy Solinger and other scholars have shown that capital shortages, competition for capital, and economic shocks during global economic integration recalibrate political compacts and shape and reshape institutions and political relationships.[45] The domestic sector's competitive position during such exposures to the global economy becomes not insignificant to the state's role in market coordination.[46] In light of these economic pressures associated with global economic integration, the Strategic Value Framework defines *contribution to the national technology base* and the *growth and global competitiveness of domestic industry and the rest of the economy* as objective measures on the *economic dimension* of strategic value (Table 2.1).

Importantly, the Strategic Value Framework posits that state elites respond to objective economic and political pressures with *intersubjective* values and identities rooted in prior episodes of national consolidation.

---

[44] Such studies include Ó Riain (2000) and Breznitz (2007), and Levi-Faur (2013), which considers the future of "the developmental state in the age of regulation" and my scholarship on China's regulatory state (Hsueh 2011).

[45] See Solinger (1991, 2009), Appel and Orenstein (2018), and Shih (2020).

[46] See Moore (2002) and Doner (2009).

In other words, government and economic elites do not simply calculate cost-benefit ratios in how they define and rank strategic value. On the one hand, values and identities are heuristics and the "aspiration-based adaptation" of values shape rational decision-making.[47] On the other hand, sociological accounts of legal institutions show that "social worlds were built from subjective understanding and not just from objective, material circumstances" and that legal facts are inseparable from the interests and social relations in which they are contextualized.[48]

Thus, existing state-society relations and coalitional dynamics shape the intersubjectivity in which state elites respond to internal and external economic and political pressures to govern markets.[49] These include legacies of colonialism and prior developmental models such as performance legitimacy, economic nationalism, and domestic interest groups, which reveal domestic preferences and choice of peer group emulation and learning in policy diffusion.[50] The historical process-tracing from sectoral origins in chapters 3, 6, and 9 highlight objective economic and political pressures faced by state elites and show how they are interpreted intersubjectively and overtime shape and reshape the evolution and reinforcement of perceived strategic value.

Given the above conceptualization, the following expectations operationalize the impacts of *perceived strategic value* on how the state formulates goals and methods, who controls industrial policy, and what kinds of measures are employed: The higher the perceived strategic value of a sector, the more likely state elites will employ purposive and deliberate action to regulate market entry, business scope, and ownership to achieve state goals. The state will enhance state control and bring to bear

---

[47] See Simon (1985), Bendor (2010), S. K. Vogel (2006) and Weyland (2006), respectively, on economics and political science theorizing about bounded rationality.

[48] See Scheppele (2003, 2017) and Woodruff (1999, 2004), respectively.

[49] See Cammett (2007), Breznitz (2007), Solinger (2009), Kosack (2012), Kuhonta (2011), Taylor (2016), Doner and Schneider (2016), and Shadlen (2017) on existing state-society relations and coalitional dynamics. Also see Kapur (2010) and (Ye 2014) on diaspora networks vis-à-vis state action.

[50] See Cheng and Haggard (1987), Wade (1990), Haggard (1990), Evans (1995), and Woo-Cumings (1999) on the developmental state; Kohli (2004), Vu (2010), Tudor (2013), and Miller (2014) on colonial origins and legacies and their impacts, including on elite power structures and mobilization, democratization, and foreign policy; and Brooks and Kurtz (2012) on import-substitution industrialization; and Ekiert and Hanson (2003), LaPorte and Lussier (2011), and Pop-Eleches and Tucker (2017) on the impacts of Communist legacies. Simpser, Slater, and Wittenberg (2018) reviews political economy debates on legacies.

resources and state capacity to coordinate market activities. The property rights arrangements that dominate involve the state holding controlling rights and interests in ownership and public–private partnerships, and in participating in corporate governance. In the market governance typology introduced in Chapter 1, high levels of perceived strategic value can lead to the state's centralization of market coordination and controlling interests in property rights arrangements as witnessed in *centralized governance*. It can also lead to the state intervention and state capacity required of regulatory agency oversight of mixed ownership distribution in *regulated governance*.

In contrast, the lower the perceived strategic value of a sector, the more likely the state would relinquish its control to decentralized and non-state actors and employ incidental control to coordinate markets and regulate market entry and business scope. Private ownership, private–private joint ventures, and public–private partnerships are typical property rights arrangements. Lower degrees of perceived strategic value can translate to the decentralization of bureaucratic coordination and deregulation of market entry and business scope in *decentralized governance*. It could also lead to the private regulation by private owners of *private governance*.

Table 2.1 summarizes the conceptualization and operationalization of *perceived strategic value* with economic and political dimensions and in objective and intersubjective terms. To test and validate the first step of the Strategic Value Framework, the process tracing from national sectoral origins in chapters 3, 6, and 9 (China, India, and Russia, respectively) historicize and periodize the scope and extent of strategic value orientation and assessment, the immediate and lasting imprints on state goals and methods, and the application for and contribution of industrial sectors.

2.2.2 Sectoral Structures and Organization of Institutions

The Strategic Value Framework, in the second step, contends that how market governance details actually unfold given the *perceived strategic value* to maintain or relinquish state control in market coordination and property rights arrangements is shaped by *sectoral structures and organization of institutions*. Herbert Kitschelt has shown that the nature of *technological properties* and *core competencies* of sectors influence the choice and efficiency of governance structures and innovation strategies, which, once established, are predisposed to solve certain types of

TABLE 2.2. *Sectoral characteristics: Structural attributes and organization of institutions*

Sectoral Structural Attributes

- Nature of technological properties: Complex versus linear technology, low versus high asset specificity, labor versus capital intensity, and tangible versus intangible assets
- Nature of core competencies: Design and marketing, manufacturing, R&D
- Type of commodity chain (buyer driven or producer driven) and domestic sector's competitive position in the global economy
- Users and purposes of services and products (Is the user, consumer or enterprise/industry? Is service or product, an infrastructure? Or does it operate on or plug into infrastructure?)

Sectoral Organization of Institutions (Nation-specific)

- Pre-existing sectoral bureaucratic and corporate stakeholders, coalitions, state-society relations
- Land, labor, and capital endowments reflecting as factor/asset flexibility

Shapes:

- How government goals are implemented
- What kinds of measures are employed

technologically complex problems.[51] Furthermore, Gary Gereffi and other scholars have found, the *type of commodity chain* dominant in a sector in the expanding scope of global production networks, which incorporates capital intensity, asset specificity, and global learning, also shapes how market governance structures vary.[52] Related key questions include what are the purposes and who are the users of services and products: Is service or product, an infrastructure? Does it operate on or plug into infrastructure? Is the user, consumer or enterprise/industry? Thus, the relevant *structural sectoral attributes*, which shape the methods of state control, are complex versus linear technology, low versus high asset specificity, labor versus capital intensity, tangible versus intangible assets, and nature of commodity chain (Table 2.2).

Importantly, the sectoral logic also incorporates the relative political weight of *pre-existing sectoral bureaucratic and corporate stakeholders* on market governance details. Existing scholarship by Robert Campbell and J. Rogers Hollingsworth and their co-authors show that the pre-

---

[51] See Kitschelt (1991) and Shafer (1994).
[52] See Gereffi (2001). Also see Yeung (2016) on global production networks.

existing sectoral-level organization of political economic relationships creates political interests, embodies complex motivations and interdependencies, and engages in qualitatively different types of transactions.[53] Specifically, existing sectoral institutions and attendant political struggles for strategic control and power within economic exchange (and not necessarily the search for efficiency) affect the political choices of state elites that manipulate property rights and ratify or select particular market governance structures. This organizational conception of sectoral structural and institutional attributes captures land, labor, and capital endowments and implications for sectoral governance and development.[54]

The Strategic Value Framework expects *sectoral structural attributes* and *nation-specific organization of institutions of sectors* to have the following impacts on about how government goals associated with *perceived strategic value* are implemented and what kinds of measures are employed: The state is more likely to impart deliberate market coordination and enhance its regulatory authority when a service or product entails complex technology because of the high investment required in the learning by trial and error of technology with highly uncertain causal structures. Moreover, when the drivers of producer-driven commodity chains are industrial capital, when research and development (R&D) and production are core competencies, and when main network links are investment based, the government is more likely to mobilize investment and coordination of industrial activities to maximize domestic exposure to R&D. These measures and implementations are observed in *centralized governance* or *regulated governance*.

Conversely, incidental coordination by the state is more likely for products or services comprising linear technology because of the lower investment required in the incremental and programmed learning of less ambiguous technological structures. Likewise, when the drivers of buyer-driven commodity chains are commercial capital, core competencies are design and marketing, and main network links are trade based, the state is less likely to mobilize investment and coordinate industrial activities. These measures and implementations manifest in *decentralized governance* or *private governance*. Importantly, the less competitive a

---

[53] Campbell and Lindberg (1990) and Hollingsworth, Schmitter, and Streeck (1994) focus in particular on sectoral organization. See Kurth (1979) on a sector's position in the product cycle and international market and timing of industrialization as the "political tendency of industry."

[54] Gregg (2015) on factor endowments and Gaddy (1996) on spatial dynamics.

domestic sector is during exposures to economic reverberations, the more likely the state would exercise deliberate control; that is, the more resources the state would devote to promote industrial development and to direct market competition. Likewise, the more competitive a domestic sector is during such exposures, the more likely the state will exercise incidental control.

Table 2.2 identifies the structural and organizational sectoral attributes shaping market governance details. The book's sectoral and subsectoral cases reflect the identified variations in *sectoral structures and nation-specific sectoral organization of institutions,* in addition to objective and intersubjective measures of *perceived strategic value.*

2.2.3 Interaction Effects: Strategic Value and Sectoral Logics

The Strategic Value Framework theorizes, in two-steps, the interaction effects of the strategic value and sectoral logics, which operate at the sectoral and subsectoral levels. Expectations for interactive strategic value and sectoral logics include that products or services involving complex technology in buyer-driven chains situated within strategic industries, such as consumer telecommunications equipment, or that are inputs in strategic industries will experience sector-specific intervention by the state and will involve state-owned or public–private enterprises. The higher perceived strategic value to the Chinese government of telecommunications infrastructural/terminal equipment versus consumer-oriented smart phones for national security and the national technology base, for example, shapes the state-owned carriers' balancing of infrastructural equipment procurement from various sources, in addition to the R&D and licensing of homegrown of technical standards (Chapter 4). In contrast, central-level bureaucracies are much more hands off on the market entry and business scope of consumer equipment makers.

On the flip side, a decentralized bureaucracy and a variety of property rights arrangements are more likely to become involved in the coordination of investment and industrial activities in producer-driven chains involving complex technology, such as synthetic manmade fiber, within what are perceived as less strategic industries. Nevertheless, country-specific sectoral organization of institutions (be they existing bureaucratic and market stakeholders, state-society relations, or resource endowments) in strategic and nonstrategic industries alike will refract the effects of objective sectoral technological conditions. This is exemplified in the Indian Ministry of Textiles' divestment of nonperforming textile mills in

FIGURE 2.2. Conceptualizing strategic value, sectoral structures, and market governance

the post-1982 union strikes versus the continued subsidization of handlooms and power looms associated with the national self-reliance through tariff and nontariff barriers (Chapter 8). The book's detailed sector and subsector case studies show how *perceived strategic value* interacts with *sectoral structures and organization of institutions,* in response to internal and external pressures. Figure 2.2 presents the rough positioning of the predicted of type of market governance of the book's main country-sector cases as a function of strategic value and sectoral logics. The sector and subsector case studies reveal the details and full complexity of their interaction and effects.

2.3 RESEARCH DESIGN AND METHODS

This book employs multilevel comparative case analysis to examine how macro-level internal and external forces, and microlevel sectoral, structural, and institutional conditions, shape dominant national and sector-specific patterns of market governance. Across case- and within case-paired comparisons at different levels of analysis (country, time, sector and subsector, company) conduct "parallel demonstration" of the Strategic Value Framework, in addition to showcasing "contrast of contexts" as a function of the interaction between structural and agential factors.[55] Importantly, cross-time process-tracing from sectoral origins empowers causal process observations.[56]

The combined approach of the multilevel comparative case studies and historical process-tracing tests and refines the general propositions of the Strategic Value Framework about the role of objective and intersubjective national and sectoral level conditions motivating state and market actors. Significantly, it empowers case specific explanations about the emergence of *national configurations of sectoral models* of globalization and development.[57] In doing so, the multilevel comparison of China to India and Russia joins other recent innovative research engaged in crisscrossing the traditional boundaries of area studies, and advocates the additional leverage of the sectoral level of analysis.[58]

The key dependent variable is market governance structures (role of the state in market coordination and dominant distribution of property rights arrangements). Industrial outcomes are also discussed in the longitudinal country and sector case studies as implications of the mediation of market governance structures in the relationship between globalization and development. The key independent variables are *perceived strategic value* and *sectoral structures and organization of institutions*. The basic units of analysis are country, sector, firm, and time. The interacting strategic value and sectoral logics of the Strategic Value Framework also apply to subsectors and market segments within them. Incorporated into the analysis are the central and subnational level governments within each country.

---

[55] See Skocpol and Somers (1980). Also, see Levi-Faur (2004) on combining two or more comparative approaches to identify patterns of similarities and differences. See George and Bennett (2005), Mahoney (2000), and Seawright and Gerring (2008) on benefits of cross-case comparisons. See Locke and Thelen (1996) and Slater and Ziblatt (2013) on analytical utility of paired comparisons and Falleti and Lynch (2009) on causal mechanisms.

[56] Collier, Brady, and Seawright (2004) on the inference leverage of process-tracing.

[57] Barnes and Weller (2017) on how combining different methods, such as process-tracing and comparative case studies, maximize their analytical utility and Saylor (2020) on case specific explanations coupled with general claims of an ideal type.

[58] Sil (2018) on the analytical leverage of "comparative area studies." Recent such research include Bardhan (2010), Kennedy (2011), Hsueh (2012), Dimitrov (2013), Ye (2014), Chen (2016), Hurst (2018), Bartley (2018), Frazier (2019), Ho (2019), and Evans and Sil (2020). See Hsueh (2012, 2020) on combining comparative area studies and sectoral level of analysis.

2.3.1 Multilevel Comparative Case Studies and Historical Process-Tracing

To begin with, the selection of the country cases (China, India, and Russia) controls for the timing of global economic integration, country size, and existing industrial base, which capture factor and resource endowments and global markets and norms. In doing so, the country-level analysis tests the *perceived strategic value* hypothesis and shows national divergence in response to internal and external pressures for the same sectors (telecommunications and textiles). Comparing the same industries across countries controls for *sectoral structural attributes* and demonstrates country-level perceived strategic value arguments, in addition to providing analytical leverage to examine regime type effects.[59]

Secondly, initiating national-level analysis at sectoral origins allows history to make assignments on the independent variables of perceived strategic value and sector structures and organization of institutions, creating "as if" randomization of the intranational sector and subsector cases and increasing the validity of the interacting logics.[60] Unraveling the causal process, process-tracing sectoral developments uncovers the origins and evolution of *perceived strategic value* and the ways in which the strategic value logic is reflected and refracted by *sectoral structures and organization of institutions*. The longitudinal analysis (historically and from 1980 to 2020 in the country and sector cases) periodizes key episodes of internal and external pressures and their relationship to the interacting strategic value and sectoral logics. These include historical events since sectoral origins, and more recently, involving the Multi-Fiber Arrangement, the General Agreement on Tariffs and Trade, and the WTO, and economic and political reverberations (such as debt and economic crises, including the 2008 Financial Crisis, and the Emergency in India, the Tiananmen Square Incident, and the collapse of the Soviet Union).

Thirdly, the sectoral level of analysis controls for regime type and state and political structures when the comparative analysis is within country; and controls for *sectoral structures and organization of institutions* when the comparative analysis is across countries. Doing so uncovers,

---

[59] Scholars debate whether Russia is today a hybrid or authoritarian regime. The longitudinal process-tracing of the Russia case studies captures and maps the political shifts to changes and continuities in perceived strategic value.

[60] The comparative process-tracing of origin stories reveals "dose effects" and mitigates the problematics of recorded history, identified by Lustick (1996) and Trachtenberg (2009) as mere reflections of historical interpretation and the logics of theoretical frameworks.

respectively, the fixed effects of *sectoral structures and organization of institutions*, in addition to the intranational "dose effects" of levels and scope of *perceived strategic value*.[61] The systematic comparison of telecommunications and textiles, consisting of sectors and subsectors with different institutional legacies, structural attributes, and perceived strategic value, provides analytical leverage in examining the true nature of market governance and how they vary within country. Subsectoral analysis (and illustrative company case studies) increases the number of observed cases and further demonstrates the Strategic Value Framework.

The analytical leverage of the sectoral structural and institutional attributes of the selected sectors and subsectors are as follows.[62] The telecommunications industry comprises comparatively new political and economic stakeholders in capital-intensive, manufacturing sectors operating complex interactive technology in producer driven chains; and technologically advanced and knowledge-intensive service sectors with lower asset specificity and consumer and industrial/enterprise users. Both services and manufacturing contribute to the national technology base and the competitiveness of the economy and have national security applications.

On the one hand, telecommunications services, which facilitate communication and disseminate information to users, are differentiated between basic service providers that operate backbone infrastructure with high asset specificity and value-added service providers with lower asset specificity that operate on top of wireline infrastructure or wireless networks connected by cell phone towers. The software running the services is physically less tangible, but involves complex technology and intensive knowledge. On the other hand, telecommunications equipment manufacturing involves the production of terminal/infrastructural equipment with complex technology, dual-use defense implications, and installed into the network infrastructure. The production of consumer-oriented equipment, such as cell phones and smart phones, involves lower technological complexity and asset specificity.

---

[61] Notably, cross-sector analysis can serve different purposes. S. K. Vogel (1996)'s sectoral comparisons primarily test whether theorized national patterns hold across sectors. Likewise, Murillo (2001, 2009) compares same sectors across countries to test her theories' applicability across countries and time. Hsueh (2011), in contrast, shows how sector and subsector variations reveal the causal impacts of sectoral structures and organization of institutions in addition to shedding light on national level factors.

[62] The study's classification of sectors and subsectors aligns with the OCED's technological classification based on ISIC Rev 3. Tables 3.5, 6.4, and 9.4 depict nation-specific sectoral organization of institutions in China, India, and Russia, respectively.

TABLE 2.3. *Comparable cases selected based on independent variables*

Regime Type	Perceived Strategic Value (High)	Perceived Strategic Value (Low)	Sectoral Structures and Organization of Institutions
Authoritarian	China Telecoms	China Textiles	China Technical Textiles
Hybrid Regime	Russia Telecoms	Russia Textiles	Russia Fixed-Line Telecoms, Russia Technical Textiles
Democracy	India Textiles	India Telecoms	India Fixed-Line Telecoms, India Apparel & Clothing

In contrast to telecommunications services and manufacturing, the textile industry consists of labor-intensive and politically and developmentally established manufacturing sectors, technical sectors with higher asset specificity and presided over by old and new political economic stakeholders, and trade services that serve internal and external consumer and industrial markets. Textile manufacturing subsectors – from fiber processing to apparel and clothing – are comparatively labor intensive, have low capital requirements and less complex transactions, and belong to predominately buyer-driven commodity. Yet, they contribute to local employment and enhance the local industrial base.

Industrial and technical textiles, including geosynthetics and other man-made fibers and high-tech materials, in contrast, are composed of high-technology contents with product categories that are inputs for construction, fire safety, green technology, space, and aviation, which contribute to infrastructural development and have policing and military or defense applications. Finally, textile trade and distribution contributes to the macroeconomy and are significant for foreign economic relations. Table 2.3 summarizes the analytical leverage of the country (China, India, and Russia) and sector cases (telecommunications and textiles and their subsectors) and Table 2.4 presents the sectoral structural attributes of telecommunications and textiles.

2.3.2 In-depth Fieldwork and Data

Substantiating the multilevel comparative case studies is the triangulation of in-depth semi-structured interviews conducted with key domestic and foreign stakeholders at the sector, company, and different levels of

TABLE 2.4. *Telecommunications and textiles and subsectors: Sectoral structural attributes*

Telecommunications	Structural Attributes	Textiles	Structural Attributes
Manufacturing	Capital-intensive, Complex technology, Producer Driven Commodity Chain, High Capital, Requirements	*Manufacturing*	Labor-intensive, Buyer-driven Commodity Chain, Low Capital Requirements
Terminal Equipment (High-Tech)	Asset Specificity, Plugs into Backbone Infrastructure, Enterprise Users	Apparel and Clothing (Low Tech)	Low Asset Specificity, Consumer Users, Fast vs. High Fashion
Consumer Equipment (Medium-High Tech)	Lower Asset Specificity, Consumer Users	Technical Textiles (Medium-High Tech and Medium-Low Tech)	Capital-intensive, Higher Asset Specificity
Services	Knowledge-intensive, Facilitate Communication and Disseminate Information, High Capital Requirements	*Trade and Distribution*	Buyer-driven Commodity Chain, Low Capital Requirements
Basic (Land-line and Mobile)	Asset Specificity, Operate Backbone Infrastructure	Internal	Macroeconomic Implications, Wholesale vs. Retail
Value-added	Lower Asset Specificity, Operate on top of Backbone Infrastructure	External	Foreign Economic Relations, Imports and Exports

government and nongovernment organizations, qualitative and quantitative data, and primary and secondary historical documents collected during iterations of in-depth fieldwork. Immersive fieldwork between 2005 and 2021 across regions (to test potential local and regional variation) and capital- and labor-intensive sectors and subsectors (telecommunications and textiles) in China, India, and Russia, and in Silicon Valley, New York City, and Washington, DC, uncovers how *perceived strategic value* and *sectoral characteristics* interact and shape dominant national sector-specific patterns of market governance and development.[63]

2.4 HOW NATIONS GLOBALIZE: NATIONAL CONFIGURATIONS OF SECTORAL MODELS OF DEVELOPMENT

The Strategic Value Framework examines the intersection of globalization and macrolevel national politics and microlevel sectoral structures and institutions and identifies *national configurations of sectoral models* of development. It contends that dominant patterns of market governance, which vary by country and by sector within country, are shaped first and foremost by how state elites respond to contemporary political and economic pressures with values and identities rooted in prior episodes of national consolidation. In turn, *perceived strategic value* interacts with *sectoral structures and organization of institutions* to shape how market governance details vary by sector.

The historical process-tracing of Part II of the book shows the origins and evolution of perceived strategic value through significant historical moments of internal and external pressures. It further maps interactions with sectoral structures and organization of institutions starting at mechanized sectoral development through the introduction of market competition and subsequent reregulation. This establishes the *historical constructiveness* and *intersubjectivity* of perceived strategic value. From there, comparative national and intranational sectoral analysis, taken to the sector and subsector, in the rest of Part II, tests and evaluates the interacting strategic value and sectoral logics and impacts on dominant patterns and details of market governance.

The China sector case studies, which depart from the expectations of conventional wisdom on the causes and effects of market liberalization

---

[63] See Gallagher (2013) on the value of qualitative interviews to capture meaning and measurement and Lynch (2013) about interviewing sampling based on analytical goals in Mosley (2013).

and globalization, motivate the identification of objective and intersubjective dimensions of strategic value and the structuring effects of sectoral technological properties and country-specific organization of institutions. They show that China's system has not transitioned in a unilinear manner toward Western-style capitalism, nor is it straightforward state capitalism that employs an industrial policy in the traditional sense. Chapter 3 traces across time (from sectoral origins historically to the 1978 Open Door Policy and beyond) how Chinese state elites have adopted *bifurcated capitalism* grounded in imperatives of *techno-security developmentalism* as a response to the impacts of internal and external pressures. The merging of state goals of economic development and national security shape and reshape the role of the state in market coordination and diverse ownership types and how they vary across industries.

The *centralized governance* of strategic industries, such as telecommunications presented in Chapter 4, demonstrates how state elites perceive application for *national security* and contribution to the *national technology base* as paramount imperatives to alleviate authoritarian regime insecurities and resolve China's power asymmetries with the outside world. State-owned carriers run and manage state-owned communications infrastructure, on which high-tech, value-added service providers and equipment makers of variegated ownership type operate. In contrast, *decentralized governance* and *private governance* of nonstrategic industries, such as labor-intensive and less value-added textiles, presented in Chapter 5, reveal the central state's willingness to relinquish control in areas outside of the economic and security nexus. Extensive deregulation has had adverse effects on market overexpansion and environmental degradation. The interacting strategic value and sectoral logics of the role of the state in market governance extend to subsectors, such as technical textiles, and when social and political stability are called into question in labor-intensive apparel and clothing and highly polluting chemical fibers.

From there, the India sector cases show how the interacting strategic value and sectoral logics can be informative even in a democratic context. Showcasing the analytical leverage of examining sector-specific roots of national variation, Indian telecommunications and textiles refine our understanding of and affirm the effects of the historical rootedness of perceived strategic value and organization of sectoral institutions. They also examine the relative weight of political institutions on market governance structures and show electoral politics' incremental and cumulative effects on dominant patterns of market governance. Nationalist imagination dating to social mobilization before India's independence interacts with the emergence of a global liberalizing coalition in the 1980s and beyond, as shown in Chapter 6, to govern strategic and non-strategic sectors.

On the one hand, Chapter 7 discloses, in the context of the electoral rise and fall of dominant national and subnational parties, *regulated governance* administrates property rights arrangements dominated by a neoliberal private business class in globally integrated high-tech sectors without entrenched bureaucratic industrial stakeholders, such as telecommunications. On the other hand, in labor-intensive textiles, perceived strategic as a function of agrarian self-reliance rooted in post-Independence nationalism, profiled in Chapter 8, *centralized governance* characterizes government interventions to protect and shelter predominantly privately held small-scale industry from neoliberal development; and the nationalization of struggling textile mills during economic crises. The resultant dominant sectoral patterns of market governance produce *bifurcated liberalism* grounded in the *neoliberal self-reliance* of the interacting perceived strategic value and sectoral logics of state goals and methods.

The cross-time Russian sector and company cases in a market-transitioning context regulated by a hybrid political regime probe the liberalizing role of international norms and organizations particularly after the collapse of the Soviet Union, examine the relative weight of regime type versus path-dependent sectoral institutions, and sharpen the conceptualization of economic and security nexus identified in the China cases. The Russia cases also explore the impacts of resource endowments on perceived strategic value. The Soviet defense industrial complex, and historically rooted values of *national security* and *resource management* born of perceived pressures faced by state elites, examined in Chapter 9, interact to shape dominant sectoral patterns of market governance.

Telecommunications, perceived strategic for national security concerns in response to anti-regime protests and conflicts with neighboring countries, experience *centralized governance* in the context of post-Soviet political centralization during the Putin era. Contrary to conventional wisdom, the telecommunications backbone infrastructure in Russia was never privatized; yet amidst the state's business scope and ownership interventions to control information, private competition in mobile and value-added services remains liberalized. Shown in Chapter 11, deregulated during the Gorbachev era and impacted by the disintegrating Soviet regionalization of production, Russian textiles experiences *private governance*. The state and subnational authorities intervene in technical textiles, whereby petroleum inputs are perceived strategic for resource management. A *bifurcated oligarchy* grounds Russia's *resource security nationalism*.

PART II

NATIONS AND SECTORS: PATTERNS OF MARKET GOVERNANCE

3

China and Sectoral Variation

*Evolution of Techno-Security Developmentalism
and the Rise of Bifurcated Capitalism*

The Strategic Value Framework posits that a country's *perceived strategic value* orientation originates from the state's responses to internal and external pressures during critical junctures of exposures to the global economy. The theoretical model further contends that *sectoral structures and organization of institutions* interact with perceived strategic value to shape market governance structures. Tracing historically from the sectoral origins of telecommunications and textiles (the main industry cases), this chapter periodizes and unravels the evolution of the perceived strategic value of *national security* and the *national technology base* in China, showing through periodization how Chinese state leaders *intersubjectively* responded to *objective* economic and political pressures. It shows how since the Open Door Policy in 1978, state goals of political and social stability (1980–2010), in the aftermath of the Cultural Revolution and reinforced by the Tiananmen Incident, evolved to incorporate *national sovereignty* (2010–2020) as well. The latter began under Hu Jintao and Wen Jiabao and extended into the Xi Jinping era as China solidifies authoritarian regime legitimacy at home and vis-à-vis the world. In parallel, the perceived strategic value of the *national technology base* has evolved from considerations of developing indigenous industrial capacity from Deng Xiaoping and Jiang Zemin to Hu-Wen (1990–2010) to a renewed focus on the global economic competitiveness of domestic industry under Xi (2010–2020).

These dual forces have given rise to *techno-security developmentalism* and its relationship to the *bifurcated* nature of the micro-institutional foundations of Chinese capitalism identified in this chapter. The paired comparisons of representative strategic and nonstrategic sectors (telecommunications and textiles, respectively) before and after China's 2001 accession to the World Trade Organization (WTO) through the 2008 Global Financial Crisis and the U.S.-China trade war and the COVID-19 global pandemic (2018–2020), in the next two chapters, uncover the dominant sectoral patterns of *centralized* and *decentralized governance*, respectively, and attendant developmental outcomes in the context of similar resource endowments, global market and ideological pressures, proliferating non-state interests, and economic decentralization and Xi-era political centralization. Investigation at the subsectoral level shows less state control in telecommunications value-added services operating on top of state-owned backbone infrastructure and more in technical textiles (in comparison with other textile subsectors), which contribute to the national technology base and have defense applications.

China's Open Door Policy, in 1978, launched the reform era, and since that juncture, scholars of the Chinese political economy have debated the relative importance of the liberalizing influences of China's participation in global markets and international organizations and forums; the entrepreneurial or predatory nature of the local developmental state; institutional reforms; participation in global supply chains, which activate the direct involvement of domestic and foreign sectors; and the role of non–state interests in shaping policy and institutional change.[1] Scholars also debate the extent and scope and capacity of the central government and the role of the Chinese Communist Party. The state continues to possess interventionist tendencies but lacks regulatory capacity, is increasingly rationalized as an adept regulator, or has transformed and employs legal and non-legal mechanisms to manage increasingly pluralistic actors.[2] Governance and policy-making are shaped by elite factional politics between Communist party generalists and technocrats; a lack of

---

[1] See, respectively, Jacobson and Oksenberg (1990), Shirk (1993), Fewsmith (2001), Peerenboom (2001), Moore (2002), and Yang (2004) on China and international markets and organizations; Perkins (1986), Nolan and Dong (1989), Parris (1993), Oi (1992, 1999); and Blecher and Shue (1996, 2001) on local corporatism and the local developmental state; Montinola, Qian, and Weingast (1995), Lau, Qian, and Roland (2000), and Qian and Weingast (1997) on federalism, Chinese style, and Mertha (2005a, 2005b) on the "soft centralization" of the 1990s, which builds on studies of "fragmented authoritarianism" by Lampton (1987), Lieberthal and Okensberg (1988), and Lieberthal and Lampton (1992); and Kennedy (2005), Zweig (2002), Gallagher (2005), and Mertha (2008) on non–state interests and FDI liberalization.

[2] See Pearson (2005) and Yang (2004) on varying accounts of the regulatory scope and capacity of the Chinese government. Recent studies on pluralistic actors and regulatory mechanisms include Stern (2013), Wang (2013), and Van Rooij, Stern, and Furst (2014).

linkage mechanisms in scale politics; bureaucratic fragmentation and subnational politics; and revenue-seeking local officials driven by fiscal recentralization, regional competition, and industrial linkages.[3]

Recent scholarship on state-market interactions, particularly since Xi Jinping became the Communist Party general secretary and the head of the state in 2013, debates the nature and direction of market reforms, including institutional change and continuities, and the depiction of their variation based on firms and sectors' position in the party-state hierarchy and subnational variation.[4] One line of inquiry contends that the state, in order to ensure regime survival, has presided over "massive privatization," where private ownership is a mainstay in the reality of a mixed economy nearly four decades after the Open Door Policy.[5] In this understanding, China's economic performance has resulted mainly from market forces and China's large and growing private sector, and reforms announced at the Third Plenum of the Chinese Communist Party in November 2013 indicated that the trend of relying on market forces would continue.[6] In contrast, existing research across industries shows steady marketization comes hand in hand with more authoritarian state control, and explicates how this varies by sector, layers of the political economy, state-ownership, and political leadership at the organization level.[7]

What explains, how and why has the Chinese state directed fifth-generation technology standard (5G) telecommunications networks and technical textiles through state-controlled corporate shareholding and government-coordinated research and development (R&D) well before the rise of Xi Jinping and the U.S.-China trade war highlighted the technological competition between the two countries? Moreover, notwithstanding debates on the extent of China's innovative achievements, the dominant pattern of market governance in the high-tech, value-added sectors diverge markedly from predominantly privately held labor-intensive, less value-added textiles, which witness only incidental central state control if any at all. The *centralized governance* of high-tech, value-added sectors with application for national security and contribution to the national technology base is contrary to the expectations of open economy politics. The *decentralized governance* of nonstrategic labor-

---

[3] See Shih (2008), Yasuda (2017), Lin (2018), and Su, Tao, and Yang (2018), respectively.
[4] Representative studies include Naughton and Tsai (2015), Pearson (2015), Pearson, Rithmire, and Tsai (2020), Chen (2018), ten Brink (2019), and Tan (2020), respectively.
[5] See Lin (2017).   [6] See Lardy (2014).
[7] See Hsueh (2011, 2015, 2016), Eaton (2015), Zheng and Huang (2018), Leutert (2020), and Yeo (2020).

intensive, less value-added sectors reveals the limits of regime type and state capitalism explanations.

These dominant sectoral patterns have given rise to a *bifurcated capitalism* shaped by *techno-security developmentalism,* discussed in comparison with the other country and sector cases in Chapter 12. Section 3.1 of this chapter shows how China's *perceived strategic value* orientation took root in the political and economic insecurities experienced during critical junctures of internal and external pressures (from the Opium Wars and Sino-Japanese War to the Soviet-Chinese split and the Cultural Revolution and Great Leap Forward), which connected *national security* with the development of the *national technology base.* The historical process-tracing also shows state elite responses cannot be disconnected from *structural and organizational sectoral attributes.* Section 3.2 explicates the political context of emerging *techno-security developmentalism* in the post-Open Door Policy period from the Tiananmen Square Incident to Deng Xiaoping's Southern Tour and implications for sectoral divergence in market governance. The bifurcation in market governance as a function of strategic and nonstrategic industries becomes most explicit after China's accession to the WTO and was reinforced by the rise of Xi Jinping shown in Section 3.3. Section 3.4 previews the dominant sectoral patterns of market governance presented in their full complexity in Chapters 4 and 5.

3.1 PERCEIVED STRATEGIC VALUE AND IMPACTS OF SECTORAL CHARACTERISTICS (SECTORAL ORIGINS AND BEYOND)

The industrial origins of Chinese telecommunications and textiles can be traced to the first and second Opium Wars (1839–1842 and 1856–1860, respectively), which originated in trade disputes over opium imports from India by the British that later involved other European powers. The association of national insecurity with underdevelopment of industry rooted in these industrial origins will come to have acute significance on successive generations of state elites and will shape dominant patterns of market governance. Thus, the evolution of the perceived strategic value of *national security* and the *national technology base* is shaped by the internal and external pressures experienced by state elites during moments of national consolidation from the Qing to the Chinese Communists.

The Opium War treaties permitted an influx of wool and cotton and foreign-machined yarn and cloth into Chinese markets. To balance opium trade, the Qing dynastic regime relied on comprador-reformers, who enriched themselves and the state through the promotion of commodities in "official and joint merchant-management" arrangements.[8] In the 1870s, these entrepreneur-officials facilitated steam-powered silk filatures, using French and Italian machinery, as part of a series of projects to improve Chinese industry, arguing "conquering the foreign powers by appropriating their science and technology."[9] Cotton spinning soon followed with the establishment of cotton textile mills such as the Shanghai Cotton Cloth Mill and the Dah Sun Cotton Mill as early "government supervision and merchant management" companies.[10]

Meanwhile, the telegraph first arrived in the 1860s when the Qing permitted telegraph cable construction, first in treaty ports by the Great Northern Telegraph Company of Denmark, and then later network expansion elsewhere by the official-entrepreneurs.[11] Initially, Qing officials responded to the telegraph infrastructure with suspicion and fear of the effects of information dissemination on the Qing government's authority over society.[12] Moreover, local populations resisted their construction and attempted to bar the line extensions inland because of disturbances on "feng shui," or natural harmony.

Soon, however, the Qing regime, under the influence of the Self-Strengthening Movement, began to realize the utility of telecommunication networks for strategic purposes such as the centralization of control and military use.[13] By the 1870s, the telegraph became a common means of communication, and major lines connected major cities. The Imperial Telegraph Administration (ITA) was established, in late 1881, as a

---

[8] See Chan (1980), 416–462 and Liu (2020), 196–230.

[9] See Finanane (2008). See quote from Rado (2016). Chao (1977) on the survival of the handicraft weaving industry without the use of intermediate technology, slowing indigenous innovation despite possession of elements of advanced spinning technology.

[10] Chan (1980), 423. Xi Jinping characterized Zhang Jian of Dah Sun as a "patriotic entrepreneur" and ten days after the state stopped the IPO of the fintech company Ant Group in November 2020, detailed in Chapter 4, toured a museum exhibition, which featured Zhang.

[11] Baark (1997), 84.   [12] Harwit (2008) and Baark (1997).

[13] Known also as the *yangwu (Westernization) movement*, it was "a network of different constituencies, who shared, in various degrees, a vision of the Western nationals as a source of inspiration for the revitalization of [China], given appropriate forms of skillful diplomacy and a selective transfer of technology and advanced knowledge from the West" (Baark 1997), 3.

government–supervision and merchant- management company that was composed of private capital and government loans from provincial treasuries. The ITA controlled the direction of development and functions of the telegraph networks, such as the delivery of military messages alongside private commercial communications. This early government-controlled, privately owned enterprise, in the same model as the textile mills, was owned and staffed by the Qing government associates and given monopoly control of telegraph communications. State exemption of import duties on building materials and funds from provincial governments extended the telegraph lines to coastal and inland cities.

The Treaty of Shimonoseki between China and Japan, in 1895, further liberalized foreign machine imports and permitted textile manufacturing by foreigners in all treaty ports across the country. By the early 1900s, external pressures had propelled the fledging establishment of an industrial base in banking, shipping, telegraphs, and textiles. Two decades after the British merchants first laid a telephone line, Qing-era official-merchants had constructed a telephone network in 1900. Up to that point, however, the lack of imperial planning and the dominance of provincial official-entrepreneurs in modern industry contributed to the fragmented integration of nascent industrial sectors with credit facilities, capital formation, and tax structure.

Importantly, the Qing regime experienced internal pressures, which launched peasant rebellions and regional militarism. On the one hand, political economic agents included the varieties of local elites: Landlords, who served as rural administrators; official-entrepreneurs; traders and grain merchants; moneylenders; autonomous municipal governments; and mobilizers of revolutionary movement.[14] On the other hand, the majority peasantry was ripe for agrarian uprisings. "Prosperous tenant farmers" and the middle peasants and poor peasants alike were subjected to varying levels of land rent, land taxes, and usury.

The Taiping Rebels, mobilized by a mixture of chiliastic ideologies, Chinese millenarian and Christian alike, fermented in southern China and agitated through the Xiang Jiang system to central China by the mid-nineteenth century. Regionalism spawned warlordism, creating competing nonstate powers vying for national consolidation. The lack of political penetration into society of the Qing regime shaped political dynamics and various interactions between political and economic agents from above

---

[14] See Bianco (1971).

and below. This gave birth to perceptions of national insecurity and the criticality of national technological development.[15]

3.1.1 National Insecurity and Uneven Development During Qing and Republican Rule

In an attempt to centralize government control over telecommunications infrastructure in the face of internal and external pressures, the Qing government established the Ministry of Posts and Communications (in late 1906) and nationalized ITA and divested private shareholders in 1909, two years before the dynasty's collapse. The ministry combined the telegraph industry with railroads, shipping, and the postal system and became the only Imperial ministry to maintain a stable annual revenue. The nationalized ITA controlled over 14,000 miles of telegraph lines, with an additional 20,000 miles managed by the provinces. By the Qing dynasty's collapse in 1911, the Qing network had 7000 plus phone subscribers. Mainly run by the Japanese and Russians in Manchuria, foreign companies had similar subscribers on foreign-built infrastructure.

The political reforms adopted in the last decade of the Qing regime contributed to Chinese efforts at industrial development," but it also gave rise to modernizers turned nationalist revolutionaries. Official merchants, scholar officials, intellectuals, and exiled students of varying ideological stripes exposed to Western ideas through transnationalism and foreign interventions and united by nationalism, agitated their frustrations at the lack of economic modernization and national development in the May Fourth Movement in 1919. The movement of strange bedfellows – Qing-era intellectuals who supported the Kuomintang (KMT) and early founders of the Chinese Communist Party (CCP) – took place a few years after the founding of the Republic of China by the KMT, first organized in Tokyo in 1905 under the leadership of Sun Yat-sen, "the traveling salesmen of the Chinese revolution."[16]

The CCP established in Shanghai as a party for the working class in 1921. They organized unions in the textile factories invested in by foreigners and the wealthy official-entrepreneurs, who benefited from the treaty ports of the few urban cities.[17] The CCP also targeted wealthy Chinese industrialists who controlled dozens of cotton and flour mills. By the end of the 1920s, over 120 mills, operating with European machinery,

[15] See Johnson (1962) and Wakeman (1991).   [16] See Bianco (1971), 11–152.
[17] See Yeh (1996).

dotted urban centers. In Shanghai, British-, Japanese-, and Chinese-owned mills dominated industry.[18] There, textile and apparel industries focused on silk and weaving, and training institutes provided expertise in textile technology, engineering, and management. The number of Japanese looms exceeded Chinese ones, leading to conflicts between Japanese and Chinese employees in Japanese-owned mills. Emboldened by the National Products Movement, the China Cotton Mill Owners' Association organized to respond to and influence the increasing authoritarian KMT on taxation and labor management.[19]

Meanwhile, the KMT targeted Communist organizers and sympathizers during the White Terror period. Labor strikes and anti-foreign demonstrations fomented the May 30 Movement of 1925. In the Northern Expedition, which followed, the KMT attempted to consolidate control over warring landlords in the Nationalist Revolution of 1928.[20] The parallel purge of left-leaning factions, however, ended the Soviet-negotiated united front with the CCP. Under the aegis of Mao Zedong, the CCP turned to focus on organizing the majority peasantry in the context of internal political chaos and the geopolitical insecurity of the encroaching Japanese intervention.[21] Poor peasants and subproletariat, owning no land, were the most receptive to Communist mobilization; however, tenant farmers, because of land rents and taxes subject to irregularities, inconsistencies, and arbitrariness, were the most negatively affected by the KMT regime and their bureaucratic and entrepreneurial agents.

3.1.2 Internal Conflict and External Intervention: Collapsing Industry and Fragmented Infrastructure

In the first decade of KMT rule, regional warlords damaged or destroyed much of the country's telephone and telegraph lines. It took until the late 1920s for the KMT to retain control, under the Ministry of Communications, and set out to reconstruct damaged infrastructure under central government ownership and regulation of the industry. Because of the lack of national integration, however, local authorities controlled the expansion of telephones. Provincial telecoms administrations established their own long-distance departments. By the mid-1930s, major coastal and inland cities and the KMT capital Nanjing experienced

---

[18] See Bergère (1990).   [19] See Bush (1982) and Bergère (1990).
[20] See Wilbur (1984).   [21] See Johnson (1962).

local phone service and long-distance connections with each other. On the eve of the Sino-Japanese war, a telephone network ran across nine provinces, and the country had some 47,000 kilometers of long-distance phone lines.

In the 1930s, economic malaise gripped urban centers, such as Tianjin, where textile mills idled and prices of finished products tumbled.[22] During the economic recession of 1931–1936, the domestic textile industry suffered an imbalance between fixed assets and working capital despite profiting from the anti-Japanese boycotts during 1928–1929. Domestic mills languished due to price deflation, the drying up of Japanese commercial credit, the increasing price of America credit, and the northeast occupation by the Japanese. Japanese cotton mills outcompeted the Chinese, contributing to the perception of national insecurity under occupation.[23]

Moreover, between 1937 and 1945, the Japanese took control of the communications network and expanded and improved the system to strengthen their rule. Through the 1940s, the KMT's ineffective economic policies such as cotton procurement to stabilize supply, price freezes on cotton threads and textiles, and conversion of gold to government scripts led to out-of-control inflation. Capital flight; the relocation of facilities among businessmen to Hong Kong and Taiwan, where Japanese colonialism since 1895 built an industrial base; and businesses' withdrawal of support further contributed to the weakening of the KMT. The civil war between the KMT and the Communists ended in 1949, and the KMT retreated to Taiwan under Allied protection.

National insecurity and technological underdevelopment came to underscore the internal and external pressures afflicting state-society interactions. Through the Long March, the Sino-Japanese War, and the Chinese Civil War, Mao Zedong and CCP cadres in rural guerilla bases inculcated mass nationalism by appealing to the socioeconomic realities of peasant drudgery. Insecurities of China's majority peasantry were further reinforced by the lack of KMT state penetration outside of key cities due to corruption within the ranks and concentrated resources on Communist eradication during Japanese occupation, particularly in the northern region.[24]

---

[22] See Bergère (1990). See also Hirata (2020) on the Japanese investment and KMT reorganization, which laid the industrial foundations of the steel industry later further reorganized by the CCP.
[23] See Mitter (2000).   [24] See Johnson (1962) and Wu (1995).

3.1.3 Internal Disarray, Cold War Insecurity, and Technological Imperatives Under Mao

During the first decade of the People's Republic of China, Mao adopted the Soviet-style Five-Year Plan under the aegis of Soviet advisors and blueprints. Mao permitted petty capital formation in the rural countryside (which helped finance urban industrialization) and private enterprise to exist alongside the state-owned economy in urban centers. The "leaning to one side" years of Soviet-Chinese relations focused on post-war reconstruction of urban areas and the implementation of heavy industry. Just as the peasant-mobilization stage in the guerrilla bases during the Sino-Japanese War and the Chinese civil war discarded slogans of class warfare and unfair distribution of property, flexible, moderate social policies such as rent control and lending and borrowing mobilized the human capital required for infrastructural development in the cities centered on mixed property rights.

During the first few years, the mostly private owners held what remained of the textile industry. Soon, however, to attain desired production levels and realize industrialization amidst ineffective policies in response to poor harvests, the state nationalized textile enterprises.[25] Thus, between the "leaning to one side" of the 1950s and Deng Xiaoping's Southern Tour in 1992, an overarching sector-specific ministry supervised textile manufacturing and internal market developments across subsectors.[26] The MTI-owned textile mills that processed raw and manmade materials and manufactured fabric, supervised the distribution of raw materials and domestically produced inputs, and owned and controlled trading companies, including the China Textile Resources Group Company, an importer of textile inputs. In addition to managing the textile supply chain and coordinating internal trade and distribution, the MTI intervened on the company level, exercising bureaucratic influence on issues ranging from the allocation of capital and equipment to decisions involving pricing, which the planning ministry also supervised.

To build a nationwide telecommunications network under the 1st Five-Year Plan, the Communist government established the Ministry of Posts and Telecommunications (MPT), in 1949, to effectively take control of

---

[25] See Finanane (2008), p. 206 and Perkins (1966), pp. 34–35.

[26] The MTI ceded control to provincial and city-level authorities during the Great Leap Forward, but regained the power to operate and tax textile factories in the 1960s.

ownership, regulation, and operation of existing infrastructure.[27] Joint ministry measures issued in 1951 declared telecommunications infrastructure a public security issue, which would require the intervention of relevant government organs.[28] Total fixed assets of the telecommunications sector grew over 9 percent annually, and as many as one million Chinese worked as forced laborers on telecommunications projects.[29] Soviet-style plans directed the production of telecommunications equipment under the Ministry of Electronics Industry, reviewed and approved by the State Planning Commission and other higher-level central authorities, including the State Council and the Central Committee of the Communist Party.

Mao soon grew weary of the reliance on the Soviet Union and the priorities of the Soviet plans and sought for "Standing on Two Feet," leading to Soviet withdrawal in the mid-1950s. Soon followed were two-plus decades of revolutionary fervor departing from the Soviet model: The economic deviation of the Great Leap Forward and the political deviation of the Cultural Revolution. As a function of telecommunications' high asset specificity and complex technology, in addition to public security designation, the MPT was exempt from complete decentralization of industrial production and fiscal resources. Nevertheless, the ministry suffered from poor construction and inaccurate accounting of assets. During a brief return to economic planning in the early 1960s, the MPT moved to acquire Western knowledge and technology from Western Europe and Japan. The Cultural Revolution soon disrupted the infrastructural modernization, however, and the MPT was abolished in 1970 and subsumed under the Ministry of Transportation managed by the People's Liberation Army (PLA).

Industrial development in telecommunications, however, did not cease entirely. In Third Front areas in China's inland regions and mountainous areas, Cold War insecurity drove development in electronics, electricity generation, and electricity grids, which powered local and long-distance telephone lines, radio, and rail, linking provincial capitals and large towns

---

[27] See Harwit (2008), p. 30.
[28] "公安部、中央邮电部、燃料工业部关于保护人民输电线路电信线路及管制线路旧料暂行办 [Interim Measures of the Ministry of Public Security, the Ministry of Posts and Telecommunications of the Central Committee, and the Ministry of Fuel Industry on the Protection of People's Transmission Lines and Telecommunication Lines]," *The Maoist Legacy*, accessed July 22, 2020 at https://www.maoistlegacy.de/db/items/show/5399.
[29] Harwit (2008), p. 30.

under their jurisdictions.[30] In 1970, China launched its first satellite and established significant electronics personnel and manufacturing facilities. Concentration on the development of oil products in the Third Front areas between 1965 and 1980, as a response to the Cold War, moreover, laid the groundwork of a petrochemical industry, which produced chemical and other synthetic fibers.[31]

By the 1970s, several decades of "high-target, quantity-centered, rapid growth" emphasis on heavy industry, combined with the political and economic disruptions of the Cultural Revolution, led to economic stagnation and uneven development. Driven by a perception of economic crisis and in search of steady sources of foreign exchange during a time of global political opening, post-Cultural Revolution state elites shifted factors of production (funds, raw materials, fuel and energy, transport capacity, labor, and foreign exchange) to emphasize light industries producing consumer goods and textiles for exports.[32] The factoral shift, combined with agricultural reforms and the deregulation of light industry not perceived strategic for national security and the national technology base in the 1980s, foreshadowed the *decentralized governance* of less strategic industries in the 1990s and beyond.

In contrast, as the Cultural Revolution drew to a close and China began to open its door to the outside world, the Ministry of Post and Telecommunications was re-established, in 1973, to manage the telecommunications monopoly. Until the early 1990s, the MPT ceded service administration, network planning, and procurement to provincial and local post and telecommunications authorities (PTAs). The decentralized PTAs made day-to-day operating decisions with their business performance linked to a system of contractual responsibility. Several ministries operated special networks for government use. The Ministry of Electronics Industry supervised the development of telecommunications equipment, but the MPT also owned and operated several large equipment makers.

Table 3.1 maps the evolution of the *perceived strategic value* of *national security* and the *national technology base* to internal and external pressures faced by state elites across significant moments of national

---

[30] See Meyskens (2020), 201–226 on industrial development in Third Front areas.
[31] See Meyskens (2020), 201–228.
[32] Quote from Solinger (1991), p. 57. See Solinger (1991) on "economic readjustment" of the Open Door Policy, which shifted industrial policy to a focus on efficiency and consumption, represented by light industrial growth and development.

TABLE 3.1. *China: Perceived strategic value and techno-security developmentalism (1860–1980s)*

Sectoral Origins and Beyond	Telecommunications 1900 First Telephone Network	Textiles 1860s First Mechanized Textiles
Perceived Strategic Value *National Security*	*External Pressures* • First and Second Opium wars • The Treaty of Shimonoseki (1895) • Sino-Japanese War (1930s–1945) • Soviet Withdrawal (mid-1950s) *Internal Pressures* • Peasant rebellions and regional militarism • Kuomintang-Warlords • Kuomintang-Communists • Cultural Revolution (1960s–1970s) • Tiananmen Square Incident (1989)	*External Pressures* • First and Second Opium wars • The Treaty of Shimonoseki • Sino-Japanese War (1930s–1945) • Northeast Japanese occupation *Internal Pressures* • Peasant rebellions and regional militarism • Kuomintang-Communists • Cultural Revolution (1960s–1970s) • Tiananmen Square Incident (1989)
National Technology Base	• Cold War • China-Soviet Relations (1950s) • Third Front Areas (1960s) • Open Door Policy (1978) • Economic sanctions (post-Tiananmen) • Self-Strengthening Movement (1890s) • May Fourth Movement (1919) • 1st Five-Year Plan (1950–1955) • Great Leap Forward (late 1950s) • Deepening reforms and economic troubles (1985–1988)	• Great Depression (1931–1936) • China-Soviet Relations • Third Front Areas (1960s) • Open Door Policy (1978) • Economic sanctions (post-Tiananmen) • Self-Strengthening Movement (1890s) • May Fourth Movement (1919) • China Cotton Mill Association (1930s) • 1st Five-Year Plan (1950–1955) • Great Leap Forward (late 1950s) • Economic stagnation and uneven development (1970s) • Deepening reforms and economic troubles (1985–1988)

political development. Analysis begins at the developmental origins of modern industry in our main composite sector cases (textiles and telecommunications).

3.2 POLITICAL CONTEXT OF NATIONAL SECURITY AND NATIONAL TECHNOLOGY BASE (1980–2000)

In the context of the end of the Cultural Revolution and the death of Mao and the normalization of foreign relations in the late 1970s, the Open Door Policy (in 1978) launched market reforms. Deng Xiaoping focused on building competitive advantage through maximizing the benefits and minimizing the costs of a more open economy through relying on empiricism and trial and error.[33] For reform-era China, however, technological advancement and infrastructural development cannot be disconnected from the state's concerns for national security, both internal and external in nature. In the period since Mao's death in 1976, especially after the 1989 Tiananmen Square Incident, successive generations of Chinese leadership have sought to identify and manage the political, economic, and social forces that could derail regime stability and China's growth and development. Thus, the protracted but sharp and steady reorganization of state power in China, as shown in Chapters 3–5, is bifurcated in nature and has varied by sector.[34]

The introduction of competition and devolution of economic decision-making, which varied by sector (as shown in our sector case studies in Chapters 4 and 5), focused first on the agricultural sector, then light industry, and heavy industry. Deepening economic reforms and the accompanying economic adjustments, from 1985 and 1988, led to deflationary pressures and agitation for political reform by intellectuals, students, and workers. Inspired by political reforms in the Soviet Union and activated by the death of former general secretary Hu Yaobang in April 1989, university students mobilized an anti-regime protest in Tiananmen Square, in Beijing, staged in June 1989 during the visit of Soviet leader Mikhail Gorbachev, the first between the two countries since the Sino-Soviet split in 1959. The protest agitated against the lack

---

[33] See Shirk (1993) and Naughton (1995). Huang (2008) contends that 1980s reforms were liberal but the state reversed directions.

[34] China's gradualism is compared to India's Big Bang liberalization and the shock therapy launched by Soviet collapse; all the same, the dominant patterns of market governance in India and Russia also varied by sector.

of political liberalization and the corruption and inflation developed during ten years of "reform and opening" and quickly spread across the country, joined by workers and other social sectors.[35]

The CCP leadership initially disagreed on how to respond, with Hu's successor Zhao Ziyang supportive of political reforms opposed by the then premier Li Peng and other hardliners. Ultimately Li Peng and his allies convinced Deng Xiaoping and the Standing Committee to repress and violently quash open dissent and keep inner-party battles within acceptable limits. State elites believed that in the absence of a stable environment, China "would not be able to achieve anything and might even lose what had been accomplished."[36] In the shadow of the Cultural Revolution and the political confrontations leading up to the Tiananmen Square Incident, the Chinese leadership prioritized national security and social political stability (Table 3.2).

Between 1989 and 1991, following the Tiananmen Square Incident, many countries enacted economic sanctions against China, and trade came to a halt. Concerned with Communist Party legitimacy in the aftermath of Tiananmen, Deng Xiaoping rejuvenated private and foreign investment and market activities during his Southern Tour in 1992. The coastal development strategy and with it the establishment of industrial parks and trade zones spurred the influx of foreign direct investment (FDI). In parallel, Deng "repeatedly called for strengthening central authority to help maintain stability and prevent chaos." In response to the collapse of the Soviet Union, Deng's successor Jiang Zemin reaffirmed the hardline by claiming that "class struggle" would continue for a period of time within "certain parts" of China.

Shaped by prior episodes of national consolidation in response to internal and external pressures, the Chinese leadership perceives the end of the cold war, in 1991, as the dawn of American military leadership in East Asia. State security imperatives have responded to China's status as the only major "Communist" power in the world with a regional security system positioned against it.[37] Government officials, leaders of sector and business associations, and managers of state- and privately owned enterprises stress the connection between acquiring national technological

---

[35] See Wright (2001, 2018).   [36] See Yang (2004), 4.
[37] External and internal security overlap (Christensen 2003; Segal 2006) and external threats are perceived in the context of aggravating domestic instability (Shambaugh 2002).

competence and "making China rich and strong" in the face of unnamed threats.[38]

Informants identify security considerations and "royalties, profits, and relative economic gains" as drivers of deliberate state control.[39] Funding programs, such as the State High-Tech Development Plan (863) centrally initiated and implemented from 1986 to 2016, jumpstarted basic science and commercialization initiatives, including R&D in telecommunications and other information technology sectors. The National Development and Reform Commission's various five-year and fifteen-year plans and catalogs for guidance of foreign investment targeted the modernization of infrastructure in high technology sectors, with applications for maintaining political stability and contribution to the national technology base and economic competitiveness (Table 3.4).

In this context, while a fragmented administrative structure governed telecommunication in the Mao era, with provincial, municipal, and prefectural governments controlling the planning of telecommunications in their jurisdiction, in the 1980s and 1990s, business reorganization, institutional reform, and government directives asserted central control of regulation and industrial strategy. The telecommunications ministry became the dominant administrator of nationwide post and telecommunications and formally separated business from bureaucracy.[40] These developments set the stage for the introduction of competition and the consolidation of state control over the entire network infrastructure in telecommunications, an industry perceived strategic for national security and the national technology base, detailed in Chapter 4.

In contrast, a sector-specific ministry for textiles, perceived less strategic for national security and the national technology base despite existing bureaucratic stakeholders, was dismantled in 1993. These developments foreshadowed decentralized and deregulated market coordination of variegated property rights arrangements in the 1990s and beyond as shown in Chapter 5. When the 1997–1999 financial crisis, which afflicted China's Asian neighbors, led to a slowdown in FDI and a deflationary spiral in the domestic market, it prompted Jiang Zemin and Zhu Rongji to green light WTO negotiations despite resistance from party

---

[38] In-depth, semi-structured interviews during extensive fieldwork between 2005 and 2019, in China. Quote from a September 8, 2008 communication in Beijing with an official at the Research Development Center of the National Development and Reform Commission.
[39] Hsueh (2016), p. 92.   [40] See Hsueh (2011).

leadership in the early 1990s in response to GATT member states' "disenchantment with China in the wake of the 1989 Tiananmen Square violence."[41] The liberalizing details of the accession protocol agreement in 1999, however, varied by sector, according to their perceived strategic value. For example, shortly after the WTO accession, a demoted and reorganized internal trade ministry, which oversaw textile trade, was merged with the non-sector-specific commerce ministry in 2003.

The 1997–1999 financial crisis briefly precipitated state interventions to ensure the global competitiveness of domestic industry including the razing of spindles in state-owned mills in already decentralized labor-intensive, less value-added textiles. More significantly, the state consolidated central control of capital-intensive, value-added telecommunications when it forced the divestment of FDI in basic telecommunications services and merged the equipment and service ministries following the Asian financial crisis. Likewise, the reinforced strategic value of the national technology base and economic competitiveness following the 2008 global financial crisis and subsequent economic slowdown led to the restructuring of state-owned telecommunications carriers and the formation of a supraministry. What is more, the 2008 anti-monopoly law targeted FDI to promote domestic industry, similar to the forced FDI divestment a decade earlier. Reregulation based on a strategic value logic will occur again during the U.S.-China trade war a decade later.

Parallel to China's accession to the WTO in 2001, part and parcel of the imperatives of Chinese Communist Party legitimacy and social and political stability are the constitutional enshrinement of business entrepreneurs in Jiang Zemin and Zhu Rongji's "Three Represents" in 2002 and the recognition of the use, sell/transfer, alienation, and derivation of income of property of different ownership types in the 2007 Property Law. Moreover, Hu Jintao and Wen Jiabao went a step further in stressing regime stability in their advocacy of a "harmonious society" in rural reforms. Explicitly linking *internal stability* and *national technological development*, the Hu-Wen era (2002–2012) also introduced the "Scientific Development Concept" and "indigenous development," which served as rationale for state intervention to promote industries that contribute to the national technology base and competitiveness of the domestic economy.

---

[41] Quote from page 86 of Solinger (2009), also 85–86 and 119–220. Also, see Lampton (2001) and Lardy (2002).

3.3 RISE OF TECHNO-SECURITY DEVELOPMENTALISM AND SECTORAL VARIATION (2000–2020)

The political context of national security and national technology base as paramount perceived strategic value in the post-Open Door Policy era is shaped and reshaped by the internal and external pressures experienced by Chinese state elites, as shown in Table 3.3. Rules and regulations concerning the role of the state in market coordination and property rights arrangements in strategic and nonstrategic industries demonstrate the perceived strategic value of *techno-security developmentalism* in the context of globalization (Table 3.4 and tables in the sectoral case chapters). The imperatives of national security and the national technology base are apparent in China's "liberalization two-step," defined as macroliberalization and sector-specific reregulation, in the post-WTO era and reenforced by Xi Jinping's political ascendancy in 2013.[42]

With the 2008 Beijing Olympics as the backdrop to globally showcase China's globalization and development, the 11th Five-Year Plan (2006–2010) during Hu-Wen enshrined into policy the "import-substitution-cum-FDI strategy" adopted and enforced by various bureaucracies in strategic industries with application for national security and contribution to the national technology base.[43] The dual strategy explicitly "courts, digests, absorbs, and innovates upon" foreign knowledge and technology. "Absorbing and digesting" FDI as knowledge and technology transfers, and as market discipline and diversification, are means to achieving government imperatives of national security, advancement of the national technology base, and economic competitiveness.[44] This approach differs from the "market-based import-substitution strategy" pursued in Russian textiles, which aims to actively replace imports with liberalized domestic industry, as discussed in Chapter 11.

Characterizing what he calls the "paradox" of welcoming FDI and developing world-class industries, an official from the Ministry of Science and Technology explained, "Import substitution is an economic policy that cannot be concrete because some industries still require foreign imports and expertise."[45] He further elaborated that domestic production cannot improve without allowing and sometimes even courting foreign participation. The National Development and Reform Commission (NDRC) regularly offered analyses on the development of foreign-

---

[42] See Hsueh (2011, 2012).   [43] See Hsueh (2015).
[44] See Ma (2005) and Sun and Zhang (2005).   [45] Quote from Hsueh (2015), p. 634.

invested companies, complete with information on their "tactics" and profit margins, with instructions on utilizing FDI to reorganize and restructure SOEs.[46]

The Ministry of Commerce (MOFCOM), whose bureaucrats are generally the most economically liberal, maintained that, "in a globalized world, we can't shun foreign investment" even while emphasizing that "China cannot rely on FDI alone and must address unemployment directly with other measures."[47] MOFCOM studies issued warnings about the impact of becoming "totally foreign-funded" and proposed, "For every U.S. dollar invested, China should match with 6 RMB."[48] One analysis warned about the detrimental impact of mergers and acquisitions involving foreign equipment makers on domestic ones, two years before the release of the Monopoly Law in 2008 and well before Xi Jinping became paramount leader.[49]

The Development Research Center of the State Council further warned that, "China had better adopt effective measures – before it is too late – to augment her staying power of increasing GDP on her own."[50] Thus, the central government provides economic incentives to attract FDI to invest in value-added, export-oriented production at the same time it issues trade tariffs, localization rules, and subsidies, which mimic "import-substitution" policies in strategic industries. The China-based manufacturing and imports of inputs by foreign companies have increased, showing that macro-liberalization and sectoral-level reregulation necessitate both the absorption of foreign inputs and government support of indigenous development. An NDRC official intimated that the Chinese government "doesn't really care if private Chinese companies or SOEs innovate. It simply wants to see domestic Chinese innovation."[51] Figure 1.3 in Chapter 1 shows how FDI as a percentage of GDP for China has witnessed a steady decline since the initial surge in 1992 and well before the 1997 and 2008 economic crises.

3.3.1 Macro-Liberalization and Techno-Security Reregulation by Sector

By the mid-2000s, variation in the dominant patterns of market governance according to the interacting strategic value and sectoral logics

---

[46] See Wang (2005).   [47] See Sang (2005) and Zhou (2005), respectively.
[48] See Chen (2005) and Han (2005), respectively.   [49] See Sang (2006).
[50] See Zhao (2006).
[51] Conversation on January 16, 2006, with official of National Development and Reform Commission.

became solidified (Table 3.2). New policy pronouncements reinforced the dominant patterns in identified strategic sectors. In the context of the introduction of competition, the State Council, in September 2006, clarified the realignment of the state sector as directed by the 1999 fourth plenum of the CCP's 15th Central Committee. The "Guiding Opinion on Promoting the Adjustment of State-owned Capital and Reorganization of State-owned Enterprises" identified key sectors critical for national security and the survival and global competitiveness of the domestic

TABLE 3.2. *China: Market governance mechanisms in strategic and less strategic sectors (1990 and beyond)*

Strategic Sectors/Assets	Less Strategic Sectors/Assets
Centralized Governance	*Decentralized and Private Governance*
• Decoupling of state-owned enterprise from government office, corporatization, business restructuring (merge, spin-off, or consolidate businesses)	• Permitting of small-scale enterprise of the Household Responsibility System
• Public listing (domestically or globally, with the state holding majority shares)	• Divesting of state assets to former managers, corporatization, business restructuring, (and public listing)
• Introduction of competition between SOEs and sometimes private companies, including FDI	• Introduction of competition and liberalization of market entry
• Strict rules on market entry and investment level (either no private entry at all or private domestic but no FDI or FDI in joint ventures)	• Vibrant "private sector" comprising of town and village enterprises, quasi-state enterprises, and FDI
• Assets and property rights held by the State-owned Assets Supervision and Administration Commission (SASAC)	• Local state discretion and decision-making on market entry and business scope
• China-specific standards-setting by national-level sector-specific associations, with ambitions for global standards-setting	• Market coordination by business and sector associations, formerly government bureaucracies
• Industrial policy via anti-monopoly and corporate governance interventions	• Private sector and company-level initiatives in standards-setting and adoption of global standards
• Strict rules on approvals of outward FDI at sector, firm, and project levels	• Private sector participation in China's "go global" policy (such as OFDI and Belt and Road Initiative)
	• Rules on approvals of OFDI

TABLE 3.3. *China: Political context of national security and national technology bvase (1980–2020)*

Perceived Strategic Value	External Pressures	Internal Pressures
National Security *Political Social Stability/Regime Legitimacy* (1980–2010) *National Sovereignty* (2010–2020)	• Normalization of foreign relations (1970s) • Soviet leader Gorbachev's visit to China, first between two countries since 1959 (1989) • Fall of Soviet Union (1991) • Hong Kong Umbrella Movement (2014, 2019) • Economic sanctions after Tiananmen Square (1989–1991) • Member states's opposition of China in the GATT due to Tiananmen Square violence (early 1990s) • Post-Cold War politics • Various Chinese government-sponsored computer hacks • China's building of artificial islands and drilling in gas fields in disputed waters of the East China and South China seas • Various disputes with countries, including in 2020 with Australia during the COVID-19 global pandemic and India over China's border intrusions	• Student and related social movements and death of Hu Yaobang and dismissal of Zhao Ziyang leading up to Tiananmen Square Incident (1986–1989) • Laid-off workers and under employment (mid-to-late 1990s) • Tiananmen Square Incident (1989) • Jiang Zemin's Three Represents • Formation and quash of Democracy Party and banning of Falun Gong (late 1990s) • Zhu Rongji state sector reforms/industrial bureaucratic conflicts in lead up to WTO accession (late 1990s) • Anti-Japanese protests (2005, 2012) • Hu-Wen Harmonious Society (2007) • Xinjiang/Urumqi protests (2009) • Interdepartmental telecoms disputes (2011) • Xi Jinping Anti-Corruption Campaign (2013) • Xinjiang Uighur "Reeducation" camps • 996.icu campaign (2019) • Slowest economic growth since Asian financial crisis (2012-ongoing) • "Wealth Hating" complex • CCP moderates' opposition of Xi's anti-corruption campaign • Citizen and worker protests of corruption and workplace and environmental safety

(continued)

TABLE 3.3. *(continued)*

Perceived Strategic Value	External Pressures	Internal Pressures
National Technology Base *Indigenous Industry* (1990–2010) *Economic/Global Competitiveness* (2010–2020)	• Coastal Development Strategy/influx of FDI • Slowdown in FDI during Asian financial crisis (1997–1999) • Asian financial crisis (1997–1999) • WTO accession protocol agreement (late 1999) • WTO Accession (2001) • Global financial crisis (2008) • 2008 Beijing Olympics • Belt and Road Initiative • Infrastructure-for-resources and Infrastructure-for-markets bargains in Global South • U.S.-China Trade War (1998–ongoing) • Global tech competition • COVID-19 Global Pandemic (2020-ongoing) • "Xinjiang Cotton Boycott" and foreign sanctions and entity lists in response to Xinjiang human rights abuses (2020-ongoing)	• Open Door Policy/Agricultural Sector Reform (1980s) • Zhao Ziyang and Hu Yaobang become premier and party secretary alternately (1980) • Deepening reforms and economic troubles (1985–1988) • 1992 Deng Xiaoping Southern Tour • Decision on Issues Concerning the Establishment of a Socialist Market Economic Structure (1993) • Deflationary pressure (mid-1990s) • Zhu Rongji state sector reforms/Industrial bureaucratic conflicts in lead up to WTO accession (late 1990s) • Industrial overexpansion during Asian financial crisis (1997–1999) • Yangtze River floods (1998) • Shenzhou Space Launch (first and last launched in 1999 and 2006, respectively) • Hu-Wen Scientific Development Concept (2006) • Sichuan Earthquake (2008) • 2008 Beijing Olympics • Stock Market Turbulence (2015–2016) • Slowed Economy (2019-ongoing) • "Patriotic purchases"/nationalist responses to foreign opposition against Xinjiang human rights abuses (2020-ongoing)

TABLE 3.4. *China's techno-security developmentalism: Law and political economy*

Globalization	National Security	National Technology Base
• 1978 Open Door Policy	• Fourth Plenum of the 15th Central Committee (1999) on state sector realignment	• Economic zones; Coastal, Western, Central China development strategies (1980, 1992, 1997, 2004)
• Laws on Sino-Foreign Cooperative Joint Venture (1979, 1988)		
• Law on Wholly Foreign-Owned Enterprises (WFOE) (1986)	• WTO protocol and accession (1999 and 2001)	• Laws on Sino-Foreign Cooperative Joint Venture (1979, 1988)
• Deng Xiaoping's Southern Tour (1992)	• State Council Guiding Opinion on national security sectors (2006)	• State High-Tech Development Plan (863) (1986–2016)
• Decision on Issues Concerning the Establishment of a Socialist Market Economic Structure (1993)	• State Council Decision on Accelerating the Development of Strategic Emerging Industries (SEIs) (2010)	• 908 and 909 Projects (1991–1995; 1996–2000)
		• Western Development Strategy (1997)
• Economic zones; Coastal, Western, Central China development strategies (1980, 1992, 1997, 2004)	• National Security Review (2011) per Anti-Monopoly Law	• WTO Accession Protocol (1999)
	• Xi Jinping's Anti-Corruption Campaign (2013)	• Jiang Zemin's Three Represents (2002)
• "Go Global" policy first articulated (1998)	• Third Plenum of the 18th National Congress of the CCP (2013)	• Regulation of private enterprises (2003)
• WTO protocol and accession (1999 and 2001)		• "Rise of Central China" Strategy (2004)
• Foreign Trade Laws (1994, 2004)	• 13th Five Year Plan (2015)	• Hu-Wen "Scientific Development" Concept for indigenous capacity
• 11th Five Year Plan: import substitution-cum-FDI strategy (2006–2010)	• Made in China 2025 (2015)	
	• Counterterrorism Law (2015)	• National Medium- and Long-Term Science and Technology Development Plan (2006–2020)
• Anti-Monopoly Law (2008, 2020 revisions)	• National Security Law (2015)	
	• Cybersecurity Law (2017)	• Anti-Monopoly Law (2008, 2020 revisions)

(*continued*)

TABLE 3.4. (*continued*)

Globalization	National Security	National Technology Base
• Third Plenum of the 18th National Congress of the CCP (2013) • Xi Jinping Speech World Economic Forum (2017) • Catalogues for Guidance on Foreign Direct Investments and Outward Investments (various years) • "Dual Circulation" (2020) in 14th Five-Year Plan • Opinions on Building a More Complete System and Mechanism for the Market-oriented Allocation of Factors (2020) • Anti-Foreign Sanctions Law (2021)	• Amendments to PRC constitution on presidential term limits (2018) • CCP dominance in state structures (2018) • Xi Jinping Thought (2018) • Anti-Monopoly Law (2008, 2020 revisions)	• State Council Decision on Accelerating the Development of Strategic Emerging Industries (2010) • Xi Jinping's China Dream (2013) • Made in China 2025 (2015) • Five Year and Fifteen Year plans (various years) • Catalogues for Guidance on Foreign Direct Investments and Outward Investments (various years) • Guiding Opinions on State Sector Reform (various rounds) • 11th Five Year Plan: import substitution-cum-FDI strategy (2006–2010) • China Standard 2035 (2020) • "Dual Circulation" (2020) in 14th Five-Year Plan • Opinions on Building a More Complete System and Mechanism for the Market-oriented Allocation of Factors (2020)

industry: Military production, electricity (grid and power generation), petroleum, telecommunications, coal, civil aviation, and shipping. Moreover, various catalogs for guidance on FDI and outward investments (OFDI) have reinforced the centralized approval process for encouraged, restricted, and prohibited sectors. The latter catalogs have diplomatically set conditions; aligned China's development aid with investment; and disproportionally distributed capital to SOEs, which make up the majority of OFDI.

Then in October 2010, the "State Council Decision on Accelerating the Development of Strategic Emerging Industries (SEIs)" identified the specific industries the central government would target: Energy efficient and environmental technologies, next generation information technology (IT), biotechnology, high-end equipment manufacturing, new energy, new materials, and new-energy vehicles (NEVs). The 2010 decision also established a quantitative target for SEIs to account for 8 percent of GDP by 2015 and 15 percent by 2020.

When Xi Jinping became the CCP general secretary the Third Plenum of the 18th National Congress in 2013 reiterated China's "opening up" and promised "comprehensively deepening reforms." At the same time, state leaders identified national security, with emphasis on internal security; social and environmental consequences of reform; and innovation and global competitiveness of Chinese business as critical issues. The 13th Five Year Plan, approved in late 2015, further sustained the dominant sectoral patterns of market governance based on *perceived strategic value* and *sectoral attributes.*

The 13th plan sought to modernize infrastructure, guarantee national security, and ensure social and political stability during a period of slowed growth and sustain China's increasing per-capita income. This would be achieved through the introduction of competition and deliberate regulation (of market entry, business scope, investment, ownership, capital markets, and standards-setting), employing new and time-tried methods to support industrial upgrading and indigenous innovation in agriculture and emerging industries. Emerging industries identified include renewable energy and civil-military integration and service sectors, such as healthcare and information communications technology.

To protect and promote indigenous industry, the Chinese government has also taken antitrust actions under the 2008 Anti-Monopoly Law against global competitors, indicting them for overcharging, price manipulation, and abusing their market position. Between 2008 and 2012, the NDRC investigated twenty pricing-related cases and, in 2013, undertook eighty. In June 2014, a State Council directive announced that MOFCOM, NDRC, the State Administration of Industry and Commerce (SAIC), and the State Intellectual Property

Office would oversee an effort to intensify "severe punishment" of "monopolistic and anti-competitive behavior."[52] Soon after, the SAIC began investigating U.S. software provider Microsoft and the NDRC, foreign-invested automakers.

Between 2011 and 2015, foreign companies or their joint ventures paid 76 percent of the more than Rmb3bn (US$480m) in antimonopoly penalties handed down by the NDRC since 2011. The U.S. Chamber of Commerce in Beijing stated in September, 2014, "China seeks to strengthen such [state] companies through the anti-monopoly law (AML) and, in apparent disregard of the AML, encourages them to consolidate market power, though this is contrary to the normal purpose of competition law."[53]

The Made in China 2025 released in May 2015 outlines the new frontier technologies prioritized by the Chinese government and sets goals of 40 percent indigenous production of "essential spare parts and key materials" in advanced industries by 2020 and of 70 percent by 2025.[54] The process-tracing of telecommunications sectors in Chapter 4 shows the connection between security concerns and government goals of advancing and controlling China's technology infrastructure, disseminating information, and managing labor markets before 2015 and its reinforcement thereafter.

The sectoral cases also reveal how the "Guiding Opinions of the Central Committee of the Communist Party of China and the State Council on Deepening State-Owned Enterprise Reform," released in August 2015, reiterates the party's central role in the internal supervision of SOEs and in the state's market coordination and ownership of priority sectors.[55] The "Guiding Opinions" differentiates between "public" versus "commercial" state-owned enterprises (SOEs), which operate on political versus market logics, respectively, and underscores the state's controlling interest in strategic sectors even as the state permits private shareholding. This is observed in the state's role in corporate governance in telecommunications equipment, including semiconductors along the supply chain.

The State Council edict, along with "Guiding Opinions on the Restructuring and Reorganization of Central State-Owned Enterprises"

---

[52] "State Council to Promote Fair Market Competition and Protect Normal Market Order," PRC State Council Directive #20 (June 4, 2014).
[53] "China: Monopoly Position," *Financial Times* (January 25, 2015).
[54] Official Translation of Made in China 2025 released by the State Council on July 7, 2015.
[55] Li (2020) on the dual role of the Chinese Communist Party, within the party and in the state.

released in July 2016, outline state methods for SOE reform to promote global competitiveness, national security, and national technological development: The cleaning up of failing SOEs through forced exit; the restructuring of SOEs through consolidations and mergers; development and innovation of SOEs; and the fortifying and strengthening of a group of central SOEs vital to the national economy and national security, including defense, nuclear power, basic communications infrastructure, power grids, oil and gas pipelines, and reserves of strategic materials such as oil and grain.

In parallel, Xi's anti-corruption campaign and an extensive coercive apparatus for maintaining social order have aimed to stop bureaucrats from lining their pockets – and tackle uneven development, industrial overexpansion, and runaway pollution.[56] Xi also intensified party guidance and supervision of executives and increased inspection and auditing of firms from a range of industries and the government has also taken private entrepreneurs into custody. The 2018 revision of Party regulations on disciplinary action for the first time in three years stipulates the importance of "resolutely" upholding Xi's core status in the Party.[57] Constitutional amendments and policy pronouncements related to the ending of term limits and Xi Jinping Thought on a variety of topics from the military to ecological civilization and foreign policy and socialist economics, further reinforced the perceived strategic value of *national security* greatly defined.[58]

These political interventions to bolster regime legitimacy and maintain authoritarian rule have occurred in the context of legalization and the increased use of personal connections among firms, which have moved beyond local protectionism to the national government, to navigate legal procedures and institutions.[59] Xi's critics in the Chinese Communist Party and moderate intellectuals, however, have openly criticized his tightening of political power and the party's apparatus of stability maintenance.[60] The anti-corruption campaign has left those with personal ties

---

[56] See Wang and Minzner (2015) on the "security state."

[57] "Xi Jinping Drops Surprise Hint Over Secret Feud," Nikkei Asian Review (September 6, 2018).

[58] "Xi Jinping Thought Explained: A New Ideology for a New Era," *New York Times* (February 26, 2018).

[59] See Ang and Jai (2014), Wang (2016), and Hou (2019).

[60] "Xi Jinping Drops Surprise Hint Over Secret Feud," *Nikkei Asian Review* (September 6, 2018) and "Does a Stronger Xi Mean a Weaker Chinese Communist Party?," *New York Times* Opinion (March 2, 2018). See Xu (2018)'s critique of Xi published online by now-

to him largely untouched.[61] Moreover, the Chinese government has silenced the dissenters with marginalization and arrest.[62] Nevertheless, Xi's responses to the U.S. trade war between 2018 and 2020 bolstered his popularity in the eyes of the Chinese citizenry.[63] The rift with the United States shifted attention away from the slowing economy and domestic scandals involving tainted vaccines and protests over online investments gone sour in shadow banking.[64]

The "dual circulation" strategy announced in mid-2020, similar to Xi's globalization speech at the 2017 World Economic Forum, reinforces the *techno-security developmentalism* orientation, which has shaped dominant patterns of market governance in strategic and nonstrategic industries. Thus, a reflection of continuity rather than of change, dual circulation's inflows and outflows centered on indigenous development and domestic consumption in the context of global economic integration recapitulate the 11th Five Year Plan (2006–2010), Made in China 2025, and China Standard 2035 to reduce import reliance and advance the national technology base. The "import-substitution-cum-FDI strategy" analyzed earlier exemplifies "dual circulation." Any subsequent reregulation and their details following FDI liberalization adheres to the dominant patterns of market governance in strategic and nonstrategic sectors.

3.4 STRATEGIC VALUE FRAMEWORK AND SECTORAL PATTERNS OF MARKET GOVERNANCE

The longitudinal case studies of Chinese telecommunications and textiles, representative of strategic and nonstrategic sectors presented in the next two chapters, expose the importance of understanding the strategic value and sectoral logics of property rights arrangements and the extent and scope of the state's role in market coordination, particularly in a large,

---

shuttered liberal Unirule Institute of Economics, and Wang and Minzer (2015) on stability maintenance.

[61] See Lorentzen and Lu (2018).

[62] "A Specter is Haunting Xi's China: 'Mr. Democracy'," *New York Times Review of Books* (April 19, 2018).

[63] "Chairman Xi crushes dissent but poor believe he's making China great," *The Guardian* (October 14, 2017).

[64] See "The Deleted WeChat Post That Fueled China's Vaccine Scandal," *The Atlantic* (July 25, 2018) and "As Chinese Investors Panic Over Dubious Products, Authorities Quash Protests," *New York Times* (August 8, 2018).

TABLE 3.5. *Perceived strategic value and sectoral patterns of market governance: China*

Industrial Sector	Telecommunications	Textiles
Perceived Strategic Value	Strategic for *national security*, contribution to the *national technology base*, and the *competitiveness of domestic industry* in service of post-Cultural Revolution and Tiananmen Square Incident imperatives	Strategic for *sociopolitical stability* and the *competitiveness of domestic economy*; less strategic for national security and contribution to the national technology base in service of post-Cultural Revolution and Tiananmen Square Incident imperatives
Sectoral Structural Attributes	Capital intensive, complex interactive technology, producer driven commodity chain	Labor intensive, linear technology, buyer-driven commodity chain
Country-specific Sectoral Organization of Institutions	During Mao and Deng eras, separate equipment and services ministries and bureaucratic and provincial networks managed fragmented telecommunications systems with stakeholders requiring accommodation during market opening; the state merged sectoral bureaucracies in 1997 and created a supraministry in 2008 in the post-WTO era and during the Global Financial Crisis.	During Mao era, until 1993, sector-specific ministry managed vertical supply chains and horizontal subsectors in manufacturing and services; ministry dismantled in 1993, and – despite reassertion of regulatory authority during the 1997 Asian financial crisis – all central sector-specific bureaucracies became sector associations after China's accession to WTO in 2001.
Dominant Patterns of Market Governance	*Centralized Governance* (Telecoms Basic Services, Value-added Services, and Telecoms Equipment)	*Private Governance* (Apparel & Clothing), *Decentralized Governance* (Technical Textiles, Trade and Distribution)

(*continued*)

TABLE 3.5. (*continued*)

Industrial Sector	Telecommunications	Textiles
Coordination Mechanisms		
Level of State Control	Central goals; central-level bureaucracies and state-owned and state-controlled firms	Local and central goals; local governments and relevant central level bureaucuracies
Issue Scope	Sector-specific rules and regulations on market entry, investment level, technical standards, business scope, and ownership and corporate governance	Local enforcement of economy-wide macroeconomic rules; central level funding for specific high-tech, value-added topic areas focused on basic R&D and commercialization
Distribution of Property Rights	State-owned infrastructure; state-controlled, through corporate governance, private and foreign-invested value-added services; and equipment makers of diverse ownership structures, including public–private joint ventures	Diverse and various ownership structures across subsectors

complex globalized economy helmed by an authoritarian regime such as China. Chapter 4 shows that the introduction of competition in telecommunications occurred a decade before the WTO accession in 2001. China's WTO commitments boosted and intensified efforts to promote competitive pressures and gain access to technology. In parallel, the state took decisive steps to consolidate central control of market governance of this industry of high importance to national security and high contribution to the national technology base and the competitiveness of the rest of the economy.

Two decades after the WTO accession, the Chinese government has yet to implement many of its market entry and business scope commitments in telecommunications. The state governs telecommunications with centralized coordination by a supraministry of government-owned and fixed-line and mobile carriers and privately owned but government controlled value-added service providers and equipment makers. The dominant pattern of *centralized governance* enables the state to achieve its security and developmental goals even while introducing competition and exposing the industry to global integration. To develop a "homegrown" semiconductor industry, for example, the Chinese state strategically courted FDI through foreign-invested joint ventures and Chinese state-owned microelectronic institutional and firm-level initiatives. Importantly, the sector and company cases also uncover how FDI liberalization in the 2000s was followed by deliberate state interventions in corporate governance by the early 2010s.

In contrast, the Chinese government has introduced competition in labor-intensive, less value-added sectors, as shown in Chapter 5 on textiles. The lower degree and narrower scope of the *perceived strategic value* of more labor intensive and less value-added textiles shape the decentralized market coordination of predominantly quasi-state and private ownership. Less concerned about controlling products or services that have few applications for national security and low contribution to the national technology base, the central state introduced competition in textiles in the 1980s and devolved market coordination to local governments and commerce bureaus by the early 1990s. Findings reveal that the interacting strategic value and sectoral logics apply at the subsector, such as the more deliberate market coordination of technical textiles by local governments and central level bureaucracies and more varied distribution of property rights. *Private governance* in apparel and clothing and *decentralized governance* in technical textiles are the institutional foundations confronted by market actors of all stripes, which shape their economic behavior.

Table 3.5 summarizes the dominant sectoral patterns of market governance shaped by the interacting effects of China's *techno-security developmentalism* and sectoral structures and organization of institutions. It outlines how perceived strategic value and sectoral characteristics during significant moments of internal and external pressures shape coordination mechanisms and distribution of property rights in strategic and less strategic industries, represented by telecommunications and textiles, respectively.

4

Security Imperatives, Infrastructural Development, and High-Tech Sectors

Centralized Governance in Chinese Telecommunications

Following Chapter 3's examination of the evolution and transformation of the paramount imperatives of *national security* and *national technology base* in China, this chapter applies the Strategic Value Framework to investigate formal and informal institutions of market coordination and property rights across the capital-intensive, producer-driven, and asset-specific service and manufacturing sectors of Chinese telecommunications. This chapter's longitudinal case studies of telecommunications services and manufacturing, illustrated by company cases, present (in their full complexity) that the higher the scope and extent of *perceived strategic value* of a sector, the more likely the central state will intervene to coordinate markets and control property rights arrangements. Infrastructural modernization, indigenous development, and state control of information dissemination grounded in the perceived strategic value orientation of *techno-security developmentalism* shape *centralized governance* in Chinese telecommunications. Subsectoral variation in contribution to the national technology base and the competitiveness of the rest of the economy and applications for internal security and authoritarian resilience and legitimacy, interacting with *sectoral structural and institutional attributes* determine state-ownership of telecommunications infrastructure and variegated property rights arrangements in value-added services and telecommunications equipment.[1]

The initial introduction of competition in telecommunications occurred in the 1990s. China's World Trade Organization (WTO)

---

[1] See Table 2.4 for sectoral structural attributes.

accession in 2001 further boosted and intensified the efforts to promote competitive pressures and gain access to technology.[2] Two decades after the WTO accession, in 2020, the Chinese government, however, is yet to implement many of its telecommunications market entry and business-scope commitments. From the 11th Five-Year Plan's focus on indigenous innovation and China's "go global" policy accelerated after the Global Financial Crisis to the Made in China 2025, the institutional landscape of *centralized governance* introduced competition in parallel to decisive and deliberate state intervention to consolidate central control of infrastructure and service provision, as shown in Section 4.1. This entails sector-specific regulation and market coordination by a supraministry and competing state-owned mobile and fixed-line operators detailed in Section 4.2.

Experiencing a more liberalized market, value-added services (VAS) in Section 4.3 and equipment makers in Section 4.4 operate in variegated property rights arrangements on state-owned backbone infrastructure. However, rules and regulations on the market entry, business scope, and content of Internet service and content providers and the social media business; and discretionary state intervention in corporate governance, ownership structures, mergers and acquisitions, and technical standards in new generation technologies, such as fifth-generation technology standard (5G) and the semiconductor value chain in equipment sectors – demonstrate the interacting *strategic value and sectoral* logics. Not to be outdone, regulatory developments in electronic commerce and the platform economy, such as financial technology, are representative of encroaching state intervention in the market coordination and property rights arrangements of more liberal subsectors of strategic industries (telecommunications and finance). The global rise and scrutiny of Huawei and the fates of Alibaba and Ant Group (in digital retail) and SMIC (in semiconductors) illustrate how the Chinese state's purposive and deliberate actions in the service of national security greatly defined and the national technology base have shaped the development and global competitiveness of Chinese telecommunications.

4.1 STRATEGIC VALUE AND SECTORAL LOGICS: CENTRALIZED GOVERNANCE

China became undisputedly the most anticipated supplier of 5G networks in developed and developing countries through Chinese

---

[2] See Doner, Noble, and Ravenhill (2007. 2020) on effects on automotive sectors.

telecommunications equipment maker Huawei by the late 2010s. The company during the COVID-19 global pandemic topped Samsung and Apple to become the world's largest supplier of phones. Huawei's early connections with the People's Liberation Army and unverifiable ownership and corporate governance structures and assumed government ties, however, have resulted in global backlash. In recent years, countries, including the United States and the United Kingdom, have banned Huawei's networking equipment, restricted financing the company could receive, and labeled it a national security threat, in addition to monitoring who can sell to Huawei and Chinese firms through export control and entity lists.[3]

Undeterred, Huawei, along with Chinese state-owned equipment makers Datang and ZTE, possess more than 10 percent of 5G-essential intellectual property rights in total.[4] Less than fifteen years ago, the Chinese government coordinated technology and knowledge transfers through cooperation between the three aforementioned Chinese companies and foreign equipment makers, namely German-owned Siemens and the U.S. company Motorola, to develop TD-SCDMA, a homegrown 3G standard. TD-SCDMA, however, never became widely adopted domestically, much less globally, despite government-enforced adoption of the 3G standard by state-owned China Mobile, which strengthened in subscribers and geographical scope through several rounds of state-orchestrated corporate and regulatory re-organization.

How did China reach the apex of global telecommunications, arguably the world's most liberalized and economically integrated industry? The Strategic Value Framework shows that *perceived strategic value* and *sectoral structures and organization of institutions,* in the context of China's global economic integration, have translated into state goals of indigenous technological development and information control, and determine the *centralized governance* of telecommunications. Telecommunications is an industry of high importance to the Chinese government in terms of application for authoritarian resilience, contribution to the national technology base, and the competitiveness of the rest of the economy. The high capital and knowledge requirements of the

---

[3] "Huawei Ban Timeline: Company Takes Samsung Crown as No. 1 Phone maker," *CNET* (July 30, 2020). Interview on January 31, 2021 in San Jose, CA, with an engineering director of a U.S.-based global semiconductor company.

[4] "Telecom Services the Geopolitics of 5G and IoT," *Jefferies Franchise Note* (September 14, 2017).

manufacturing and services subsectors, marked by capital-intensity, complex technology, and producer driven commodity chains and knowledge-intensive communication and information dissemination, respectively, further shape the role of the state in market coordination and property rights arrangements.

Today, the Central Cyberspace Affairs Commission of the Central Committee of the Communist Party of China makes the telecommunications policy enforced by the Cyberspace Administration of China and the Ministry of Industry and Information Technology (MIIT) under the State Council. Other related central-level authorities with purview of telecommunications sectors include state-backed investment funds, such as the China Integrated Circuit Industry Investment Fund. The scope and methods of market governance in Chinese telecommunications and other strategic sectors are not the standard neutral regulation of price and entry to ensure an equal playing field or free competition. Sector-specific rules and practices maximize the benefits of competition; at the same time, they enhance central state management of network infrastructure, information dissemination, and technology. The distribution of property rights arrangements ranges from state-owned carriers to public–private joint ventures (JVs) and privately held value-added service providers and equipment makers.

Throughout the 1990s, to modernize infrastructure and rationalize service provision, the state broke up the telecommunications monopoly and introduced competition. The Chinese government also permitted FDI, which was officially banned, to partner with state-owned entities to build new (second-) generation mobile networks through what were then known as Chinese-Chinese-Foreign (CCF) joint venture arrangements.[5] These variable interest entities (VIEs), referred to as the "Sina.com Model" in value-added services, permitted FDI in restricted sectors to enter the domestic market through a registered wholly foreign-owned enterprise (WFOE)'s domestic contractor and conversely, Chinese companies to turn into a foreign one with shares that foreign investors can buy.[6]

By the end of the decade, however, at the height of China's WTO protocol agreement negotiations, the government had begun to reinforce

---

[5] 2005 and 2006 interviews in Beijing and Shanghai with principals involved in special investment vehicles, which circumvented formal rules banning FDI.

[6] The cross-time subsector case studies show VIEs continue to operate in restricted sectors, despite formal bans on ownership types, as a function of sector-specific state goals.

central state ownership and management of backbone infrastructure and regulatory authority over basic service provision. In 1998, during a phase of state intervention in industrial activities orchestrated by Jiang Zemin and Zhu Rongji (in parallel with the ongoing WTO negotiations), top leadership ordered the divestment of FDI and private capital. The state further merged what were at that time separate telecommunications equipment and service ministries and created the Ministry of Information Industry (MII). The MII resolved bureaucratic conflict and consolidated state control over telecommunications policy. These actions coincided with the call to reform the state sector by the fourth plenary session of the CCP's 15th Central Committee, refining the 1997 call to "grasp the large, let go of the small" state-owned enterprises (SOEs) during the East Asian financial crisis.

Shortly before the WTO accession, between 1998 and 2002, the state corporatized and restructured state-owned carriers to create fixed-line and mobile duopolies. In the post-WTO era, the State-owned Assets Supervision and Administration Commission (SASAC) retains the assets of the operators. Subsidiaries of the carriers are publicly listed in Hong Kong and New York but direct private entry in basic telecommunications services is prohibited. In spite of China's WTO commitment of up to 49 percent foreign equity ownership, the state-owned parent holding companies retain 70–75 percent of all outstanding shares of the operators, and no single investor possesses more than 10 percent of the remaining shares in the publicly traded entities.[7]

Today, SASAC regularly rotates company executives to manage competition and retain control of the carriers.[8] Corruption scandals notwithstanding, party reforms, such as the "CPC Central Committee Notice on Strengthening and Improving Party Building in State-owned Enterprises," released in 1997, have strengthened the Chinese Communist Party's role. Under the Hu-Wen leadership, the creation of the MIIT and carrier-restructuring, in 2008, during the global financial crisis further enhanced regulatory authority and consolidated policymaking. A former telecommunications ministry official opined, "Conflicts and struggles between bureaucracies are the norm, but coordination ultimately happens when

---

[7] The globally accepted definition for FDI is foreign investment over 10 percent with an effective voice in management.

[8] The CCP institutionalizes rotations and exchanges to control the *nomenklatura*, placing trusted lieutenants in key positions and rotating officials to prevent them from building personal fiefdoms (Yang 2004). These mechanisms enable the CCP to extract revenue, remedy interregional disparity, and maintain central rule (Sheng 2007).

the iron fist of the central leadership manifests."[9] Foreign and domestic stakeholders of the Chinese telecommunications industry maintain, "It may be difficult to separate national security imperatives from the desire to possess strategic economic assets, but national security concerns always trump money arguments."[10]

4.2 BASIC SERVICES: INFRASTRUCTURE MODERNIZATION AND MANAGEMENT VIA STATE OWNERSHIP AND SECTOR RESTRUCTURING

The Ministry of Industry and Information Technology restructured the duopolies of fixed-line and mobile services in 2008 into integrated carriers providing nationwide services on state-owned backbone infrastructure. Leading up to the showcase of China's growth and development to the outside world during the 2008 Beijing Olympics, the MIIT further assigned the implementation of TD-SCDMA, a homegrown third-generation networking standard, to the newly restructured China Mobile, which is the most competitive state-owned carrier by subscriber. "Now the party said, development has occurred, we want to create orderly development and we don't want to step down," explained the managing principal of a venture capital (VC) research firm, who participated in the technically illegal foreign capital CCF joint ventures in telecommunications in the 1990s.[11]

"Going forward the government will continue to safeguard industries with high profitability and of national security concern. Having foreign capital won't be so important anymore," intimated a former research and development (R&D) executive at Motorola China, who also served as director of the Beijing-based United States Information Technology Office and vice chair of the China Association of Standards.[12] In 2011, the State Council established a cross-ministerial National Security Review regime for mergers and acquisitions (M&As) by foreign investors and involving Chinese companies as per the 2008 Anti-Monopoly Law.[13] Reviews of

---

[9] March 2, 2006 interview in Beijing with a former telecommunications ministry official.

[10] Quote from interview in Shanghai on November 3, 2005 with vice president of a privately owned Chinese telecommunications VAS provider.

[11] Interview on March 13, 2013 in Beijing.

[12] Interview on September 29, 2008 in Beijing.

[13] "China Publishes Final Rules on the National Security Review of Foreign Investment in Chinese Companies," *Jones Day Commentaries* (September 2011). The Anti-Monopoly Law's overhaul in 2020 targeted Internet service provision.

M&As are supposed to consider implications of national security, economic stability, social order, and research and development capabilities relating to key technologies.

Shortly before the ten-year anniversary of China's WTO ascension in December 2011, the MIIT announced an investigation of China Telecom and China Unicom, two of the state-owned carriers, for monopolistic practices in national broadband pricing. The general consensus among government and firm-level industry insiders deemed this well-timed move to "order competition," which followed carrier restructuring to manage competition and implement TD-SCDMA, to be more about resolving interdepartmental disputes between incumbents and new entrants than a genuine attempt to ensure a truly level-playing field or decrease tariffs for consumers.[14]

In 2017, privately owned companies, including Alibaba, Tencent, and ride-hailing company DiDi Chuxing, purchased shares of China Unicom. Investors received a combined 35.2 percent stake in China Unicom's Shanghai-listed unit and were allocated three board seats. "The mixed ownership will raise the innovation capability of the company...allowing us to transform from a traditional operation to an integrated operator," said Lu Yimin, president of China Unicom Hong Kong.[15] Reforming SOEs with mixed ownership structures is in line with the 2015 party guidelines for deepening reform discussed in Chapter 3. This strategy of utilizing private capital through mixed ownership structures first upgraded the state-owned carriers in the late 1990s. This is when the Chinese government courted private and foreign minority shareholders to invest, but later forced them to divest after the state had restructured the sector and modernized infrastructure.

4.2.1 State-Owned Blockchains: Infrastructure for Interconnectivity Across China and Beyond

In the second decade of the twenty-first century, another backbone infrastructure in which the Chinese government has retained centralized coordination and government ownership is digitization through

---

[14] Interviews with various informants, including government bureaucrats, managers of state-owned carriers, and foreign-invested companies and sector associations between 2013 and 2019.

[15] "State-owned China Unicom to Raise $12 billion From Alibaba, Tencent, Others," *Reuters* (August 16, 2017).

blockchain technology.[16] Similar to the telecommunications operators, blockchains are perceived as a basic telecommunications service by the Chinese government. The Chinese government's development and governance of Blockchain Services Network (BSN), therefore, mirrors the *centralized governance* of the telecommunications backbone infrastructure. In 2018, China Mobile established BSN, together with state-owned payment and settlement provider UnionPay, China's first financial-level pre-authorization service for secured transactions. They partnered with the State Information Center of the National Development and Research Commission and the main blockchain architect Red Date Technology, which catered to smart cities.

With 45 percent of all blockchain projects coming from China in 2020, the state-backed initiative has integrated blockchain technology across governments, individuals, businesses, and emerging markets to transfer digital assets via decentralized applications.[17] Designated the Digital Silk Road, the BSN aims to link China and its trading partners in the ambitious Belt and Road Initiative to establish infrastructure networks and promote trade throughout Asia and beyond. At least for now, BSN's operating environment and public city nodes are open to the public for connecting and uploading. Time will tell whether the transfer of digital assets on BSN will come under state surveillance and management, similar to Russia's approach toward RuNet to control information dissemination and bar non-Russian-sanctioned Internet activity, as shown in the Russian telecommunications case studies in Chapter 10.

4.3 VALUE-ADDED SERVICES: CONTROL OF INFORMATION AND SECTORAL DEVELOPMENT VIA RULES ON OWNERSHIP STRUCTURE AND BUSINESS SCOPE

Telecommunications value-added services (VAS), which operate on top of national-security sensitive infrastructure already owned and managed by the state, experience more decentralized market coordination and rampant nonstate market activity. To promote the development of VAS, the state first licensed nonstate providers in 1994. During Zhu Rongji's

---

[16] Blockchains, a growing list of records linked by cryptography, are "an open, distributed ledger that can record transactions between parties efficiently and in a verifiable and permanent way." See "Truth About Blockchain," *Harvard Business Review* (January–February, 2007).

[17] "China-Backed Crypto Guru Wants to Unify World's Blockchains," *Bloomberg* (July 26, 2020).

interventionist activities in strategic sectors from telecommunications basic services to energy sectors in the late 1990s, the central state did not crack down on foreign investors entering the Chinese market through the CCF special holding company investment vehicle, which skirted an official ban in telecommunications. When the government forced FDI divestment in basic services in 1998, it did not enforce the ban in VAS, which was a fledgling subsector.[18] Early VAS providers included Sina.com, Sohu.com, NEtease.com, and Tom Online, which were founded by foreign-invested JV partners. By the early 2000s, the telecommunications ministry had devolved licensing and certification of VAS and equipment makers to provincial branches.

As domestic industry matured, in the mid-2000s, the authoritarian state judged the politically and socially disruptive potential of the business of information dissemination and began to consolidate state control over the business of the Internet. The telecommunications ministry directed bureaucratic energies to enhancing its regulatory authority in restricting market entry through centralizing license approvals, enforcing licensing rules, regulating business scope and interactions with consumers, and expanding carrier oversight of service providers operating on government-owned infrastructure. To ensure orderly development, the MIIT periodically issues regulation to enhance its discretion over the business scope and product development of VAS providers. FDI must form JVs, whereby state-owned or state-sponsored partners retain majority ownership and management control.[19] Foreign investors are further required to obtain special operating licenses, the discretionary approval process for which is cumbersome and routinely delayed.

4.3.1 State-sponsored Rise and Control of Digital Retail: Regulatory Boosts *and* Interventions

Such state interventions to order and consolidate state control of "runaway" competition and to promote "orderly" sectoral developments in the context of state priorities to develop the national technology base and

---

[18] Two decades after its first use, the special investment vehicle came under regulatory scrutiny in 2020 in the context of the state's crackdown on horizontal consolidation in fintech, discussed later in the VAS case study.

[19] Interviews in Beijing and Shanghai with general managers and foreign partners of VAS providers between 2006 and 2013.

tackle national security imperatives have occurred at least twice in digital retail to Chinese entrepreneur and billionaire Jack Ma, the co-founder and former executive chairman of Internet commerce company Alibaba Group and the spun-off financial technology company Ant Group. For years, Ma and his businesses operated without much state intervention and scrutiny. If anything, the state courted FDI and then reregulated to benefit the fintech's growth and development. Yet the stakes changed when Ma pushed the envelope by questioning the state's handling of regulatory issues in 2020. Ant Group's monopoly position came to be perceived as disrupting state control of banking, telecommunications, and, importantly, Communist Party rule.

In 1999, Jack Ma founded Alibaba with venture capital from American investment bank Goldman Sachs and Japanese-owned Softbank during the period, before China's WTO accession, described above, when the Chinese government did not enforce the official ban on FDI or variable interest entities. A few years later, in 2003, Ma founded Alibaba's e-payment subsidiary Alipay, which was launched by Alibaba's online shopping platform Taobao. Significantly, Alipay attracted \$1 billion in investment from American web services provider Yahoo.

In 2010, under pressure from the Chinese government, Alibaba unilaterally spun off Alipay, forcing Yahoo and Softbank out of the most lucrative part of their JV with the group's publicly traded company. Alibaba justified the move on the grounds that it was simply complying with a government rule stipulating that only Chinese-owned companies could be licensed to engage in e-payment. But Alipay had operated for years without the government requiring and enforcing licensure. What changed is that now that the domestic e-payment sector has developed, in part due to Western expertise, existing rules are being enforced and new rules are being introduced to favor the domestic industry.[20]

Without foreign investors as controlling partners, Alipay became rebranded as Ant Group in 2014; the company, in 2015, raised \$4.5 billion from Chinese state-owned banks and state-controlled VCs, including China Investment Corporation and Primavera Capital Group, respectively. Ironically in 2020, a decade after regulatory boosts benefited the rise of Alipay, and two decades after Alibaba's first use of the VIE special

---

[20] See Hsueh (2015, 2016). Ant-itrust activities in 2013 and 2014 against foreign auto-makers and manufacturers of auto parts, including Daimler and Volkswagen, and high technology companies, such as Qualcomm and Microsoft, fall under the same pattern of market governance.

investment vehicle, regulatory scrutiny of the horizontal consolidation of fintech by Tencent and Ant Group under the 2020 updates to the monopoly law halted the dual initial public offering of the Ant Group in Hong Kong and Shanghai.

The government rested the crackdown on the Ant Group on the antimonopoly revisions, which included rules barring the VIE model dating back to the high-speed development of value-added services through CCFs in the early 2000s.[21] The latest round of reregulation, however, is unlikely the definitive crackdown on these investment structures nor of monopolies per se. The variable interest entities have benefited "too many highly placed people" and the Chinese government "does not have access to enough domestic real risk capital to sustain their innovation/invention requirements." The VIEs are the means to increasing the national technology base and not the main target of reregulation. Moreover, the largest monopolies, such as China Mobile and the Industrial and Commercial Bank of China, are after all state-owned.

Under scrutiny are the increasing size and influence of private companies what heretofore had been state-sponsored, including Alibaba, in strategic industries, such as fin-tech, which straddle the financial and telecommunications infrastructures. The state is interested in ordering sectoral developments and retaining discretionary control at the firm level in the business of the Internet and the business of finance, which are industries with implications for the national technology base and national security. The Antitrust Law overhaul, proposed in early 2020 and released in November, includes language specifically targeting the Internet business and horizontal consolidation. Regulators are vested with the responsibility to monitor the impact that Internet companies have on the online sector, their scale, and the digital platforms' ability to control products and services, including in other industries.[22] In response to increasing horizontal consolidation by the fintech industry, penalties may force violators to divest assets,

---

[21] The VIE model was popularized by Sina.com in the pre-WTO era when foreign-invested enterprises in strategic sectors were officially banned but FDI entered China nonetheless through holding company structures, detailed in Hsueh (2011).

[22] "China Targets Internet Giants in Antitrust Law Overhaul," *Bloomberg* (January 6, 2020); "Draft Revision of Anti-Monopoly Law of the People's Republic of China (Draft for Public Comment) 《中华人民共和国反垄断法》修订草案（公开征求意见稿），" State Administration of Market Regulation (January 2, 2020).

intellectual property or technologies, open up their infrastructure, and adjust their algorithms.[23]

At the China Wealth Management 50 Forum in December 2020, former finance minister Lou Jiwei, who sits on the National Committee of the Chinese People's Political Consultative Conference, pointed to the systemic risk of the mixed operations in data-based financial platforms (such as Alipay and WeChat) as what the state cannot risk losing control.[24] Lou also attributed the 2015–2016 stock market turbulence to the need for more robust regulation of the "chaotic" bond market and the excess leverage incurred by the financial industry's increasing segmentation.

Unsurprisingly then is the announcement, in April 2021, that under the "comprehensive, viable rectification plan" of four regulatory agencies (banking, securities, foreign exchange, and the Ministry of Industry and Information Technology), the Ant Group will restructure as a financial holding company under the same regulatory control as banks, which in China are state-owned except in very limited market segments.[25] Doing so would involve the liquidation and mergers and other reorganizations of money market and personal lending businesses, which generated for Alipay the "equivalent of more than $17 trillion of digital-payment transactions in the year to June 2020, originated unsecured short-term loans to roughly 500 million people and [sold] many insurance policies, mutual funds and other investment products."

In spring 2021, the State Administration for Market Regulation (SAMR), the Cybersecurity Administration of China, and the State Tax Administration of China targeted 34 technology companies for investigation into market "concentration operation." This incurred fines for Alibaba, Tencent, and Didi Chuxing and other technology companies for acquisitions and mergers dating back a decade. The fines were in relation to data security, consumer privacy, and anticompetitive practices covered in the updated anti-monopoly law.[26] The Cybersecurity

[23] "China Clampdown on Big Tech Puts More Billionaires on Notice," *Bloomberg* (November 10, 2020).

[24] "楼继伟发言全文'深圳先行示范区首届金融峰会' [The full text of Lou Jiwei's speech at 'Shenzhen Pioneer Demonstration Zone First Financial Summit']," *Sina.com* (December 20, 2020).

[25] "Jack Ma's Ant Group Bows to Beijing with Company Overhaul," *The Wall Street Journal* (April 12, 2021).

[26] "China Steps Up on Anti-Trust Pressures on Internet Firms," *Wall Street Journal* (June 17, 2021) and "China's Antitrust Watchdog Punishes Alibaba, Tencent and Didi for Merger Irregularities after Digging into Old Deals," *South China Morning Post* (July 7, 2021).

Administration of China also began an investigation of Didi's handling of customer data two days after its US$44 billion IPO in New York, which suspended new user registrations and removed the Didi app in China.[27]

4.3.2 Information Control via Intervention in Business Operations and Self-Censorship of Internet Service and Content Providers

The Anti-Monopoly Law of 2020 has enhanced the government's ability to control the business operations of value-added service providers at the intersection of telecommunications and finance. In electronic-commerce, in particular, the state perceives at stake big data and mass surveillance for authoritarian control. The control of the information business extends to the Social Credit Systems (SCS) launched by e-commerce platforms, such as Alibaba and Ant Group's Sesame Credit and Taobao, in collaboration with local governments and the Chinese state to collect personal, financial, and behavioral data. SCS systems, centralized by the People's Bank of China in 2018, reward and punish citizens, organizations, and companies based on assessments of their trustworthiness, in addition to track and restrict movements of dissidents and political activists.[28]

The enhanced controls on the business of Internet and related financial technology in the digitization of payment and financial processing via the Anti-Monopoly Law of 2020 join state ownership and management of basic services. They also augment rules on the market entry and business scope of VAS providers to facilitate the blockage of the Internet and telecommunications and the dissemination of state sponsored propaganda during and after episodes of social and political unrest.[29] Driven by concerns of internal and external political challenges to Communist Party legitimacy and authoritarian rule, laws on counterterrorism (2015), national security (2015), and cybersecurity (2017) tightly supervise how information is shared and exchanged and impose strict Internet censorship. These laws also terminate business operations if and when security or developmental objectives become paramount.

While the state permits variegated property rights arrangements, market coordination mechanisms to control information dissemination

---

[27] "Didi Says Had No Knowledge of Cyberspace Investigation Before IPO," *Reuters* (July 5, 2021).

[28] Cao, Kostka, and Xu (2020) shows that information control on the Social Credit System is achieved clandestinely, exacerbating citizens' information problem.

[29] These include anti-Japanese protests in 2005 and 2012, Xinjiang protests in 2009, the leadership transition in 2012, and the advent of reeducation camps in 2018.

and sectoral development include rules and regulations on licensure based on business scope and consumer Internet usage. "A WFOE [wholly foreign-owned enterprise] or other foreign-owned entity cannot obtain a commercial ICP license in China. There are no exceptions to the rule. If a WFOE or foreign entity wants to offer its software in China though a SaaS system, it must use an indirect method such as licensing the software to a licensed Chinese entity using an 'Internet portal.'"[30] In an attempt to contain widespread piracy of its products and check the Chinese government's anti-monopoly scrutiny described in Chapter 3, the American software company Microsoft partnered with state-owned China Electronics Technology Corporation in 2017 to produce a government-approved version of Windows.[31] The military contractor is a major vendor of surveillance technology in Xinjiang, where reeducation camps imprison hundreds of thousands of the local Muslim minority Uighurs.

Even then, foreign companies are required to replicate their code base with China-specific configurations and state-authorized global standards in databases physically located in China.[32] Chapter 10 discusses similar data localization rules in Russia. In 2018, the MIIT established mirrored copies of the Domain Name System under the claim that homegrown root servers can eliminate the perceived threat of the United States, Europe, and Japan cutting access to the root name servers operated by organizations in those countries.[33]

Importantly, foreign-invested and domestic Chinese VAS providers have routinely engaged in "self-censorship" to escape the scrutiny of the MIIT, state-owned carriers, and other state agencies engaged in content control. In the early 2000s, foreign-invested Sina.com, Sohu.com, NEtease.com, and Tom Online began the practice of signing the "Public Pledge on Self-Regulation and Professional Ethics for the China Internet Industry."[34] The founder of a foreign-invested VAS provider based explained: "Censorship is the baseline in this business. We make sure to

---

[30] "How to Form a WFOE in China, Part 9: Forming a WFOE Subject to Industry Specific Regulation," *China Law Blog* (December 5, 2015).

[31] "China Appears to Block Microsoft's Bing as Censorship Intensifies," *New York Times* (January 23, 2019).

[32] See interview in Mountain View, CA on February 20, 2021 with marketing director of a global medical device company with sales and marketing in four locations in China. Also, see Hsueh (2011).

[33] "China's Imaginary Root Server to Fix Imaginary Threat," *Technode* (December 24, 2019).

[34] See Hsueh (2011), 105–110.

avoid hardcore porn, gambling, and politics, including content on Taiwan and Tibet. Operators are motivated by money, not humanistic reasons, so we don't touch the above-mentioned topics."[35] In an attempt in 2017 to return to the Chinese market, nearly a decade after exiting, due to regulatory hurdles, Google developed a censored search engine internally code-named Project Dragonfly that the company has since terminated, which would filter websites and search terms that are blacklisted by the Chinese government.[36]

The development of a software to suppress certain posts by Facebook, which is banned in China since 2009 following the use of Facebook by Xinjiang activists at the time of the Urumqi protests, however, did not bring the social media company closer to government approval to operate a subsidiary, much less release a social media app, which would require separate licensure.[37] The revocation by the Cyberspace Administration of China, established in 2014, of a corporate license granted to Facebook by the Zhejiang provincial government in 2018 more accurately captures state methods to achieve security imperatives. Moreover, in actions above and beyond self-censorship are the daily coordination between government agencies and privately owned VAS providers, such as Alibaba, Baidu, and Tencent, in the state's outsourcing of data analytics, including of stolen information, such as from the 2014 breach of the U.S. Office of Personnel Management by Chinese military units and Chinese hacker attacks on Marriot, Equifax, US healthcare giant Anthem, and a navy contractor.[38]

4.3.3 Social Media Business, Content Control, and User-Level Responses

Restrictions on foreign-invested value-added service and content providers due to rules and enforcement on them related to market entry,

---

[35] See interview with David Turchetti, founder and CEO of 21 Communications, a foreign-invested value-added service provider, on December 9, 2005.

[36] See "Google, Seeking a Return to China, Is Said to Be Building a Censored Search Engine," *New York Times* (August 1, 2018) and "Confirmed: Google Terminated Dragonfly, Its Censored Chinese Search Engine," *Forbes* (July 19, 2019).

[37] "China Said to Quickly Withdraw Approval for New Facebook Venture," *New York Times* (July 25, 2018).

[38] "Chinese Hackers Pursues Key Data on U.S. Workers," *New York Times* (July 9, 2014) and "China Hacked a Navy Contractor and Secured a Trove of Highly Sensitive Data on Submarine Warfare," *Washington Post* (June 8, 2018).

business scope, and ownership structures have witnessed the boom of indigenous Chinese social media applications, which have adopted and localized global technology. The rise of Chinese social media businesses, however, uncovers how the state has responded to the popularity of Internet and mobile social media with new methods to control business scope and information dissemination at the company and user levels. In parallel are the Internet and social media users and their responses to information control by the state. For virtually every globally dominant service provider, there is a Chinese equivalent in the Chinese market.

To name a few, Google's search engine has Baidu; E-Bay has Alibaba-owned Taobao in e-commerce; Facebook and Facebook Messenger, social networking apps, have RenRen and QQ; and video sharing platform YouTube has Youku and Tudou. Videoconferencing company WebEx has the U.S.-headquartered Zoom, which relies on a 700-member R&D team based in multiple locations in China.[39] Moreover, Zoom's China-based servers, which are governed by the Chinese government's rules and regulations, including the 2017 Cybersecurity Law, generate encryption keys for North American users.[40] During the COVID-19 pandemic, Zoom has emerged as the dominant online meeting platform even as the global media reported potential security risks.

Chinese homegrown social media businesses, such as Bytedance, also proactively and directly censor users in response to what the state might deem unacceptable, a common practice of VAS providers as discussed above. In November 2018, platform moderators of the Bytedance-owned video-sharing social media app TikTok censored the accounts of an Afghan American who used "makeup tutorial" videos to draw attention to Uyghur concentration camps in Xinjiang.[41] They also routinely suppress broadcast streams about Chinese state organs such as the police and military that "defame civil servants," and other materials that might threaten "national security" and show "rural poverty, slums, and beer bellies and crooked smiles."[42] In April 2019, Douyin, also owned by Bytedance, banned livestreamers for speaking Cantonese while

---

[39] "Zoom's Encryption Keys Are Sometimes Being Sent to China, Report Finds," *PC Magazine* (April 3, 2020).

[40] "Move Fast and Roll Your Own Crypto: A Quick Look at the Confidentiality of Zoom Meetings," *Citizens Lab Report* (April 3, 2020).

[41] "TikTok 'Makeup Tutorial' Goes Viral with Call to Action on China's Treatment of Uyghurs," *The Guardian* (November 27, 2020).

[42] "Invisible Censorship: TikTok Told Moderators to Suppress Posts by Ugly People and the Poor to Attract New Users," *The Intercept* (March 16, 2020).

responding to state narratives on what constitutes proper and normative Chinese language, particularly sensitive in the light of the Umbrella Movement in Hong Kong in 2014 and 2019.

Because Chinese social media businesses operate in a marketized environment, whereby private companies operate side-by-side with state-owned and state-controlled entities, Chinese social media businesses, which serve diverse users who are apolitical, critical of the state, or cater to the state, are important constituents of the state's management of online activism for authoritarian control.[43] In an Internet monitoring system known as the "Great Firewall of China," the state typically employs myriad security agencies, including an Internet police taskforce to monitor and censor content. At least fourteen government organizations, including the Ministry of Industry and Information Technology, Cyberspace Administration of China, Ministry of Culture, Ministry of Public Security, and People's Bank of China, regulate content and the business of content, including Internet cafés and online games and social media.[44]

The 2017 Cybersecurity Law and related guidelines and measures are ambiguously written and necessitate "critical information infrastructural operators," including telecommunications services as well as other strategic sectors, such as finance, transportation, and utilities, serving the domestic market to store information within China. The draft "Measures for Security Assessment of Cross-border Transfer of Personal Information and Important Data" released in mid-2019, for public consultation, empowers the state to conduct regular "security assessments." Around the same time, the draft "Measures for Data Security Management" extends such assessments to cover data pertaining to national security, economic security, social stability, and public health.[45] Such information as that on the COVID-19 pandemic in China would presumably fall under these measures. These measures are comparable to those in Russia enacted in the mid-2010s after the Crimea intervention (Chapter 10).

To distract and distort information in service of ensuring regime stability, similar to other authoritarian regimes around the world, the state has deployed paid online commentators, known as the "fifty-cent army," to influence and guide public opinion during sensitive times.[46]

---

[43] Yang (2009, 2015), Han (2018), Roberts (2018).   [44] See Hsueh (2011).

[45] "China Data Protection Regulations (CDPR)," *The China Law Blog* (May 20, 2018) and "More Changes on the Horizon: New Cross-Border Transfer Restrictions and Personal Information Requirements in the PR," *Mayer and Brown Note* (August 22, 2019).

[46] See Han (2018), 152–174 and Roberts (2018), 190–221, respectively.

The Chinese government has also taken advantage of netizens, who spontaneously and autonomously rise to defend the regime's role in unifying and building the nation with wordplay and narratives.[47] Nevertheless, whether anti-regime, apolitical, or privately anti-regime, Chinese netizens have skirted around the CCP's control of information through wordplay and ironic framing and other creative means.[48] Moreover, journalists in a fluid and strategic collaboration with the party-state, have adopted "guarded improvisation" as creative adjustments to confront censorship restrictions of lower-level authorities.[49] Everyday users use virtual private network (VPN) and other software, though in recent years the Great Firewall of China has interfered with outgoing VPN connections.

In early 2019, on the global open-source software platform Github, Chinese high-tech workers launched the 996.icu campaign against the twelve-hours-a-day, six-days-a-week schedule. Organizers called only for the enforcement of labor laws and ultimately engaged in a company-level approach instead of collective mobilization, which would have triggered a government crackdown.[50] High-tech workers and entrepreneurs have benefited from China's sprint to high-tech development, yet they may be the most influential critics of Xi Jinping, who has faced the lowest economic growth since the Asian financial crisis in the late 1990s further worsened by the U.S.-China trade war.[51] The regulatory crackdown on the Ant Group, in 2020, discussed above, can be viewed as the Chinese Communist Party tapping into societal resentment against the likes of Alibaba/Ant Group cofounder Jack Ma, wealthy and well-off, disconnected from the people, and perceived by the state to be too influential in sectoral development.[52]

The state tapping into and inciting nationalist sentiments yet quickly quashing mass mobilization have occurred periodically, such as in the 2005 and 2012 anti-Japanese protests. Swiftly organized and publicized via Internet chat rooms, instant and text messages, and other forms of

---

[47] See Han (2018), 93–98.
[48] See Stockmann and Gallagher (2011) and Fu (2017), respectively.
[49] See Repnikova (2018).
[50] See Fu (2017) on mobilizing strategies to minimize risks and King, Pan, and Roberts (2013) on government crackdown on collective mobilization.
[51] "Chinese Economy Slows to Lowest Growth Rate in 28 years," *Washington Post* (January 21, 2019).
[52] "Li Yuan: Why China Turned Against Jack Ma," *New York Times New World Column* (December 24, 2020).

mobile communication, the 2005 protests began with a labor strike at a Japanese company in the Pearl River delta that expanded into the dispute over Japanese history books' coverage of China and joined by anti–industrial pollution and anti–political corruption protestors.[53] The 2012 protests centered on territorial disputes concerning the Senkaku (Diaoyu) Islands around the time of the anniversary of the Mukden Incident of 1931, a pretext for Japanese invasion of Manchuria. In both incidents, once the protests escalated, the state deemed at stake foreign economic relations and Internal political stability and stepped in and quickly quashed the protests.[54]

4.4 TELECOMMUNICATIONS EQUIPMENT: INDIGENOUS DEVELOPMENT AND GLOBAL COMPETITIVENESS VIA INDUSTRIAL POLICY, STANDARDS-SETTING AND CORPORATE GOVERNANCE INTERVENTIONS

In spite of the global scrutiny of Huawei and China's dominance in supplying 5G networking equipment as mentioned earlier in the chapter, the state is less concerned with controlling ownership and business scope in telecommunications equipment because this subsector is perceived to be less sensitive on national security grounds. Telecommunications equipment plugs into and does not have direct jurisdiction over the state-owned and managed communications infrastructure. The state formally liberalized equipment imports in the late 1980s during the period of diminishing foreign exchange and trade sanctions after the Tiananmen Square Incident. State regulation permitted FDI through JVs in the 1990s and wholly foreign-owned entities after WTO accession. In the context of liberalized market entry, the state promotes indigenous development through infrastructural procurement, standards setting, and corporate governance interventions.

Many foreign equipment makers operating in Chinese markets have retained domestic JV partners in order to navigate complicated distribution networks and the numerous central- and local-level bureaucracies granted regulatory authority to manage subsectors perceived less strategic to national security yet making important contribution to the enhancement of the national technology base. In this context, state-owned

---

[53] See Hsueh (2011), 97–98.

[54] See Weiss (2014) on the motivations of external signaling and domestic stability, which prompt the Chinese state to allow or stifle protests.

operators balance procurement among domestic and foreign telecommunications equipment producers to ensure network modernization. "ZTE and Datang are gaining market share when they had none before. Huawei is not gaining as much as they believe they deserve—they bitterly complained about not gaining more TD orders. So there's a balance among domestic equipment makers," explained a former director of the Global Innovation Research Center, Peking University.[55]

To develop the national technology base, indigenous capacity in particular, investment incentives and state subsidies have promoted domestic equipment makers in information communications technology.[56] JVs with FDI, state subsidies, including the 863 Program, and the more intense and frequent interactions with government bureaucracies and financial institutions, including founders who are well connected to state and party officials, have facilitated domestic sector development.[57] Moreover, the state retains discretion to intervene in market coordination and shareholder control of state-owned or state-controlled private companies in new technology sectors to manage domestic sector development and global competitiveness. In semiconductors, for example, authorities at different levels of government are required by law to participate in the market coordination and the negotiations of ownership arrangements of FDI in state-owned and state-controlled enterprises.[58]

Notably, to control the technologies that operate telecommunications infrastructure and to promote indigenous technology, the state coordinates and manages technical standards-setting in terminal equipment. The Chinese government signed the APEC Mutual Recognition Agreement for Conformity Assessment of Telecommunications Equipment in 1998; however, China-specific standards plague the conformity assessment process, and licensing schemes favor domestic industry and enhance state authority in market coordination. State-owned equipment makers, under the leadership of research organs affiliated with the telecommunications ministry, routinely collaborate with private domestic and foreign companies, motivated by market access and economic and political capital, to transfer and incubate technology.[59]

---

[55] See interview on September 28, 2008 in Beijing.
[56] Suttmeier (2005) associates civilian-based technology initiatives, national security imperatives, and post-Mao economic reform.
[57] Huawei, its ownership and controlling interests in constant debate, is a standout example.
[58] See Hsueh (2011).
[59] May 19, 2006 interview in Chongqing with vice president of a JV between domestic and foreign-invested telecommunications equipment makers.

Foreign equipment makers Siemens' and Motorola's participation in incubating TD-SCDMA with Datang and ZTE, led by the telecommunications ministry in the 2000s, is an early representative case of deliberate market coordination involving public–private collaboration. When technical difficulties delayed the release of TD-SCDMA, the state postponed the licensing of other 3G technologies and restructured the carriers into integrated operators to ensure its smooth implementation. The MIIT then assigned TD-SCDMA, in 2008, to the newly strengthened China Mobile. These actions maximized nationwide network resources and service operation capabilities and granted existing and new domestic equipment makers the time to commercialize technology.

Before TD-SCDMA and later 5G, a prominent state-sponsored attempt, which ultimately failed, to promote indigenous technology for domestic and global adoption through state intervention in market coordination was WAPI (Wired Authentication and Privacy Infrastructure), a wireless LAN standard, between 2004 and 2010.[60] In the mid-2010s, the MIIT again delayed licensing the next 4G technologies until after the state-owned carriers successfully rolled out TD-LTE, which is China's homegrown 4G standard. Despite Beijing's regulatory efforts, the third- and fourth-generation standards TD-SCDMA and TD-LTE, respectively, are not widely adopted outside of China.[61]

4.4.1 State Regulatory Interventions: Telecommunications Next Generation Technologies (5G)

The strategic value logic of market governance to modernize infrastructure and enhance indigenous capacity has also applied to telecommuni-

---

[60] Hsueh (2011) on TD-SCDMA, WAPI and other standards-setting episodes to promote domestic industry development and global competitiveness.

[61] Nahm and Steinfeld (2014) locate China's success as contract manufacturers in the intense interaction between upstream research and development and downstream manufacturing; in contrast, Steinfeld (2004), Fuller (2016), and Brandt and Rawski (2019) show mixed results and failures in technology and commercialization across industrial sectors. The failure to gain traction of TD-SCDMA and TD-LTE "reflects the difficulty of creating a protected industry ecosystem for national firms in an industry that is increasingly dominated by global platforms" (Thun and Sturgeon 2019). Rather, the firms that have thrived are those value-added service providers, under less state control because they do not produce or operate the national security-sensitive communications infrastructure as discussed in Section 4.3 of this chapter, which have adopted and localized the global technology.

cations fifth-generation network technology.[62] The Made in China 2025 industrial policy, which identifies strategic emerging sectors like autonomous driving vehicles, green technology, and semiconductors, also emphasizes breakthroughs in 5G. The new network technology is expected to significantly boost data transfer and wireless speeds and lower lag times between network and device. Chinese companies own in total about 10 percent of 5G-essential intellectual property rights (IPR).[63] The companies, which rank among the top ten contributors of IPR are Huawei, state-owned ZTE, the Chinese Academy of Telecommunications Technology under the MIIT, and Guangdong Oppo Mobile Telecommunications, a subsidiary of the privately held BBK Electronics.[64]

The 2017 adoption of Huawei's Polar coding methodology by 3GPP, the global wireless standards-setting body, has likely raised that number as telecommunications carriers around the world, including in Canada and India, began to deploy Huawei technology for 5G networks. Moreover, within the Chinese market, in 2018, the Chinese government has again considered restructuring the national carriers for 5G rollout.[65] Additionally, the U.S. chipmaker Intel, which operates two assembly and testing factories in Chengdu, has partnered with Huawei and China Mobile to conduct interoperability trials and will work with China Unicom to roll out 5G at the 2022 Winter Olympics in Beijing.[66]

Part and parcel of the strategic value logic of market governance to enhance the national technology base is how Chinese regulators and courts exert influence over domestic and global markets, with numerous multinational corporations doing significant business in China. In 2013, following a complaint filed by the government-sponsored Mobile Phone China Alliance, alleging several questionable practices, the NDRC launched an anti-monopoly investigation against the U.S. wireless technology company Qualcomm, accusing it and other such foreign companies of receiving "profits through discriminatory pricing or high

---

[62] See interview on March 12, 2013 in Beijing with official at the Ministry of Science and Technology.

[63] "Telecom Services the Geopolitics of 5G and IoT," *Jefferies Franchise Note* (September 14, 2017).

[64] "Chinese Manufacturers Still Lead 5G Standard Essential Patent List," *GizChina* (February 27, 2020).

[65] "China Explores Megamerger of Mobile-Phone Carriers," *Bloomberg* (September 4, 2018).

[66] "Intel Makes 5G Push across China with Huawei," *ZDNet* (September 26, 2018).

royalty fees."[67] Legal decisions favor Chinese companies in intellectual property disputes, such as the 2015 case involving American company Vringo, which had accused Chinese state-owned telecommunications equipment maker ZTE of using patented mobile technology for years without paying license fees.

In 2018, the State Administration for Market Regulation, established that year, delayed the merger between two rival chipmakers: Qualcomm, a U.S. company whose China business accounts for nearly two-thirds of its revenue in 2017, and NXP of the Netherlands.[68] The deal would have increased Qualcomm's competitiveness in the Internet of Things, including connected cars. Later in the year, the IPR tribunal of the Fuzhou Intermediate Court banned the sale of older iPhone models after ruling earlier that Apple infringed on Qualcomm patents covering wireless networks and devices.[69] Chinese handset makers like Xiaomi, Vivo, and OPPO compete with Apple and license Qualcomm's 4G and 5G technologies.[70] OPPO, in 2020, ranks among the top ten companies in the world with contribution to essential 5G technology. In 2017, its parent company, BBK Electronics, ranked just behind Samsung as the second largest smartphone manufacturer.[71]

In the U.S.-China trade war that commenced in 2018 China countered with tariffs that target sectors and products, including soy, cars, and chemicals, which are produced in regions within the United States where President Trump had the most ardent supporters. Joining the multi-sector alliance of the U.S. businesses protesting the trade war were high-tech companies (such as Qualcomm, Intel, and Apple) that worried about their bottom line with chips, networking equipment, and smartphones assembled and sold in China, and many of their inputs produced there.[72] They claimed the trade war would slow down the United States' own 5G development.[73]

---

[67] "Monopoly Position: China," *Financial Times* (January 26, 2015).

[68] "Qualcomm Ends $44 billion NXP Bid after Failing to Win China Approval," *Reuters* (July 25, 2018).

[69] "iPhone Ban in China May Push Apple, Qualcomm Toward Settlement," *Bloomberg* (December 10, 2018).

[70] "Qualcomm Differentiates Itself and Smartphone Partners from Apple and Huawei with the Snapdragon 855," *Forbes* (December 10, 2018).

[71] "BBK is Second Largest Smartphone Manufacturer," *Electronics Weekly* (May 26, 2017).

[72] "In China Trade War, Apple Worries It Will Be Collateral Damage," *New York Times* (June 18, 2020).

[73] "Tech Firms Say China Tariffs Will Set Back U.S.'s 5G Goals," *Wall Street Journal* (September 7, 2018).

4.4.2 Semiconductor Supply Chain: State Funds, Initial Joint Ventures, and Corporate Governance Interventions

The development of indigenous Chinese capacity in microelectronics, which contributes to critical inputs in telecommunications equipment, offers another case study of the state's deliberate role in market coordination and property rights arrangements in the *centralized governance* of sectors perceived strategic for the national technology base. Government subsidies, tax incentives, FDI liberalization, and centrally managed firm-level collaborations between state-owned and foreign-invested enterprises aimed to establish an indigenous semiconductor industry. They are outlined in the 908 and 909 Projects of the 8th and 9th five-year plans (1991–1995 and 1996–2000, respectively,), the various Catalogs for the Guidance of Foreign Investment Industries, *Policies to Encourage the Development of Software and IC Industries* in 2000, the *National Medium- and Long-Term Science and Technology Development Plan* for 2006–2020, and the "Guidelines for the Development and Promotion of the Integrated Circuit Industry" in 2014. By the 2015 release of Made in China 2025, the courting of private investment and FDI and later acquisition through corporate governance interventions by centrally managed state-owned enterprises at the company level have become prevailing market governance mechanisms.

The 9th Five Year Plan's 909 Project established state-owned Huahong Microelectronics in 1996. Soon after, Huahong collaborated with Japanese equipment maker NEC in the joint venture Shanghai Huahong NEC Electronics, which focused on bringing dynamic random access memory (DRAM) chips to market. The SOE-FDI collaboration represented an advancement from China's first foundry Huajing of the 908 Project, which had purchased equipment from Lucent and employed technology from Toshiba and Siemens. The first IC production of Shanghai Huahong NEC Electronics came on line in 2001, around the time the government released *Policies to Encourage the Development of Software and IC Industries*. Still industry experts attribute Huahong's success to Japanese engineers and fabrication plans rather than indigenous capacity.[74]

In 2011, Huahong acquired the majority shares of Grace Semiconductor, founded by Taiwanese entrepreneur Winston Wong with

[74] See Fuller (2016), 122–126.

Jiang Minheng, the son of former president Jiang Zeming.[75] At the time of Grace's founding in 2000, Jiang Minheng served as one of the vice presidents of the Chinese Academy of Sciences (CAS).[76] The merger of Huahong and Grace, in 2011, added another Chinese state-controlled company to join Semiconductor Manufacturing International Corporation (SMIC), as competitors to the world's top two contract-chip manufacturers by revenue, Taiwanese-owned United Microelectronics Corporation and Taiwan Semiconductor Manufacturing Corporation (TSMC), also the largest independent foundry by market share.

The founding and development of SMIC followed the same dominant pattern of market governance of strategic utilization of foreign-invested private assets and eventual central state intervention in corporate governance. "The government wanted to attract high-end semiconductor manufacturing since demand is super strong but there was less supply from within China," explained the China manager of a U.S.-based venture capital firm, who has served SMIC's board since its founding.[77] In 2000, SMIC was founded by Richard Chang, a Texas Instruments veteran and former executive of TSMC, who teamed up with Wang Yangyuan, a Peking University professor, at the Zhangjiang High Technology Park, managed and run by the Ministry of Science and Technology and the Shanghai government.[78] The company dual listed at the New York Stock Exchange and in Hong Kong in 2004. Five years later, after settling an intellectual property lawsuit in the United States with TSMC, corporate governance interventions and massive financial infusion from the Chinese central state and local governments culminated in the takeover of SMIC by the Shanghai government in 2009. The Taiwan-born Chang, co-founder and CEO, resigned shortly thereafter.[79]

Ten years later, in 2020, state-owned Datang Telecom Technology & Industry and China Investment Corporation (CIC), the country's

---

[75] See Mengin (2015), 197.

[76] The year before, in 1999, CAS had teamed with the Shanghai government, the State Administration of Radio, Film, and Television, and the Ministry of Railways, to establish China Netcom, which later merged with China Unicom in 2000 (Hsueh 2011).

[77] Interview on October 10, 2005.

[78] Interview with Richard Chang at SMIC Headquarters in Shanghai on December 12, 2005.

[79] "Changes in Directorate and Authorized Representatives," *Semiconductor Manufacturing International Corporation* (Press Release, November 10, 2009); "SMIC Trading Halted After Chairman's Death," *EE Times* (June 30, 2011); and "SMIC Founder Says 'Optimistic' China Can Catch Up with U.S. in Semiconductors," *Reuters* (August 5, 2020).

sovereign wealth fund, have become SMIC's main shareholders, and SMIC is referred to as China's largest semiconductor foundry in public and private. The Peking University professor served as honorary chairman and scientific advisor of SMIC until 2021. During the U.S.-China trade war, in May 2019, President Trump signed an executive order that effectively blocked as a U.S. supplier Huawei, a minority shareholder of SMIC's R&D arm. SMIC voluntarily delisted from the New York Stock Exchange, citing low trade volume and high listing costs.[80]

In mid-July 2020, with China spending more on importing semiconductor chips than it does on oil, SMIC debuted in Shanghai as the biggest initial public offering in a decade since the state-owned Agricultural Bank of China.[81] The Shanghai listing occurred just as TSMC readied to commercialize 5-nanometer technology, two generations ahead of SMIC's capabilities. The MIIT's China Integrated Circuit Industry Investment Fund, Singapore's sovereign fund GIC Pte, and the Abu Dhabi Investment Authority are among the institutional investors.[82]

It is no coincidence that both Grace Semiconductor and SMIC have employed and poached senior industry veterans in their 40s and 50s, who have in-depth knowledge of current manufacturing processes, from Taiwanese, Japanese, and Korean companies. Under them are typically recent graduates, who are considered young talent apt for training. "For those in their 40s and 50s, it is a no-brainer: They get offered the same figure salary but in RMB instead of NT$, which means four times as much," explained an executive at TSMC.[83] In 2017, SMIC hired its current co-CEO Liang Mong Song, formerly of TSMC, from Samsung. Two years later, another former TSMC executive, Chiang Shang-yi, left SMIC, after joining the company in 2016, to become the CEO of Wuhan Hongxin Semiconductor Manufacturing Company, which has since been taken over by the Wuhan government after running into delays and

---

[80] "China's Biggest Chip Maker, SMIC, to Withdraw from New York Stock Exchange as Trade Spat With US Spills Over to Technology Sector," *South Morning China Post* (May 24, 2019) and "Chinese Chipmaker SMIC to Delist from NYSE, Focus on Hong Kong," *Caixin Global* (May 24, 2019). Also, see "Executive Order on Securing the Information and Communications Technology and Services Supply Chain," *White House Executive Order* (May 15, 2019).

[81] "China's National Champion Chipmaker Becomes Its Biggest Listing in a Decade," *Fortune* (July 16, 2020).

[82] "Top China Chipmaker SMIC More than Triples in Shanghai Debut," *Bloomberg* (July 15, 2020).

[83] "US Fears Attempts by Chinese Chipmakers to Grab Top Talent," *Financial Times* (November 2, 2018).

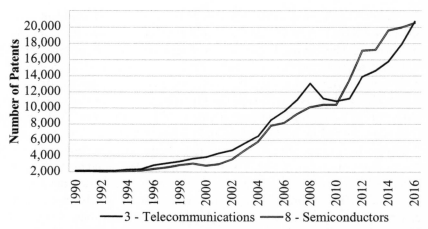

FIGURE 4.1. China patent publications by technology (Telecommunications and Semiconductors) (1990–2016)
Source: World Intellectual Property Organization (2019).

financial troubles.[84] State-sponsored Tsinghua Unigroup hired Charles Kau, who was the former head of Inotera and who had also worked at Fairchild Semiconductor, Intel, TSMC, and Macronix as the Vice Chairman and the Global Executive Vice President. Inotera is Micron's joint venture in Taiwan. In 2018, at least 1,000 Taiwanese engineers worked in Chinese chip companies.

Figure 4.1 shows that patent publications in semiconductors increased significantly in the 2000s, when strategic utilization of FDI began. On this measure, indigenous development in semiconductors surpassed telecommunications in 2010, when state interventions consolidated control over the corporate governance of SMIC. The growth in telecommunications patent publications maps the strategic utilization of FDI via the CCF model in the mid-1990s.

4.4.3 Indigenous Development of Integrated Circuits Design and Memory Chips

The twist-and-turn developments of Huahong Grace and SMIC under *centralized governance* of China's semiconductor industry are not exceptions but the norm up and down the supply chain. If wafer fabrication is

---

[84] "Beijing-backed Tsinghua Unigroup's Chip Projects Hit by Delays," *Nikkei Asia* (November 30, 2021).

the infrastructure of the semiconductor industry, the integrated circuits (IC) sector (design and manufacturing) is the DNA that runs it and the Chinese government was determined to establish the entire supply chain. Not to mention semiconductors, in general, are critical inputs for AI, 5G, autonomous driving, electric vehicles, computer information systems, biometric recognition, the Internet of Things, and edge computing. "The IC industry chain is very long, from design, manufacturing, packaging, testing, to materials," said Wei Xu, the secretary of the Shanghai Integrated Circuit Industry Association (SICA) and the executive vice president of Shanghai Huahong Grace Semiconductor. "There is no single country that can dominate the world. China should consider the integrity and construction of the industrial chain, but in a completely closed environment."[85]

With funding from local governments, state-owned banks, and the China Integrated Circuit Industry Investment Fund, established in 2014, state-backed manufacturers of RAM and NAND memory technologies represent the mandate of the "Guidelines for the Development and Promotion of the Integrated Circuit Industry" and Made in China 2025 to establish a full-fledged domestic semiconductor value chain. In the mid-2010s, not a single Chinese company was among the six companies – Samsung Electronics, Kioxia, SK Hynix, Western Digital, Micron Technology, and Intel – which make up nearly 100 percent of the integrated circuit (IC) market. China's top telecommunications equipment makers – Huawei Technologies, ZTE, Xiaomi, Alibaba Group Holding, and Lenovo – relied on imported technology. In 2020, many homegrown memory chipmakers have joined global competition.

The state's role in the coordination and funding of R&D in privately and state-initiated production of memory chips, however, began much earlier. An incubator of memory chip production, Tsinghua Unigroup, the subsidiary of Tsinghua Holdings, a state-owned assets management enterprise of Tsinghua University, was established in 1988, shortly before the *Policies to Encourage the Development of Software and IC Industries* in 2000. Under the *National Medium- and Long-Term Science and Technology Development Plan* for 2006–2020, Tsinghua Unigroup officially became a "mixed ownership state holding enterprise based on market mechanism" in 2009 when it restructured with 49 percent owned

---

[85] "Countdown: How Close is China to 40% Chip Self-Sufficiency?," *EE Times* (April 11, 2019).

by Beijing Jiankun Group, a private investment firm founded in 2004 by Zhao Weiguo.[86]

Zhao, the current CEO of Tsinghua Unigroup, set out to use China's tried-and-true strategy of "using foreign know-how as a shortcut to building an advanced chip sector for China."[87] Zhao's methods have involved strategic partnerships with Intel Corporation (the U.S.-based semiconductor-chip manufacturer) along with domestic and foreign investment and acquisitions, including stakes in PowerTech Technology and ChipMOS Technologies (Taiwanese IC packaging and testing companies) and purchases of Spreadtrum Communications and RDA Microelectronics (NASDAQ-listed domestic companies). Tsinghua Unigroup gained global notoriety when it attempted to acquire U.S. rivals Micron Technology Inc. and Western Digital Corp., which fell apart amidst concerns that the U.S. regulators would not approve based on national security grounds.[88] Tsinghua Unigroup succeeded in acquiring a 51 percent stake in data networking business H3C. The stake was acquired from Hewlett-Packard, in 2016. In 2018, Tsinghua Unigroup acquired another 51% stake in French chipmaker Linxens from private equity firm CVC.[89]

Production never ceased during the COVID-19 pandemic at Wuhan-based Yangtze Memory Technologies, China's first homegrown memory chipmaker and a subsidiary of Tsinghua Unigroup, and Changxin Memory Technologies, another state-backed memory chip producer.[90] Yangtze employs around 6,000 people and has offices in Shanghai, Beijing, and Silicon Valley. In eastern Wuhan, the company runs a campus the size of more than 160 football fields.[91] Yangtze's Hubei facility joins more than 25 plants in China, which went into production in 2017 and continued through 2020, representing 40 percent of the

---

[86] Tsinghua Unigroup website, accessed on August 15, 2020 at http://en.thholding.com.cn/2016-08/10/c_55629.htm.

[87] "Meet Tsinghua's Zhao Weiguo, The Man Spearheading China's Chip Ambition," *Forbes* (July 29, 2015).

[88] "US Fears Attempts by Chinese Chipmakers to Grab Top Talent," *Financial Times* (November 2, 2018).

[89] "China's Unigroup Buys French Chipmaker Linxens for $2.6bn," *Financial Times* (July 25, 2018) and "France Not Objecting to Sale of Linxens to Chinese Group," *Reuters* (July 26, 2018).

[90] "How China's Chip Industry Defied the Coronavirus Lockdown," *Nikkei Asian Review* (March 18, 2020).

[91] "Chinese Chipmaker Tsinghua Unigroup Agrees $22bn in State Financing," *Financial Times* (March 28, 2017).

global total. In 2019, China's semiconductor industry grew 14 percent, even while the global industry shrank by 13 percent. In April 2020, the company announced that it now builds 128-layer 3D NAND flash memory chips, which match the most advanced offerings of international industry leaders. Industry experts, however, question whether mass production will be possible.[92] Moreover, two-high profile memory chip projects of the Unigroup have hit delays amid mounting debt and bond payments.

4.4.4 Authoritarian Digital Surveillance: State-Private Partnerships in Artificial Intelligence

The continued relevance of the strategic use of foreign and private investment to develop sectors and subsectors, perceived to be of strategic value for the national technology base and national security imperatives, extends to digital surveillance. A significant case of the intersection between sectoral development and authoritarian control is the collaboration with state-owned and state-controlled value-added service providers to develop the Social Credit Systems for mass surveillance, which Wen Jiabao officially sanctioned in 2011. In 2015, the state licensed eight fin-tech companies, including Alibaba and Ant Group's Sesame Credit, Tencent, and ride-sharing and online-dating services, Didi Chuxing and Baihe.com, respectively, to develop software and algorithms used to calculate credit. By 2018, to retain control of data management, the state centralized under the People's Bank of China what had become more than 135 commercial credit reporting platforms.

The People's Liberation Army's significant partnerships with foreign companies and educational institutions, including the Massachusetts Institute of Technology and the Michigan State University, in the R&D of artificial intelligence applications in facial recognition and audio-visual tracking, also exemplify the strategic use of state-market partnerships for authoritarian control.[93] Representative cases include the University of Technology Sydney's partnership with China Electronics Technology

---

[92] "China's Top Chipmaker Says It Can Match Samsung on Memory Tech," *Nikkei Asian Review* (April 13, 2020).
[93] "What about Whataboutism," *Made in China Journal* (July 7, 2020).

TABLE 4.1. *China: Laws, rules, and regulations governing telecoms subsectors*

Market Coordination	Property Rights Arrangements
Telecommunications Writ-Large	

Market Coordination	Property Rights Arrangements
• 908 and 909 Projects of the Eighth and Ninth five-year plans (1991–1995 and 1996–2000)	• *Siye danwei*, quasi-government organizations embedded in state bureaucracies, such as sector-specific associations Internet Society of China, China Communications Standards Association (1970s and beyond)
• Ministry of Information Industry, which merged Ministry of Equipment Industry (MEI) and Ministry of Post and Telecommunications (MPT) (1998)	
• World Trade Organization protocol and accession (1999 and 2001)	• CPC Central Committee Notice on Strengthening and Improving Party Building in State-owned Enterprises (1997)
• National Medium- and Long-Term Science and Technology Development Plan (2006–2020)	• Three Represents (courted private entrepreneurs as representatives of local and national People's Congresses) (2002)
• Ministry of Industry and Information Technology (MIIT) (2008)	
• State Council Cross-Ministerial National Security Review regime for M&As (2011)	• State-owned Assets Supervision and Administration Commission (SASAC) (2003)
• "Opinions of the State Council on Promoting Fair Market Competition and Maintaining the Normal Market Order," State Council Directive #20 (June 4, 2014)	• Anti-Monopoly Law (2008, 2020 revisions)
• Cyberspace Administration of China (also known as Central Leading Group for Cyberspace Affairs) (2014)	• Guiding Opinions of the Central Committee of the Communist Party of China and the State Council on Deepening State-Owned Enterprise Reform (2015)
• Made in China 2025 (2015)	
• China Standard 2035 (drafted 2018, 2020)	• Guiding Opinions on the Restructuring and Reorganization of Central State- Owned Enterprises (2016)
• Infrastructure-for-resources and infrastructure-for-markets bargains abroad (2000 and beyond)	• Cross-time variation in enforcement of ban against Variable Interest Entities (VIEs)
• Catalogues for the Guidance of Foreign Investment Industries (various years)	
• Special Administrative Measures for Foreign Investment Access (Negative Lists) (various years)	

Market Coordination	Property Rights Arrangements

Telecommunications Basic Services

- Various rounds of executive "musical chairs" of state-owned carriers
- Carrier restructuring, technology standards licensure delays, and central state assignments of tech rollout (2008, 2010s)

- Chinese-Chinese-Foreign (CCF) joint venture arrangements permitted (1990s)
- Forced divestment of Chinese-Chinese-Foreign joint ventures, which coincided with "Grasp the large, let go of the small" SOEs (1997)
- Various rounds of reorganization and restructuring of state-owned carriers (1998–2002, 2008, 2010S)
- Private investment permitted in state-owned carriers per state sector reform guidelines (2015)

Telecommunications Value-Added Services

- Public Pledge on Self-Regulation and Professional Ethics for the China Internet Industry (2002 and beyond)
- Cyberspace Administration of China (2014)
- Ministry of Culture
- Ministry of Public Security
- Law on National Security (2015)
- Law on Counterterrorism (2015)
- Social Credit Systems (2011 launch, 2015 licensure, 2018 state centralization)
- Cybersecurity Law (2017)
- Draft Measures for Security Assessment of Cross-border Transfer of Personal Information and Important Data (2019)
- Draft Measures for Data Security Management (2019)

- Company Law of the PRC (1994)
- Contract Law of the PRC
- Three Foreign-Invested Enterprises (FIE) Laws: Sino-foreign Equity Joint Venture Enterprise Law (adopted 1979, 1990, 2001, 2016); Wholly Foreign-Owned Enterprise Law (adopted 1986, revised 2000); Sino-foreign Cooperation Joint Venture Enterprise Law (adopted 1988, revised 2000, 2017)
- Foreign Investment Law – replaced Three FIE Laws (2019)
- Government Outsourcing of Intelligence related Data Analytics
- Corporate Governance Interventions

(*continued*)

TABLE 4.1. (*continued*)

Market Coordination	Property Rights Arrangements
Telecommunications Equipment	
• China-specific standards despite APEC Mutual Recognition Agreement for Conformity Assessment of Telecommunications Equipment • Policies to Encourage the Development of Software and IC Industries (2000) • "Guidelines for the Development and Promotion of the Integrated Circuit Industry" (2014) • China Integrated Circuit Industry Investment Fund (2014) • Approval of new technology standards after state-owned carrier restructuring and carrier successful rollout	• Anti-Monopoly Law (2008, 2020 revisions) • Provisions on Mergers and Acquisitions of Domestic Enterprises by Foreign Investors (2009) • Catalog of Industries for Guiding Foreign Investment, the Special Administrative Measures (Negative List) for Foreign Investment Access • Certain Provisions on Change of the Equity Interests of the Investors of a Foreign-Invested Enterprise (FIE) • Public–Private Partnerships in Digital Surveillance, Artificial Intelligence • Corporate Governance Interventions

Corporation, which is the state-owned military tech parent company of Hikvision, which has developed public security surveillance cameras used by Chinese security forces to track and detain Muslim Uyghurs.[94] Moreover, the Chinese police used genetic material provided by a Yale geneticist and equipment by the U.S. equipment company Thermo Fisher to bolster the DNA database and tracking ability of a nationwide system of surveillance and control employed most recently in Xinjiang.[95]

Table 4.1 shows temporal and subsectoral variation in laws and regulations governing telecommunications, as analyzed in this chapter. Table 4.2 maps dominant patterns of market governance and development outcomes in telecommunications.

---

[94] "UTS, Curtin Unis Announce Reviews Over Links to Surveillance Tech Used by Chinese Government," *Four Corners* (July 15, 2019). The U.S. government, under Trump, placed Hikvision on the Entity List requiring government licensure in October 2019 and in its Executive Order prohibiting U.S. investment of PLA linked companies in November 2020.

[95] "China Uses DNA to Track Its People, with the Help of American Expertise," *New York Times* (2019).

TABLE 4.2. *China telecommunications subsectors: Strategic value, market governance, and development*

Centralized Governance	Dominant Coordination Mechanisms	Dominant Distribution of Property Rights	Development Outcomes
High Strategic Value Infrastructure Modernization and Technology Control	**Basic Services** Centralized, sector-specific regulation and coordination by supraministry of entry, business scope, technical standards, investment level, corporate governance, and carrier restructuring	**Basic Services** State-owned carriers with foreign equity investment in strategic partnerships	**Basic Services** World-class fixed-line and mobile infrastructure, state-owned carriers partner with global telecom operators to tap developing country markets
Medium High Strategic Value Control of Information and Sectoral Development	**Value-added Services** Centralized, sector-specific regulation and coordination by supraministry, state-owned carriers, and courts of entry, business scope, including data management and content, technical standards, investment level, corporate governance, and user-level control mechanisms	**Value-added Services** Variegated market players with restrictions on the business scope, investment level, and ownership structures of foreign direct investment	**Value-added Services** Domestic privately owned and state controlled VAS providers, including social media companies, dominate domestic market and have ambitions to tap global markets

(continued)

TABLE 4.2. (*continued*)

Centralized Governance	Dominant Coordination Mechanisms	Dominant Distribution of Property Rights	Development Outcomes
Medium Strategic Value Indigenous Technology and Global Competitiveness	Equipment Sectors Centralized, sector-specific regulation and coordination by supraministry and courts of entry, business scope, technical standards, investment level, corporate governance, and concessional financing and state-firm bargains abroad	Equipment Sectors Variegated market players, with the state retaining majority or minority shareholder control of corporate governance of select state-owned and state controlled privately owned companies	Equipment Sectors Indigenous technology, competitive equipment makers with domestic market share, national champions tap global markets, and protracted indigenous development in semiconductors

5

Political Stability, Local Goals, and Labor-Intensive Sectors

Decentralized Governance in Chinese Textiles

Applied to the China-sector cases, the Strategic Value Framework expects that the lower degree and narrower scope of the *perceived strategic value* of labor- intensive and less value-added sectors, represented by textiles, for *national security* and the *national technology base* will shape the decentralized role of the state in market coordination and the dominance of subnational state and private actors in property rights arrangements. Indeed parallel to the centralization of market governance in telecommunications based on interacting strategic value and sectoral logics uncovered in Chapter 4, this chapter's cross-time case studies of labor-intensive and capital-intensive sectors of textile manufacturing and trade and distribution show how the introduction of competition in the 1980s and subsequent reregulation during the 1998 and 2008 economic and financial crises reinforced the decentralized role of the state in market coordination and competing interests of subnational state authorities and predominately private economic actors.

The dominant pattern of *decentralized governance* has led to China's high ranking in the global textile industry in low tech, low value-added apparel and clothing and high-tech, high-value-added technical textiles even as deregulation has resulted in overexpansion and runaway pollution. Illustrated by company case studies, *techno-security developmentalism* interacts with *sectoral structural attributes and organization of institutions* and shapes the role of the military in cotton production, and science and technology bureaucracies and subnational state authorities in promoting export-oriented industrialization in technical textiles, which contribute to the national technology base and have defense applications.[1] Sector-specific micromanagement, however, are replaced by macroeconomic rules and regulations and foreign economic policy responding to periodic diplomatic and trade disputes. The global pandemic was no exception.

For example, the import demand from the United States decreased since the start of the U.S.-China trade war in 2018.[2] The COVID-19 pandemic further slowed demand and shut down a major percentage of textile production for several weeks in early 2020. The manufacturing of medical masks and other textile-related safety wear, however, never ceased. The Chinese government briefly banned their export, including from foreign-invested companies manufacturing in the country, until early April that year.[3] Meanwhile, in the face of the coronavirus, textile industries around the world shut down production for several months, and global demand dampened.[4] Surveys conducted, in March and April 2020 by the International Textile Manufacturers Federation (ITMF), on affiliated companies and associations reported an average of 27 percent global decrease in orders.[5]

Section 5.1 of Chapter 5 shows how China's entry into the World Trade Organization (WTO) reinforced the deregulated and market-based nature of textile governance but that the strategic value and sectoral logics interact to shape how the degree and scope of state control and dominant property rights arrangements vary by subsector. On the one hand, as shown in Section 5.2, local government and private stakeholder initiatives characterize the governance of labor-intensive apparel and clothing, dominated by privately owned enterprises, such as Hong Kong listed Bosideng. The utilization of labor inputs in apparel and clothing has consequences for local social and political stability. On the other hand, Section 5.3 documents the varying will and capacity of local governments and central level science and technology bureaucracies to harness limited resources in technical sectors.

---

[1] See Table 2.4 for sectoral structural attributes.
[2] "US Textile and Apparel Import Demand Still Collapsing in Jan 2020," *CCF Group* (March 11, 2020).
[3] "The World Needs Masks. China Makes Them, But Has Been Hoarding Them," *New York Times* (April 1, 2020). France and Taiwan also had official export bans.
[4] "Pandemic Hits Spending Hard: 79% Dive in Clothing Sales Leads a Record Plunge," *National Public Radio* (March 15, 2020).
[5] "ITMF Survey About the Impact of the Corona-Pandemic on the Global Textile Industry," *Textile World* (April 30, 2020).

Such selective state interventions also operate in cotton production, as illustrated by state-owned Xinjiang Productions and Construction Corps. This *modus operandi* has persisted throughout the reform era, further reinforced by the emphasis on high-tech materials of the Made in China 2025 and the National Development and Reform Commission (NDRC)'s Textile Industry Development Plan (2016–2020). Section 5.4 discusses the Chinese government's deregulated governance of textile trade and distribution, which permits foreign-invested enterprises to operate independently and compete in the cutthroat, price-cutting domestic market marked by periodic overexpansion and reactive government intervention in response to economic reverberations and political crises.

5.1 STRATEGIC VALUE AND SECTORAL LOGICS: DECENTRALIZED GOVERNANCE

In 2020, Oxford-trained economist Yu Yongding, a member of the NDRC's National Planning Committee and the Foreign Policy Advisory Committee of the Ministry of Foreign Affairs, who served as the president of the China Society of World Economy, advocated for an "independent industrial system," which is integrated into global supply chains even while China's economic growth is anchored by domestic consumption and less dependent on external demand.[6] The Chinese textile industry, in many ways, already fits into this aspiration of domestic consumption-driven demand and Chinese domination of the global supply chain.

The Chinese textiles and clothing industry, which includes everything from fiber and yarn to fabrics, made-ups, and readymade garments made of cotton, silk, wool, and synthetic yarn, is today marked by world-class production and global market dominance in contract manufacturing. Globally, China ranks first in the production of clothing and textiles.[7] Between 2013 and 2017, on an average, China accounted for nearly 40 percent of global exports of apparel and textiles, compared to 26 percent a decade earlier.[8] By 2018, accounting for nearly 50 percent of global

---

[6] See "Yu Yongding: How to Realize the Transition from 'international cycle' to 'double cycle'?," *China Wealth Management 50 People Forum* (August 16, 2020). In Chinese.

[7] According to the WTO's *World Trade Statistical Review*, in 2018, China is followed by the European Union, India, and the United States in textiles, and EU, Bangladesh, and Vietnam in clothing.

[8] Statista 2020, accessed August 19, 2020 at www.statista.com/statistics/1036081/china-textile-clothing-leather-import-export-share-in-global-trade/.

textile exports, at U.S. $276.73 billion, Chinese textile exports comprised nearly seven times that of India, the second largest exporter.[9]

Moreover, Chinese manufacturers also produce high-tech nonwovens and geosynthetics and attempt to commercialize nanotechnology in nonwoven fiber applications, and apply artificial intelligence to digitize design and manufacturing in addition to producing smart textiles. Disaggregated, apparel and clothing accounts for 60 percent of Chinese textile exports. Nonetheless, fiber, yarn, and fabrics reached an all-time high in growth in 2018, when China reached top three in the global supply of cotton and chemical fiber.[10] Sourcing diversification strategies to reduce dependence on China during the U.S.-China trade war and geopolitics notwithstanding, reshoring has not become a mainstream practice in the United States or the European Union.[11]

The path to which China has achieved domestic consumption and global competitiveness in labor-intensive and less value-added textiles, however, is not through centralized government coordination and predominant state sponsorship and ownership, as shown in Chapter 4 for telecommunications. Rather, the regulatory and industrial trajectory of textiles shows that the state relinquished central-level market coordination to decentralized state bureaucrats and nonstate economic actors by the early 1990s, and the textile ministry and related bureaucracies became sector and business associations. Macroeconomic rules and regulations, disconnected from micro-level sectoral management, along with the predominately private sector govern the industry.

Less concerned about the production and marketing of goods or services with few applications for national security and low contribution to the national technology base, and turning to light and textile industries as a source of foreign exchange, the Chinese government introduced competition in the textile industry in the 1980s. Shortly after the *Decision on Issues Concerning the Establishment of a Socialist Market Economic Structure* officially eliminated the planning system and aimed to establish a modern market system and incorporate international institutions, the dismantling of the Ministry of Textile Industry (in 1993) relinquished central-level coordination of production. The "grasp the

---

[9] "India Overtakes Germany and Italy, is New World No. 2 in Textile Exports," *The Times of India* (June 3, 2020).

[10] Ranking according to Statista Data (2020), with India and the United States rank far behind in chemical fiber and close behind in cotton.

[11] See "Five Ways World Textile and Apparel Trade is China," *Just-Style Apparel Sourcing Strategy* (August 12, 2020).

large, let go of the small" policy, in 1997, further deregulated less strategic sectors, such as textiles, while it retained centralized market coordination in strategic sectors shown in Chapter 4. The downgrading of the Ministry of Internal Trade, in 1998, to a bureau-level department devolved economic decision-making in the trade and distribution of raw materials and processed textiles. State-owned trading companies separated from bureaucracy and became corporatized.

The effects of path-dependent *sectoral organization of institutions* in apparel textiles became apparent during the 1997 Asian financial crisis and the WTO protocol negotiations in the same period. With the WTO accession and the expiration of the Multi-Fiber Arrangement (MFA) impending, former textile bureaucrats, still powerful within the Communist Party, convinced the central leadership that overexpansion in chemical and natural fiber-processing sectors and the slow development of technical sectors were harmful for the global competitiveness of Chinese textiles. The demoted State Administration of Textile Industry (SATI) entered state-owned textile mills to destroy spindles and forced the closure of failing manufacturers, mergers of weak and strong companies, and industrial upgrading across subsectors.[12] The 1998 Yangtze River floods further justified the attempt to strengthen productive capacity in technical textiles. That the State Council had dismantled the textile ministry, however, affected SATI's efforts. Decentralization had empowered local and provincial governments, which restructured state- and collectively owned textile enterprises based on local agendas in response to slowed export growth during the East Asian crisis and not the weakened textile bureaucracy.[13]

Nevertheless, the implications of China's WTO protocol negotiations in 1999, on less strategic sectors for national security and the national technology base, reveal the *perceived strategic value* logic driving China's leaders. The decentralized nature of market governance in Chinese textiles became reinforced by a political bargain brokered by state leaders in its WTO protocol agreement. In order to secure lower foreign investment ceilings for telecommunication sectors, the development of which is perceived paramount for authoritarian resilience on political and economic grounds, the Chinese government agreed to a four-year safeguard mechanism for textiles after the phase-out of the MFA and the 2005 expiration

---

[12] See Hsueh (2011), 156–192.   [13] See Hsueh (2011).

of the WTO's Agreement on Textiles and Clothing.[14] The "compromise" reiterated the fifth Sino-American textile agreement (1997–2008) and had little additional economic impact.[15]

Immediately before the WTO accession in December 2001, the remaining offices of the textile bureaucracy became sector and business associations. Soon after, the commerce ministry delegated the administration of licensing and quota distribution to local commerce bureaus and sector and business associations. "Textiles is no longer considered a pillar industry and thus was one of the first to undergo the process of deregulation," explained Li Jinbao, director of Science and Technological Development at the China National Textiles & Apparel Council (CNTAC).[16] "The numerous central incentives are policies of the past. Government support to encourage [multinationals] to source and procure in China has all but stopped. Any encouragement of manufacturing, which is dominated by private Chinese firms, are on the local level," explained a former China general manager for Liz Claiborne, an American apparel brand marketer.[17]

Sector and business associations work with local governments and private entrepreneurs to increase investment and solidify China's leading role in the global production network, but they "typically lack resources to execute many of [their] ideas and [have] no management authority."[18] "These *xiehuei* [associations] develop opinions to assist government and also provide assistance to enterprises," explained Gao Meizhen, the general manager of Bosideng, a Hong Kong-listed garment manufacturer and brand marketer.[19] Funding for the associations derives primarily from membership fees and revenue generated from trade shows and export consulting.[20] One informant, the R&D director of a textile association, explains the extent of state involvement in setting technical standards across industries: "Guobiao (national standards) deals with more

---

[14] Interviews in Beijing on October 26, 2005 with official from the U.S. Commercial Service and on February 25, 2006 with official from the U.S. Embassy's Economic Section.

[15] Quote from interview on May 26, 2006 in Jiangsu with general manager of Chenfeng Apparel, a privately owned domestic contract manufacturer.

[16] Interview on April 24, 2006, in Beijing.   [17] Interview on May 23, 2005, in Shanghai.

[18] Interview on March 8, 2006 in Shanghai with Gu Qingliang, professor of textile economics, Glorious Sun School of Business and Management.

[19] Interview on March 10, 2006 in Changshu, Jiangsu province.

[20] Interview on March 13, 2013 in Beijing with Yang Jun, Vice President and Secretary General, Federation of China Textile and Garment Enterprises.

important security-related issues, whereas industrial or company standards govern textiles [a less strategic sector]."[21]

Today, the dominant pattern of devolved market coordination and dominance of quasi-state and private ownership governs textile sectors, which have few applications for national security and limited contribution to the national technology base. Manufacturers of various ownership stripes operate linear technology in commodity chains, which respond to consumer and global industrial demands. The actual degree and scope of the role of the state in market coordination and property rights arrangements vary by subsector according to interacting strategic value and sectoral logics shown in the subsector case studies. Labor- and capital-intensive textiles comprise varying degrees of complex interactive technology, asset specificity, and global learning and are buyer- and producer-driven commodity chains, respectively. Moreover, the development and use of technology in technical textiles have national security applications and contribute to the national technology base.

5.2 APPAREL AND CLOTHING: SECTORAL DEVELOPMENT AND LABOR RELATIONS VIA DECENTRALIZED GOVERNANCE

Institutional restructuring before and after China's WTO accession set the stage for private sector development and local-stakeholders-initiated FDI throughout the 1990s and beyond.[22] Following China's 2001 WTO accession, the 16th CPC Central Committee's 3rd Plenary Session in the *Decision of the CCP Central Committee on Certain Issues Concerning the Improvement of the Socialist Market Economy* (in 2003) announced regulation to facilitate private enterprise, the effects of which were most greatly felt in less strategic sectors, such as apparel and clothing. Many garment manufacturers owed their establishment to the devolution of economic decision-making to local governments, de facto recognition of private property, and market entry and FDI liberalization in less strategic sectors from the 1990s. They operated as quasi-private collective enterprises and served as contract manufacturers working closely with foreign brand marketers and foreign-invested manufacturers, many from Taiwan and Southeast Asia. Typically, foreign partners managed the supply

---

[21] Interview on April 24, 2006 in Beijing with Lin Jinbao, vice president charged with science and technology at the National Textile and Apparel Council.

[22] See Mertha (2009) on the role of nonstate interests in shaping policy and institutional change.

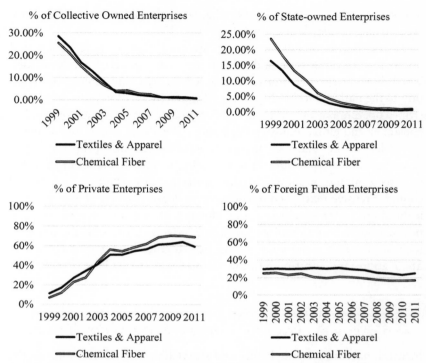

FIGURE 5.1. China textiles and apparel vs. chemical fiber: Enterprise type (1999–2011)
Source: Annual Industrial Statistics, China Data Online, 2019.

chain, helped set up production processes, and dictated production standards. The central government encouraged value-added production in garment production, but it did not support that policy with concrete industrial programs or financial resources, which they left up to local authorities.[23]

By the WTO accession in the early 2000s, the proportion of domestic privately owned textile manufacturers, many of whom divested to managers-turned-owners by collectively owned enterprises, dominated the variegated property rights arrangements across textile sectors (Figure 5.1). Into the 2010s, state-owned enterprises accounted for less than 1 percent of textile enterprises even as foreign investment remained steady, between 25 percent–30 percent in textiles and apparel and fallen to less than 20 percent in high-polluting chemical fiber processing (see Section 5.3).

---

[23] See Oi (1992, 1999) and Ang (2016).

Bosideng Corporation, currently one of China's largest upmarket brand marketers, operated in the decentralized institutional environment. Gao Dekang, Bosideng's CEO, party secretary of his hometown and representative in the National People's Congress, established Bosideng with a few sewing machines during the heyday of the Household Responsibility System in the late 1970s.[24] From a *getihu* comprising less than seven people in a business to an international listing by way of several mergers and acquisitions with local town and village enterprises during economic slowdowns, Bosideng transformed into one of China's leading producers of goose down jackets and branded winter coat apparel.[25]

Today, Bosideng and other apparel and clothing manufacturers, traders, and retailers respond to global economic and market conditions rather than to government calls to purchase domestic inputs or curtail or increase production to achieve the state's often reactive imperatives and less deliberate actions in industries with few implications for China's perceived vulnerabilities and aspirations. "Over 90 percent of fabric producers are privately owned companies, and they can do whatever they want, such as import yarn from Pakistan," explained Yang Jun, the vice president and secretary general of the Federation of China Textile and Garment Enterprisers.[26]

In this deregulated environment, updated labor laws to curb citizen and administrative grievances in the context of worker layoffs and cuts in social benefits in labor-intensive sectors, such as apparel and clothing, reflect the interaction between strategic value and sectoral logics. When citizen and worker protests of corruption and workplace and environmental safety in labor-intensive industries do not escalate into regime-destabilizing social unrest, local authorities and economic stakeholders govern market coordination and property rights arrangements.[27] The laws, including the Labor Contract Law of 2008, enhance the job security of workers (e.g., ensuring that full-time employees work under a contract) and ensure judicial fairness in the commercial realm for private

---

[24] See Hou (2019) on how pragmatism, such as protection from official predation, drives private entrepreneurs to participate in the National People's Congress.

[25] China produces about 80 percent of the global supply when combining duck and goose down, according to Journal of Prauden of Korean premium goose down brand (June 13, 2019).

[26] Interview on March 13, 2013, in Beijing.

[27] See Gallagher (2017) on effectiveness of worker protections and patterns of legal mobilization.

entrepreneurs that control valuable and mobile assets.[28] These new rules do not always achieve the declared goals of labor protections in practice. They do, however, increase the discretion of local governments and local branches of the state-controlled All-China Federation of Trade Unions in handling labor disputes through mediation (before reaching arbitration committees and courts at higher levels of authority).[29]

5.2.1 Pluralistic Market Stakeholders in Digitization of Textile Design and Manufacturing

Applications of intelligent manufacturing serve to maintain China's global competitiveness in apparel and clothing in the context of rising labor wages and raw material costs, which in recent years has led to the relocation of manufacturing to other developing countries. General industrial upgrading and the development of the digitalization of apparel and textile design and production have occurred in the context of the deregulation and dominance of private actors of *decentralized governance*. The lower sunk costs involved in consumer-electronics applications of smart textiles further contribute to their development and growth. The mass production and trade of nonsecurity applications of smart textiles, which contribute to the national technology base and regional and national economic competitiveness, have proliferated in the 2010s and beyond.

Heartdub, based in Beijing and founded in Seattle by graduates of the Massachusetts Institute of Technology in 2013, adopts ICT applications to cut cost and streamline production in textiles. Applying artificial intelligence, Heartdub uses data on textile materials gathered by software to mimic properties of real fabric to enable fabric makers "to complete the steps up to preorder presentation at no cost, thereby cutting their overall development cost by about half. Fashion brands also need to make fewer clothing samples because they can see how they will look thanks to the virtual models."[30]

Smart Fabric, founded in Shenzhen in 2014 by Junchao Fu, also represents the mostly privately owned and invested enterprises, which have benefited from market-based incentives and received government

---

[28] Solinger (2009) shows laws recalibrated political compacts between state and labor. Also, see Wang (2016).

[29] See Minzner (2011) on mediation practices that represent "China's turn against the law."

[30] "Chinese Startup Brings AI to the Apparel Industry," *Nikkei Asia Review* (January 13, 2020).

and private funding designed to enhance productive efficiency. The company develops a software-as-a-service cloud enterprise resource system, which leverages the Internet of Things and enterprise resource planning to connect suppliers with customers along the upstream and downstream industry chain. "The [global] textile market, despite being valued at [a] trillion dollars, [bears problems] like extreme dispersion of productivity, inefficient usage of resources, and a low degree of information technology popularity," said Jeffrey Li Zhaohui, managing partner of Tencent Investment, which with CBC Capital, Alibaba's Vision + Capital, and Sequoia Capital China invested US$100 million.[31] According to Fu, Smart Fabrics has "decrease[d] 5 percent to 10 percent of procurement costs for garment markers on average and contract[ed] order delivery time by 30 percent (around 2–3 weeks). For factories in cooperation with the company, their weaving and knitting machinery operates more than 300 days annually from 200 days before. Occupancy of dying machines has improved to 95 percent from 60 percent."[32]

5.3 INDUSTRIAL AND TECHNICAL TEXTILES: TECH UPGRADING AND ENVIRONMENTAL MANAGEMENT VIA DECENTRALIZED AND CENTRALIZED INTERVENTIONS

Market coordination by subnational governments and nonstate market actors and property rights arrangements of predominantly privately owned enterprises characterize market governance in the more capital intensive, valued-added technical textiles. Because of the subsector's national security applications and contribution to the national technology base, the central state and local governments promote industrial upgrading and high-tech sectors through preferential fiscal policies and direct subsidies. The Made in China 2025 industrial policy, released in 2015, and the China Standard 2035 in 2020, fortified the dominant pattern of market governance in strategic sectors, which include strategic segments of nonstrategic industries, such as technical textiles. The development of a raw material base (cotton and chemical-fiber processing) for China's growing dominance in global textile supply chains and the more upstream manufacturing of high-tech materials reveals variation in the actual will

[31] "Tencent, Sequoia Lead $100M Round in Smart Fabric to Disrupt Traditional Textile Sector," *China Money Network* (September 12, 2019).
[32] "Tencent and Sequoia Weave the way in Textiles," *Equal Ocean* (September 13, 2019).

and capacity of the central versus subnational state in market coordination and property-right arrangements.

The period between 1998 and 2001 witnessed tremendous growth in
technical sectors such as geosynthetics. In addition to economy-wide state
intervention to encourage industrial restructuring in response to the East
Asian financial crisis, nonwoven sectors grew overnight after Zhu Rongji
visited flood sites along the Yangtze in 1998 and commented about the
"shoddy dike construction and levees made of bean curd and turtle
eggs."[33] The Ministry of Textile Industry created the Nonwoven
Manufacturers Association (now CNITA) in 1984, but the nonwoven
sector did not receive mass attention until Zhu's 1998 visits. Hao Jianxiu,
a former minister of textiles and vice minister of the State Development
and Planning Commission, further encouraged investments in geotextiles
when she became vice chairwoman of the China International Committee
for Natural Disaster in 2000.

After the WTO accession, the former textile ministry's science and
technology (S&T) units became the China Nonwovens & Industrial
Textiles Association (CNITA) and its local branches and the dozen textile
colleges and engineering institutes renamed and merged with other universities. The structuring effects of existing *sectoral organization of
institutions* became apparent when the latter established as the already-
assembled faculties in chemical and material science conducting research
on technical textiles. These university and college units apply to and
receive funding to tackle various national- and provincial-level S&T and
industrial development plans.

Moreover, today CNITA is the sole textile organization designated as a
central-level association. "CNITA is a national-level association that does
not have a role in policymaking. However, the central government has
placed more emphasis in technical textiles," explained Li Lingshen, the
chairman and president of CNITA.[34] "Government intervention involves
money to promote technical transformation. Market development and
state promotional activities are in the model rather than just the state
prohibiting activities and restricting and discouraging them with standards difficult to meet," Li further remarked.

---

[33] Quoted in Hsueh (2011), 143. Nonwoven fibers are inputs for geotextiles, which have
applications in construction. That summer, extreme rains flooded the valleys of the
Yangtze, Nenjiang, and Songhua rivers, and the government sent PLA troops to assist
after embankment bursts along the Yangtze River in Jiangxi and Hebei provinces.

[34] Interview on March 12, 2013 in Beijing.

In accordance with the strategic value logic, the central state retains supervision of industrial developments in technical textiles through various market-based measures and identifies specific areas in various five-year and S&T plans for government funding. On the one hand, market-based measures include oversight of technological development through the national technical standards committees of State Council ministries, such as the Ministry of Science and Technology (MOST), the Chinese Academy of Science, and the Ministry of Housing and Urban-Rural Development. To strengthen domestic capacity in manmade fabrics and geosynthetics, relevant central-level bureaucracies and standards-setting associations, including the China National Color Technical Standardization Committee, exercise discretionary distribution of limited central funding for R&D and retain control of intellectual property through standards, licensure, and patents.

On the other hand, the National Reform and Development Commission (NDRC) has continued to release textile plans to transform fiber processing and dyeing to technical textiles. NDRC studies also address environmental consequences and "real effects of economic slow-down and hardship though not all are indeed bankrupt" during the 2008 global financial crisis, for example.[35] Shortly after the WTO accession, the Catalog for the Guidance of Foreign Investment Industries of 2004 listed the production of special textiles for engineering use, weaving, dyeing, and post dressing of high-grade loomage face fabric as encouraged sectors. It also removed the treatment and production of urethane elastic fiber and polyester from the encouraged category due to the aforementioned subsectors' tendency to overheat. To pursue efficiency gains due to cheaper labor costs and lax environmental regulations, many global chemical fiber processers shifted production to China even before China's WTO entry. Through the 1990s and 2000s, knowledge and technology transfers via joint ventures adopted by these foreign producers helped to develop indigenous capacity in the lower-tech, less value-added sectors of industrial textiles.

As investment catalogs discouraged or forbade high-polluting sectors, various national level five-year plans distinguished technical textiles. The 11th Five-Year Plan (2006–2010)'s emphasis on indigenous innovation and industrial upgrading led to the promotion of R&D in textile machinery and nonwoven fiber. The 12th Five-Year Plan (2011–2015) guided

[35] Interview on September 23, 2008 in Beijing with Zhao Hong, the Vice President of China National Textile and Apparel Council.

the NDRC's textile bureau to include "filters as an important product," explained Li of CNITA.[36] The inclusion of filters for indigenous development has shaped how China became a global leader in medical textiles, including surgical masks, by the outbreak of the COVID-19 pandemic in 2020. Only a decade earlier, "Chinese companies mainly still produce at the low and middle ends. High-end textiles are still mainly in the domain of foreign companies importing to China," explained a former general manager for TenCate, a foreign-invested producer of woven and nonwoven geosynthetic fabrics.[37]

Other central-level research funding through the 2000s and 2010s also focused on technical and industrial transformation and innovation. In 2005, the MOST added high-performance chemical fiber processing to the eight areas designated for development under the 863 Program (1986–2016). The 863 Program routinely sponsored collaborative efforts between chemical fiber processors, technical textile manufacturers, and universities and research institutes. The program supported such basic research as the development of Bt cotton strands, the commercialization for which the state authorized through farms owned and operated in the 2010s with forced Uyghur labor by the People Liberation Army's Xinjiang Productions and Construction Corps discussed below. The fifteen-year Medium-to-Long-Term Plan for Science and Technology (2006–2020) called for special funding for producers of industrial fabric with applications for airplanes and other aviation equipment for civilian use.

Equipped with central-level institutional support, local governments responded by providing investment incentives and subsidies for the manufacturing of chemical fiber and synthetic fabrics.[38] Local authorities offered free land, tax rebates, bank loans, and ad hoc technical standards dictated by major domestic players in the fledgling industry. Domestic private and foreign investors were drawn into technical textiles, including from other subsectors. "Many Chinese companies that produce construction textiles began in apparel or other textiles, producing carpet weaving, sacks, and building insulation," exclaimed the former general manager of

---

[36] Interview on March 12, 2013, in Beijing.
[37] Interview on February 9, 2006, in Beijing.
[38] Interviews in 2006 and on March 11, 2013 in Shanghai with Wang Yimin, professor of material science at Donghua University and senior scientist at the State Key Laboratory of Modification of Chemical Fibers and Polymer Materials.

TenCate.[39] "They tweaked their equipment to enter new markets and new revenue streams."[40]

The varying experiences of domestic and foreign-invested companies illustrate how government-company bargains, in the setting of technical standards, tended to favor the domestic sector even in the decentralized, deregulated industry with less intentional and deliberate state intervention.[41] Foreign-invested companies, which entered the domestic market by forming alliances with local manufacturers with established clienteles, describe their experiences with the "unregulated collusion between architects, developers, and trade associations that set technical standards for bridges, roads, and buildings" and engage in collusive price-fixing.[42]

5.3.1 Domestic Cotton Production: State Intervention in Strategic Segment of Textile Chain

In the late 1990s, with China's WTO accession being negotiated and amidst slowed global demand due to the 1997 Asian financial crisis, when the State Administration of Textile Industry, the demoted ministry, forced spindles in state-owned mills to shut down across the country and mandated the restructuring of the textile industry, state elites identified domestically produced cotton as part and parcel of China's integration into the global economy. The *perceived strategic value* of domestic cotton production extends to the state's economic interests as well as internal security imperatives, reminiscent of the Soviet era designation discussed in Chapter 9. The state has imparted centralized market coordination in this strategic segment of a largely decentralized and deregulated textile industry. State-owned and state-controlled producers dominate this segment of the domestic textile chain.

The People Liberation Army's Xinjiang Productions and Construction Corps (XPCC) is a dominant producer in domestic cotton production. XPCC saw its rise with the large-scale relocation of textile mills by central bureaucracies to Xinjiang in the late 1990s. Well before Made in China

---

[39] Interview in Beijing on February 9, 2006.
[40] Interview in Beijing on September 21, 2008.
[41] See company case studies of Shenzhen-based Ocean Power, which produced mixes for soft-serve ice cream before entering R&D in geosynthetics, and foreign retailer of non-woven fabric Polyfelt, which later became TenCate, on standards-setting in a more strategic subsector of a nonstrategic sector in Hsueh (2011), pp. 169–177.
[42] Interview on September 21, 2008 in Beijing with former general manager for PolyFelt/TenCate.

2025, the 863 Program funded the development of Bacillus thuringiensis (Bt) cotton strands, which XPCC's Xinjiang farms helped to commercialize.[43] In 2020, XPCC produced more than 7 percent of the global supply and roughly one-third of China's.[44] The PLA-owned and operated company gained notoriety in the late 2010s when reports revealed that XPCC's cotton income is derived from the use of forced labor and contributes to the construction of surveillance infrastructure and "reeducation" camps, which have imprisoned Uyghur Muslims and other ethnic minorities.[45]

The Better Cotton Initiative (BCI), the largest cotton sustainability program, with its own label that certifies producers around the world, in March 2020, suspended its Xinjiang operations with licensed farmers, including XPCC's production, after coming under global pressure. BCI also removed privately owned Huafu Fashion Company, listed in Shenzhen, which operates the world's largest mixed-color cotton yarn spinning mill in Xinjiang, from the BCI Council.[46] In summer 2020, the Trump administration placed XPCC on the U.S. Treasury's sanctions list, along with the value-added telecommunications service provider TikTok, a video sharing social network, discussed in Chapter 4.[47] A year later, in July 2021, Biden put import bans on cotton, tomatoes, and some solar products originating from Xinjiang, and added 14 Chinese enterprises to the Department of Commerce's Entity List involved in alleged human rights abuses in Xinjiang, the dismantling of freedoms in Hong Kong, and a threatening posture on Taiwan.[48]

The National People's Congress Standing Committee issued China's first comprehensive Export Control Law (in October 2021) and the Anti-Foreign Sanctions Law (in June 2021) in response to the series of "unjustifiable" laws and sanctions imposed by foreign governments. The latter gives the state broad powers to seize assets from – and deny visas to –

---

[43] Chinese scientists engineered Bt crops to resist insects while posing limited threats to other organisms. Interview in Beijing with official of the Ministry of Science and Technology, on March 2, 2006. Also, see Rozelle et al. (2002).

[44] "Sanctions on China's Top Cotton Supplier Weave a Tangled Web for Fashion Brands," *Washington Post* (August 22, 2020).

[45] "Coalition Brings Pressure to End Forced Uyghur Labor," *New York Times* (July 23, 2020).

[46] "BCI Pulls Out of Xinjiang," *Ecotextiles* (March 27, 2020).

[47] "Sanctions on China's Top Cotton Supplier Weave a Tangled Web for Fashion Brands," *Washington Post* (August 22, 2020).

[48] "U.S. Slaps Curbs on 34 Entities, Faults China Firms on Abuses," *Bloomberg* (July 9, 2021).

those individuals or entities from countries that have sanctioned China for human rights violations.[49] Additionally, similar to the nationalist sentiments driving the anti-Japanese protests in 2005 and 2012, Chinese consumers have responded to what is perceived and framed as a foreign-led "Xinjiang cotton boycott" with a counter campaign to buy local.

The surge of patriotic purchases has raised the profile of Chinese popular and little known brands alike. Hong Kong-listed Chinese apparel producers and retailers have witnessed stocks at the highest level in five years. The 2022 Beijing Olympics is expected to further boost domestic firms that have supported using materials from Xinjiang. In contrast, shares of foreign brands, such as the U.S.-based Nike and the U.K.-based Adidas, have underperformed and sales have cooled in comparison. "The sentiment to buy homegrown brands will continue," said Steven Leung, the executive director at UOB Kay Hian (Hong Kong) Ltd. "In the short-term, the stock prices of Li Ning and Anta will continue to rise."[50]

5.3.2 Central Level Funding and R&D in Upstream High-Tech Materials and Smart Textiles

Just as in upstream cotton production (cotton being a raw material for apparel and clothing), in the most high-technology and security-sensitive upstream sectors of technical textiles, such as new materials incorporating nanotechnology applications and artificial intelligence, central state participation in the coordination of market entry and the exit of the predominantly privately owned enterprises most closely approximates the *centralized governance* of strategic sectors. High-performance fiber as key inputs, such as in medical masks and other safety textiles, is of particular interest to national-level bureaucracies, targeting funding for basic research and commercialization in new materials.[51] Smart textiles, which are able to detect changes in their surroundings and react to them, are at the intersection of high-tech materials and intelligent manufacturing, identified by Made in China 2025 as critical for the development of the national technology base. Their various applications include green

---

[49] "China to Set Up Special Group to Enforce Anti-Sanctions Law," *South China Morning Post* (June 11, 2021).
[50] "Nike Shares Lose Out to Chinese Sneaker Rivals After Xinjiang Cotton Boycott," *Bloomberg* (July 6, 2021).
[51] Interview on March 11, 2013 in Shanghai with Wang Yimin.

production of traditional industries, ICT, energy, transportation, and civil-military integration.[52]

The ministries of Science and Technology, Housing and Urban-Rural Development, Industry and Information Technology, Transport, and other central-level bureaucracies coordinate export-oriented industrialization and state-controlled enterprises dominant in these sectors. The Textile Industry Development Plan (2016–2020) released by the NDRC explicitly building on 11th to 13th five-year plans and Made in China 2025, specifically identifies the strategic value of high-performance fiber and intelligent home textiles for the global competitiveness of Chinese textiles.[53] These subsectors are also listed as encouraged sectors in the foreign investment catalogs.

Most technical textile enterprises are privately owned; however, many receive state funding or are state-sponsored through close relationships with the national-level technical bureaucracies. The state-owned China Textile Investment Development Co., which acquired Anxin Securities Co. in a megamerger in 2014, for example, shares R&D personnel and facilities with the State Key Laboratory of Modification of Chemical Fibers and Polymer Materials, housed at Donghua University, formerly East China Textiles Institute of Science and Technology. Moreover, the Institute for Composite Materials of Tianjin Polytechnic University, until 2000 the Tianjin Institute of Textiles, has produced material for the Shenzhou spacecraft (first and last launched in 1999 and 2016, respectively) and receives funding for basic research in carbon fiber at the nanolevel (e.g., high-performance fiber for military and national security applications).

The academic journal *Nano Energy* publishes a high number of papers by Chinese academics representing science and technology bureaucracies. Its editorial board comprises many scholars based at Chinese institutions, including the Chinese Academy of Sciences and Zhejiang University School of Material Science and Engineering. Notwithstanding the central-level government coordination and state-controlled or state-owned assets absent in the labor-intensive textile sectors, "commercialization is at least five to ten years away in nanoparticle finish, stain-resistant fabrics. Even then, the non-security market is small domestically

---

[52] "Chinese Scientists Design Power-Generating Fabric for Wearable Electronics," *Xinhuanet* (February 27, 2019).
[53] "Textile Industry Development Plan Issued," 世界服装鞋帽网 World Apparel and Footwear Network (January 10, 2016).

TABLE 5.1. *China: Textile production by subsector (2013 and 2014)*

Textile Fiber Production in China: 2013

Product	World	China	Share of China
Chemical fiber (unit: 10,000 tons)	6,377.2	4,092.9	64.2%
Synthetic fiber (unit: 10,000 tons)	5,897.1	3,778.4	64.1%
Cotton (unit: 10,000 tons)	2,553.8	669.9	26.2%

Apparel Production in China: 2013 and 2014

Year/Product	2013 # of firms	Output (unit:10,000)	2014 # of firms	output (unit:10,000)	2013 vs. 2014 # of firms	output
Total apparel	10,222	2,710,070	10,916	2,992,060	6.8%	10.4%
Woven apparel	7,090	1,392,237	7,554	1,550,700	6.5%	11.4%
Knit apparel	3,947	1,317,682	4,224	1,441,360	7.0%	9.4%

Source: China Textile Industry Development Report (2013/2014; 2014/2015)

and globally," explained Pan Ning, Professor of Biological and Agricultural Engineering at the University of California, Davis, who served in the now defunct Ministry of Textile Industry.[54]

Table 5.1 shows how Chinese producers, state-controlled and privately owned, in 2013 and 2014, represented over 64 percent of global production in chemical and synesthetic fiber. Figure 5.2 presents China's exponential growth in technology patent publications in different market segments of technical textiles. Microstructural nanotechnology and chemical polymers both classify as medium high-tech by the OECD, and Figure 5.3 shows China's export growth in that category of products vis-à-vis other categories of technology intensity. Notably, from 1990 to 2014, both low-tech and medium low-tech exports have fallen, whereas China has witnessed growth in high-tech and medium high-tech product categories. In turns of imports, all categories of tech intensity have fallen with the exception of medium high-tech products, which include chemical raw materials and products and chemical fiber, important inputs of non-woven manmade textiles, such as rubber and plastics and other high-tech materials (Figures 5.3 and 5.4).

[54] Interview on October 14, 2013 in Davis, California.

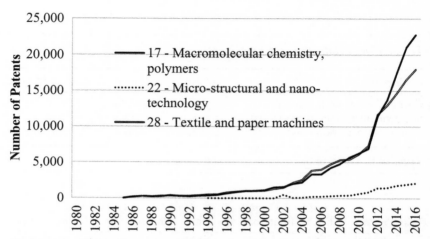

FIGURE 5.2. China: Patent 4 publications by technology (textiles technical sectors) (1980–2016)
Source: World Intellectual Property Organization (2019).

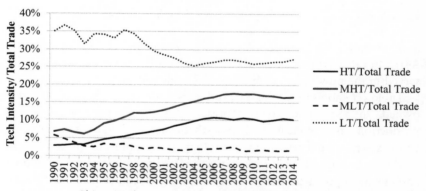

FIGURE 5.3. China: Tech intensity of exports as % of total trade (1990–2014)
Source: World Trade Organization (2017) with OECD Tech Intensity Definition.

5.3.3 Reactive Local State in High-Polluting and Overexpanding Chemical Fiber and State-Market Collusions

The path dependency of earlier rounds of decentralization and deregulation shapes actual industrial and market developments, including reactive local state interventions motivated by political and economic interests in high-polluting chemical fiber processing and collusive economic behavior in a pluralistic landscape of state and market actors.[55] High-polluting

---

[55] Hsueh (2011), 227–252, shows this incidental and reactive intervention in other non-strategic, highly polluting sectors, such as coal power plants and paper mills.

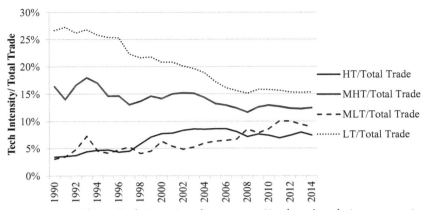

FIGURE 5.4. China: Tech intensity of imports as % of total trade (1990–2014)
Source: World Trade Organization (2017) with OECD Tech Intensity Definition.

and overexpanding downstream sectors, including chemical fibers, routinely appear on the negative lists of foreign investment catalogs. In response, in the context of weakly institutionalized environmental regulations and the private regulation of government offices-turned-textile sector and business associations in the WTO era, local state authorities simply close down or, at best, half-heartedly attempt to restructure them.[56] Chinese Communist Party career promotions and other professional benefits tied to achievements related to central imperatives on technological upgrading and climate change, and the interests of groups with local political influence, further motivate such incidental and reactive local state practices.[57]

Moreover, central-level S&T plans and funding initiatives to target industrial upgrading and invest in basic research, combined with lax enforcement of rules and regulation in a deregulated institutional environment, have led to collusion between universities and enterprises.[58] "Academics are used to obtaining funding from the government. It is all about papers and publications and lots of talk and investments," explained Yimin Wang, professor of chemical engineering at Donghua.[59]

---

[56] Kostka (2015) on the state's "command without control" and Van der Kamp (2020) on the local government's "blunt force" attempts at regulation.
[57] Kostka and Hobbs (2012) and Su, Tao, and Yang (2018).
[58] Interview in Shanghai with Wang on April 15, 2006.
[59] Interview in Shanghai with Wang on March 11, 2013.

5.4 TEXTILE TRADE AND DISTRIBUTION: DECENTRALIZATION AND FOREIGN ECONOMIC POLICY

The trade and distribution of apparel and textiles and related raw materials and inputs for export and domestic consumer and enterprise consumption became decentralized and liberalized with the demotion of the Ministry of Internal Trade in 1998 and China's WTO accession in 2001. Similar to the market landscape of the rest of textiles, perceived to be less strategic for national security and the national technology base, domestic and foreign retailers and brand marketers alike fiercely compete in the internal market with few formal regulatory barriers, on the one hand. This contrasts markedly with the strict regulation of internal textile trade for FDI in India, as shown in Chapter 8. On the other hand, macroeconomic tools and foreign economic diplomacy and disputes affect imports of raw material and other inputs and exports of apparel and technical sectors.

5.4.1 Apparel Retail: Liberalized Internal Trade and Local State-Company Bargains

Bestseller Fashion Group China, a wholly foreign-owned enterprise (WFOE), founded by two Danish entrepreneurs, is a strong case – if not quite representative of all FDI because of its hyper success – of liberalized and competitive markets in apparel and clothing in China. In 2015 alone, more than 100 foreign brands across different retail, consumer products, and food and beverages markets entered China for the first time.[60] They typically enter China by setting up a physical store or a Chinese language online shop, partnering with China's third party e-commerce or mobile platforms, such as Tmall, JD.com, Yihaodian, and Mengdian, or through a multichannel sales approach. Earlier entrants, such as Bestseller, pursued multichannel sales.

Half a decade before the WTO accession, in 1996, during a period of de facto liberalization in the already-decentralized textiles, longtime expatriates Allan Warburg and Dan Friis convinced Anders Holch Poulsen, owner of Denmark's apparel brand marketer Bestseller, to enter

---

[60] See "Report on Domestic and Foreign Brands Who Enter China for the First Time in 2015," *Soupu.com* (January 4, 2016).

the Chinese market to source for export and to sell domestically.[61] Today Bestseller China is one of China's leading fashion retailers operating more than 7,000 stores in over 500 cities. The company markets the various brands of Denmark's Bestseller, in addition to SELECTED, which was launched exclusively in China in 2008. It has also purchased foreign brands, such as J.Lindeberg.

Nearly a decade before the 2004 rules on trade and distribution (promulgated as part of China's timetable of WTO commitments) permitted foreign retailers to distribute products not manufactured domestically, Bestseller China broadly interpreted in its favor trade laws, which permitted foreign-invested companies to trade "self-manufactured" products. Bestseller China easily obtained a license to operate as a WFOE that outsourced garment manufacturing for exports. To sell in the domestic market, Bestseller Denmark and Bestseller China signed contracts that granted Bestseller China the rights to Bestseller Denmark's brands, trademarks, and other technology and intellectual property. To independently market and distribute garments produced by its contract manufacturers, Bestseller engaged in "value-added production" by adding stickers and tags and repackaging the already manufactured garments to bear Bestseller's brands.

What is more, taking advantage of the abolishment of sector-specific control of the internal supply chain and relaxed enforcement of the prohibition against FDI in apparel retail, Bestseller China distributed its apparel products via Bestseller-owned retail centers and franchises by building good relationships with local authorities across the country. As early as 1996, Bestseller China operated in department stores and stand-alone shops by renting spaces stocked with its own inventory and staffed with its own salespeople. Customers paid department stores, which then paid Bestseller China after deducting rent, and issued Bestseller China VAT invoices each month. Stand-alone stores, in contrast, operated as Bestseller China's branch offices. The establishment of each branch office required that Bestseller China interact with local commerce and tax bureaus to obtain business licenses and rental contracts. This process, repeated in each location, proved cumbersome and exposed Bestseller to the vagaries of local state protectionism.

---

[61] Povlsen owns 50 percent stakes of Bestseller China. The rest of the shares are divided between Warburg and Friis, who made it to the 2019 Hurun China Rich List. In 2020, Warburg is based in Hong Kong, and he and his wife own the California Donum wine estate.

Bestseller China also operated franchises since 1997 with a "one brand, one city, and one franchise taker" strategy despite the absence of a franchise law, prior to 2004. Bestseller China set sales targets, waived franchise fees, and earned revenue when franchisees bought its products. Bestseller did not change its franchise model, which minimized competition between franchisees, despite rules promulgated in 2004 that permitted FDI in franchising. According to Warburg, "The 2004 rules enhance bureaucratic oversight and introduce competition in ways that include cumbersome entry requirements."[62]

In the same regulatory context, other foreign-invested fashion retailers adopted a different strategy. Hong Kong-based Esprit Corporation joined forces, in 1997, with the China Resources Enterprises, the Hong Kong subsidiary of state-controlled China Resources Holdings with a minority stake, to open Esprit outlets five years after performing poorly with a market-entry model similar to that of Bestseller China. Seeking to maximize China Resources's central and local state connections, Esprit set up the JV after the promulgation of Tentative Measures on Establishment of Sino-Foreign Joint Venture Trading Enterprises on an Experimental Basis.

After years of lackluster growth within China (1/3 of the growth of Esprit's other markets), in 2009, Esprit, the world's seventh largest fashion group by market value at the time, bought out China Resources's 51 percent stake in the hopes of expanding its China business.[63] A decade later in 2019, the company's struggles during the global financial crisis and beyond had them enter another JV as a minority shareholder at 40 percent, this time with the investment holding company of retail and online platforms Mulsanne Group Holding Ltd. (MGH) of Ningbo.[64] In fact, finding a reliable local partner continues to be the business model for foreign-invested apparel retailers. In 2015, Macy's partnered with Fung Retailing Ltd. to form a JV company, Macy's China, to pilot e-commerce on Alibaba's Tmall Global. Unfortunately, by June 2020, during the COVID-19 pandemic, lagging sales led Esprit to shutter its stores in the

[62] Interview on April 26, 2006 in Beijing with Allen Warburg, general manager of Bestseller Fashion Group (China).
[63] "Esprit Receives a Dressing Down: Analysts Say the Clothing Giant's China Operation is Lacking Ambition Despite Impressive Global Earnings," *Financial Times* (September 22, 2004).
[64] "Esprit Partners Mulsanne Group! Focus on Mainland China Business," *Apparel Resources* (December 2, 2009).

country, after having already closed most of its stores around the world, including the rest of Asia, Australia, New Zealand, and Europe except Germany.

5.4.2 Exports and Raw Material Imports: Macro-Economic Tools and Diplomacy and Disputes

To enhance the national technology base, the central government indirectly subsidizes textile sectors by securing raw materials and other inputs through foreign economic bargains and by calibrating fiscal policies on income, trade, energy, and high-tech content. The central government has ensured that chemical fiber processors obtained stable and inexpensive access to raw and processed material inputs.[65] These include oil and processed inputs procured from countries that China has directed investments, loans, and aid. For example, Chinese state-owned Sinopec has invested in and signed a distribution agreement with Russian company SIBUR to procure polyethylene, a material input for technical textiles, as discussed in Chapter 11. Fiscal methods include levying an export tax on energy and metal products and raw materials to discourage the growth of energy-intensive and pollution-prone exports, and reducing import fees to ensure domestic access to critical production inputs, except during trade and diplomatic disputes.[66]

On the latter point, China's restriction on cotton imports from Australia during an international dispute illustrates how textile trade and distribution can become sites of contention whereby *perceived strategic value* in response to political pressures shapes the state's role in market coordination. In October 2020, the Chinese government ordered cotton mills to stop purchasing supplies from Australia, considered the highest quality among cotton imports.[67] The government threatened quota restrictions and 40 percent tariffs for noncompliance. This occurred at the height of diplomatic tensions between China and Australia over

---

[65] See Hsueh and Nelson (2018) on China's infrastructure-for-resources and infrastructure-for-markets bargains in developing and resource-rich countries to secure raw materials for the purposes of industrial development at home; and Frick and Hsueh (2021) on the relationship between China's OFDI patterns and state goals.

[66] "Beijing Raises Tax on Energy and Metals Products," *South China Morning Post* (October 28, 2006); Group of Twenty (2016); and "Factbox: China's Tariffs on U.S. Commodities and Energy," *Reuters* (August 26, 2019), respectively.

[67] "China Tells Cotton Mills to Stop Buying Australian Supplies – Sources," *Reuters* (October 16, 2020). China also imposed a restriction on coal imports and anti-dumping and anti-subsidy duties totaling 80.5 percent imposed on Australian barley.

TABLE 5.2. *China: Laws, rules, and regulations governing textiles subsectors*

Market Coordination	Property Rights Arrangements

Textiles Writ-Large

Market Coordination	Property Rights Arrangements
• 1978 Open Door Policy • Economic zones; Coastal, Western, Central China development strategies (1980, 1992, 1997, 2004) • Decision on Issues Concerning the Establishment of a Socialist Market Economic Structure (1993) • Ministry of Textile Industry dismantled and demoted into State Administration of Textile Industry (SATI) (1993) • All-China Federation of Trade Unions • World Trade Organization protocol and accession (1999 and 2001) • Former state bureaucracies, now business associations, such as the China National Textile and Apparel Council, disconnected from state organs (1990s, 2001, and beyond)	• Household Responsibility System, which permitted privately initiated *getihu*, comprising less than seven people in a business (1978 and beyond) • Laws on Sino-Foreign Cooperative Joint Venture (1979, 1988) • Law on Wholly Foreign-Owned Enterprises (WFOE) (1986) • Three Represents (courted private entrepreneurs as representatives of local and national People's Congresses) (2002) • Regulation on private enterprise (*Decision of the CCP Central Committee on Certain Issues Concerning the Improvement of the Socialist Market Economy*) (2003)

Apparel and Clothing

Market Coordination	Property Rights Arrangements
• Fifth Sino-American Textile Agreement (1997–2008) • WTO's Agreement on Textiles and Clothing (2001–2005) • Labor Contract Law (2008)	

Nonwovens and Industrial Textiles (including Chemical Fiber and Geosynthetics)

Market Coordination	Property Rights Arrangements
• China International Committee for Natural Disaster (2000, after floods along Yangtze in 1998) • China Nonwovens & Industrial Textiles Association (CNITA) (established in 1984, only national-level association) • Catalog for the Guidance of Foreign Investment Industries (2004, and various years) encouraged special textiles for engineering use, weaving, dyeing, and post-dressing of high-grade loomage	• Wholly Foreign-Owned Enterprise Law (adopted 1986, revised 2000) • Most FDI partnered with local companies to enter the byzantine market to navigate domestic standards and local- and central-level interventions to promote indigenous capacity

Market Coordination	Property Rights Arrangements
• 11th, 12th, and 13th Five Year Plans (2006–2010, 2011–2015, and 2016–2020, respectively, encouraged medical textiles, such as filters and skin grafting • Five-Year and Science & Technology Plans of sector and standard associations • Made in China 2025 (2015) • Textile Industry Development Plan (2016-2020) • China Standard 2035 (2020)	

Textile Trade and Distribution

• Ministry of Internal Trade downgraded (1998) • Multi-Fiber Arrangement (MFA) (1974–1994) • Fifth Sino-American Textile Agreement (1997–2008) • Interim Measures for Administration of Commercial Franchise Operations (1997) • World Trade Organization protocol and accession (1999 and 2001) • Foreign Trade Laws (1994, 2004) • Export tax on energy and metal products and raw materials to discourage high-polluting, energy-intensive production • Import tariffs and/or export restrictions on raw materials and commodities during trade and diplomatic disputes • Infrastructure-for-resources and infrastructure-for-markets bargains abroad (2000 and beyond)	• Wholly Foreign-Owned Enterprise Law (adopted 1986, revised 2000) • Foreign-invested joint ventures between FDI and local retailers/ partners

allegations of Chinese intervention in Australia's domestic affairs and the call by the Australian prime minister for a probe into the Wuhan origins of the COVID-19 pandemic. According to a China-based trader, the restriction on cotton imports "is very supportive to the price of high-grade cotton," in a year with a small domestic crop of high-grade fiber.

TABLE 5.3. *China textiles subsectors: Strategic value, market governance, and development*

Decentralized Governance	Dominant Coordination Mechanisms	Dominant Distribution of Property Rights	Development Outcomes
Low Strategic Value Local Economic Growth and Social and Political Stability	Apparel and Clothing Decentralized regulation and nonstate private market coordination	Apparel and Clothing Variegated market players dominated by the private sector	Apparel and Clothing World class production and global market dominance in contract manufacturing; adoption of ICT applications and artificial intelligence in apparel and textile design and production
Medium Strategic Value Indigenous Industrial Development and Environmental Management	Industrial and Technical Textiles Mix of central and decentralized market coordination and funding by central and local state science and technology bureaucracies and nonstate market actors; central state intervention in the most high-tech subsectors, such as nonwoven nanofibers and smart textiles	Industrial and Technical Textiles Variegated market players, with state investment in favored private sector players involved in high-tech materials with security and infrastructural applications	Industrial and Technical Textiles Global market players in chemical and synthetic fiber processing; limited commercialization in high performance fiber and high-tech nonwovens; mass production of consumer electronics embedded smart textiles; proliferation of market players in high-polluting market segments

Decentralized Governance	Dominant Coordination Mechanisms	Dominant Distribution of Property Rights	Development Outcomes
Medium Strategic Value Export-oriented Industrialization and Foreign Economic Policy	Trade and Distribution Non-sector-specific regulation by commerce ministry; export tax to discourage high-polluting, energy-intensive production; import and export tariffs and/or restrictions on raw materials and commodities during diplomatic and/or trade disputes	Trade and Distribution Variegated market players; local government and FDI bargains; and foreign-invested joint ventures with local partners	Trade and Distribution Top exporter of clothing and textiles, including technical sectors; top global market for foreign-invested retailers and brand marketers

Periodic external pressures shaping central government actions notwithstanding, decentralized market stakeholders, from local governments and technical and industrial textile associations to state bureaucracies in charge of high-tech and raw material inputs, view their primary role as sponsors and promoters of industrial upgrading in subsectors with construction, military, shipbuilding, aviation, and other industrial applications. Inside the halls of the dilapidated building that formerly housed the Ministry of Textile Industry, the pervasive conviction among former textile bureaucrats, now heads of sector associations, is that China relied too much on imports of manufacturing equipment and high-tech fabrics and that when Chinese companies produced high-value fabrics, they relied too heavily on expensive raw material imports. China National Textile and Apparel Council officials also expressed concern that FDI and foreign-invested JVs dominated the domestic production of equipment components and spare parts. They believe export restrictions of high-tech industrial fabrics imposed by advanced industrialized countries justified their calls to substitute imports and reward domestic companies that satisfy intellectual property thresholds.[68]

Table 5.2 shows temporal variation and subsectoral variation in laws and regulations governing textiles, as presented in this chapter. Table 5.3 maps dominant patterns of market governance structures and development outcomes in textiles.

---

[68] For example, technical textile products, including manmade nonwoven fabrics, are on Lists 2–4 of the tariffs imposed by the U.S. government under the Trump Administration during the ongoing U.S.-China trade war. Also, interview in Beijing on September 14, 2006 with Baiyi Wang, High Technology R&D Center, Ministry of Science and Technology.

6

India and Sectoral Variation

Evolution of Neoliberal Self-Reliance and the Rise of Bifurcated Liberalism

The Strategic Value Framework proposes that the *perceived strategic value* of state elites, as they respond to internal and external pressures, interacting with *sectoral structures and organization of institutions*, explicate the dominant intranational sectoral patterns of market governance as countries integrate into the global economy. The historical and contemporary evidence, process-tracing from sectoral origins, of this chapter, shows how Indian state leaders *intersubjectively* respond to *objective* internal and external pressures on the country's political legitimacy and political and economic stability. The chapter develops, through periodization, the argument that successively elected governments' interpretation of Independence legacies for political gain in response to conflicts with neighboring countries, internal sectarian clashes, and economic crises joined imperatives of *national self-reliance* with *neoliberal development*.

The political significance of *small-scale industry* for *national self-reliance* is embraced by coalition governments led by the National Congress Party and the Bharatiya Janata Party (BJP) in the 1980s and beyond, with *national industrial development* viewed as increasingly important in 2000, when Congress returned to government. In parallel, the *perceived strategic value* of *neoliberal development* first took root when state elites, responding to internal political pressures introduced domestic competition (1980–2000) to maintain political stability, and later (1990–2020), incorporated external competition when faced with the impacts of economic crisis brought on by external pressures. The comparative cross-time analysis at the national and sectoral levels provides analytical leverage to reconsider dominant perspectives about global economic integration, regime type, and subnational characteristics.

The regulatory and developmental trajectories of telecommunications and textiles and their subsectors, in the next two chapters, uncover how *neoliberal self-reliance* shapes *bifurcated liberalism* resulting from the interacting strategic value and sectoral logics. Contrary to China and similar to Russia in certain subsectors, deregulation in telecommunications, perceived less strategic in the post-Independence nationalist imagination, is characterized, since Big Bang liberalization in 1990, by the *regulated governance* of an independent regulator and dominated by variegated property rights arrangements, on the one hand. On the other hand, *centralized governance* in sectors associated with *national self-reliance* and dominated by privately held rural small-scale industry, such as textiles, is marked by central-level regulation to introduce competition and promote export-oriented industrialization and protect select subsectors connected to the nationalist imagination. Interacting strategic and sectoral logics apply at the subsector, with central level bureaucratic management of telecommunications equipment, galvanized by the China Factor in the 2010s, and subnational state coordination and private sector governance of technical textiles.

"Big Bang Liberalization" of the 1990s launched market reforms in India, which followed decades of an import substitution strategy and severe fiscal and balance-of-payments crises.[1] Scholars of India's political economy have debated the impetus for economic liberalization. De-emphasizing immediate economic conditions as the cause of liberalization, political scientists contend that the following factors explain why India introduced competition and deregulated in the post-1990 period: Formal and informal institutional arrangements and decentralization; international economic marginalization as a function of India's post-Independence insular policies; and proliferation of nonstate interests as a result of competition in the political system, including identity politics and civil society, and party and interest group politics.[2] Studies show the shift toward a pro-market orientation and away from import-substitution industrialization (ISI) to more outward-facing, export-oriented policies

---

[1] See Joshi and Little (1994) and Frankel (2004) on the extent of insularity of India's economic policies across time and Herring (1999) on the momentary autonomy afforded the state for economic liberalization by the external payment crisis.

[2] See Jenkins (1999), Sinha (2004), Bussell (2012), Nayar (2005), Varshney (1998), Desai (1999), Kohli (1990, 2012), Thachil (2014), and Chhibber and Verma (2018), respectively.

taking root in the 1970s, with distributional and political consequences.[3] Scholars debate the relative importance of internal versus external factors in the radical changes in India's trade regime and economic policies, the role of nonresident Indian returnees, and whether the produced changes vary by subnational governments, industry, or firm-level characteristics.[4]

The India sector and subsector case studies, in the next three chapters, show that Big Bang Liberalization in the 1990s and beyond did not apply evenly across the economy. Process-tracing from sectoral origins (historically and from Independence to the present day) reveals that despite the activation of macro-level economic liberalization, the creation of new actors and interests, and with it, transnational diffusion in India's vibrant democratic politics, do not fully explain why the Indian government has extensively relinquished state control in certain sectors and continues to intervene in market entry and exit, business scope, and investment level in others. Section 6.2 of this chapter delineates the political context of *national self-reliance* and *neoliberal development* in the Emergency period through Big Bang Liberalization. State imperatives emerging from the nationalist imagination and transnational liberalizing elites interact with path-dependent *sectoral structures and organization of institutions* during intense internal political and economic crises.

Section 6.3 shows how the rise of the perceived strategic value orientation of *neoliberal self-reliance* has profound implications in 2004 and beyond, affecting both the Singh and Modi governments. Emergent are the decentralized, deregulatory role of the state and the dominant distribution of public and private actors governing sectoral development in high-tech, globally integrated sectors and the converse in labor-intensive, small-scale industry. Section 6.4 previews the regulatory and developmental trajectories of telecommunication and textile sectors and subsectors presented in their full complexity in Chapters 7 and 8, respectively. These dominant sectoral patterns have given rise to a *bifurcated liberalism* shaped by *neoliberal self-reliance*, discussed in comparison with other country and sector cases in Chapter 12.

6.1 PERCEIVED STRATEGIC VALUE AND IMPACTS OF SECTORAL CHARACTERISTICS (SECTORAL ORIGINS AND BEYOND)

The evolutionary emergence of state imperatives of *national self-reliance* and *neoliberal development* as constituent priorities of *perceived strategic*

---

[3] Subramanian (2008), Kohli (2012), Ahmed and Varshney (2012), and Mukherji (2014).
[4] Kapur (2010), Ye (2014), Sinha (2005, 2016), and Naseemullah (2017), respectively.

value in India is linked to significant periods of national consolidation dating to the beginning of sectoral development. Cannot be underestimated are the profound impacts of the association of rural small-scale industry, represented by cotton spinning and Indian textiles, with the real and perceived suppression of Indian indigenous industry big and small by British colonialism. Moreover, neoliberal ideas introduced to India, during critical moments of economic and political turmoil in the 1970s and beyond, have shaped the governance of globally integrated sectors with complex interactive technology.

For centuries, nonindustrial cotton textiles produced in India were synonymous with the subcontinent's insertion into the global economy. The expansion of railways helped Indian producers in central and south India to enter into British mercantilist trade.[5] As early as the 1690s, English manufacturers pushed for protections against cotton fabric produced in India, which began the "movement of British cotton cloth" to India by the British East India Company.[6] Even before the British Empire officially incorporated India in 1858, machine-made yarn and cloth imports began to erode Indian producers' competitive advantage in the domestic market.[7] The governor-general of India, William Bentinck, included a memo written by a John Walker: "The exportation of Manchester and Glasgow cottons and muslins to India has so deluged the Indian markets, that many thousands of native weavers are ruined, and in the great distress."[8]

Mechanized Indian textile industry first developed capacity, with imported British machinery, in the Bombay cotton mills in the early 1850s before formal British occupation. By the late nineteenth century, over 100 textile mills had established in Bombay and elsewhere.[9] In 1914, India housed the world's largest jute industry, fourth largest cotton textile industry, and the third largest railway network.[10] With the second largest yarn industry, Indian cotton mills supplied textile producers in China and Japan.[11]

---

[5] See Arnold (2011), 654.

[6] By the late eighteenth century, "triangular trade" between Britain, China, and India comprised British trade monopolies in Chinese tea, British textiles, and Indian opium. See Liu (2020), 33–35.

[7] This included chopping the thumbs of weavers to prevent the quality of Indian textiles from surpassing those of British manufactures. See Miller (2014), 6 and 24.

[8] See Liu (2020), 89.   [9] See Katzenstein (1979).   [10] See Chandavarkar (2003), 35.

[11] See Arnold (2011), 655.

Once under colonial rule, Indian industrialists protested the privileged market access of British textile mills and advocated protective tariffs. In parallel, beginning in the 1910s, the *Swadeshi* ("one's own land") movement spearheaded by Mahatma Gandhi boycotted foreign-made goods, especially British goods, including textiles. The Gandhi-led movement called for the revival of small-scale, labor-intensive domestic production processes of traditional spinners of hand- spun yarn and their product the *khadi* cloth, replaced by British imports and the products of Indian textile mills. The British initially refused to protect Indian industry, but once India became strategically important in the 1920s, shortly after World War I, the colonial government fiscally restricted non-British imports and financed continued defense and other public expenditures. During World War II, colonial government expenditures promoted textiles, along with iron and steel, cement, paper, and sugar in order to supply ammunition and garments from India.[12]

The Gandhi-led *Swadeshi* movement understood British colonialism as seizing and subordinating the Indian system of making and selling cotton textiles and decimating it in favor of the steam-powered factories in Manchester, England.[13] The massive Gujarat textile center in Ahmedabad served as a base where Gandhi expounded ideas, such as the Village Industries Reconstruction, which tied small-scale industries with employment for the "idle masses" and the life and death of those villages with that of India.[14] Thus *Swadeshiism* gave birth to the *perceived strategic value* of *small-scale industry* as related to *national self-reliance* in the Indian nationalist imagination.

The championing of Indian and small-scale production to achieve *national self-reliance* reconciled with the Hindu nationalist view of the caste system's division of occupations as an organic, legitimate labor system. For Gandhi, it was about recognizing the greatest self-sacrifice of the untouchables rather than challenging the legitimacy of the caste system. In contrast, B. R. Ambedkar, the pre-eminent first law minister, who was also a Dalit, who wrote the Indian constitution, viewed the caste system as unequal division of "laborers," or "graded inequality."[15]

Significantly, Gandhi stressed that his nationalist message of Indian *self-reliance* incorporated the demands of textile capitalists alienated by

---

[12] See Kohli (2004), 253–254 on colonialism and origins of patterns of state construction and intervention in Brazil, India, Nigeria, and South Korea.

[13] See Arnold (2011), Jackson (2016), and Bassett (2017).   [14] See Gandhi (1960).

[15] See Thachil (2014), 44.

British protectionist policies.[16] He judiciously stressed that this was not a war against machines but that "machinery to be well used has to help and ease human effort" in the "India [that] lives not in a handful of her big cities but in her 7,00,000 villages."[17] In 1930, Gandhi declared, the "purest form of *swadeshi* [economic independence] to the extent it is practicable is *kadhi* [hand spun cloth]. If this is not possible, then *swadeshi* should mean cloth made in mills owned and controlled by Indians out of yarn spun in those mills."[18] The boycott of foreign cloth advocated by the Non-Cooperation and Civil Disobedience movements of the 1920s and 1930s halved British and other foreign textile imports to the delight of textile magnates.[19] Influenced by nationalist sentiments, early Indian industrialist and founder of the Tata Group, today India's largest conglomerate, J. N. Tata, for his part, renamed his first textile mill from Empress Mills after Queen Victoria to Swadeshi Mill.[20]

6.1.1 National Self-Reliance: Small-Scale Industry and the Role of National Industrialists

Gandhi's champion of the demands of the Indian capitalists during the early days of the nationalist movement helped launch the long-term political alliance between business groups and the Congress Party.[21] The integration of Indian-owned production and textile mills into the Congress Party's nationalist appeal rationalized the role of large-scale business in any future textile policy, in addition to solidifying the long-term alliance between the Congress Party and business groups in contemporary Indian politics.[22] The sectoral case studies, in Chapters 7 and 8, show that the aforementioned early public–private institutional arrangements in response to internal and external pressures came to shape and reshape the role of the state and the dominant distribution of property rights in the *national self-reliance* and *neoliberal orientation* of capitalist development in India.[23]

---

[16] See Bassett (2017), 147. Western-trained engineers transformed from would-be techno-nationalists to supporters of Gandhi's "freedom movement" and ultimately struck each their own balance.

[17] See Gandhi (1960). Reorganization of production into small units that employed wage labor, adoption of technology, and use of imported dyes rebounded weaving and handicraft production. See Arnold (2011).

[18] Quoted in Tudor (2013), 111–112. See also Gandhi (1958).   [19] See Tudor (2013).

[20] See Sood and Arora (2006), 7.   [21] See Kohli (2004), 253–254.

[22] See Kohli (2004) and Tudor (2013).   [23] See Kohli (2004), 269.

After Independence in 1947, as India's first prime minister, Jawaharlal Nehru promoted state infrastructural projects through tapping into *Swadeshi* imagination of self-sufficiency, small-scale industry, and the interdependence of a national collective (in a context of religious and ethnic diversity). Importantly, the Congress Party worked closely with national industrialists in launching India's series of five-year plans in 1951. The first and second five-year plans adhered to the Bombay Plan of 1945–1946 initiated by eight leading industrialists, who envisioned a mixed economy with a growing private sector alongside the public sector focused on national development. The 1st Five Year Plan emphasized state intervention with a significant role for the public sector and focused on agricultural development, while the 2nd Five Year Plan focused more on the development of heavy industry. The national strategy under Nehru combined "import-substitution industrialization, foreign-exchange control, reservations for and protection of small-scale enterprises, and industrial license and quota systems for 'raw material' production."[24]

The strategy of ISI in favor of national industrialists and the *Swadeshi* protection for small-scale industry was left largely unchanged and unchallenged through the 1960s and 1970s, despite liberalizing pressures in the context of economic crisis, natural disaster, and external wars. The Textiles Committee Act of 1963 denoted the importance of textiles by creating a sector-specific body to oversee related rules and regulations. The 1963 Act replaced Section 72 of the 1935 Government of India Act, which had created the Cotton Textile Fund Ordinance to supervise external trade and promote industrial development.

To promote small-scale industries and maximize rural employment, the Textile Committee issued policies that curtailed the development of textile mills in favor of the nonmechanized, labor-intensive "unorganized" weaving sector of handlooms and power looms.[25] The Nehru government also required large mills to provide a significant portion of their output to poor consumers at controlled prices. Additionally, when

---

[24] See Sood and Arora (2006), 7.

[25] See Goswami (1990), Roy (1998), Misra (2000), and Bagchi (2004). See also Iyer, Kanna, and Varshney (2012). "Unorganized" sectors, handlooms and power looms in textiles, are entities not officially registered with government agencies, not subject to labor laws or environmental regulations, and barred from access to institutional sources of finance. All the same, Chapter 8 shows that the actual governance of organized and unorganized textiles alike implicates the central state in market coordination in specific sector and market segments.

less efficient producers faltered, the government nationalized them "to end the misery of workers."[26]

In the context of the *perceived strategic value* of labor intensive, small scale industry, "adhering to Gandhian critique of technology as luxury... for a nation where the vast majority of citizens live in poverty in rural areas, social policy dictated public expenditure prioritized other infrastructure—such as roads and power, as well as social services like sanitation, education, and health—over expanding telecommunications."[27] "India acquired its first telegraph in the 1850s, when the British brought it to India fifteen years after its first invention. India had its first Telegraph Act in 1885 and the predecessor to state-owned carrier MTNL, Bombay Telephone established its first mutual exchange in Mumbai in 1882 and in Delhi in 1911," noted S. D. Saxena, a member of India's telecommunications administrative service and the former chief financial officer of state-owned service providers BSNL and MTNL.[28] Despite an early start, on the day of its Independence, the country possessed 82,000 telephones lines, mostly in urban areas and left behind by the British, for a population of 350 million.[29] "Few households possessed phones. Villages had grocer telephones through the 1970s and MSNL had monopoly in two major cities until 1992."

Successive five-year plans, following Independence, characterized communication as a tool for improving education, encouraging civic cooperation, and raising living standards. However, adhering to the less *perceived strategic value* of telecommunications compared to other infrastructure for rural development, Indian telecommunications remained underdeveloped and teledensity remained very low through the 1980s. Similar to China in geographical size and significant rural population, India's communications infrastructure was in comparison inefficient and unevenly distributed, centered mainly in cities.

Until Big Bang Liberalization, the telecommunications services and equipment sectors were strictly the purview of the state, restricted from nongovernment, including foreign, participation and investment. Nehruvian techno-nationalism nurtured state-owned carriers and domestic equipment makers and imposed limits on foreign equity and restrictions on technology imports and investment.[30] The Department of

---

[26] See Kohli (2004), 276–277, Nayar (1989), 309 and 352, Joshi and Little (1994), 52.
[27] See Chakravartty (2004), 233.   [28] Interview on February 18, 2013, in Delhi, India.
[29] See Harwit (2008), 22.
[30] See Singh (1999) for the nurturing of domestic equipment makers during Nehru.

Telecommunications owned, supervised, and regulated the telecommunications services monopoly, and the Department of Electronics managed the suppliers that wired the infrastructure.[31]

After Nehru's death in 1964, Lal Bahadur Shastri succeeded Nehru as prime minister. First the 1962 Sino-Indian War and then the War with Pakistan (1965–1966) disrupted the 3rd Five Year Plan, shifting focus from agriculture to the defense industry. The National Congress Party elected Indira Gandhi as the prime minister, when Lal died in 1966. Upon her election, Gandhi devalued the rupee and liberalized trade during a balance-of-payments crisis in the context of two wars and a severe drought. The deregulation was brief, however, as Gandhi faced opposition from her advisors and organized capital, who behind the scenes sought protection and lobbied for subsidies grounded in ISI.[32] In the late 1960s onward, Gandhi's policies emphasized self-sufficiency and South-South cooperation, championed by her advisors.

Under the 4th Five Year Plan, Gandhi nationalized fourteen major national banks and launched the Green Revolution in 1966–1967 to advance agriculture. The policies associated with the Green Revolution introduced technological change, modernized agricultural sectors, and "strengthened the incentives and capacity of a politically excluded group, in this case agricultural producers, to seek greater political representation."[33] The emergent *sectoral organization of institutions* sowed the seeds for regional party development, including the pro-farmer Janata family of parties and other regional populist ones that catered to farmers.[34]

Gandhi also established the state-owned National Textile Corporation (NTC) in 1968. The subsequent once- or twice-a-decade rounds of "revival schemes" led by the Board of Industrial and Financial Reconstruction, including nationalization, modernization, and privatization, further underscored the "social objective" to save textiles via the Acts of Parliament. These acts included the 1974 Sick Textile Undertakings Act and the 1976 Laxmirattan and Atherton West Cotton Mills (Taking Over of Management) Act, in addition to textile undertaking acts enacted into the 1990s.

The Multi-Fiber Arrangement (MFA) negotiations, in the early 1970s, further exposed the *perceived strategic value* of India's protection of

[31] See Chowdary (1998).   [32] See Mukherji (2014).   [33] See Dasgupta (2018).
[34] For regional party development, see Harriss (1982), and Kohli (1987, 1990), Varshney (1998), Frankel (2004), and Ziegfeld (2016).

small-scale industrial development as a function of nationalist imagination.[35] The Indian government negotiated the exclusion of handloom
and cotton industry products, but did not initially seek concessions for
manmade fibers. At the end, a clause prevented discrimination against
entrants in new fibers.[36] The subsequent slow development of textiles saw
that India did not fully utilize MFA quotas, distributed by business
associations established before Independence.

The 5th Five Year Plan continued the focus on *national self-reliance* in
agriculture and defense production, including telecommunications satel-
lite development, which began under the 4th Five Year Plan when the
Indo-Pakistan War and Bangladesh Liberation War broke out in 1971. In
1974, India also tested its nuclear capacity in response to the United
States' intervention in the conflict with Pakistan. The 5th Five Year
Plan's stress on poverty alleviation and employment rationalized the
government's entry into power generation and transmission under the
Electricity Supply Act. The Indian government also established the Indian
National Highway System and launched the Minimum Needs Program
(MNP). The MNP joined the Pay Commission, first founded in 1946, to
provide recommendations to the government on the pay structure of its
civil and military divisions.

Between 1975 and 1977, for an eighteen-month period, Gandhi pro-
claimed and presided over a state of Emergency, under the pretext of
threats to national security after a war with Pakistan and in the context of
a poor economy, exacerbated by the 1973 oil crisis and challenges due to
drought. Evoking Article 352 of the Indian constitution, Gandhi launched
a massive crackdown on the widespread protests against the Emergency,
which she extended twice. The government imprisoned protestors and
strikers and thousands of Jana Sangh members and other agitators across
the country. Among those arrested were critics within the National
Congress Party, such as Acharya Kripalani, as well as founders and
leaders of the Janata family of parties, including future prime ministers
Morarji Desai and Charan Singh, referred to as champion of peasants,
and Atal Bihari Vajpayee, the first prime minister under the Bharatiya
Janata Party (BJP).

---

[35] See Aggarwal (1985) on the "liberal protectionism," which guaranteed global markets in
a competitive environment, of the the MFA's quota allocation. The ten-year phaseout of
all quotas by 2005 of the Agreement on Textile and Clothing in 1995 replaced the MFA.
[36] See Sinha (2016), 176.

During this time, the Janata family of parties gained strength regionally and then nationally. After Gandhi withdrew the Emergency, in 1977, and held general elections, the Jana Sangh merged with parties from across the political spectrum, including the Socialist Party, the Congress, and the Bharatiya Lok Dal, to form the Janata Party and defeated Gandhi. Between 1978 and 1980, the Janata Party's coalition government under Morarji Desai and Charan Singh rejected a 6th Five Year Plan in lieu of a Rolling Plan, which comprised an annual project and flexible targets.

6.1.2 Post-Emergency Merging of National Self-Reliance and Neoliberal Development and Sectoral Variation

The reconciling of *national self-reliance* through public–private initiatives with *neoliberal development* began to take shape, in the 1980s, in response to rising political opposition to the Congress Party and the 1970s oil and economic crises and wars with Pakistan. Though Indira Gandhi scrapped the defeated Janata Party's plan after the Congress Party returned to power in 1980, to expand political support under internal pressures, her 6th Five Year Plan emphasized industrial efficiency, technological upgrading, and internal market liberalization, including freeing certain key industries from antimonopoly actions and raising the exemption limit for licensing of new enterprises.[37] The plan eliminated price controls and closed ration shops. Following Thatcherism spreading across the world, including sending officials to Great Britain for training, the Indian government divested and merged public sector enterprises to create specialized corporate entities.[38]

To cultivate political support among a *transnational liberalizing coalition* of nonresident Indians and business groups, Gandhi also relaxed controls for market entry and investment in technology sectors, such as computers, electronics, and telecommunications equipment.[39] The permissible range of industries open to foreign investment accompanied with sophisticated technology expanded on a case-by-case basis under the

---

[37] See Rosen (1992), 65.

[38] Interviews in 2013 and 2017 in Gurgaon, India, Berkeley and San Francisco, California with Pradip Baijal, retired official of the Indian Administrative Service, charged with power sector and telecommunications reforms.

[39] Kapur (2010) on interacting effects of Indian diaspora and favorable government policy and Ye (2014) on the "propitious mix of external and internal networks" in the development of software informatics.

Foreign Exchange Regulation Act in 1982.[40] Nonresident Indians received special privileges to bypass controls on foreign investment and remission of foreign exchange, during which time the Center for Development of Telematics was set up by G. B. Meemamsi and Indian returnee Sam Pitroda.

Notwithstanding the reoriented *perceived strategic value* of *national self-reliance* to incorporate *neoliberal development*, Gandhi further expanded reservations for small-scale industry.[41] During this time, the eighteen-month-long textile strikes between 1982 and 1983 in Mumbai, without the support of the officially recognized union, dealt a near death-blow to the already struggling textile industry. To resolve the crisis, the state relied on its long-term alliance with industrialists dating to Gandhi's *Swadeshi* movement to end the strikes with the support of mill owners. "Mill owners discovered it was easier to simply close down the mills."[42] The National Textile Corporation took over the management of those mills, which did not shutter, under The Textile Undertakings (Taking Over of Management) Act of 1983.[43]

Table 6.1 maps the evolution of the *perceived strategic value* of *national self-reliance* (of small-scale industry and national industrialists) and *neoliberal development* to internal and external pressures faced by state elites across significant moments of national political development. Analysis begins at the origins of modern industry in our composite sector cases.

6.2 POLITICAL CONTEXT OF NATIONAL SELF-RELIANCE AND NEOLIBERAL DEVELOPMENT (1980–2000)

State elite responses to internal and external economic and political pressures during various phases of national consolidation reinforced and transformed path-dependent values and identities. Rooted in *Swadeshi self-reliance* and reinterpreted by Nehru's emphasis on industrial infrastructure and public sector investment, the politics of the Emergency era and beyond merged with it the perceived strategic value of *neoliberal development*. Reform-era India, which began in the 1980s, is thus shaped and reshaped by the dual imperatives.

---

[40] See Rosen (1992).   [41] See Rosen (1992), 65–66.
[42] Interview on February 18, 2013, with an Indian Administrative Service bureaucrat.
[43] See Sigeman (1995), 175.

TABLE 6.1. *India: Perceived strategic value and neoliberal self-reliance (1850–1980s)*

Sectoral Origins and Beyond	Telecommunications 1882 First Telephone Network		Textiles 1850s First Mechanized Textiles	
Perceived Strategic Value	*External Pressures*	*Internal Pressures*	*External Pressures*	*Internal Pressures*
Self-Reliance (Small-Scale Industry and National Industrialists)	• World War I • World War II • South-South Cooperation (1960s) • Indo-Pakistan War (1971) • Bangladesh Liberation War (1971)	• Five-year plans and public infrastruture • Nuclear Capacity • Drought (1970s) • Nonresident Indian returnees (1980s and beyond)	• "British cotton cloth to India" movement by British East Indian Company • 1858 British incorporation • World War I • World War II • South-South Cooperation (1960s) • Multi-Fiber Arrangement (1970s)	• *Swadeshi* ("one's own land") Movement • Gandhi's Village Industries Reconstruction • Bombay Plan of 1945–1946 • Green Revolution (late 1960s)
Neoliberal Development	• Balance-of-payment crises (mid-1960s and late 1980s/early 1990s) • Oil and economic crises (1970s) • Thatcherism (1980s) • Gulf War (1991)	• State of Emergency (1975–1977) • Assassination of Indira Gandhi/Election of Rajiv Gandhi (1984) • Transnational liberalizing coalition (1980s and beyond)	• Sino-Indian War of 1962 • War with Pakistan (1965–1966) • Balance-of-payment crisis (mid-1960s) • Founding of Janata family of parties (1970s)	• Death of Lal/Election of Indira Gandhi • State of Emergency (1975–1977) • Bombay Textile Strikes (1982–1983)

State intervention, in 1983, ended the textile strikes and nationalized assets of failing textile mills. In the aftermath, with the actual growth rate exceeding what was targeted by half a percentage point, Rajiv Gandhi, who succeeded his mother as the prime minister following Indira Gandhi's assassination, touted the 6th Five Year Plan as successful. The 7th Five Year Plan (1985–1990), which heeded largely to the scope of reforms already in motion, further exposed India's evolving *perceived strategic value*. In this political context, sectoral variation in market governance as a function of *perceived strategic value* became amplified, incorporating the seemingly dueling state imperatives.

On the one hand, the government delicensed, permitted manufacturing, and raised investment limits in a number of industries previously monopolized by the public sector, including telecommunications, synesthetic fibers and filament yarn, textile machinery, and chemical industries. Notably, the government permitted private sector investment in telecommunications equipment production. The government also liberalized the imports of goods not produced in India as a step toward technological upgrading, to reduce licensing procedures for export-oriented enterprises, and to allow greater and speedier access to foreign exchange for imports of raw materials and components used in export production.

On the other hand, the government increased the number of products reserved for production in the small-scale industry from 500 to 800, though limits on capacity of large-scale mills were removed.[44] Relatedly, the imports of consumer goods remained largely banned, and imports of capital goods liberalized in one year were restricted the next, except in electronics and communications. Moreover, sector-specific national policies for textiles, sugar, electronics, and computers were introduced.[45]

Though under the 7th Five Year Plan, India's 6 percent GDP growth rate further exceeded the target of 5 percent, in 1991, India experienced a balance-of-payments crisis, exacerbated by the Gulf War, which decreased remittances and increased prices of oil imports and withdrawal of savings by nonresident Indians. India was left with less than US $1 billion in foreign exchange reserves. During the political turmoil and economic crisis, the 8th Five Year Plan (1992–1997) became delayed. Annual Plans instead covered the period (1989–1992) during the presidencies of first the Janata Dal-led National Front and then the Samajwadi Janata Party coalition with the National Congress Party.

---

[44] See Rosen (1992), 65–66.   [45] See Rosen (1992), 70.

The National Congress Party returned to office in 1992, and Narasimha Rao became the prime minister. Finance minister Manmohan Singh quickly moved to hasten the pace of public sector divestment and the liberalization of internal competition, aided in part by a loan from the IMF.[46] To offset the burgeoning deficit and foreign debt, the 8th Five Year Plan (1992–1997) also ushered in economic reforms that expanded the scope of India's global economic engagement to accompany the internal market reform begun a decade earlier. "Macroeconomic stabilization and fiscal adjustment alone cannot suffice; they must be supported by essential reformism economic policy...(facilitating) a transition from a regime of quantitative restrictions to a price-based mechanism...over-centralization and excessive bureaucratization have proved to be counter-productive," Singh exclaimed in a July 1991 Budget Speech to the Lok Sabha lower house.[47]

In 1997, after two years of United Front coalitions under the umbrella leadership of Janata Dal (helmed by H. D. Deve Gowda and Inder Kumar Gujral), the BJP returned to political power heading the National Democratic Alliance of center-right and rightwing political parties. Influenced by a distinct liberal wing, which had emerged within the BJP, Prime Minister Atal Bihari Vajpayee marshaled Gandhian nationalism's *Swadeshi self-reliance* and interdependence of community and advocated for the mobilization of national resources and the reduction of the state's role to engage the global economy (rather than boycotting foreign goods).[48] The BJP advocated for global engagement even as the Rashtriya Seva Sangh (RSS), the movement's nonelectoral wing, remained wedded to economic nationalism. The wedding of values emerging from the nationalist imagination and the transnational liberalizing coalition gave rise politically to the urban middle class, upper caste elites who had been left out of the Congress Party's patronage machine, which had privileged globally oriented industrialists.[49]

During Vajpayee's term, India's compliance requirements for the WTO, for which the country is a founding member, further propelled the BJP to continue macro-level liberalization. To settle cases that India lost through dispute settlement at the WTO concerning quantitative restrictions, intellectual property rights, and tariffs, the government

---

[46] See Sinha (2019).   [47] See Quote in Ahmed and Varshney (2012), 38.
[48] See Thachil (2014), 51–53 and 86.
[49] See Chhibber (1997) on the urban middle class left out of the Congress Party's patronage machine.

eliminated quotas and increased the ceiling for foreign direct investment (FDI) through the automatic route in many industries from tourism and pharmaceuticals to mining and advertising. During this time, the government also reduced state equity to 26 percent in most industries. The Indian government introduced competition in mobile telecommunications with the issuance of licenses, including to FDI, after having corporatized and commenced the restructuring of state-owned service providers. The Rakesh Mohan Infrastructure Committee of 1996, on which former C-DOT director S.D. Saxena served, recommended public–private partnerships and the issuance of commercial bonds to fund urban infrastructure.

6.2.1 Big Bang Liberalization and Path Dependence of Sectoral Organization of Institutions

Sectoral variation, however, remained on the actual level of foreign investment permitted. Moreover, during this time, the BJP government emphasized technological upgrading and indigenous development, but at the expense of labor. "We want to make the country self-reliant and strong. In the changing world economic scenario, it would not be possible to stay aloof and prosper. The transitional problems should and could not be seen in isolation and resolved. Rigid labor laws would have to be relaxed after due deliberations," Vajpayee explained in 2001. For example, in telecommunications, the BJP-led government liberalized market entry in national long-distance service and corporatized the public carrier BSNL and separated it from the Department of Telecommunications, despite resistance from state workers and their supporters in other state-owned enterprises. This occurred in the context of the establishment of the Telecommunications Regulatory Agency of India (TRAI) in 1998 and the New Telecom Policy in 1999, which also rationalized the tariff structure and introduced a revenue sharing regime for service provision.

Not to be outdone, the "long political shadow on India's textile policy" cast by Gandhi's populist commitment to "love the small people" and the accommodation of large scale, mechanized production owned and controlled by Indians, which adhered to Nehru's "socialist proclivities" for the production of cheap cloth for mass consumption, began to shift toward *neoliberal development*. The National Textile Policy of 2000 "de-reserved" small-scale industry for garment manufacturing, and various policies, including the 1999 Technology Upgradation Fund Scheme, the 2001 Finance Bill, and the 2003–2004 Union Budget, provided fiscal and infrastructural incentives and subsidies to invest in value-added, high-tech production and promote textile and apparel exports.[50] In 2002, the government established a "High Powered Steering Group" to implement policies and programs outlined in the National Textile Policy and to devise further measures if necessary.[51]

In spite of macro-liberalization intact are the path-dependent effects of the *sectoral organization of institutions*. For example, in telecommunications, equipment makers under the jurisdiction of the Department of Telecommunications and the emphasis there on the manufacturing of networking equipment for rural backbone infrastructure, in addition to the civil service bureaucracy Indian Telecommunications Service (ITS) as part of and distinct from the Indian Administrative Service, represent interacting strategic value and sectoral logics. Importantly, Gandhian legacies' impacts on economies of scale in textiles are apparent in the continued dominance of small-scale industries in Indian textiles, with its lasting institutional and policy impacts.[52]

6.3 RISE OF NEOLIBERAL SELF-RELIANCE AND SECTORAL VARIATION (2000–2020)

Internal and external pressures experienced by state elites shape and reshape the political context of *national self-reliance* and *neoliberal development* as paramount *perceived strategic value* in post-Big Bang Liberalization, as shown in Table 6.2. The perceived strategic value of *neoliberal self-reliance* in the context of globalization are reflected in the rules and regulations on the role of the state in market coordination and property rights arrangements governing strategic and less strategic industries (identified in Table 6.3 and tables in the sectoral case studies in Chapters 7 and 8). The National Congress Party's return to head coalition government from 2004 to 2014, under the United Progressive Alliance (UPA), solidified the political context of *national self-reliance* and *neoliberal development*. With promises of governmental transparency and accountability and economic sustainability for the poor rural farmer and the business entrepreneur alike, the UPA's "National Common Minimum Program" became perceived as a corrective to the liberalization

[50] See Verma (2002) and Tewari (2006) on export competitiveness and post-MFA adjustments in India's textiles and apparel.
[51] See Sinha (2016), 188–189, and quote from page 189.
[52] Teitelbaum (2007) contends agrarian mobilization led to incentives for small-scale industries, with adverse impacts on urban workers and organized labor.

TABLE 6.2. *India: Political context of self-reliance and neoliberal development (1980–2020)*

Perceived Strategic Value	External Pressures	Internal Pressures
National Self-Reliance *Small-Scale Industry* (1980–2020) *National Industry* (2000–2020)	• Sectarian conflicts (2000s) • Mumbai attacks (2008) • Expiration of the Multi-Fiber Arrangement and Agreement on Textile and Clothing (2005) • Import competition from China and South Asia (2000s and beyond) • Inflows of Chinese FDI (2010s and beyond) • Himalayan border dispute with China (2020)	• Labor resistance/Mumbai union strikes (1980s) • Mobilization of marginalized groups (1980s) • Supreme Court mandate on green technology (1996) • Rashtriya Seva Sangh (RSS), nonelectoral wing of Bharatiya Janata Party (1997) • Power loom protests against hank inclusion in excise (2002) • United Progressive Alliance (UPA) of National Congress Party's promises of economic sustainability for the poor rural farmer and the business entrepreneur (2004) • 2G scandal (2008) and Supreme Court ruling (2012) • Election of Narendra Modi (2014) • Supreme Court ruling against private telcos' revenue sharing model (2014) • Land disputes and corruption resulting from government divestments • Save Handlooms campaign (2015) • Protests against CENVAT, Good and Services Tax, demonetization (various years) • Protests against multi-brand retail liberalization (2011–2012) • Protests against abolishment of handloom, power loom boards
Neoliberal Development *Domestic Competition* (1980–2000)	• Gulf War (1991) • Founding member of World Trade Organization (1995) • Global Financial Crisis (2008)	• Second term of Indira Gandhi, after the Emergency (1980–1984) • Mill closures and weakened labor (1980s and beyond) • Balance-of-payments crisis (1991) • Electoral opposition to National Congress Party: short-lived

Perceived Strategic Value	External Pressures	Internal Pressures
External Competition (2000–2020)	• U.S.-China trade war (2018–ongoing) • Brexit (2016-ongoing) • U.S. objection of RoSCTL on grounds of WTO Agreement on Subsidies and Countervailing Measures (2019) • COVID-19 global pandemic (2020)	governments of Janata Dal-led National Front and Samajwadi Janata Party (1989–1992) coalition with Congress • Growing deficit and foreign debt (1992) • United Front coalitions of regional parties under umbrella leadership of Janata Dal (1995–1997) • United Progressive Alliance (UPA) of National Congress Party (2004)

policies launched by Rao over a decade earlier.[53] In August 2004, during a meeting with the Associated Chambers of Commerce and Industry of India, Manmohan Singh (then prime minister) evoked the Bombay Plan of 1944 to reassure business of their grand bargain with the government.

Singh identified J. R. D. Tata, along with other industrialists, including Ghanshyam Das Birla, Purushottamdas Thakurdas, Lala Shri Ram, Ardeshir Dalal, A. D. Shroff, and Kasturbhai Lalbhai, as critical for the plan's "great emphasis on public investment in the social and economic infrastructure, in both rural and urban areas...the importance of agrarian reform and agricultural research, in setting up educational institutions and a modern financial system. Above all, it defined the framework for India's transition from agrarian feudalism to industrial capitalism, but capitalism that is humane, that invests in the welfare and skills of the working people."[54]

The following month, in September, the UPA appointed a National Commission for Enterprises in the Unorganized Sector (NCEUS). At the time of NCEUS's establishment, 86 percent of all employed worked in the small-scale, unorganized sector in 2005; the number remained above 80 percent in 2018.[55] Moreover, during the same period, the number of informal workers in the organized sector rose from 46 percent to 51

---

[53] "The Common Minimum Programme: The Complete Document," *The Economic Times* (May 27, 2004).

[54] See "Bombay Plan and Mixed-up Economy," *The Hindu Business Line* (September 7, 2004).

[55] See India Ministry of Statistics and Program Implementation (2020).

TABLE 6.3. *India's neoliberal self-reliance: Law and political economy*

Globalization	Self-Reliance (Small-scale Industry and National Industry)	Neoliberal Development
• Multi-Fiber Arrangement negotiations (1970s) • Big Bang Liberalization (under Rao/Singh) • 8th Five-Year Plan (1992–1997) • Founding member of World Trade Organization (1995) – 26% FDI permitted on macro-level • FDI Policy liberalization (various years) • Protracted FDI restrictions in retail and distribution (wholesale, single-brand, multi-brand, e-commerce) • Citizenship Law – de-nationalization of Muslims, privileging Hindus (2019) • Requirement of government registration, approval, and certification for FDI hailing from border countries, targeting China (2020) • Schemes of Rebates and Levies on Exports (various years)	• Negotiated Terms of Multi-Fiber Arrangement • BJP (under Vajpayee) wedding of national resource mobilization, reduced role of the state, and global economic engagement • Micro-sectoral policies on Industrial upgrading and indigenous development • Congress-led United Progressive Alliance (2004–2014) • National Common Minimum Program (2004–2014) • Bombay Plan of 1944 (evoked by Singh) (2004) • National Commission for Enterprises in the Unorganized Sector/Arjun Sen Gupta Commission (2004) • Micro Small and Medium Enterprises Development (MSMED) Act	• Second term of Indira Gandhi, after the Emergency (1980–1984) • Creation of Specialized Corporate Entities (1980s–ongoing) • 6th Five-Year Plan (1980–1985) • Merger and Divestment of Public Sector Enterprises (1980s–ongoing) • 7th Five-Year Plan (1985–1990) • Public Sector Divestment and Internal Liberalization • Singh Budget Speech to Lok Sabha (1991) • Labor policies • Indian National Congress under Rao (1991–1995) • 8th Five Year Plan (1992–1997) • Removal of Constitutional preamble restricting states' fiscal powers (2012) • United Front alliance of regional parties (1996–1997) • Rakesh Mohan Infrastructure Committee (1996) • BJP-led National Democratic Alliance (1997–1998, 1999–2004) • Congress-led United Progressive Alliance (2004–2014) • National Voluntary Guidelines (NVG) on Social, Environmental and Economical Responsibilities of Business of 2011 • Companies Act of 2013 Section 135 Corporate Social Responsibility

• Modi's 2017 India Independence Day Speech	• National Institution for Transforming India (NITI-Aayog) (2014)
• Companies Act of 2013 Section 135 Corporate Social Responsibility	• 5-year National Development Agenda
• Made in India, Skill India, and Startup India (2015)	• Demonetization (2016)
	• Goods and Services Tax (2017)

percent. According to the NCEUS, "The unorganized sector consists of all unincorporated private enterprises owned by individuals or households engaged in the sale and production of goods and services operated on a proprietary or partnership basis and with less than ten total workers."[56] Those who do not receive social security benefits provided by employers are informal workers, and those who do are classified as formal workers.[57]

6.3.1 National Self-Reliance and Regulation of Unorganized/Small-Scale Industry

In evoking the Bombay Plan and creating the NCEUS, Singh reinforced the essential role of industrialists and small-scale industry alike in the *perceived strategic value* of *national self-reliance*. In doing so, the UPA government sought to centralize the regulation of both organized industry and unorganized small-scale industry in ways never done before. The Labor Ministry of India, in 2006, established the Arjun Sen Gupta Commission to provide recommendations to the NCEUS. That year, the Micro Small and Medium Enterprises Development (MSMED) Act became India's first-ever legal framework to introduce the concept of "enterprise" for rural, small-scale sectors in manufacturing and services; to define medium enterprises; and to integrate micro, small, and medium enterprises.

---

[56] See NCEUS (2007), 3.

[57] The NCEUS presents the first step to recognize and account for unorganized sectors and informal workers predominate in labor-intensive industry.

In 2007, the Ministry of Small-Scale Industries and the Ministry of Agro and Rural Industries merged to establish the Ministry of Micro Small and Medium Enterprises (MSME). The National Institute of Micro Small and Medium Enterprises (NI-MSME), under the new ministry, provides guidance on the procedures of and consulting on shouldering the impacts of new regulations, such as the Goods and Services Tax and Intellectual Property Rights. The NI-MSME also has programs on micro enterprise development, clean technologies, and agro entrepreneurship.

Around the same time that the government centralized the governance of unorganized sectors with the formation of the MSMED, it established a Centralized Value-Added Tax (CENVAT), a predecessor to the 2014 Goods and Services Tax, which levied taxes on the manufacture or production of movable and marketable goods. The CENVAT theoretically equalized taxation among the various sizes of textile enterprises along the supply chain, from large-scale mills to power looms and handlooms producing gray and interlining fabrics and synthetic fibers. Historically, tax and excise varied along the Indian textile supply chain, with the effect of unorganized power loom and handloom sectors avoiding taxes and excise duties. In practice, the CENVAT as applied to textiles granted exemptions and credits to gray fabric manufacturers (which tended to be small scale power looms), a move opposed by the larger textile mills. To compensate the organized sector, the government instituted an Asset Reconstruction Fund for "sick but viable textile mills."[58]

6.3.2 Neoliberal Development and Deregulation of Industrial Capital and Organized Industry

Even as reregulation protected small-scale industry, such as the power loom sector in textiles, the state continued to deregulate industrial capital, as shown in the evolution of corporate social responsibility from a voluntary scheme to a legal mandate with loopholes. The National Voluntary Guidelines (NVG) on Social, Environmental and Economical Responsibilities of Business of 2011 and the Companies Act of 2013 renewed the dominance of industrial capital in the organized sector (which comprises

---

[58] "Cenvat Credit for Textiles May Go," *The Economic Times* (February 11, 2003) and "No Change in CENVAT Rules on Excise Duty for Textile Goods," *Fiber2Fashion* (July 29, 2015). Also, see Indian Budget 2016–2017 on excise duty and CENVAT for made up articles of textiles and garments.

formally licensed enterprises and employs just shy of 20 percent of all employed in India) in the context of the role of the state in labor regulations. The NVG, which accorded particular activities exemptions from specific labor regulations, and the Companies Act increased "vulnerability of employment in the organized manufacturing sector" and "impacted the bargaining power of labor through increased usage of contractual labor, decreasing wage shares, reduced trade union participation, and low coverage of workers under any form of social security benefits."[59]

In 2014, Narendra Modi, who had served as the chief minister of Gujarat, India's fifth largest state known for liberal market reforms, became elected as the next prime minister under a BJP government. On August 15, 2014, Modi, in his Independence Day speech as Prime Minister (atop the Red Fort), dissolved the Planning Commission and replaced it with the policy think tank National Institution for Transforming India (NITI-Aayog). Nonetheless, Modi evoked Gandhi and cotton nationalism, three years later, in his Independence Day speech: "Politicians cannot be against small scale traders for electoral reasons. These rhetorical appeals still work. Gandhi is a ritual, one of the directions you pray, like east, west, south and north, and Gandhi."[60]

A 2019 amendment of Section 135 of the Companies Act, regulated by the Ministry of Corporate Affairs (MCA), embodies the emerging *perceived strategic value* of neoliberal self-reliance. The amendment, which mandated Social Corporate Responsibility (CSR), reflects the uneasy melding of the *Swadeshi* nationalist imagination's "inclusive growth and equitable development" and the dominance of business and family groups of national industrialists advocating *neoliberal development*. The CSR "[disengages] from the popular discourse on labor reforms and instead [engages] in seemingly harmless norms of voluntary action and corporate social responsibility to facilitate accumulation" in favor of business.[61] During the COVID-19 pandemic in 2020, the MCA declared funds spent to tackle COVID-19 as CSR activity. The MCA also declared funds donated to the Prime Minister Citizen Assistance and Relief in Emergency Situations (PM CARES Fund) as counting toward the CSR

[59] See Sood, Nath, and Ghosh (2014).
[60] Interview in Philadelphia with Sanjoy Chakravorty, Professor of Geography and Urban Studies, Temple University on March 12, 2020. Also, see Chakravorty (2019) on India's national narratives and narrators.
[61] See Sood, Nath, and Ghosh (2014).

mandate and tax exemptible under the Income Tax Act of 1961.[62] According to MCA, 18,000 companies had filed paperwork affirming their readiness to contribute to CSR efforts.[63]

The pro-business orientation reflects how industrialists benefited from dominant sectoral patterns of market governance, whereby the introduction of competition in the internal market for organized manufacturing and services, beginning in the 1980s, reinforced the decentralized nature of the role of the state in enforcing labor regulations, leaving employment in organized sectors – not dissimilar to small-scale industry – without guarantee of de facto protection. The post-Independence incorporation of industrialists in the Indian nationalist principles of collective *self-reliance* became personified in the private family groups dominant in deregulated industrial sectors, such as information communications technology, automobiles, and pharmaceuticals.

6.4 STRATEGIC VALUE FRAMEWORK AND SECTORAL PATTERNS OF MARKET GOVERNANCE

"Swadeshi is Made in India, whether it is steel or machine tools under Nehru or indigenous textiles, there's nothing wrong with what Modi is saying. We have domestic, internal markets so we go to the globe to trade in order to buy oil," explained Vivek Prabhu, a technical textile entrepreneur.[64] This popular response to Made in India, one of Narendra Modi's signature policies, is echoed by the BJP and the National Congress Party supporters alike. Also evoked by both is the Minister of Parliament and Congress member Shashi Tharoor's speech at the Oxford University in 2015, characterizing the impacts of British colonialism on India, stoking economic nationalism.[65]

These sentiments, along with the election of Narendra Modi in 2014, reflect the "nationalist legitimacy" of Indira Gandhi's early populist and anti-capitalist rhetoric *and* the "pro-business" neoliberal consensus of the 1980s and beyond. Contrary to a straightforward shift toward a pro-business consensus dominant in existing literature on the Indian political

---

[62] See appeal by Injeti Srinivas, the Head of Ministry of Corporate Affairs, published on MCA website.

[63] "Corporate Affairs Ministry to Count Funds Spent to Tackle COVID-19 under CSR Activity," *The Economic Times* (March 23, 2020).

[64] Interview on January 8, 2020.

[65] See "Shashi Tharoor's Oxford Speech: Make Reparations, Free India," *The Economic Times* (July 28, 2015).

economy, the historical process-tracing of the origins and evolution of *perceived strategic value* in this chapter has uncovered the emergence of *neoliberal self-reliance* rooted in the values of *national self-reliance* and *neoliberal development*. This *strategic value orientation* is a function of state elite responses to internal and external pressures during significant moments of national consolidation, including economic crises and labor resistance.

The emergence of *neoliberal self-reliance* interacting with *sectoral structures and organization of institutions* has shaped the bifurcation in market governance as applied to strategic and less strategic sectors. The role of the state and the dominant property rights arrangements in high-tech, globally integrated sectors, such as telecommunications, are characterized by *regulated governance* as shown in Chapter 7. The initial introduction of competition in telecommunications occurred during Big Bang Liberalization supported by pro-liberalization industrial stakeholders disconnected from existing post-Independence bureaucratic power brokers. Today a central-level ministry makes policy and an independent regulator enforces the market entry and business scope of a state-owned fixed-line operator and fiercely competitive mobile carriers and value-added service providers.

The perceived strategic orientation of *neoliberal self-reliance* applies at the subsectoral level. Nehruvian interpretation of Gandhian Swadeshi self-reliance has retained bureaucratic oversight of the development of state- and privately-owned equipment makers, which concentrated on rural automatic exchanges and low-tech inputs. In response to increasing inflows of Chinese capital and the dominance of Chinese competition in the 2000s, however, the state has pivoted to incorporate private sector participation in the development of indigenous new-generation mobile consumer and terminal telecommunications equipment.

Importantly, at a time when centralized market coordination in labor-intensive, less value-added textiles is eliminated around the world, India created a central ministry and other sector-specific bureaucracies in textiles associated with nationalist narratives of self-reliance in the 1980s, following internal political and economic crises. Chapter 8 discloses that endowed with limited resources and regulatory capacity, the *centralized governance* of the textile ministry has both introduced extensive competition in the neoliberal era and deliberately intervened in market developments. In addition to subsidizing industrial upgrading and deregulating trade, the India central government has nationalized large-scale textile mills of the organized sector during economic downturns. It has also

TABLE 6.4. *Perceived Strategic value and sectoral patterns of market governance: India*

Industrial Sector	Telecommunications	Textiles
Perceived Strategic Value	Strategic for *neoliberal development* in response to transnational liberalizing coalition during economic crisis and instability; less strategic for *national self-reliance* as a function of Nehru's interpretation of Gandhi's *Swadeshiism* on infrastructural development for collective gain	Strategic for regime legitimacy and economic development: post-independence *nationalist imagination* of *Swadeshiism self-sufficiency* of India's rural, small-scale industry and employment and interdependence of community sensitive to sectarian conflict
Sectoral Structural Attributes	Capital intensive, complex interactive technology, producer-driven commodity chain	Labor intensive, linear technology, buyer-driven commodity chain
Country-specific Sectoral Organization of Institutions	Beginning in 1980s, infusion of nonresident Indian capital combined with dominance of government bureaucracy in manufacturing sectors; until Big Bang liberalization, sector-specific administrative service presided over services; in 1990 and beyond, the introduction of competition, including foreign direct investment, and privatization undermined regulatory authority; regulatory agency created in 1998 presides over bidding wars and spectrum allocation scandals, with occasional politically motivated intervention by central-level policy ministry	Until mid-1980s, a sector-specific committee issued policies, implemented by separate bureaucracies, that protect unorganized, small-scale, nonmechanized handlooms and power looms and large-scale textile mills; central ministry created in 1987 introduced competition and industrial upgrading though slowed growth of integrated mills through 1990s; in 2004 and beyond, export-oriented industrialization parallels protections and subsidies of *khadi* and small-scale production; subnational governments operate special economic zones and promote industrial upgrading

Industrial Sector	Telecommunications	Textiles
Dominant Pattern of Market Governance	*Regulated Governance* (Telecoms Services, *Centralized Governance* (Telecoms Equipment)	*Centralized Governance* (Apparel & Clothing; Trade), *Decentralized Governance* (Technical Textiles)
Coordination Mechanisms		
Level of State Control	Central goals; central-level ministries, regulator, and Supreme Court rulings Liberal rules and	Central and local goals; central-level sector-specific ministries and subnational governments
Issue Scope	regulations on market entry and business scope overseen by regulator	Sector-specific rules and regulations on trade and distribution
Distribution of Property Rights	Diverse and various ownership structures across subsectors, with state ownership of fixed-line networks	Private ownership dominant across subsectors; state ownership of distressed textile mills in different phases of economic and political crises

cushioned the survival of small-scale, labor-intensive, and highly polluting handlooms and power looms dominant in apparel and clothing and technical sectors alike through fiscal and protectionist trade policies.

Table 6.4 summarizes the dominant sectoral patterns of market governance shaped by the interacting effects of India's *neoliberal self-reliance* and sectoral structures and organization of institutions. It outlines how perceived strategic value and sectoral characteristics during significant moments of internal and external pressures shape coordination mechanisms and distribution of property rights in strategic and less strategic industries, represented by telecommunications and textiles, respectively.

7

Pro-Liberalization Transnational Business and High-Tech Services

Regulated Governance in Indian Telecommunications

The Strategic Value Framework expects that the higher the *perceived strategic value* of a sector, the more likely the state will intervene to coordinate markets and the distribution of property right arrangements will reflect state power; and the details of goals and methods are shaped by *sectoral structures and organization of institutions.*[1] Tracing the origins and evolution of the perceived strategic value orientation of state elites in response to internal and external pressures, Chapter 6 has periodized the rise of *neoliberal self-reliance* in India and identifies sectoral variation in impacts on dominant patterns of market governance. This chapter shows how the perceived strategic value of capital-intensive and globally integrated sectors, such as telecommunications, during episodes of political and economic uncertainty during neoliberal ascendence has interacted with sectoral characteristics, and shapes the dominant pattern of *regulated governance.* Interacting strategic value and sectoral logics determines how market governance and development outcomes have varied by subsector, as illuminated by the company cases.

Indira Gandhi, responding to internal political pressures, shortly after the Emergency of 1975–1977, first legitimated the Indian returnees, who collaborated with state bureaucrats in high-tech sectors, including telecommunications. Examined in Section 7.1, the transnational liberalizing coalition, further nurtured by Rajiv Gandhi during a period of economic uncertainty, launched infrastructural modernization oriented toward the development of automatic exchanges for rural small towns, in accordance

[1] See Table 2.4 for sectoral structural attributes.

184

to the value of development for the masses rooted in Independence legacies examined in the previous chapter.

Whereas the state retained ownership and management of landline networks, market liberalization in mobile services and value-added services (VAS), in the 1990s, has led to intense competition amongst dominant domestic and foreign-owned carriers. Section 7.2 analyzes the liberalizing role of the state and the variegated property rights arrangements, which characterize market governance in mobile and VAS. Since the 1980s, policies and regulations have weakened central-level supervision and coordination of industrial and market developments; and periodic spectrum scandals have questioned the independence of the telecommunications regulator, as shown in Section 7.3.

In contrast, Section 7.4 shows the Nehruvian interpretation of indigenous technological development for *national self-reliance* in the context of *Swadeshiism* championed by Mahatma Gandhi has shaped the state's supervisory role in the development of telecommunications equipment. State-ownership of landlines and research and development (R&D) focused on rural automatic exchanges led by state science and technology bureaucracies, since the 1980s, has shaped the protracted technological advancement of telecommunications equipment slowed to capture the gains of technological convergence. In the 2010s, Modi-era responses to the increasing dominance of foreign direct investment (FDI) from China and other internal and external pressures oriented around perceived national security and developmental concerns have galvanized calls for indigenous development of telecommunications equipment and regulation on Big Data.

7.1 STRATEGIC VALUE AND SECTORAL LOGICS: REGULATED GOVERNANCE IN TELECOMMUNICATIONS

Today, the Indian telecommunications industry exemplifies the zenith of a globalized India. Legally, few regulatory barriers and an independent regulator govern competition between market players. In 1980, India had 0.3 telephone lines per 100 people, compared to China's 0.2 and Russia's 7.[2] At the start of the Big Bang Liberalization in 1990, China and India had similar teledensity of 0.6 per 100 people and Russia had 14. A decade later, India had 3 telephone lines per 100 people, compared to China's 11 and Russia's 22 (Figure 7.1). The slow growth of fixed-line subscriptions in India is offset in part by the growth of mobile subscriptions

---

[2] See World Development Indicators (World Bank 2021).

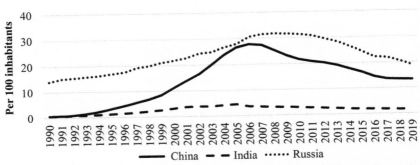

FIGURE 7.1. Fixed phone subscriptions per 100 inhabitants, China, India, and Russia (1990–2019)
Source: International Telecommunication Union (ITU) Statistics (2021).

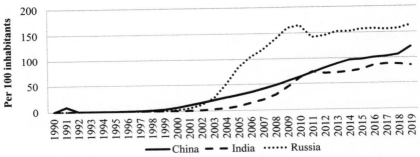

FIGURE 7.2. Mobile subscriptions per 100 inhabitants, China, India, and Russia (1990–2019)
Source: International Telecommunication Union (ITU) Statistics (2021).

in the 2000s and beyond, with India at 62 per 100 people, China 63 and Russia 165 in 2010, according to the International Telecommunications Union (2015) (Figure 7.2).

The high-speed development of Indian mobile networks in the post-Big Bang liberalization era appears to adhere to conventional wisdom on the relationship between economic liberalization and development outcomes, on the one hand. On the other hand, the continued state-ownership of fixed-line networks may well explain why fixed broadband development is slow and protracted (Figure 7.3). The dominance in India's global software outsourcing sector, disconnected from bureaucracy but facilitated by favorable government policies and dominated by the globally networked private sector, also seemingly conforms to this understanding (Figure 7.4).[3] State-owned networks in both China and Russia, however,

---

[3] In 2019, India ranked number 1 worldwide in offshore business services, according to Statista.

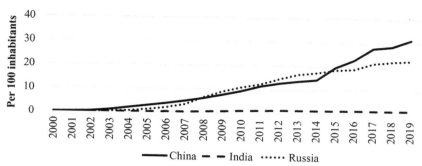

FIGURE 7.3. Fixed broadband subscriptions (per 100 people), China, India, and Russia (2000–2019)
Source: International Telecommunication Union (ITU) Statistics (2021).

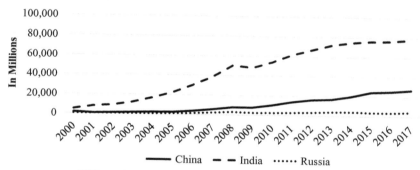

FIGURE 7.4. ICT service exports, China, India, and Russia (BoP, current US$) (2000–2017)
Source: International Telecommunication Union (ITU) Statistics (2021).

witnessed exponential broadband growth amidst exposure to the global economy. How do we explain subsectoral variation in the role of the state and ownership structures within Indian telecommunications in the context of economy-wide and sector-specific introduction of competition? What explicates cross-national variation in development outcomes despite similarities in property rights arrangements?

Telecommunications services in India are composed of state-owned fixed-line infrastructure and public and private mobile service providers, which are governed by a policymaking central ministry (Telecom Commission of the Department of Telecommunications, Ministry of Communications) and an institutionally separate regulator (Telecom Regulatory Authority of India) with dispute arbitration mechanisms and judicial contestation. Telecommunications equipment manufacturers come under the joint regulation of the telecommunications ministry and central-level science and technology bureaucracies, including the Center for the Development of Telematics.

The dominant pattern of *regulated governance*, characterized by the centralized role of the state in market coordination and variegated property rights arrangements, is representative of Indian high-tech sectors dominated by pro-liberalization industrial stakeholders disconnected from post-Independence bureaucratic power brokers. In practice, however, the telecommunications regulator and the various telecommunications bureaucracies are not independent of each other or of political interests. The politics of market governance as a function of the *perceived strategic value* of *neoliberal self-reliance* and the path-dependent *sectoral organization of institutions* shape subsectoral variation in governance mechanisms.

Up until the 1980s, the Indian government perceived telecommunications infrastructure to be of secondary importance compared to other rural infrastructure. This occurred in the context of the promotion and protection of small-scale, labor-intensive development championed by *Swadeshiism* principles of *national self-reliance*, which Nehru interpreted through techno-nationalism. S.D. Saxena, formerly of the Indian Telecommunications Service (ITS) and a retired chief financial officer of incumbent state-owned and managed networks BSNL and MTNL, explained: "Telecommunications was a public sector but not one prioritized by the planning commission when deciding the allocation of resources. The telecommunications administrative service used to be ridiculed for asking for money for the growth of telephones. 'Why not water?' was the planners' retort as they fixated on rural development."

In the 1980s, government policy began to shift in the aftermath of the Emergency when Indira Gandhi faced political opposition from growing regional parties, as discussed in Chapter 6. This set the stage for sweeping liberalization in telecommunications in the 1990s and beyond. The path-dependent effects of the existing sectoral organization of institutions created by the *perceived strategic value* of *national self-reliance*, however, have shaped the protracted liberalization and reregulation of market entry, business scope, and technology adoption in the services and equipment subsectors in favor of state-owned and Indian firms over global ones, respectively. Eager to expand existing networks to rural areas with a large electorate, the Rajiv Gandhi government's liberalization discourse combined Nehruvian techno-nationalism with Gandhian values of *self-reliance*.

Sam Pitroda (a nonresident Indian [NRI] who had returned to India at the invitation of Indira Gandhi) and a coalition of government technocrats and other NRI returnees convinced the Rajiv Gandhi government to set up the Center for Development of Telematics (C-DOT) under the Ministry of Science and Technology, in 1984, to develop rural automatic exchanges for wireline infrastructure. Village autonomy and social equity became connected to the "appropriate technology...the great social leveler second only to death."[4] "The government focused on making telecommunications a device for the masses because private enterprises already had access to the communications infrastructure. The government viewed telecommunications as a very powerful technology, such as Iridium 77 circling the globe, but only for the rich if the problem of connectivity is not addressed," exclaimed Saxena, credited for introducing the Electronic Switching System in India when he worked with Pitroda and G.B. Meemamsi at C-DOT.[5]

The creation of the C-DOT under the urging of transnational forces and the corporation of state-owned equipment makers and service providers represented how the evolution of *perceived strategic value* amalgamated *national self-reliance* and *neoliberal development*. The Department of Electronics convinced the Ministry of Posts and Telegraphs to accord higher priority to the modernization of telecommunications infrastructure. The ministry had previously emphasized postal services and had considered advanced switch technology and user equipment to be elitist.[6] Following the establishment of C-DOT, the Department of Telecommunications (DoT) was created in 1985 within the Ministry of Communications and the Telecommunications Commission ("Telecom Commission") formed in 1989 to formulate policy and prepare the DoT's budget. In 1990, government bureaucracy officially separated from the operation of telecommunications services in Delhi and Mumbai and international long-distance, respectively, with the corporatization of Mahanagar Telephone Nigam Limited (MTNL) and Videsh Sanchar Nigam Limited (VSNL).

7.2 BASIC SERVICES: UNIVERSAL SERVICE PROVISION AND NETWORK DEVELOPMENT VIA MOBILE LIBERALIZATION AND STATE-OWNED WIRELINES

"The wheels of liberalization began with Rajiv Ghandi and the C-DOT scheme with Pitroda, but market access was not allowed in services until

---

[4] Sam Pitroda quoted in Chakravartty (2004), 238.
[5] Interview in Delhi on February 18, 2013. See also Saxena (2008).
[6] See Mukherji (2014), 112.

1994," explained Rajat Kathuria, Chair of the Indian Council for Research on International Economic Relations.[7] In the context of the *perceived strategic value* of post-Independence *national self-reliance*, the Indian government frames the delivery of local, national, and international telecommunications as making such services "affordable for the common man," grounded in the view of telecommunications as a "mass-based business." "The mindset of introduction of competition, which was the change sweeping all over the world started in Britain by Thatcher, escalated government getting out of telecommunications, but the romanticism of India's values for rural development for the collective good drives government behavior in telecommunications," Saxena elaborated.[8] All the same, in 1993, there were only about 8 million phone lines for India's 900 million people.

From the 1980s, successively elected governments introduced competition and followed with reregulation amidst a pluralistic landscape of stakeholders, including those opposing liberalization and those demanding network modernization and expansion.[9] The union government created the state-owned Bharat Sanchar Nigam Limited (BSNL), under the DoT's supervision, after corporatization had established MTNL and VSNL. The DoT served as regulator and service operator and helped manage equipment manufacturing until the early 1990s. Protests by unionized government workers halted internal competition and foreign participation in the industry.[10]

The licensing of VSAT (Very Small Aperture Terminal) by DoT in 1993, however, permitted the access of private dedicated satellite links to Information Technology (IT) services companies, transnationally networked and disconnected from the telecommunications bureaucracy.[11] This inadvertently promoted the development of IT services, a sector of Information Communications Technology (ICT) in which India has become a global leader. The VSAT licensure had followed the establishment of Software Technology Parks, in 1991 and beyond, by the Department of Electronics.

---

[7] Interview on February 21, 2013 in New Delhi, India.

[8] Interview on February 18, 2013 in Delhi, India.

[9] See Singh (2000, 2005) and Sethi (2006).

[10] Interview with former telecommunications administrative service officer on February 19, 2013 in Delhi.

[11] Commissioned in 1983, the Indian National Satellite System is a joint venture of the DoT, Department of Space, India Meteorological Department, All India Radio, and Doordarshan.

Then, between 1994 and 1998, under the banner of the National Telecommunications Policy of 1994, governments (headed by the United Front coalition of regional parties and the National Democratic Alliance [NDA] formed by the Bharatiya Janata Party) granted licenses to nonstate carriers and VAS providers, including FDI, with the licenses going to the highest bidders, such as AT&T and HFCL, then a domestic private manufacturer of telecommunications equipment. In 1994, "The [Rao] government permitted AT&T, in a joint venture with privately owned Birla Communications to enter the market after the Americans bargained for AT&T entry when the Indian prime minister visited the United States," said Kathuria.[12] By January 1995, the Rao government liberalized mobile services in a unique competition model of twenty circles.[13]

7.2.1 State Capacity, Political Interference, and the Rise of the Regulator

The Telecommunications Regulatory Agency of India (TRAI), in 1998, became established under the Telecommunications Regulatory Authority Act of 1997. "Those who obtained licenses at low prices won; however, in those early years, state incumbents made it difficult for private operators to enter. Impediments and barriers included high interconnection fees and high carry fees as the government didn't have the withdrawal nor technical ability to calculate interconnection fees," described Pradip Baijal, who, renowned for his efforts in the government's disinvestments in power, steel, finance, and telecommunications, served as the third chairman of TRAI until his retirement in 2006 during the Congress-led United Progressive Alliance (UPA).[14] "Private players went to high courts and the courts advised the creation of an independent regulator."[15]

Sunil Dhar, founder of the Global Internet Group, explained, "Once you open the Pandora's box of economic liberalization, it's very difficult to put it back in. Politicians want to stay in power, and one way to do so is to satisfy disparate interests in telecoms."[16] Between 1998 and 2004, under Arun Shourie as the minister of Communications and Information

---

[12] Interview on February 21, 2013, in New Delhi, India.   [13] See Sinha (1996).

[14] Interview on February 21, 2013, in Gurgaron, India. Baijal spent a sabbatical year at Oxford during the height of Thatcher reforms.

[15] See Thiruvengadam and Joshi (2013) on the distinctive role played by the Indian judiciary in the development of telecommunications regulation.

[16] Interview on January 29, 2010.

Technology, the introduction of competition went beyond India's commitments to the World Trade Organiation (WTO). The New Telecom Policy (NTP) also liberalized FDI in Internet service provision, which had been monopolized by state-owned VSNL, rationalized the tariff structure, and introduced a revenue sharing regime.

Atal Bihari Vajpayee, the first prime minister under the BJP, further liberalized market entry in National Long Distance Service and corporatized incumbent BSNL in 2000, and separated the state-owned operator from the DoT despite resistance from state workers and their supporters in other state-owned enterprises.[17] Disconnected from the low castes that dominated the telecommunications bureaucracy, the BJP pushed privatization and FDI liberalization in the face of a massive national telecommunications scandal, series of strikes by organized labor and service and equipment trade unions, and public interest cases launched by civil rights groups, regional rights groups, and others.[18]

The creation of TRAI was supposed to resolve complaints that the telecommunications ministry regularly licensed the highest or favored bidders and imposed high charges for interconnection between public exchanges and private ones, and that corruption ran rampant at lower levels within state-owned carriers.[19] The lasting suspicion that TRAI, staffed by bureaucrats from the Indian telecommunications and administrative services, was not quite politically independent, further motivated the BJP-led NDA government under Vajpayee (in 2000) to establish the Telecommunications Dispute Settlement Appellate Tribunal (TDSAT) to arbitrate technical standards and disputes between licensor, licensee, service provider, and consumer.[20]

7.2.2 Liberalization that Advantaged Some and Disadvantaged Others

The corporatization of BSNL plunged the state-owned carrier into the competitive mobile services market, on the one hand. On the other hand, the state introduced regulation in the incumbent's favor. To the chagrin of carriers operating GSM networks, the introduction of Unified Access Service license regime, in 2002, lifted the artificial restrictions on mobility

---

[17] Saxena interview (February 18, 2013).   [18] Singh (1999) and Chakravatty (2004).
[19] Desai (1999). See also Bussell (2012) on the impact of grand and petty corruption on the delivery of public services and related policy outcomes.
[20] Kathuria interview (February 21, 2013).

technology. CDMA technology, previously limited to fixed-line use, now competed as mobile. That year, BSNL rolled out its first mobile network, a decade after the first private carriers received licenses. Because of crowded urban markets, BSNL chose to wire highways and expressways and to connect the semi-urban poor.

Around the same time, the Tata Group entered the long-distance market when it acquired 25 percent stake of VSNL. Tata became the sole owner in 2008, renaming VSNL to Tata Communications. In parallel, between 2000 and 2003, several global carriers exited India. Though FDI ceiling in basic services increased from 49 percent to 74 percent and in some services, allowing up to 100 percent, between 2000 and 2003, AT&T, Southwestern Bell, Swiss Telecom, and France Telecom divested interests, some to domestic players that held licenses. Foreign investors grew weary of what they viewed as a lack of transparency in the licensing and tendering processes of appropriate local partners and of low market demand.[21] This differed from China, where in the late 1990s after network modernization, the Chinese government forced the divestment of FDI in variable interest entity models to gain full control shortly before the country's WTO accession (see Chapter 4). Rather, questions of regulatory independence within the existing *sectoral organization of institutions* have stifled FDI entry, not the failure to comply with WTO commitments, anti-FDI regulation, or non-tariff barriers, as further elaborated below.

As the early FDI entrants exited, Indian companies, including Bharti Airtel; Southeast Asian investors, including SingTel and Whampo; and other European firms, such as Orange, began acquiring licenses. "While the motivations were to promote new entrants and upgrade networks, the unified, tech-neutral licensing benefited those who obtained licenses at low prices and enjoyed low interconnection charges, such as Tata and Reliance," Baijal explained.[22] This remained true when later, Reliance Jio, which the telecoms ministry granted a tech-neutral pan-India license to operate in 2015, was further advantaged by historical license fees that its consolidated competitors Bharti Airtel and Vodafone Idea had to pay.[23]

---

[21] See Jenkins (1999), 99 and Desai (2006), 47–53.

[22] Baijal interview (February 21, 2013).

[23] The Supreme Court ruled in favor of the government on the fees in 2009. "Factbox: India's telecom sector on the ropes after $13 billion levy ruling," *Reuters* (November 29, 2019).

7.3 WITHER AN INDEPENDENT REGULATOR: THE IMPLICATED POLITICS OF SPECTRUM ALLOCATIONS

In the 2000s and beyond, the civil servants of the Indian Telecommunications Service hold administrative and management positions in the state-owned carriers and TRAI and its dispute settlement body, and they direct policy in the DoT under the Ministry of Communication and Information Technology. In the context of their *regulated governance*, whereby policy bureaucracies and a regulator legally autonomous of them coordinate the market entry and exit of a diversity of public and private players, questions of political independence and conflicts of interest abound. The combination of multiple institutions as market coordinators and India's federal parliamentary system, whereby the majority party or coalition government dominates politics, has resulted in an unevenly streamlined and rationalized reform process.

Policies that induced fierce competition in a crowded market soon called the independence of the regulator into question. "The political party in power matters because the party in power determines who leads the Ministry of Communications and the leadership (or lack thereof) taken during crisis, such as the 2G scandal which rocked India and attempted to drag my good name down with it,"[24] explained Baijal. "The sheer ambiguity of the [liberalization] process provides ample scope for politicians to engineer the transition in ways beneficial to themselves and associates."[25] The Unified Access Service attracted new market players and launched the privatization of state-owned value-added service provider VSNL, which Tata acquired. Non-state competition quickly dominated the market. This included Reliance Telecommunications, which, already dominant in CDMA, was granted a GSM license in 2007.

The Cellular Operators Association of India (COAI), representing the GSM industry body, filed a complaint to TDSAT opposing the crossover allocation of spectrum on the grounds that carriers should not be permitted to dominate both GSM and CMDA networks.[26] The DoT argued that TDSAT did not have jurisdiction because this was a policy matter outside

---

[24] Interview on May 10, 2013, in San Francisco. See Kohli (2012) on the relationship between the narrow nature of ruling alliance and business interests in pursuit of economic growth.

[25] See Jenkins (1999).

[26] Interviews between 2013 and 2017 with COAI officials and company members familiar with such disputes. Also, "GSM Lobby Challenges New Spectrum Policy," *Mint* (November 20, 2007).

of regulatory purview. Then in 2008, a scandal erupted when members of the sitting United Progressive Alliance were found to have manipulated spectrum management by awarding 122 2G spectrum licenses at prices lower than previous valuations. "Andimuthu Raja, the communications minister, and Dayanidhi Maran and Kanimozhi Karunanidhi, two other members of the Dravida Munnetra Kazhagam, were accused of taking under-table payments and manipulating spectrum management. Instead of first come, first serve, various change of dates took place for people behind the queue, and they granted licenses at knocked down prices," explained Rajan Mathews, Director General of the Cellular Operators Association of India from 2010–2020, who previously served as an executive for several foreign-invested carriers, including AT&T Wireless and NTT DoComo.[27]

The retroactive deadline announcement favored at least eight bidders, two of which promptly turned around and sold their licenses to FDI, garnering them $1.3 billion in instant profits.[28] At the time of the 2G scandal, each of India's twenty-three circles had close to twelve players.[29] The hyper-competition contrasts with the five to six players that existed when liberalization came into place in 1994. In 2010, the spectrum allocation of 3G airwaves reflected not so much corruption but arbitrariness in selection method. Critics contended allocations favored regional interests and resulted in "patchwork" rather than nationwide mobile coverage. At the end of the 2000s, TRAI bureaucrats took trips abroad to auction spectrums and seek input from those involved in global telecommunications.[30]

In 2012 the Supreme Court canceled all 122 licenses in a ruling on a Public Interest Litigation filed by a host of activists, including the India Against Corruption Movement. Describing telecom spectrum as a natural resource, the litigation questioned whether the government had a right to distribute spectrum in a manner that was not "fair and transparent" in accordance with the "fundamentals of the equality clause enshrined in the Constitution." The court ruled the spectrum allocation method by

[27] Interview on February 22, 2013.

[28] "India's Telecom Scandal: Can You Prepone My 2G Spot?" *The Economist* (February 3, 2012).

[29] It was estimated that of the 122 licenses canceled, 53.31 million connections were affected, which is around 8.24 percent of India's active connection base. See "Table: Supreme Court 2G Scam Verdict Impacts Over 53.31M Connections in India," *MediaNama* (February 2, 2012).

[30] Communication with Indian industry insiders based in Silicon Valley in fall 2009.

Andimuthu Raja as flawed and that he had acted to "favor some of the applicants" and had "virtually gifted away the important national asset at throw away price."[31] The case became a symbol of crony capitalism in India, even making the *Time's* list of Top Ten Abuses of Power in 2011, and became the BJP's rallying cry in the lead-up to the 2014 Lok Sabha election.[32] Then in 2017, a special Central Bureau of Investigation court acquitted all accused and claimed that the 2012 ruling was made under "public perception created by rumor, gossip and speculation," where "some people created a scam by artfully arranging a few selected facts and exaggerating things beyond recognition to astronomical levels."[33]

7.3.1 "Liberalization of Access" and Universal Access or Protection of State-Owned Incumbents

The *perceived strategic value* of telecommunications as a means to *national self-reliance* to address rural backwardness, however, continued to shape the state's role in market coordination, now fused with the value of *neoliberal development*. In the context of macro-liberalization of the Indian economy in general and telecommunications in particular, specific policies address state goals of universal service provision and rural network development. The *sectoral organization of institutions* has determined the policy specifics, which guaranteed market share for the public carriers.

The revenue sharing model introduced by the New Telecom Policy, in 1999, replaced high interconnection fees and led to an increase in government coffers for network development when subscriber base increased exponentially.[34] It required telecommunications operators to pay 6–10 percent of their annual revenues as license fees, and an additional 2–3 percent spectrum usage charges. The aftermath witnessed the subsidization of towers by DoT and enforcement of low termination charge by TRAI to attract carriers to extend to rural areas. In 2014, the High Court ordered the Comptroller and Auditor General to investigate the revenue sharing model of private telecom operators after it was found in private

---

[31] "If There was No 2G Scam, Why Did the Supreme Court Cancel 122 Spectrum Licenses in 2012?," *Scroll.in* (December 22, 2017).

[32] "Top Ten Abuses of Power in the What They Were Thinking Category: India's Telecoms Scandal," *The Time Magazine* (May 17, 2011).

[33] "2G Spectrum Verdict: No Proof of Scam, Says Court. A Scam of Lies, Says Congress," *Times of India* (December 22, 2017).

[34] See Baijal interview (February 21, 2013).

audits, including ones ordered by the DoT in 2007–2008 of five telecom companies – Bharti Airtel, Vodafone India, Reliance Communications, Tata Teleservices, and Idea Cellular – of routine under-reporting of revenues.[35]

The NTP also sanctioned the Universal Access Levy, a percentage of the revenue earned by operators under various licenses, which converted to a statutory fund by the 2003 Indian Telegraph Amendment Act, and contributed to the Universal Service Obligation. Under these auspices, the Public Call Offices converted to Public Teleinfo Centers that offered multimedia services.[36] Relatedly, in the late 2010s, to further achieve the DoT's goal of "expanding the reach of Internet, and the employment and revenue opportunity it provides to those so-called 'agents' reselling Wi-Fi plans of telcos, which could even be local 'paan' or tea shops," the TRAI proposed a countrywide interoperable WANI (Wi-Fi Access Network Interface) architecture.[37]

Billed as "liberalization of access," WANI would set up Public Data Offices where Wi-Fi would be available on demand. According to T.V. Ramachandran, president of the Broadband India Forum, it separates access from the networks, promoting the survival of India's small-scale enterprises, from MVNOs (mobile virtual network operators) to street- and village-level entrepreneurs.[38] A competing plan, the "Bharat Wi-Fi" model, is jointly proposed by all telecom companies, Internet service providers, and virtual network operators who will work together to offer Wi-Fi through public hotspots via roaming agreements.

The Indian government also instituted policies specifically targeted to compensate state-owned carriers for providing universal access. To compensate BSNL for the differential between the cost of providing basic fixed-line access in underserved areas and the revenue earned by the operator, the TRAI instituted the Access Deficit Charge (ADC) from 2003 to 2008. The ADC's combined fee was paid to BSNL by calling parties and operators for termination of international long-distance calls. Initially set at 30 percent (versus the global average of 6–7 percent), it was

---

[35] "With Revenue Sharing Model under Scanner, Telcos Woes are Far from Over," *Business Standard* (January 13, 2014).
[36] Privately owned STD stations, many of which offer Wi-Fi, also proliferate in India.
[37] "Wi-Fi on the Go: Government Pushes to Keep Bharat Connected," *The Economic Times* (July 16, 2019).
[38] "Can WANI Be to Telecom What UPI is to Payments?," *Financial Express* (November 12, 2019).

reduced to 10 percent over the years. Inaccurate calculations of deficits and lines installed in upmarket neighborhoods and wealthy households soured public perception of the ADC, however. The exponential growth of mobile services to serve the unconnected also made such subsidization increasingly unpopular. The discovery that BSNL incurred massive loss due to illegal efforts, including security breaches, to avoid fees further propelled the TRAI to eliminate the charge.[39]

Moreover, in 2019, the Modi government announced Rs 70,000 crore revival packages for BSNL and MTNL. The revival packages included monetizing assets, raising funds, spectrum for the Chinese technology standard TD-LTE, and a voluntary retirement scheme for employees. It also announced plans to merge the two state-owned carriers. The potential of an untenable debt, without first reorganizing so that BSNL could be granted 2G and 4G spectrums in Delhi and Mumbai and offer pan-India services in addition to its twenty circles, delayed an immediate merger in the midst of the COVID-19 pandemic.[40] In October 2020, the DoT released a Cabinet mandate requesting "all ministries/departments. . .to issue necessary instructions including to CPSEs/Central Autonomous organizations under their control for mandatory utilization of BSNL/MTNL networks for internet/ broadband, landline and leased line requirements."[41]

7.4 TELECOMMUNICATIONS EQUIPMENT: BUREAUCRACY-LED WIRELINE MANUFACTURING AND PROTECTIONISM IN 2010S AND BEYOND

Industrial bureaucracies exercise more intentional supervision and regulatory capacity due to high priority in the development of infrastructure, rooted in Nehruvian techno-nationalism's interpretation of Gandhian values of self-sufficiency. The priority placed on other infrastructure, such as electricity, due to the Gandhian critique of technology and luxury, of which telecommunications was associated during British colonialism, however, meant that public sector allocations up until the 1980s deemphasized the development of telecommunications. At that time, the shifting priority given to *neoliberal development* in response to internal

---

[39] "End of the Era of Access Deficit Charge," *Times of India* (October 3, 2008).
[40] See "BSNL-MTNL Merger May Get Delayed as Govt-appointed Panel Wants Spectrum First," *The Financial Express* (July 5, 2020).
[41] See "Centre Mandates All Ministries, Public Depts, CPSUs to Use BSNL, MTNL Services," *The Hindu* (October 14, 2020).

political and economic pressures launched the adoption of rural network technologies promoted by transnational Indian returnees. Nonresident Indians were allowed to bypass controls on foreign investment, which were permitted on a case-by-case basis accompanied with sophisticated technology.

Since initial government promotion of Indian returnee innovations in rural automatic telecommunications exchanges, however, the development of domestic manufacturing capacity has been marked by path-dependent bureaucratic inertia and lean budget allocations. In the 2000s and beyond, sectarian conflicts and the China Factor (growing market dominance of Chinese telecommunications equipment makers and border security disputes) have regenerated the state's purposive orientation toward developing a domestic manufacturing industry in the name of national self-sufficiency with liberal and protectionist methods.

7.4.1 Transnational Networks, Bureaucracy, and Manufacturing of Rural Automatic Exchanges

As analyzed earlier, in the early 1980s, the higher strategic value of telecommunications equipment for rural development provided the jump-start for the modernization of telecommunications writ large. Almost immediately, centrally run science and technology bureaucracies facilitated the direction and development of domestic manufacturing capacity. At the behest of Pitroda, the Center for the Development of Telematics was established in 1984. An autonomous telecommunications technology research center, C-DOT became registered as a publicly funded research institution under the Department of Scientific and Industrial Research of the Ministry of Science and Technology.

C-DOT worked with state-owned equipment producer India Telephone Industries Limited (ITI), which was founded in 1948 under Nehru and managed by the Ministry of Industries, to develop rural automatic exchanges for villages and larger switches for small towns. C-DOT licensed the technology to the domestic private sector to supply the telecoms operators.[42] The government also sourced from domestic private enterprises. The Telecom Engineering Center under the Ministry of Communications certified the producers for ITU/IEEE standardization.

---

[42] Rosen (1992), 73. Sharma interview (February 20, 2013).

The institutional organization of R&D in telecommunications equipment under the aegis of C-DOT and ITI affected the Indian domestic sector's manufacturing capacity. Following their lead, domestic equipment makers focused on manufacturing products for the network expansion of state-owned fixed-line carriers, delaying investment in next-generation mobile technologies and broadband. This resulted in the rapid pace of global technological advancement, such as technological convergence and the introduction of new standards, proving more favorable for new entrants and foreign equipment makers Siemens, Alcatel, and Fujitsu, when the government permitted up to 51 percent foreign ownership in joint ventures in 1992.

C-DOT and the Telecom Equipment Manufacturers Association of India (TEMA) together resisted further liberalization because this would reduce the domestic sector's advantage in the three percent local content requirement for network infrastructure. In response to the opposition of the bureaucratic-business alliance, the central government increased the local content requirement when it fully liberalized the equipment market to FDI in 1998.[43] However "more competition in the market meant that operators met the 30 percent local inputs rule and procured the rest from global suppliers," explained Rahul Sharma, president of TEMA, who also serves as president of Vedanta and business head of Sterlite Technologies.[44]

All the same, the Indian government has used the licensing function to exercise market coordination in favor of domestic equipment makers. In 2002, the government approved the GSM technology after the Department of Telecommunications, which promoted CDMA networks, warmed toward GSM out of efficiency concerns.[45] This gave domestic mobile equipment makers markets to supply GSM-compatible components for carrier network procurement. Moreover, in a move favorable to the state-owned carriers, the DoT lifted restrictions that tied the use of CDMA technology to fixed-line networks.

"Other than cable produced by Sterlite Technologies the domestic sector is not that strong," quipped COAI director general Mathews, also chairperson of the Development Organization for Standards for Telecommunications in India.[46] With GSM technology, "India can get connected to the democracy of equipment but still have significant resources to generate IP and R&D. When it came down to it, Indian

---

[43] See Sinha (1996).   [44] Interview on February 20, 2013 in New Delhi, India.
[45] Mukherji (2008).   [46] Interview on February 22, 2013, in New Delhi, India.

companies didn't have the withdrawal. Frankly, the Indian government has not done much. Besides, Indian companies started with niche areas, and ITI and C-DOT were part of the continuum of public sector units to manufacture domestic (captured market) but never did significant R&D work. When landline died, ITI's future also faded," further explained Mathews.[47]

In the 2000s, the finance ministry threatened to cut off funding for C-DOT when the government R&D center unsuccessfully tried pivoting from rural automatic exchanges to commercially viable wireless technology. With the continued focus on the rural sector, C-DOT formed joint ventures with global equipment makers such as Alcatel to develop wireless broadband. The government expedited the approval process, granting the joint venture licensure within months of signing the memorandum of agreement by the Singh government in 2005.[48]

The C-DOT Alcatel Research Center, of which 51 percent stakes was owned by Alcatel and 49 percent by C-DOT, had aimed to employ 1000 workers and develop the latest broadband wireless technologies, building on the government's strength in landline technologies. It also hoped to facilitate the industrialization and volume production of the WiMAX solutions by domestic equipment makers. In spite of the high hopes for promoting domestic manufacturing capacity, however, when the market evolved toward LTE technology, Alcatel diluted its stake, in 2013, and shifted away from manufacturing to focus on security certification.[49]

7.4.2 (Not) Made in India: Debating the Role of Government in Industrial Development

The general assessment, among those in the infrastructural sector, is that today "India doesn't produce equipment like towers, transmitters, and cell phones. India has lost the game in producing infrastructure."[50] Asset finance and leasing infrastructural capital enterprises, instead, procure

---

[47] The telecommunications services case study in Section 7.2 examines the redefinition of CDMA as mobile, which bestowed a lifeline to state-owned BSNL heretofore had not ventured into mobile services.

[48] See "C-DOT, Alcatel to Set Up R&D Venture," *The Economic Times* (April 1, 2005).

[49] See "Alcatel-Lucent May Dilute Stake in R&D Venture with C-DOT," *The Hindu Business Line* (March 23, 2013).

[50] Interview with Rajarashi Datta, a managing director at SREI, on February 18, 2013, in New Delhi, India.

foreign-produced telecommunications equipment and tower infrastructure and then lease them to telecommunications operators, such as Tata and VIOM Networks. New entrants, such as Telenor India, previously owned by the Norwegian state-owned carrier and now by Bharti Airtel, use Huawei as a vendor. In 2016, Telenor became the first company to globally deploy Huawei's narrow-band 4G LTE/commercial lean GSM network across six telecom circles.[51] Two years later, the Chinese company completed fifth-generation technology standard (5G) trials with Bharti Airtel.

In the context of C-DOT's lackluster performance in developing new generation technologies, the domestic debate on the precise role of the government in sponsoring the development of telecommunications equipment is centered around security versus developmental concerns. State goals of national security and industrial development, however, are typically not closely tied together when implemented in practice. When the Indian government began to liberalize infrastructure (including road, power, and telecommunications) and capital markets (in telecommunications, insurance, banking, and real estate), some policies, which protected state-owned incumbents in certain equipment sectors, were instituted due to national security reasons.[52] However, "not until sectarian conflicts foment or when Chinese equipment makers Huawei and ZTE make major headway in Indian markets, is telecommunications ever characterized, much less perceived, as a security issue," underscored Saxena.[53]

In the aftermath of the 2008 Mumbai attacks, the Singh government initiated in 2009, and approved and funded in 2011, the National Intelligence Grid (NATGRID).[54] Signaling a potential boon for the domestic equipment industry, the NATGRID would permit government agencies, such as the Intelligence Bureau, local police, and revenue and custom departments, to access records related to immigration, banking, financial transactions, and telecommunications. However, in the pipeline for over a decade, opposition parties criticized the Modi government for

---

[51] Telenor India Completes Deployment of Over 10K Huawei Blade Site Wireless BTS," *The Economic Times* (June 6, 2016).

[52] Interview with Parveen Arora on February 19, 2013, General Counsel, Vestas, Guragon, India.

[53] Interview on February 18, 2013, in Delhi, India.

[54] The terrorist attacks took place in November 2008 when ten members of Lashkar-e-Taiba, an extremist Islamist terrorist organization based in Pakistan, carried out twelve coordinated shooting and bombing attacks lasting four days across Mumbai.

the politically motivated delay of the National Counter Terrorism Center and the full implementation of the NATGRID.[55] Though the Modi government signed agreements with stakeholders such as the National Crime Records Bureau in 2020, with continued opposition from others, including the Civil Aviation Ministry and airline companies, implementation remained incomplete in 2021.[56]

Another initiative, also introduced in 2011 under the UPA, is the National Optic Fiber Network project. Originally touted as the government's answer to the expansion of communication networks to rural areas, in the face of competitive pressures from Chinese equipment makers, it became framed as indirect subsidy for domestic equipment makers. "The Indian government began the national fiber optic network to reach gram panchayats. The issue became piggybacked once domestic manufacturing became the hot button issue. So now will give domestic manufacturing a preference for sourcing. The Indian government has financed this partly through the universal service obligation fund. Operators don't have commercial reasons to do this," explained Mathews. That same year, the TRAI examined the technological development of Indian equipment manufacturers, including the semiconductor sector, in "Recommendations on Telecom Equipment Manufacturing Policy."

In late 2012, the Singh government also announced preferential market access in government-funded projects for domestic equipment makers on security and self-reliance grounds "where Indian industry has capability to capture the market." In 2014, United Telecoms, a licensee of technology developed by C-DOT secured the highest competitive bid in recent years to supply the government-owned Bharat Broadband Network (BBNL) established two years earlier to wire the National Optical Fiber Network.[57] The government also appointed a task force in the Telecommunications Engineering Center to create an R&D fund to help define value and help domestic industry to develop products.

The reorganization of related bureaucracies, in 2016, aimed to promote domestic indigenous development in ICT, including equipment manufacturing. The Ministry of Communication and Information

---

[55] "P Chidambaram Asks Why BJP-led Govt 'Sitting On' NCTC, NATGRID," *Times of India* (April 3, 2019).

[56] "NATGRID to Have Access to Database that Links Around 14,000 Police Stations," *The Hindu* (July 12, 2020).

[57] See "United Telecom Pips Rivals ITI, Tejas, Sterlite, L&T with Rs 998 crore Bid for BBNL Contract," *The Economic Times* (February 4, 2014).

Technology divided into the Ministry of Communications and Ministry of Electronics and Information Technology. In 2017, the Department of Industry Policy and Promotion's "Preferential Electronics Order" and "Cyber Notification" required all state and central government procurements to mandate preferences for domestically manufactured electronic goods and cyber-security software products.

Under the Made in India banner, the C-DoT-owned ITI was awarded the three-year contract to implement the Army Static Switched Communication Network (ASCON) Phase IV in October 2020. The Defense Ministry explained the project will "involve several activities including execution of civil works, laying of optical fiber cable and tower construction, and [the generation of] employment in remote border areas. The project is also a big opportunity for the public sector to showcase its capability and provide impetus to the Indian economy and will be a step in the direction of achieving the goal of Atmanirbhar Bharat ('Self-Reliant India')."[58]

Toward such a goal, in an extensively liberalized context whereby Chinese dominance has become increasingly a concern to policymakers and Indian businesses alike, the country's largest mobile operator Reliance Jio announced the development of in-house technology to roll-out and operate 5G. Jio, which teamed with Google on a customized Android mobile operating system, has not revealed any details of its "from scratch…100% homegrown technologies and solutions."[59] Technological convergence and India's competitive advantage in digital design and software shape indigenous capacity: "Such a system entails software integration of established global vendors' components and solutions."[60] The "virtualized 5G network's" trials began soon after the DoT's auction of 4G spectrum in March 2021.[61]

Sharma of TEMA said, "C-DOT is a public sector initiative, which led to initial growth and development. However, the Indian industry was not

---

[58] See "India-China Standoff: Why the Secure Communication System Will Be a Boost for the Indian Army," *One India* (October 9, 2020).

[59] "Reliance Jio Claim: Complete 5G Solution from Scratch with 100% Home Grown Technologies," *IEEE Communications Society* (July 20, 2020) and "India Approves Google's $4.5 billion Deal with Reliance's Jio Platforms," *Tech Crunch* (November 11, 2020).

[60] Interview on March 8, 2021 in San Jose, CA, with director of engineering of a global semiconductor firm with an digital chip design verification R&D office in India.

[61] "Jio Trials HD Virtual Reality Meeting Using Homegrown 5G NR And 5G Core," *The Economic Times* (September 23, 2021).

ready for the wireless market when the opening of India's equipment market to global players in 1998 coincided with the shift from fixed line to wireless. Now it's about the promotion of domestic industry. Going forward the domestic wireless startups will not emerge without more meaningful government support."[62] With what methods is the operative question and the debate continues.

7.4.3 Securing Indian Telecommunications for Next Generation Challenges

In the 2010s, the China Factor became perceived as both developmental and security threats before the election of Modi and his framing of Atmanirbhar Bharat, a "self-reliant India." Between 2000 and 2020, imports from China, long a geopolitical rival, increased to 14 percent from less than 3 percent, and Chinese Internet companies became key investors in Indian high-tech startups.[63] "Chinese funds are playing a positive role by helping Indian start-ups to raise more capital," said Amit Bhandari, a fellow at Gateway House in February 2020. But, he continued, "China is the rival. . . . [It's] influence has not always been very positive."

Huawei revealed its source code in 2011, after Huawei and ZTE were accused of spying on India. The Chinese company also signed no-spy agreements with telcommunications carriers with provisions for penalties in case of deficiency in security mandated by the DoT. In 2019, amidst global controversy over the requested arrest of CFO Meng Wanzhou in Canada by the U.S. government, the Indian government banned Huawei from further participation in 5G trials.[64] Huawei offered to sign a "no back door" pact. No matter, in August 2020 Bharti Airtel announced plans to switch to Nokia and Ericcson from Huawei and ZTE for their 5G trials in Kolkata and Bengaluru.

Faced with potential Chinese takeovers during the 2020 COVID-19 pandemic, the Indian government extended the requirement of central government approval for FDI flowing from Pakistan and Bangladesh to

---

[62] Interview on February 20, 2013, in Guragon, India.

[63] "China Provides Record Funding for Indian Tech Start-ups," *Financial Times* (February 16, 2020).

[64] "Huawei Offers to Sign 'No Back Door' Pact with India to Allay Spying Fears," *Business Standard* (June 25, 2019); "ZTE and Huawei are to Be Excluded from India's 5G Trials," *Telecoms Tech News* (September 17, 2018); and "Airtel, Huawei Conduct Successful 5G Trial," *The Hindu Business Line* (February 23, 2018).

all countries with which India shares a land border. With the press note specifically stating the government's concerns about opportunistic acquisitions and takeovers during the health crisis, most investors and analysts suspect Chinese FDI is the prime target.[65] The COVID-19 global pandemic has sparked a sell-off in the Indian stock market, bleeding companies of funds; however, Nepal, Afghanistan, Bhutan, and Sri Lanka have shown little interest in investing in Indian businesses. In contrast, the People's Bank of China increased its shareholding to 1 percent from 0.8 percent in the mortgage company Housing Development Finance Corporation.

Moreover, in recent years, Chinese companies are investors in two-thirds of India's start-ups with $1 billion in valuation.[66] In telecommunications, the Chinese Internet commerce company Alibaba backs financial services firm Paytm and food delivery service Zomato. Incidentally, after Alibaba became its largest investor in 2016, Paytm founder Vijay Shekhar Sharma reassured users that his company remained Indian. The Chinese VAS provider Tencent has invested in car-hailing app Ola and Byju's, an education technology company. Chinese equipment maker Xiaomi owns 72 percent share of the Indian smartphone market. Chinese venture capital (VC) firms have also invested in e-commerce giant Flipkart and video-sharing service ShareChat. The relaxation of requirements on raising capital during the pandemic by the Chinese government as discussed in Chapter 4 contributes to other Chinese companies and VCs joining these investors.

The deaths of twenty Indians following a clash, in June 2020, between Chinese and Indian soldiers along the disputed Himalayan border provided further impetus for Modi-era promotion of indigenous development in the name of national security. Less than two weeks after the clash, citing data security across Indian borders as "a matter of very deep and immediate concern which requires emergency measures," the Ministry of Electronics and Information Technology banned fifty-nine Chinese-owned mobile and non-mobile Internet-enabled devices, including TikTok, WeChat, and Weibo, because of their use for activities that were "prejudicial to the sovereignty and integrity of India, security of state, and public order."[67]

[65] See the Department for Promotion of Industry and Internal Trade, Ministry of Commerce and Industry of India Press Note No. 3 (2020 Series) (April 17, 2020). Also, see "India Moves to Curb Chinese Corporate Takeovers," *Financial Times* (April 18, 2020).

[66] See "India Moves to Curb Chinese Corporate Takeovers," *Financial Times* (April 20, 2020).

[67] See "India Bans Nearly 60 Chinese Apps, Including TikTok and WeChat," *New York Times* (June 30, 2020).

Later in July, new rules required any bidder of government contracts (including state governments, state banks, and other public-sector companies from a country sharing a land border with India) to register with the Ministry of Commerce and Industry and receive "political and security clearance" from ministries of External Affairs and Home Affairs.[68] China is presumed the main target; India's finance ministry said the new rules are designed to "strengthen the defense of India and national security." Also, in the name of national security, Chinese companies are blocked from highway projects, are barred from investing in small- and medium-sized businesses, and have had shipments delayed and other additional hurdles at Indian ports.[69]

7.4.4 Data Management in a Big Data World: Internet Security, Politics, and Protectionism

In December 2018, the Ministry of Electronics and Information Technology proposed new rules on data management affecting VAS providers, including social media, digital media platforms, and streaming services. The data management rules, which went into effect in February 2021 as the Information Technology (Guidelines for Intermediaries and Digital Media Ethics Code) Rules 2021, require proactive monitoring, local presence for VAS providers with 5 million or more users, takedown of unlawful content, and tracing of content originator. The proposed rules responded to a Parliament motion in July by the BJP about the "misuse of social media platforms and spreading of fake news."[70] After the rules went into effect, American messaging platform WhatsApp, in May 2021, sued the Ministry of Electronics and Information Technology (in Delhi High Court) for enforcing traceability for identifying originator of a message, which the company said violates end-to-end encryption.[71]

---

[68] See "India to Curb Chinese Bids for State Contracts," *Financial Times* (July 24, 2020). The military standoff between India and China is seen along the disputed Himalayan border, which includes the area in proximity to the disputed Pangong Lake in Ladakh and the Tibet Autonomous Region, and between Sikkim and the Tibet Autonomous Region.

[69] See "India Unveils Rules on Chinese Firms Seeking Government Contracts Amid Row," *DW* (July 24, 2020).

[70] See "Comments/suggestions invited on Draft of "The Information Technology [Intermediary Guidelines (Amendment) Rules] 2018," Ministry of Electronics and Information Technology (December 24, 2018).

[71] See "WhatsApp Moves Delhi High Court Against New Guidelines," *Hindustan Times* (May 26, 2021).

TABLE 7.1. *India: Laws, rules, and regulations governing telecoms subsectors*

Market Coordination	Property Rights Arrangements
Telecommunications Writ-Large	
• Department of Telecommunications (1985) • Telecom Commission (1989) • National Telecommunications Policy (NTP) (1994) • Telecommunications Regulatory Authority Act of 1997 • Telecommunications Regulatory Agency of India (TRAI) (1998) • New Telecom Policy (liberalized FDI in services, rationalized tariff structure, introduced revenue sharing model) (1999) • Universal Access Levy, Universal Service Obligation (1999) • Telecommunications Dispute Settlement Appellate Tribunal (TDSAT) (2000) • Unified Access Service licensure (2002) • Indian Telegraph (Amendment) Act, 2003 • Supreme Court cancellation of 122 licenses, 2G scandal (2012) • Elimination of Access Deficit Charge (ADC) (2009) • National Intelligence Grid (NATGRID (2011) • National Optic Fiber Network (2011) • Ministry of Communication and Information Technology divided into the Ministry of Communications and Ministry of Electronics and Information Technology (2016) • Central Investigation Bureau Special Court ruling acquitting all 2G accused (2017)	• National Telecommunications Policy liberalized FDI up to 49% in services (1994) • New Telecom Policy (liberalized FDI in services and further corporatized and separated from government state-owned carriers) (1999) • Expanded "government approval" requirement of FDI from Pakistan and Bangladesh to all countries with borders with India • Bidder of government contracts required to register with Ministry of Commerce and Industry and receive "political and security clearance" from Ministries of External and Home Affair
Telecommunications Basic Services	
• Liberalization of market entry in mobile and value-added services (to nonstate providers, including FDI) (20 circles) (1995)	• Corporatization and separation from government office of state-owned MTNL and VSNL, with operations in Delhi and Mumbai and

Market Coordination	Property Rights Arrangements
• Liberalized market entry in National Long-Distance Service (2000) • CDMA redefined as mobile services under Unified Access Service regime (2002) • Access Deficit Charge (ADC) (2003–2008) • "Revival Packages" for BSNL and MTNL (2019) • Mandatory utilization by government entities of BSNL/MTNL networks for internet/ broadband, landline and leased line requirements (2020)	international long-distance, respectively (1986) • Bharat Sanchar Nigam Limited (BSNL) (1989) • AT&T in joint venture with Birla Communications became first foreign-invested carrier granted mobile license (1994) • Corporatization and separation from government office of state-owned BSNL, with domestic landline networks, except Delhi and Mumbai (2000) • Divestments by early entrant FDI (2000–2003) • New private domestic and foreign entrants, including Bharit and AirTel and Singtel and Orange, respectively (2000–2003) • Privatization of VSNL with purchase by Tata (2002–2008)

Telecommunications Value-Added Services

• Establishment of Software Technology Parks of India by Ministry of Electronics (1991) • VSAT (Very Small Aperture Terminal) licensure for IT services (1993) • Liberalization of market entry in mobile and value-added services (to nonstate providers, including FDI) (20 circles) (1995) • Liberalization of Internet service provision (1999) • Public Call Offices conversion to multimedia Public Teleinfo Centers (1999) • TRAI proposal: WANI (Wi-Fi Access Network Interface) (2018) • "Bharat Wi-Fi" proposal by telcos and value-added service providers (2018) • Ban of 59 Chinese-owned social media applications (2020)	• Bharat Broadband Network (BBNL), public sector undertaking under DoT (2012) • Information Technology (Guidelines for Intermediaries and Digital Media Ethics Code) Rules 2021 (local incorporation for entities with 5 million plus users)

(continued)

TABLE 7.1. *(continued)*

Market Coordination	Property Rights Arrangements
• Information Technology (Guidelines for Intermediaries and Digital Media Ethics Code) Rules 2021 (monitoring, local presence and takedown and tracing of original posts) (2021)	

Telecommunications Equipment

Market Coordination	Property Rights Arrangements
• Center for Development of Telematics (C-DOT), Ministry of Science and Technology (1984) • Telecom Engineering Center, Ministry of Communications • Rural Exchanges for Fixed-Line Networks (1980s) • Local Content Requirement of 3% in network infrastructure (early 1990s) • Local Content Policy 30% (1998) • United Access Service/GSM technology approval (2002) • TRAI's "Recommendations on Telecom Equipment Manufacturing Policy (2011) • Preferential market access in government-funded project for domestic equipment makers on security and *self-reliance* grounds (2012) • R&D Fund, Telecommunications Engineering Center (2012) • Made in India (2015) • Formation of Ministry of Electronics and Information Technology (2016) • "Preferential Electronics Order" and "Cyber Notification," Department of Industry Policy and Promotion (2017) • Army Static Switched Communication Network (2020)	• India Telephone Industries Limited (1948), PSU of DoT, Ministry of Communications • FDI permitted up to 51% ownership in joint ventures (1992) • FDI full liberalization in equipment (1998) • C-DOT joint ventures with FDI, including with C-DOT Alcatel Research Center • Ban of Huawei in 5G trial participation (2019)

TABLE 7.2. *India telecommunications subsectors: Strategic value, market governance, and development*

Regulated Governance	Dominant Coordination Mechanisms	Dominant Distribution of Property Rights	Development Outcomes
Medium Strategic Value Universal Coverage and Market Competition	**Basic and Value-added Services** Centralized policymaking by sector-specific central ministry, with market coordination and enforcement by separate regulator; periodic politically motivated intervention of regulator by ministry and political parties in ruling government coalitions; new rules on monitoring, local presence, and takedown and tracing of original posts	**Fixed-line Services** Government-owned backbone infrastructure and private investment in broadband **Mobile & Value-added** Fiercely competitive public, private, and foreign-invested service providers, including IT outsourcing, spurred by licensure of satellite links; fixed-line CDMA initially offered by public carriers in mobile markets	**Telecommunications Services** Telecommunications mobile reach in the most rural areas; significant consumer choice in basic and value-added services; globally competitive service providers in global markets
High Strategic Value Rural Infrastructural Development and State Bureaucratic Control	**Equipment Sectors** Centralized coordination of R&D and S&T policies related central bureaucracies; state licensing of technology and production of fixed-line equipment, including rural automatic exchanges; public-private R&D joint ventures in new generation networks	**Equipment Sectors** Dominant FDI & private domestic equipment makers; state-owned or state-invested equipment makers in niche markets (rural infrastructural equipment and other fixed-line products) created by state infrastructural development initiatives	**Equipment Sectors** Domestic equipment makers not globally competitive and slow to enter mobile markets, with focus on fixed-line networks; fierce competition from and increasing reach of Chinese FDI in next-generation technologies and start-ups

The immediate pretext to these rules is the government's concern for internal social stability; however, internal politics and developmental protectionism also motivated these rules. In 2018, WhatsApp mass messages spread falsehoods about child kidnappers, leading to the murder of two dozen innocent people by furious mobs. Moreover, the private information of 560,000 Indians from Facebook, which Cambridge Analytica of the Trump fame harvested for an Indian political consultancy, allegedly influenced the Bihar assembly elections in 2010. Importantly, the secretary of the Department of Telecommunications explained it this way when the government first proposed the rules: "We don't want to build walls, but at the same time, we explicitly recognize and appreciate that data is a strategic asset," said Aruna Sundararajan, also chairwoman of the Telecommunications Commission.[72] "There is a strong feeling in many quarters that the reason that India has not been able to develop a Tencent or Baidu or Alibaba is because we have not been nuanced in our policies." With such rules on data management favoring domestic industry's comparative advantage in ICT and software, the Indian social media app Koo became one of the first to comply when it announced the appointment of a resident grievance officer, chief compliance officer, and nodal contact officer.

Table 7.1 shows temporal and subsectoral variation in laws and regulations governing telecommunications, as analyzed in this chapter. Table 7.2 maps dominant patterns of market governance structures and development outcomes in telecommunications.

---

[72] See "India Pushes Back Against Tech 'Colonization' by Internet Giants," *New York Times* (August 31, 2018).

8

Political Legitimacy, Economic Stability, and Labor-Intensive Small-Scale Sectors

Centralized Governance in Indian Textiles

The Strategic Value Framework expects the cross-time Indian textile case studies of this chapter to show that the higher *perceived strategic value* (for *neoliberal self-reliance*) of labor-intensive and small-scale industry dominated sectors shapes the *centralized governance* by the Indian government. In the context of macro-level liberalization of the Indian economy, and parallel to the *regulated governance* in telecommunications analyzed in Chapter 7, this chapter uncovers sector-specific interventions by the federal-level Ministry of Textiles to coordinate textile markets, and divergent property rights arrangements proliferated by rural small-scale enterprises and financially dominated by large-scale mills. Interacting strategic value and sectoral logics explicate how the dual state imperatives of *national self-reliance* and *neoliberal development* affect the centralized bureaucratic regulation of textile sectors implementing export-oriented industrialization in the post-Big Bang Liberalization era.[1] Bureaucratic controls on market entry and exit, business scope, ownership, and raw materials up and down the production chain (overseen by coalition governments led by the National Congress Party and the Bharatiya Janata Party [BJP] alike from the 1980s and beyond) compensate for and provide shelter from economic liberalization driven by neoliberal development.

Protections of small-scale handlooms and power looms in weaving and fiber processing, the periodic nationalization or divestment of struggling vertically integrated large-scale textile mills in apparel and clothing

---

[1] See Table 2.4 for sectoral structural attributes.

production, and protracted foreign direct investment (FDI) liberalization and sector-specific tariff structures in trade and distribution are among the governance mechanisms founded on India's melding strategic value orientation of *neoliberal self-reliance*. Illustrated by company case studies, fiscal and regulatory impediments to environmentally friendly technological upgrading characterize the *decentralized governance* of technical textiles. Subnational government interventions reinforce the survival of small-scale industry; and the political dominance of large-scale mills of the central-level sector-specific policies undergirds industrial development up and down the value chain.

The *centralized governance* of textiles and subsectoral variation in governance mechanisms in India, today, are founded on the perceptions that British colonialism destroyed textiles weaved with cotton (hand spun by skilled Indian artisans in rural small-scale enterprises), yet India's global economic integration rests on economic liberalization and deregulation. Chapter 6 has examined how if Mahatma Gandhi is India personified, the Indian textile industry is the symbol of the country's nationalist imagination. The *Swadeshi* movement of national self-sufficiency was founded on the perception that British colonialism destroyed textiles weaved with cotton, which is hand spun by skilled Indian artisans in rural small-scale enterprises. So animating is cotton nationalism, the most recognizable depictions of Gandhi are of him wrapped in *khadi*, which is cloth made from thread spun on an age-old charkha, the hand spinning wheel. Indeed, tracing regulation and development from 1980s and beyond, Section 8.1 of this chapter shows that at a time when centralized market coordination in labor-intensive, less value-added textiles was globally eliminated at the height of the neoliberalism, India created centralized sector-specific bureaucracies under the umbrella management of the Ministry of Textiles.

At times, endowed with resources and regulatory capacity, the textile ministry has both introduced extensive competition and deliberately intervened in market developments. The actual role of the state in market coordination and the dominant property rights arrangements vary by subsector. Firm-level navigation of conflicting economic policies and practices reveals that *centralized governance* unevenly promotes export-oriented industrialization: The elimination of policies that limited the development of large-scale, mechanized textile mills, and continued protections for small-scale handlooms and power looms, as shown in Section 8.2. The textile ministry deliberately coordinates targeted protectionist policies for the "unorganized" sector of less mechanized, small-scale producers and retailers, perceived significant for regime legitimacy and contributions to rural employment.[2]

The highly specified policies have led to overexpansion in labor-intensive handlooms and highly polluting power looms and limited the development of flexibility and variability in design and lean retailing. Technical textiles, in contrast, is under the purview of subnational governments and private economic actors as they navigate central-level technology upgradation schemes and fiscal policies disclosed in Section 8.3. Illustrative company cases, such as technical fabric producer Priyafil, show that policies designed to support small-scale industry incentivize the expansion of power looms and limit the technological advancement and manufacturing scale of Indian technical textiles. Section 8.4 underscores the protracted FDI liberalization in textile trade and distribution, which transpired over two decades after the initial introduction of internal competition in the 1980s.

8.1 STRATEGIC VALUE AND SECTORAL LOGICS: CENTRALIZED GOVERNANCE IN TEXTILES

"The textile industry is important because of India's huge need for employment and growth. The industry contributes massively to GDP and is the second largest employment generator in India, particularly the handloom and power looms," declared R. K. Sharma, former chairman and managing director of the National Textile Corporation (NTC) under the Ministry of Textiles.[3] "Indian handloom is more than a potential global economic force; it is also our identity...how we treat our craftspeople represents our values," exclaimed Laila Tyabji, the founder of Dastkar, a nongovernmental organization founded to connect handicraft artisans and urban buyers.[4]

According to the World Trade Organization's World Trade Statistical Review 2020, Indian apparel and clothing exports rank third in the world. Indian statistics show that the textiles and apparel industry contributes 2.3 percent to India's GDP and accounts for 13 percent of

---

[2] The textiles "organized sector" is typified by large-scale, mechanized mills. Small-scale handlooms and power looms of the informal sector represent the "unorganized," predominately weaving sector.
[3] Interview on February 20, 2013, in Delhi.
[4] See "More Power to Skilled Hands," *The Hindu* (May 5, 2015).

industrial production and 12 percent of the country's export earnings.[5] Importantly, as the second-largest employer in India, textiles provide work for 45 million people. The number of workers, mostly employed by rural small-scale handlooms and power looms dominant in numbers in the Indian textile industry, is expected to rise to 55 million people by the end of 2020.

In the context of the *perceived strategic value* of *national self-reliance* and *neoliberal development,* and existing *sectoral organization of institutions*, government-business relations and regulatory developments in the 1980s paved the sectoral pathway to *centralized governance* today. From central-level textile undertaking acts to the establishment of the state-owned NTC, regular and periodic "revival schemes" emphasized the "social objective" to save textiles. The centralization of market coordination has sustained the coexistence of disparate non-state domestic stakeholders comprising unorganized small-scale enterprises and organized textile mills. Importantly, it has presided over India's "liberalization two-step," which follows market liberalization at the aggregate level with reregulation at the sectoral level.[6]

Regulation up to the late 1980s banned FDI and controlled the production type and volume and prohibited the modernization of large-scale, mechanized mills specializing in fiber-processing and spinning and producing inputs for the "organized" sector. These restrictions curtailed robust participation in global textile chains and the market penetration of global retailers; thus, the Indian textile industry did not fully utilize the quotas of the Multi-Fiber Arrangement (MFA) (and it had already negotiated the exclusion of handloom and cotton industry products) distributed by business associations established before Independence.

In the early 1980s, when the Indira Gandhi government liberalized market entry to permit investment from transnational Indian returnees in technology sectors, such as telecommunications, as shown in Chapter 7, sectoral variation based on interacting strategic value and sectoral logics began to take shape. Gandhi introduced competition in the internal market, which included the loosening of labor laws that introduced temporary and contractual workers. Moreover, the central government intervened in the textile strikes, which lasted for eighteen months between 1982 and 1983 in Mumbai, in favor of large-scale mill owners, congruent

---

[5] See "India's Textile and Apparel Exports to Reach USD 300 bn by FY25: Invest India," *The Economic Times* (January 14, 2020).
[6] Also see Hsueh (2011, 2012).

with the perceived strategic value of national industry in India's *national self-reliance*.

Without the sanctification of the officially recognized union Rashtriya Mill Mazdoor Sangh, nearly 250,000 workers in sixty-five mills in Mumbai participated, becoming the largest work stoppage in India's history. The protesting workers frustrated with Sangh sought better conditions under the leadership of Dutta Samant, who had earlier successfully fought for pay increases at Premiere Automobiles. Representing workers with rising expectations in an ever-shifting political climate, Samant negotiated with mill owners overseeing declining "sick" factories saddled with excess stock.[7] Eventually, the state ended the strikes with the support of mill owners and its long-term alliance with industrialists.

In the aftermath, the state barred mill owners from selling land and granted concessional rates for continued operation of factories. The 1983 Textile Undertakings (Taking Over of Management) Act sanctioned state takeovers in the remaining mills.[8] Many "mill owners discovered it was easier to simply close down the mills."[9] Others pressed for land sales in order to revive the mills. After permission was granted in 1991, however, most mill owners did little to modernize or resume production. With weakened labor unions and labor liberalization leading to the rise of contractual work in the "organized" sectors, the textile industry in Mumbai was no longer a major employment generator.

While there is no clear winner (between mill owners or laborers), the textile labor strikes reinforced the dominance of small-scale industry in the textiles value chain, further aided by expanded reservations in the Handlooms (Reservation of Articles for Production) Act, 1985. "There used to be huge textile mills in Bombay... This forgotten grief destroyed Indian textiles. Mills such as Binny, established during British India, were unable to survive. No one wanted to invest in large mills, so the industry moved to small-scale power looms."[10]

In 1987, the Ministry of Textiles became formally established under Rajiv Gandhi's 7th Five Year Plan, with textile labor strikes and an economy in crisis as the backdrop. The sector-specific ministry's establishment centralized the coordination of the fragmented interests of the various organized and unorganized sectors. The textile ministry instituted

---

[7] See Van Wersch (1992).   [8] Sigeman (1995), 175.
[9] Interview on February 18, 2013 with an Indian Administrative Service bureaucrat.
[10] Interview on January 8, 2020 with Vivek Prabhu, managing director of a synthetic fiber processing enterprise.

mechanisms to enforce the MFA and bilateral trade agreements and opened export windows to promote trade. Rajiv Gandhi also quietly passed a textile policy, which removed restrictions on the capacity of the mill sector. The centralization of separate textile bureaucracies (beneath a single roof) prepared for macro-level liberalization and fore-shadowed sectoral variation in the promotion of industrial restructuring and modernization and the sheltering of the majority of handlooms and power looms.

8.2 APPAREL AND CLOTHING: POLITICAL LEGITIMACY AND RURAL EMPLOYMENT VIA SECTOR-SPECIFIC CENTRAL INTERVENTIONS AND ECONOMIC LIBERALIZATION

Today, the dominant pattern of market governance in apparel and clothing is characterized by central policies in support of "unorganized" small-scale rural sectors, export liberalization, and upgrading and modernization of industrialized mills of the "organized sector." Bureaucratic controls on market entry and exit, business scope, ownership, and raw materials persist through caveats attached to policies and separate compensatory measures to shelter subsectors and market segments from the forces of liberalization. Privately held traditional handlooms and power looms and large-scale mechanized producers comprise the dominant distribution of property rights. The Indian government "views handlooms and power looms as strategic to the survival of Indian textiles because India is still socialized and the government needs to take care of certain segments of society," explained Sharma, formerly of the National Textile Corporation. "If [NTC] doesn't support it, the downtrodden parts of industry will vanish."[11]

The introduction of competition during the Rajiv Gandhi government, which was accelerated in the 1990s, lifted many economic controls on textile mills. As the state began to eliminate trade barriers that protected domestic textiles, at the behest of textile bureaucrats, mill owners, and garment exporters, the textile ministry set up a committee (in 1995) to evaluate the impact of the abolition of quotas in response to the expiration of the MFA and the ATC quota regimes. The government eliminated heavy excise and custom duties on synthetic products. Moreover, the Textile Undertakings (Nationalization) Act, 1995, vested the NTC power

---

[11] Interview on February 20, 2013

to acquire struggling mills to ensure "the production and distribution of different varieties of cloth and yarn so as to subserve the interests of the general Public."[12]

8.2.1 Restructuring Apparel Production: Divestments, Undertakings, and Developmental Turn

"By virtue of being the country's oldest industry, India textiles must adapt to technological changes," explained Vivek Plawat, a Ministry of Textiles bureaucrat and executive director charged with the restructuring and modernization of mills owned by the NTC throughout India.[13] The NTC began reinvesting surplus assets from the closing down of nonperforming state-owned mills into the modernization of its remaining mills and the establishment of new ones.[14] The NTC has also courted global partners through promises to assist them to meet government requirements and procurement processes. Such actions were met with less trade union resistance because of compensation packages and similar efforts from the 1980s onward.[15] The government has also kept a watchful eye on sectarian roots of industrial organization in textiles. Traditionally, Muslims and the Indo-Chinese in Calcutta dominated the leather tannery and dyeing segments, in which the government has largely divested ownership. The government remains cautious of sectarian conflicts when the restructuring of such factories involves worker displacement.[16]

Still, the divestment of government-owned assets in textiles, which has involved prominent developers, has not been without controversy, particularly when it comes to land-related issues. In 2015, controversy arose when Shankersinh Vaghela (the former Minister of Textiles from 2004–2009) and K. Ramachandran Pillai (the former chairman and managing director of NTC) sold Madhusudhan Mill's properties in

---

[12] See Textile Undertakings (Nationalization) Act, 1995.
[13] Interview on February 20, 2013, in Delhi.
[14] Interview on February 20, 2013 with R. K. Sharma, Manager Director, the National Textiles Corporation, in New Delhi.
[15] Interview with Sharma (February 20, 2013).
[16] Interview on May 29, 2013, with Sumeet Mhaskar, Associate Professor of Sociology, Jindal School of Government and Public Policy, in Stanford, California. Also, see Chandavarkar (2009). Recent research findings suggest pro-social behavior toward the "ethnic other" increases with national identification (Charnysh, Lucas, and Singh 2015).

Mumbai, Gandhinagar, Delhi, and Kolkata for "throwaway" prices.[17] The NTC took over the management of the mill during the 1980s strikes and nationalized it under the *Textile Undertakings (Nationalization) Act, 1995*. The mill, sold to the private company Hall & Anderson, came to the attention of the Central Bureau of Investigation, when apartment towers rose in Mumbai.

In the 2000s and beyond, the goals of *neoliberal development* and *national self-reliance* shaped a developmental turn in market governance. The textile ministry more aggressively shifted away from subsidizing losses and focused on affecting industrial restructuring. The 2000 National Textile Policy "de-reserved" small-scale industry from garment manufacturing. It also introduced integrated textile parks and incentivized technological upgrading with a Technology Upgradation Fund Scheme, Textile Modernization Fund, Soft Loan Scheme, and Rehabilitation Fund for workers.[18] Further facilitating the development of the organized sector, import duties and surcharges were reduced for specified textile machinery and custom duties reduced on raw materials. Moreover, the 2001 Finance Bill and the 2003–2004 Union Budget provided fiscal and infrastructural incentives and subsidies to invest in value-added, high-tech production and promote textile and apparel exports.[19] Export-oriented large-scale mills in Special Economic Zones, exempt from customs duties and internal taxes, which are tied to export performance and employment generation, have benefited from these policies designed to promote export-oriented industrialization.

In the early 2000s, the government also reconstituted (for two years) the Development Council for Textile Industry, first established under Section 6 of the Industries (Development & Regulation) Act of 1951. The Official Group for Growth in Textiles formed "to look into financial structure affecting the industry, as well as address the concern of exporters."[20] Importantly, the Steering Group on Investment and Growth in Textile Industry was established and vested with the responsibility to implement policies and programs outlined in the National Textile Policy and to devise further measures if necessary. The high-powered steering

[17] See "Towers Rise on NTC Plot Sold Cheap in Mumbai's Parel; Flats Cost Rs 5cr," *Times of India* (June 24, 2015) and "ED Registers Money Laundering Case Against Former Union Minister Vaghela, Others," *The India Express* (August 3, 2016).
[18] See Ministry of Textiles (MOT) Annual Report (2000–2001).
[19] See Verma (2002) and Tewari (2006) on export competitiveness and post-MFA adjustments in India's textiles and apparel.
[20] See Sinha (2016), 188–189 and quote from page 189.

group brought together the ministerial heads of textiles and other related bureaucracies, such as chemicals and petrochemicals; secretaries of finance, revenue, and banking; the director general of foreign trade; and representatives of industry associations.

Liberalization in market entry has sanctioned private entrepreneurs, such as the Edelweiss Group cofounded by Rashesh Shah, to invest in distressed textile assets. Shortly after the 2008 global financial crisis, Shah acquired a denim manufacturer from Ahmedabad; in 2018, textiles, along with steel, power, shipping, and construction, was one of five top sectors in Edelweiss' portfolio.[21] Since 2009, Edelweiss has invested in and managed the assets of Alok Industries, an integrated textile manufacturer with eleven factories across the country in Navi Mumbai, Silvassa, and Vapi and operating across the value chain, from spinning to home textiles, garments, and retail.

8.2.2 Supporting Handlooms and Power Looms via Liberalization Followed by Reregulation

The evolution of *perceived strategic value* to incorporate a *neoliberal understanding* of India's *national self-reliance* has also focused on coordinating handloom and power looms to "capture India's comparative advantage" in spinning and weaving and in handicraft. Policies to sustain small-scale rural industry have introduced competition and supported the modernization, design capability, and flexibility of small batch production.[22] The Jute Corporation was first established in 1971, and now operates under the textile ministry in jute-producing states of West Bengal, Bihar, Assam, Meghalaya, Tripura, Odisha, and Andhra Pradesh. The Commission for Handicrafts further promotes the marketing and export of handlooms and other textile handicrafts, along with the Powerloom Development Export Council and the Export Council for Handlooms.

Moreover, the Comprehensive Legislation for Minimum Conditions of Work and Social Security for Unorganised Workers of 2007 and the reestablishment of the Khadi and Village Industries Commission (KVIC) under the Ministry of Micro Small and Medium Enterprises soon

---

[21] See "King of Distressed Assets," *Business Today* (April 22, 2018).
[22] Communication with Rajasthan- and Haryana-based garment and textile producers and merchants in 2006 and 2013. See also Tewari (2006) on the modernization of small-scale, unorganized sectors.

followed. The KVIC has administered, at the national and state levels, the Prime Minister's Employment Generation Program and the Interest Subsidy Eligibility Certificate, which adults and institutions registered with KVIC and engaged in such rural industries can apply when in need for financial assistance. The livelihood of handlooms, power looms, weavers, and other related small-scale enterprises dominant in apparel and clothing and the second largest source of employment in India after agriculture falls squarely under the governance of these policies designed to shoulder the effects of economic liberalization on India's small-scale, rural industries.

Notwithstanding liberal and developmental tools to restructure the industry, centralized market coordination includes sector-specific requirements, which have sustained what is perceived as the distinctiveness of Indian textiles in the handloom sectors. These state interventions in labor-intensive, less value-added textiles diverge markedly from India's market governance of high-tech services in information communications technology examined in Chapter 7 and China's extensive deregulation of textiles shown in Chapter 5. The Handlooms (Reservation of Articles for Production) Act, 1985 granted the central government the "power to specify articles for exclusive production by handlooms" and "the power to enter and inspect" and "search and seize" to enforce such regulation with imprisonment and fines.[23] Moreover, the 2001 Textile Order reduced fees and streamlined the purchase of machinery for handloom and power loom sectors. The 2001 textile order also retained the specific orders on hank yarn obligation (HYO), reverse twist (adopted by the *khadi* industry in 1956 to avoid mixing mill yarn), the olive green shade, and marking on textiles. Significantly, the Textile Commissioner "can now insist on markings on the imported textile articles also."[24] Thirty-five years later, in the 2010s, "handloom reservation persists in spite of the common knowledge that most mass-consumed items are produced only on power looms."[25]

On the one hand, these sector-specific interventions are sustained by the nationalist rallying of a large, predominantly low-skilled, rural electorate: "Handlooms are India's strength, not weakness." The National Commission for Enterprises in the Unorganized Sector (NCEUS), which

[23] See full text of The Handlooms (Reservation of Articles for Production) Act, 1985.
[24] See MOT Annual Report (2000–2001), 5.
[25] See "Reservation for Handlooms Makes No Sense," Opinion *The Hindu Business Line* (August 1, 2012).

was established in 2004, estimated that 86 percent of total workers in 2004–2005 worked in the unorganized sector.[26] The number remained above 80 percent in 2018, and during the same period, the number of informal workers in the organized sector rose from 46 percent to 51 percent according to the Ministry of Statistics and Program Implementation's Periodic Labor Force Survey 2017–2018.

What is more, the emotional appeal of Gandhi and Nehru's ideological commitments transcends economic class and political party. In 2015, the online petition "Save Handlooms—Don't repeal the Handloom Reservation Act!" received 15,000 signatories in less than a week, bringing together urban professionals on social media advocating cultural heritage and the low carbon footprint; "the superrich," who can afford artisan handicraft; and the "20 million handloom workers...compared to three million in the IT industry."[27] In this social milieu, the hank yarn obligation, after a reduction in 2003, remained at 40 percent of total weaving yarn for domestic consumption until 2019, when it decreased to 30.[28]

On the other hand, the gap between regulation and actual demand represents the objective versus intersubjective in measures of strategic value. Sanjay Kumar Jain, the chairman of the Confederation of Indian Textile Industry explained in 2019, "The actual cotton hank yarn requirement by the handloom sector is less than 15 percent of the total as per the estimate based on the Handloom Census 2009–10 data. It is estimated that now the requirement for hank yarn would have fallen to about a mere 10 percent of the total weaving yarn produced for domestic consumption." Still that number may be offset by power looms. Taking advantage of the protectionist policies for handlooms, power looms have replaced them in the consumption of the bulk of the hank yarn. In turn, textile mills have also invested in handlooms and power looms.[29]

Table 8.1 shows the high and steady proportion of small-scale industry through the 2010s, despite reduced protections for the handloom and

---

[26] See "Report on Conditions of Work and Promotion of Livelihoods in the Unorganized Sector," National Commission for Enterprises in the Unorganized Sector (August 2007).

[27] Quoted from "Reservation for Handlooms Makes No Sense," Opinion *The Hindu Business Line* (August 1, 2012) and "More Power to Skilled Hands," *The Hindu* (May 5, 2015), respectively.

[28] See "CITI Hails Reduction in Hank Yarn Obligation from 40% to 30% as Historical," *The Textile Magazine* (March 13, 2019).

[29] See Hsueh (2012). Also, see company case studies in this chapter.

TABLE 8.1. *India: Subsector breakdown in cloth production*

Cloth Production

Sector	2010–2011	2011–2012	2012–2013	2013–2014	2014–2015	2015–2016
Mill Sector	4%	4%	4%	4%	4%	4%
Handloom Sector	11%	12%	11%	11%	11%	11%
Power loom Sector	62%	63%	61%	59%	59%	59%
Knitting Sector	24%	22%	23%	26%	26%	26%
% Share	24%	22%	23%	26%	26%	26%

Source: Textile Commissioner, Ministry of Textiles, 2018.

knitting sectors. The proportion of textile mills in cloth production is minuscule and marginal compared to the small-scale industry.

8.2.3 Politics of Sector-Specific Fiscal Policies and the Limited Role of Subnational Governments

"In 1996, the Supreme Court of India ordered the manufacturers to upgrade to greener technology to stem pollution. The Manufacturers Association of Tirupur and its textile mills, the single largest export hub generating a fifth of India's exports, suffered greatly after MFA quotas expired in 2005, yet the mills did virtually nothing and almost closed down."[30] Notwithstanding the court mandate, technology upgradation schemes, modernization funds, and tax incentives to restructure the industry, tax exemptions for "goods of special importance," which cover textile categories of the highly polluting small-scale power looms, have disincentivized investments in technological upgrading and environmental friendly modernization.[31]

Historically, taxes and excise duties varied along the Indian textile supply chain, with the effect of unorganized power loom and handloom sectors avoiding them. The 2003–2004 Budget restructured the fiscal system and extended the Centralized Value-Added Tax (CENVAT) to fabrics and made-ups from the yarn stage. The elimination of exemptions, which included hank yarn, followed the de-reservation of the small-scale industry for the knitting sector the year before and was a boon for the organized textile mill sector. A predecessor to the Goods and Services Tax (GST) of 2017, which unified direct and indirect taxes, CENVAT theoretically equalized taxation among the various sizes of textile enterprises along the supply chain, from large-scale mills to power looms and handlooms producing gray and interlining fabrics and synthetic fibers.

In reality, the implementation of CENVAT incorporated certain market segments and product categories, under taxation, only to include new areas of exemption. To incentivize compliance of the yarn excise by power loom producers, the government eliminated a registration requirement, which lowered the cost to do so. The Indian Cotton Mills Federation (ICMF), whose spinning mill members use power loom products, supported the elimination in order to "bring the vested interests

---

[30] Interview on February 18, 2013, with Rajarashi Datta, Vice President, Srei Infrastructure Finance Limited in New Dehli.

[31] See Harrison et al. (2019) on impacts of tax versus command-and-control regulations.

(traders, master weavers) under the tax," according to the then ICMF Chairman Chintan Parikh.[32] Importantly, anticipating power loom producers' protests that "hank yarns under excise will affect them adversely," the Ministry of Textile's steering group earlier, in 2001, explicitly recognized the potential effects on power looms of the "withdrawal of CENVAT exemption on hank yarn (plain reel and cross reel) of cotton and man-made fibres" and "recommended that CENVAT may be introduced on grey fabric stage of powerloom produced fabrics on an optional basis with a simplified procedure for assessment."[33] Exemptions and credits to gray fabric manufacturers (which tended to be small-scale power looms) stand in 2020, as does the Hank Yarn Obligation after incremental reductions in 2003 and 2019.[34]

In addition to the exemptions from excise and custom duties levied by the central government, subnational governments with the exclusive power to collect sales taxes except on "goods of special importance" designated by the central government did not tax handlooms and power looms.[35] Though the Indian constitution removed the preamble that restricted the states' fiscal powers in 2012, taxing the textile industry was unpopular. In Gujarat, Tarachand Kasat Devkishan Mangani, the Convener of the "Save Textile Struggle Committee" argued that "unlike jewelries, cloth is a necessity...is indispensable."[36] That year, when the state of Karnataka explored taxing the textile industry, the Federation of Karnataka Chamber of Commerce & Industry (FKCCI) stepped in to represent textile mills, small and medium enterprises, and small-scale producers. The FKCCI convinced the state government of the negative impacts of taxes on the industry.[37]

---

[32] See D'Souza (2012), 19.

[33] See former quote from "Cenvat Credit for Textiles May Go," *The Economic Times* (February 11, 2003) and latter ones from "No. S-4/4/2000-TPC (Pt.) Government of India Ministry of Textiles," Office Memorandum of the Ministry of Textiles (November 9, 2001).

[34] See "No Change in CENVAT Rules on Excise Duty for Textile Goods," *Fiber2Fashion* (July 29, 2015). Also, see Indian Budget 2016–2017 on excise duty and CENVAT for made-up articles of textiles and garments.

[35] Relevant laws are the Additional Duties of Excise (Goods of Special Importance) Act, 1957; the Additional Duties of Excise (Textiles and Textile Articles) Act, 1978; and the National Goods and Services Tax of 2017 of the 101th Constitutional Amendment Act, 2016.

[36] See "Textile Industry Has Suffered Loss of Rs 40,000 crore Due to Protests Against GST, Claim Traders," *India Today* (July 14, 2017).

[37] Interview with Vivek Prabhu, Priyafil Group, on January 8, 2020.

"There were the excise tax, central valuation [CENVAT] tax, lots of changes as per cursor to the GST, with pull and pushes from all sides," explained Vivek Prabhu, a Bangalore-based manufacturer of synthetic textiles active in various sectoral associations, including the All India Flat Tape Manufacturers Association and the All India Plastics Manufactures Association. He added, "Even after the GST unified direct and indirect taxes, textile products were protected with an inverted duty structure, which kept prices low. Outputs, such as readymade garments and nonwoven fabric, were taxed at a lower rate (5 percent) than raw materials inputs (18 percent)."[38]

8.2.4 Company-Level Responses in the Context of Sector-Specific Market Governance

Market players navigate market governance structures, which vary by subsector, and negotiate bargains at the subnational state and firm levels. On the one hand, local small-scale textile producers routinely seek national and subnational state protections.[39] In 2018, "the [Haryana] policy is packed with fiscal incentives and contains provisions for infrastructure augmentation, setting up of textile parks, promotion of Khadi industry, and facilities for skill training. It aims at generating 50,000 new jobs by attracting investment in the textile sector to the tune of Rs 5,000 crore," declared Vipul Goyal, Industries and Commerce Minister of Haryana.[40]

On the other hand, mill owners, taking advantage of policies that promote small-scale industry, have invested in handlooms and power looms. Such firm-level responses circumvent worker strikes that have crippled the strengths of textile mills and further support the small-scale industry and policies designed to protect them. The multiple sector-specific exceptions of the CENVAT have also incentivized the organized sector's firm-level backward and forward linkages in the value chain. Protections for small-scale industry have incentivized the mill owners' financial interests in handlooms and power looms. Moreover, taking advantage of the country's multipoint sector-specific tax structure,

---

[38] In March 2020, the Indian government moved to consider equalizing the GST; however, rationalization may adversely affect textile producers by bringing the GST to 18 percent, increasing product prices.

[39] See Jenkins (1999) on the details of bargains between producers and local governments.

[40] See "Cabinet Clears Textile Policy 2018 for Setting Up New Units in Haryana," *Times of India* (February 27, 2018).

Reliance Industries, which was founded on textile trading, parlayed into the manufacturing of textiles and fibers. That business led to investments in plastics and petrochemicals and oil refinery and stages of oil exploration.[41] In these ways, *centralized governance*, which on the surface appears to favor small-scale industry, also reinforces the political dominance of large business groups in India's political economy.

8.3 INDUSTRIAL AND TECHNICAL TEXTILES: TECHNOLOGICAL UPGRADING AND SMALL-SCALE DEVELOPMENT VIA NATIONAL AND SUBNATIONAL POLICIES

Dominated by privately owned small and medium enterprises, including power looms, technical textiles in India operates in the context of market coordination by the central ministry and subnational governments. The more *decentralized governance* entails resource allocations by the Ministry of Textiles through various technology upgradation schemes and by subnational governments and sector and business associations through the establishment of industrial clusters and state-level incentives and subsidies. To promote technical textiles in the context of the state-owned National Textile Corporation's divestment of distressed assets and dormant property, the NTC has engaged in partnerships with global players, including Skaps, Atlantic, and Tejen Japan, for technology transfers and the establishment of mills for technical production.[42] With budgetary independence from the government, the NTC, in 2013, planned to "double its capacity from the existing 675,000 spindles to 1.35 million spindles...the company board...approved diversifying into technical textiles," reported Chairman and Managing Director R. K. Sharma.[43]

The state governments of Gujarat, Haryana, Karnataka, among others, regularly release textile policies, which promote the development of technical textiles. Moreover, state governments oversee industrial

---

[41] Interview on February 22, 2013 with Muralidhar Tsunduru, Government Relations, Reliance Industries, in Delhi. One of the world's most vertically integrated and horizontally diversified groups, Reliance has also found success in retail chains and media and telecommunications. In 2014, Reliance formed a majority joint venture with Chinese-owned Ruyi Science and Technology Group in a partial divestment of its textile and apparel businesses. Also, see "Reliance Industries Ltd to Enter Textile JV with China's Shandong Ruyi," *The Economic Times* (December 10, 2014).

[42] Interview with Plawat (February 20, 2013).

[43] Interview on January 20, 2013. See "'We Will Raise Resources Through Sale of Assets," *The Business Standard* (January 23, 2013).

zones where state-owned and private companies have established manufacturing clusters. In the context of economic liberalization, starting in the 1990s, "Suraz Apparel Park, Brandex Apparel City, and other apparel parks around the country with historical strength in textiles, including Bangalore, have tried attracting Indian entrepreneurs," explained Rajarashi Datta, Vice President of SREI Infrastructure Finance.[44] Illustrative are Karnataka's textile policies of 2008–2013 and 2013–2018, which have incentivized the technological upgrading of the state's ninety-two registered enterprises producing technical textiles.[45]

The 5th International Conference and Exhibition on Technical Textiles (Texchnotex) in 2016, for example, was co-sponsored by the states of Gujarat and Karnataka and organized jointly by the Ministry of Textiles and the Federation of Indian Chambers of Commerce and Industry. Vivek Prabhu, managing director of Priyafil, a family-owned manufacturer of monofilament fabrics, explained that such gatherings represent a "major platform for business meetings between foreign and Indian companies, renewing past relations and generating new business such as joint venture collaborations, technology exchanges, enhancing export and import ties and, of course, attracting investment in the Indian industry."[46]

All the same, integrated textile parks in special economic zones have drawn limited FDI, though multinationals have set up chemical fiber processing plants, such as Dupont in Hyderabad. "Textiles have not attracted even $1 billion in the last 11 years [before 2013] even with 100 percent openness in textiles manufacturing and FDI automatic approval. This is largely due to restrictions in retail regime—no domestic market to tap into. India has an oxymoron policy in textiles, which gives the industry a lifeline but takes oxygen away," Datta added.[47] The retail and trade case study explains this seeming conundrum.

8.3.1 Technological Upgradation and Fiscal Policies: Impeded Modernization and Reinforcement of Small-Scale Industry

The slow growth and development of technical textiles in India exposes the combined effects of the dominance of small-scale rural power looms

---

[44] Interview in Delhi on February 18, 2013.
[45] "New Textile Policy on the Anvil," *The Hindu* (December 21, 2012).
[46] See *The Hindu* (December 21, 2012).
[47] From 2010–2018, India attracted US$1.4 billion in FDI in textiles, according to Statista data accessed on November 4, 2020, from www.statista.com/statistics/1036081/china-textile-clothing-leather-import-export-share-in-global-trade/.

(unlike in China and Russia, the other country cases), high capital requirements of technical textiles, and the low regulatory and developmental capacity of the textile ministry. The Prabhu family-owned Priyafil Group's experiences typify firm-level navigation of national and state policies and the interacting sectoral characteristics in the context of frequent rule changes, uneven implementation, and delays in regulatory enforcement.

The privately incorporated Priyafil, founded in 1972 as a mosquito net manufacturer, currently produces 2.5 million square meters a month of the High Density Poly Ethylene (HDPE) synthetic yarn in a production facility fifteen kilometers outside of Bangalore. Priyafil's power loom vendors weave the HDPE into fish netting, which Priyafil packages and distributes all over India. "I have 70 power loom vendors spread across India using the HDPE produced in our factory 15 miles outside Bangalore. They operate in traditional weaving towns, weaving in silicon, cotton, and polyester. There are big swings in demand, so we are able to offer vendors a steady source of income. I have worked with some vendors for almost forty years, since even before the 1982 union strikes," said Vivek Prabhu, the managing director of Priyafil.[48]

"Ours is the oldest product in the market segment, so there's brand loyalty." To maintain industry leadership, Priyafil applied twice for and received capital and interest subsidies, securing loans from banks on a list of centrally approved financial institutions. In both circumstances, "the bank will take it up to the ministry to let them know that the business has taken a loan, and if we meet all parameters, the ministry will approve the subsidies of 10 percent capital and 5 percent interest."[49] The details of the frequently revised Technology Upgradation Fund Scheme (TUFS) introduced by the Ministry of Textiles, combined with bureaucracy and delayed enforcement of intellectual property rights, however, have discouraged actual technological advancement.

Each time, Priyafil received fewer subsidies for the approved loans than anticipated. "The Modi government made changes in the application process and removed the interest subsidy. Banks are also less involved after shady deals and scandals. Companies are now required to approach the ministry directly." Undeterred, Priyafil expanded production to poly sacks, which the company exported to Africa for a time. The company also hired engineers, who invented a system to produce wefts, now patent pending, before sending to vendors. Unfortunately, Priyafil waited two

---

[48] Interview with Prabhu on December 18, 2019.
[49] Interview with Prabhu on January 8, 2020.

years for a hearing on the company's invention. Because the new system improves existing technology, Priyafil executives "worry some people have already taken it." Even so, "that's a little faster than usual." In the interim, the long wait, coupled with slowed demand and further tax changes, forced Priyafil to suspend poly sacks production.

Fiscal policies have also discouraged technological upgrading and export-oriented industrialization, disproportionately affecting the highly polluting, small-scale rural power looms. The November 2016 demonetization and the Goods and Services Tax in July 2017, both by the Modi government, influenced Priyafil's decision to downsize after investing in export-oriented expansion and technological upgrading. Demand came to a halt when banknote demonetization forced Priyfil's final customers (fishers and farmers), who typically purchase in cash, to transfer to online banking, which squeezed liquidity.[50] "Typically buyers in these sectors invest extra cash to storing products, but now they can't stock."

Then the uneven implementation of GST amplified the market uncertainties produced by demonetization across textile sectors. Because Priyafil's final products comprise outputs of power looms, traditionally not taxed as a function of the *perceived strategic value* of small-scale industry, revised GST rules after organized protests across the country require the government to reimburse 5 percent of final sales.[51] In practice, however, the state has been slow in disbursing reimbursements. "We have waited two and half years for our reimbursement, which amounts to 20 million rupees. Many companies won't survive under these circumstances. Production is down 40–50 percent, and sale is down 50 percent in some region in industry." Also affected are Priyafil's other contractors and middlemen up and down the supply chain. "Agents who book consignments for wholesalers used to visit fabric producers across India. They barely come around anymore."

Figure 8.1 and Figure 8.2 show the technology intensity, as measured by the OECD, of India's imports and exports as a percentage of the total trade volume from 1990 to 2014. The proportion of low-tech exports has fallen; however, it continues to be the largest category of India's exports. Strict rules on retail and distribution as detailed in the trade case study below contribute to why low-tech imports remain modest. Table 8.2

---

[50] See "Demonetisation Lowers Sales, Raises Textile Inventories in Q3," *Business Standard* (October 7, 2019)

[51] The GST Council, in November 2017, revised the tax rate for most textile products to 5 percent, except for luxury apparel at the 12–18 percent rate. "Textile Industry Has Suffered Loss of Rs 40,000 crore Due to Protests Against GST, Claim Traders," *India Today* (July 14, 2017).

TABLE 8.2. *India: Percentage of subsector of total textile exports*

2014–2015	2015–2016	2016–2017	2017–2018	
Readymade Garment	42.0%	43.2%	44.5%	42.6%
Cotton textiles	29.3%	28.3%	26.7%	28.5%
Man-made textiles	14.5%	13.3%	13.2%	13.7%
Wool textiles	0.5%	0.5%	0.4%	0.5%
Silk	0.4%	0.2%	0.2%	0.2%
Handlooms & Handicrafts	13.4%	14.5%	14.9%	14.5%
% Textiles of Total Exports	12.9%	15.0%	14.1%	12.9%

Source: Directorate General of Commercial Intelligence and Statistics, Ministry of Commerce, India (2018).

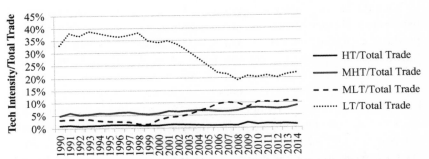

FIGURE 8.1. India: Tech intensity of exports as % of total trade (1990–2014)
Source: World Trade Organization (2017) with OECD Tech Intensity Definition.

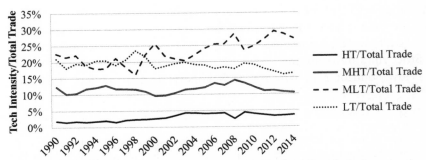

FIGURE 8.2. India: Tech intensity of imports as % of total trade (1990–2014)
Source: World Trade Organization (2017) with OECD Tech Intensity Definition.

shows the size of manmade textile exports versus handlooms and handicrafts. Bearing in mind the large proportion of small-scale power looms, which comprise the manufacture of cotton and technical textiles, and small and medium enterprises engaged in readymade garments, the actual proportion of low-tech, small-scale industry sustaining India's textile exports are likely over 50 percent.

8.4 TEXTILE TRADE & DISTRIBUTION: FDI LIBERALIZATION AND EXPORT PROMOTION VIA SECTOR-SPECIFIC TRADE AND FISCAL POLICIES

Thus far, this chapter has analyzed how *centralized governance* in textiles has followed the roadmap paved before Big Bang Liberalization, which dictated variation by sector as a function of *perceived strategic value* (see historical process-tracing in Chapter 6). Textile trade and distribution, similar to the textile manufacturing governed with economic policies that support small-scale retailers and reinforce the political influence of organized textile mills, is no exception. Even more apparent, the introduction of foreign competition did not occur until the mid-2000s. Restrictions on foreign competition in textile retail trade in the context of economywide liberalization have propelled large business groups and the organized sector to enter and dominate internal markets. For example, similar to Reliance Industries' decades-long backwards and forwards foray in the textile value chain in response to sector-specific market governance, the Birla Group, one of the globe's largest producers of Viscose staple fiber, acquired Madura Garments. With the large business group behind it, Madura has successfully launched four best-selling apparel brands like Louis Philippe, Van Heusen, Allen Solly, and Peter England.

In 2006, more than fifteen years after initial liberalization in high-tech services (as shown in Chapter 7 on telecommunications) and ten years after the approval of FDI in wholesale distribution, the Singh government under the United Progressive Alliance permitted 51 percent FDI limit in single-brand retail of labor-intensive services, including textiles and foodstuffs. Later in 2011, the Cabinet proposed an increase to 100 percent in FDI in single-brand retail and the lifting of the FDI ban on multi-brand retail. After receiving political backlash, in January 2012, the Cabinet legalized 100 percent foreign ownership in single-brand retail pending government approval but declined action on multi-brand liberalization.[52]

---

[52] See Consolidated FDI Policy, Department of Industrial Policy and Promotion, Ministry of Commerce and Industry, Government of India (April 10, 2012).

Though the 2012 Circular stipulated a government route, by 2014, the government permitted automatic approval up to 49 percent for single-brand retail, and by 2020, 100 percent automatic approval.

Following an inter-ministerial group set up by Singh, which advised that more competition would drive down inflating food prices, the government reintroduced FDI liberalization in multi-brand retail. In a September 2012 Press Note, the Cabinet permitted up to 51 percent foreign ownership, with conditions. Subject to final government approval, foreign retailers are required to invest at a minimum of US$100 million and with 50 percent in "back-end infrastructure," defined as "processing, manufacturing, distribution, design improvement, quality control, packaging, logistics, storage, warehouse and agricultural market produce infrastructure."[53] Importantly, foreign operators in both single-brand and multi-brand retail are required to source up to 30 percent from "small industries/village and cottage industries, artisans and craftsmen."

Despite what it may have seemed, however, the domestic content policy does not necessarily promote traditional small-scale industry. To begin with, the 2013 Circular stipulates "industries which have a total investment in plant and machinery not exceeding US$1 million." The valuation was subsequently revised to $2 million, which until 2020 exceeded the maximum size of small and medium enterprises defined by the Micro Small and Medium Enterprises Development Act of 2006.[54] In 2019, the government further relaxed rules by permitting domestic sourcing by global operations and by group companies or third parties.[55] Moreover, for single-brand retailers, domestic content sourced from small-scale industry is preferred but not required.[56]

The move to liberalize FDI in multi-brand retail was supported by large domestic and foreign-invested stakeholders already operating in the retail market, including the Birla Group and German wholesale retailer Metro, respectively. "The Indian market is very large. A $100 million investment in back end for a serious player, who wants to make an impact and create a supply chain, is not much. The investments required are much larger," said Ajay Sheodaan, customer management director, Metro Cash and Carry India Pvt. Ltd., which began operations in 2003. Thomas

[53] Also, see "Walmart: What Happened in India," *Forbes* (October 13, 2013).
[54] "Finance Minister Announces Revised MSME Definitions; No Difference Between Manufacturing and Service Enterprises," *The Economic Times* (May 26, 2020).
[55] See "Sourcing Relief for Single-brand Retail," *The Mint* (August 29, 2019).
[56] See Consolidated FDI Policy, Department of Industrial Policy and Promotion, Ministry of Commerce and Industry, Government of India (October 15, 2020).

Varghese, the chairman of the Confederation of Indian Industry's national retail committee and chief executive of Aditya Birla Retail, concurred: "The government has held extensive stakeholder discussions before forming these criteria. They are agreeable and should not meet with any resistance from international retailers."[57]

Among small-scale producers and retailers that thrive under the new rules and distribution of ownership arrangements governing retail and distribution are foreign-invested, small-batch apparel companies that maximize the adoption of information communications technology.[58] These companies, such as the Hyderabad-based Trupik's Connect App, which allows prior-to-purchase 3D trial of clothes, adopts technological innovations such as artificial intelligence (applying India's strength in software outsourcing). In this milieu, the transnational liberalizing coalition, comprising Indian returnees in technical sectors, plays an important role in the synergy between FDI and technical innovations in textile retail and distribution. So do the Ministry of Micro, Small, and Medium Enterprises and related bureaucracies and political constituencies. For now, FDI is restricted to business-to-business e-commerce, explicitly barring FDI in business-to-consumer e-commerce.[59]

8.4.1 Wither a Developmental State: Trade and Fiscal Policies in Export-oriented Industrialization

The politics of the Scheme of Rebate of State and Central Taxes and Levies on Export of Garments and Made-ups (RoSCTL) and the tariff structure for raw materials and semi-finished products in the manufacturing of critical inputs for technical textiles show how sector-specific economic policies complicate the Indian government's promotion of export-oriented industrialization. Introduced in March 2019 and extended beyond April 2020, the RoSCTL is designed to promote apparel and clothing exports based on credit measures. The Scheme's extension beyond April 2020 is as much about slowed global demand due to COVID-19 and other global events as it is about resilient domestic institutional arrangements.

[57] See "Cabinet Likely to Approve FDI in Multi-brand Retail," *The Mint* (November 23, 2011).
[58] Communication, in 2017, with Trupik founder Vikranth Katpally in Silicon Valley, United States.
[59] See Consolidated FDI Policy, Department of Industrial Policy and Promotion, Ministry of Commerce and Industry, Government of India (October 15, 2020).

"Textile and clothing exports this year were affected by the U.S.-China trade war, EU's struggle with Brexit, and the growing geopolitical tensions in west Asia," explained the chairman of the Cotton Textiles Export Promotion Council K.V. Srinivasan in January 2020.[60] More than that, he further explained, were the 30 percent set for handloom reservations, which needs to be further reduced. Srinivasan further implored that cotton yarn and fabric exports, important segments of the textile value chain, also need to be considered for rebates, levies and taxes, along with made-ups and garments that are 56 percent of India's textile exports.

In response, the textile ministry requested the Cotton Corporation of India, the Texprocil, and the Skill Development Ministry to jointly submit a report on further reductions on handloom reservations.[61] Consistent domestic resistance, however, has made reductions politically infeasible. A gap of more than sixteen years between Hank Yarn Obligation reductions, from 40 percent in 2003 to 30 percent in 2019, can be attributed to the power loom operators' protest against hank yarn's inclusion in the excise net. In 2002, the Power Loom Development and Export Council petitioned the central government to lower the excise duty on the cotton yarn in hank form consumed by power looms and "openly admitted that bulk of the hank yarn was indeed consumed by them."[62]

RoSCT's credit provision addressed the U.S. government's objections of the monetary incentives of previous schemes on grounds of the WTO Agreement on Subsidies and Countervailing Measures. Moreover, the capital investment subsidy, provided by the Amended Technology Upgradation Fund Scheme for which garment and technical textile manufacturers like Priyafil are eligible, serves Modi and the BJP's "Made in India" policy. Yet, it does not solve the problem of the highly polluting power looms subsisting on handloom reservations and suffering during the lowered demand of the COVID-19 outbreak. In this regulatory context, it might seem surprising that India's small-scale industries are only marginally more likely to support the BJP as opposed to those in the highest income bracket and with higher levels of education with higher

[60] See "Hank Yarn Obligation for Textile Mills Expected to Be Reduced Further," *The Hindu* (January 17, 2020).
[61] See "Hank Yarn Obligation for Textile Mills Expected to Be Reduced Further," *The Hindu* (January 17, 2020).
[62] See "Reservation for Handlooms Makes No Sense," Opinion *The Hindu Business Line* (August 1, 2012). See also D'Souza (2012).

support for the BJP.[63] The India-sector case studies reported in this book show that the perceived strategic value of labor-intensive, small-scale industry, represented by Indian textiles, cuts across political parties and time.

Regulatory developments, in August 2020, complicate the export-oriented industrialization of the labor-intensive and low-tech small-scale industry dominating India's textiles value chain. To achieve "minimum government and maximum governance, a leaner Government Machinery and the need for systematic rationalization of Government bodies," the Modi-directed central government abolished in succession the India Handicrafts Board set up in 1952, the All India Handloom Board set up in 1992, and the All India Powerloom Board set up in 1981 and reconstituted in 2013.[64] The center also withdrew textile officials from the governing bodies of the Textiles Research Associations (TRAs). The status change from "affiliated" to "approved" bodies reduced government presence; however, it retained the final approval of the textile ministry in "any disposal, sale, transfer of assets created out of central government grant."[65] Days later, on August 7, the 5th National Handloom Day, the National Federation of Handlooms and Handicrafts led a protest at the Devangapuri handloom cluster, near Chirala in the state of Andhra Pradesh.[66]

Another illustration of how India's tariff structure produces a less-than-developmental export-oriented industrialization is the tariff structure's impacts on the manufacturing of plastics, critical inputs for synthetic textiles (including polymers, such as HDPE, and products made of polymers, such as fishing nets). Increases in import tariffs for raw materials have hurt the predominantly small-scale plastics/chemical-processing sector comprising over 50,000 micro and small units, such as the Prabhu family-owned Priyafil Group, already relatively low tech compared to global counterparts and competing with imports of low-cost polymers from China and South Asian countries. Synthetic textiles is the very subsector that the Indian government's technological upgradation policies

---

[63] See the multiyear panel study ("Lok Surveys") of the Lok Foundation carried out by the Center for Advanced Studies of India of the University of Pennsylvania, in conjunction with the Carnegie Endowment of International Peace. Also, see "Being Middle Class in India," *The Hindu* (December 9, 2014).

[64] See "Resolution No.1/13/2017-DCHL/Coordn/AIHB," Office of the Development Commissioner For (Handlooms), Ministry of Textiles, Government of India.

[65] See "After Handloom, Powerloom Board Scrapped by Govt," *Times of India* (August 9, 2020).

[66] See "Reconstitute Handloom and Handicrafts Boards: Weavers," *The Hindu* (August 11, 2020).

TABLE 8.3. *India: Laws, rules, and regulations governing textile subsectors*

Market Coordination	Property Rights Arrangements
Textiles Writ-Large	
• Ministry of Textiles (1987) • The National Textile Policy of 2000 • Development Council for Textile Industry (2000s) • Official Group for Growth in Textiles • Textile Order of 2001 (streamlined processes retained hank yarn obligation, reverse twist, olive green shade, and marking on textiles) • Steering Group on Investment and Growth in Textile Industry (2002) • Special Economic Zones • Centralized Value-Added Tax (CENVAT) (2004) • Comprehensive Legislation for Minimum Conditions of Work and Social Security for Unorganized Workers of 2007 • Ministry of Micro Small and Medium Enterprises (MSME) (2007) • National Institute of Micro Small and Medium Enterprises (NI-MSME) • Demonetization (2016) • Goods and Services Tax (2017) • Cotton Textiles Export Promotion Council	• National Textile Corporation's rounds of nationalization and divestment of distressed assets and dormant property (1980s and beyond) • Micro Small and Medium Enterprises Development (MSMED) Act (2006) • Intellectual Property Rights
Apparel and Clothing – "organized" sector	
• Textile Undertakings (Taking Over of Management) Act (1983) • Textile Undertakings (Nationalization) Act, 1995 • Textile Modernization Fund (2000) • Soft Loan Scheme (2000) • Rehabilitation Fund (2000) • Special Economic Zones • WTO's Agreement on Textiles and Clothing (2001–2005) • Asset Reconstruction Fund (Textile Mills) • Centralized Value-Added Tax (CENVAT) (2004) • Scheme of Rebate of State and Central Taxes and Levies on Export of Garments and Made-ups (RoSCTL) (2019)	• National Textile Corporation • Cotton Corporation of India • National Textile Policy of 2000 – de-reserved small-scale industry for apparel and clothing (2000) • De-serving of the knitting sector from small scale industry (2003)

Market Coordination	Property Rights Arrangements

Apparel and Clothing – "unorganized" sector

<ul><li>Negotiated Exclusion of Handlooms and Cotton Industry in Multi-Fiber Arrangement (1974–1994)</li><li>Agreement on Textile and Clothing (1995–2005)</li><li>Textile Order of 2001 (streamlined processes retained hank yarn obligation, reverse twist, olive green shade, and marking on textiles)</li><li>Hank Yarn Obligation (40%) (2003)</li><li>Hank Yarn Inclusion in Excise Net/ Elimination Hank Yarn Excise Duty Exemption (2002)</li><li>Centralized Value-Added Tax (CENVAT) (2004) (extended to yarn stage and beyond; added exemptions for gray fabrics)</li><li>National Common Minimum Program of the United Progressive Alliance (2004)</li><li>National Commission on Enterprises in the Unorganized Sector (2004)</li><li>Comprehensive Legislation for Minimum Conditions of Work and Social Security for Unorganized Workers (2007)</li><li>Khadi and Village Industries Commission (and related Prime Minister's Employment Generation Program and the Interest Subsidy Eligibility Certificate</li><li>Commission for Handicraft</li><li>Jute Corporation</li><li>Hank Yarn Obligation (30%) (2019)</li></ul>	<ul><li>National Textile Policy of 2000 – de-reserved small-scale industry for apparel and clothing (2000)</li><li>De-serving of the knitting sector from small scale industry (2003)</li><li>National Commission on Enterprises in the Unorganized Sector (2004)</li><li>Ministry of Micro, Small, and Medium Enterprises (MSME) (2007)</li><li>National Institute of Micro, Small, and Medium Enterprises (NI-MSME)</li><li>Revised definition of micro, small, and medium enterprises (2020)</li></ul>

Nonwovens and Industrial Textiles (including Chemical Fiber and Geosynthetics)

<ul><li>Technology Upgradation Fund Scheme (1999)</li><li>Finance Bill (2001)</li><li>Union Budget (2003–2004)</li><li>Centralized Value-Added Tax (CENVAT) (2004)</li><li>Revised Technology Upgradation Fund Scheme (Various Years) (subsidy revisions, removal of interest subsidy)</li></ul>	<ul><li>National Textile Corporation</li><li>Ministry of Micro Small and Medium Enterprises (MSME) (2007)</li><li>National Institute of Micro Small and Medium Enterprises (NI-MSME)</li></ul>

(continued)

TABLE 8.3. *(continued)*

Market Coordination	Property Rights Arrangements
• State Level Textile Policies (various years) • All India Plastics Manufacturers Association • All India Flat Tape Manufacturers Association • Indian Technical Textile Association	• Revised definition of micro small and medium enterprises (2020)

Textile Trade and Distribution

• Textile Committee on Multi-Fiber Arrangement and Apparel & Clothing Textile trade quotas (1995) • Finance Bill (2001) • Hank Yarn Inclusion in Excise Net/ Elimination Hank Yarn Excise Duty Exemption (2002) • Union Budget (2003–2004) • Power Loom Development Export Council • Export Council for Handlooms • Scheme of Rebate of State and Central Taxes and Levies on Export of Garments and Made-ups (RoSCTL) (2019) • Amended Technology Upgradation Fund Scheme • Abolishment of India Handicrafts Board; • All India Handloom Board; All India Powerloom Board (2020) • Textile Research Association status change affiliated to approved (2020)	• Wholesale 100% FDI automatic approval (1997) • Single-Brand 51% FDI liberalization, government approval, small-scale domestic content requirement (2006) • Single-Brand 100% FDI liberalization, government approval, small-scale domestic content requirement (2012) • Single-Brand 100% FDI liberalization, automatic approval up to 51%, small-scale domestic content requirement (2014) • Multi-Brand 51% FDI liberalization, government approval, small-scale domestic content requirement (2013) • Single-Brand 100% FDI liberalization, automatic approval (2020) • Business-to-Business e-commerce 100% FDI liberalization, automatic approval

TABLE 8.4. *India textiles subsectors: Strategic value, market governance, and development*

Centralized Governance	Dominant Coordination Mechanisms	Dominant Distribution of Property Rights	Development Outcomes
High Strategic Value Small-Scale Industry and Rural Development	**Apparel and Clothing** Centralized coordination of market entry, exit, and business scope by textile ministry via sector-specific fiscal policies and subsidies; periodic divestments and nationalizations of struggling mills; and protection and subsidization of "unorganized," small-scale rural sectors	**Apparel and Clothing** Dominance of privately held, small-scale traditional handlooms and power looms and large-scale mechanized producers.	**Apparel and Clothing** Low tech, highly polluting traditional handlooms and power looms in weaving and fiber processing markets; vertically integrated large-scale mills and garment manufacturers with niche markets in apparel and clothing
Medium Strategic Value Subnational Goals and Industrial Upgrading	**Industrial and Technical Textiles** Centralized coordination of market entry, exit, and business scope by textile ministry via sector-specific fiscal policies and subsidies; and subnational promotion of industrial upgrading and development zones	**Industrial and Technical Textiles** Dominance of privately owned, small-scale producers and large business groups; state-owned mills nationalized during economic and political crises	**Industrial and Technical Textiles** Weak domestic industry with low global market penetration and production of less technologically intensive commodities in industrial clusters of small-scale manufacturers
High Strategic Value Internal Markets and Export-oriented Industrialization	**Trade and Distribution** Centralized coordination of and strict sector-specific tariff structure on imports and exports and rules on market entry, exit, and business scope of FDI in wholesale, single-brand, and multi-brand retail of non-high-tech, labor-intensive goods	**Trade and Distribution** Dominance of privately owned, small- and medium-sized retailers and large business groups; market participation of wholesale and single-brand FDI and up to 51% of multi-brand FDI	**Trade and Distribution** Slowed domestic industrial development and upgrading; low foreign entry and market penetration

and their implementation at the national and state levels have unevenly targeted.[67] "Cheap imports are coming from Bangladesh and Nepal, creating an uneven competitive environment. [In 2016] product demand from the Northeast states is down by almost 50 percent," observed Prabhu, a member of the All India Flat Tape Manufacturers Association.[68]

"The industry is currently witnessing depression in the market, which has led the industry to halt their expansion and investment plans," said Arvind Mehta, chairman of the The All India Plastics Manufacturers Association.[69] "[The] government of India is planning to enforce mandatory BIS standards on raw material. Industry felt that this move would put small enterprises to [a] disadvantage, and allowing imports of semi-finished and finished products—which are made from the very raw materials which are being denied entry by imposing non-tariff barriers to trade (NTBT)—would not be in the best interest of the nation. Industry demanded that both BIS and international standards should be considered at par. This would avoid unnecessary compliance burden on raw material suppliers and at the same time ensure import of safe and quality material."

Table 8.3 shows temporal variation and subsectoral variation in laws and regulations governing textiles, as presented in this chapter. Table 8.4 maps dominant patterns of market governance structures and development outcomes in textiles.

---

[67] Interview with Prabhu on December 18, 2019.
[68] See "TECHNOTEX 2016 Event Report," 5th International Conference and Exhibition on Technical Textiles (April 21 23, 2016).
[69] "Plastics Industry Body Urges Govt for Restructuring of Custom Duties on Imports," *Deccan Chronicle* (December 17 2019).

Russia and Sectoral Variation

Evolution of Resource Security Nationalism and the Rise of Bifurcated Oligarchy

The Strategic Value Framework expects the dominant sectoral patterns of market governance presented in the Russia sectoral and subsectoral case studies to reflect how the degree and scope of *perceived strategic value* interacts with *sectoral structures and organization of institutions*. Longitudinal periodization in this chapter, beginning from sectoral origins of labor-intensive textiles and capital-intensive telecommunications, shows the ways in which Russian state leaders have *intersubjectively* responded to *objective* economic and political pressures. From the Russian Revolution to the Soviet-era military industrial complex and Gorbachev-initiated *perestroika* and *glasnost* and Putin's Russia, process-tracing distinguishes the origins and evolution of the state imperatives of *national security* and *resource management*. On the one hand, the *national security* imperative evolved from the goals of political stability and regime legitimacy in the late Gorbachev and the Yeltsin (1990–2000) to early Putin, Medvedev, and later Putin periods (2000–2020) to focusing on national sovereignty. On the other hand, *resource management* evolved from a focus on national resources (2000–2020) to incorporating the national technology base (2010–2020) as well.

The perceived strategic value orientation of *resource security nationalism*, which emerged, and the sectoral structures and path-dependent sectoral organization of institutions, shape and reshape the *centralized governance* of strategic sectors and *decentralized* and *private governance* of nonstrategic sectors, respectively represented by telecommunications and textiles. The concomitant micro-institutional foundations of capitalism are that of a *bifurcated oligarchy* shaped, on the one hand, by the mass privatization and macroliberalization of the Soviet breakdown, and on the other hand, by the perceived strategic value of *national security* and *resource management* imperatives reinforced by internal and external political and economic crises, including the color revolutions and interventions in Georgia and the Ukraine.

After the fall of the Soviet Union in 1991, the newly formed Russian Federation adopted a "shock therapy" program of privatization, liberalization, and stabilization advocated by the Washington Consensus of the United States, the International Monetary Fund, and the World Bank. Unleashed market forces shepherded in new and old political actors and foreign participation of all stripes.[1] Overnight, new owners emerged to helm newly privatized companies where they previously served as state managers and workers. Joining the market landscape were multilateral and nongovernmental organizations, Western governments, multinational corporations, and direct and portfolio investment, touting neoliberal reforms and the dismantling of the Soviet-command economy and institutions.[2] In parallel, the United States and other Western governments supported President Boris Yeltsin and his precarious hold on political power, which questioned his commitment to democracy against the return of the Communists.[3]

Existing literature debates what followed. On the one hand, without rational legal institutions and the state capacity to enforce the rule of law and regulate equal and fair competition rent-seeking and corruption pervaded.[4] On the other hand, the reorganization of state power and any enhancement of state capacity benefited oligarchic interests and the rising power of a political strongman and his cronies.[5] Other scholarship depicts macrostabilization and fiscal policy outcomes and compliance to federal law and policy as strategic interactions between reformers and other stakeholders, including enterprises and regional governments.[6]

More recent scholarship shows that the centralization of state power is more complex than rent-seeking and capture and has combined liberal and illiberal elements to govern Russia with state-led development.[7]

---

[1] See Aslund (1995), Stiglitz (2001), Barnes (2003b), and Sachs (2005).
[2] See Boone and Rodionov (2001), McFaul (2001), Remington (2001), and Nesvetailova (2005).
[3] See Goldgeier and McFaul (2003) and Fish (2005).
[4] See Sharafutdinova (2010), Aslund (2019), and Gans-Morse (2017).
[5] See Barnes (2003a, 2006) and Rutland (2010).
[6] See Shleifer and Treisman (2000) and Stoner-Weiss (2006).
[7] See Barnes (2006), Gelman and Ross (2010), Gelman (2015), and Wengle (2012, 2015). See Szakonyi (2020) on the role of businesspeople in the context of weak parties in policymaking.

Indeed, the longitudinal sectoral case studies presented in the next three chapters, which disaggregate the Russian economy and examine micro-sectoral level developments, reveal that markets in Russia are currently governed with varying extent of state control and property rights arrangements. What explains sectoral variation in market governance and their impacts on growth and development in the context of macro-level liberalization and reregulation?

The Strategic Value Framework developed in this book explicates the dominant sectoral patterns of market governance with historical evidence presented below. Section 9.1 of this chapter traces historically the emergence of *national security* and *resource management* as paramount goals as state elites are shaped and reshaped by internal and external political and economic pressures through different political regimes (from the Russian revolution to the Soviet era). Section 9.2 shows the political context of national security and resource management and interactions with *sectoral structures and organization of institutions* in the period after Soviet collapse. Section 9.3 situates *resource security nationalism* as the perceived strategic value orientation shaping sectoral variation in market governance during the rise of Vladimir Putin aided by economic and political crises. Section 9.4 previews the centralized role of the state in market coordination and property rights arrangements in defense-origin dual use telecommunications with roots in the military industrial complex, depicted in Chapter 10, and in contrast, the decentralized and privatized textiles, presented in Chapter 11. The rise of *bifurcated oligarchy* in Russian-style capitalism shaped by *resource security nationalism* and path-dependent sectoral organization of institutions is compared with the new capitalisms of the book's other country and sector cases in the conclusion chapter.

9.1 PERCEIVED STRATEGIC VALUE AND IMPACTS OF SECTORAL CHARACTERISTICS (SECTORAL ORIGINS AND BEYOND)

Beginning from sectoral origins of capital-intensive telecommunications and labor-intensive textiles in mid-nineteenth century to the founding of the Soviet Union and through its collapse, emergent are the perceived strategic value of *national security* and *resource management*. Process-tracing identifies the historical roots of state responses to regime insecurities from within and without, in the context of technological requirements and existing governmental capabilities for the defense of national integrity. The *perceived strategic value* orientation reinforced by state elite responses to significant moments of internal and external pressures has shaped and reshaped dominant sectoral patterns of market governance at the fall of the Soviet Union in 1991, through the political crisis faced by Yeltsin, and after the 1998 economic crisis, which led to the rise of Putin and subsequent political centralization.

Textile mills date as far back as 1722 in pre-revolutionary Imperial Russia, which aspired supranational governance as an "imperial, religious, ideological" power over various peoples within a large territorial span.[8] From the beginning, the ownership, machinery, and organization of textile mills in spinning and weaving were predominantly English, not unlike the Indian and Chinese industrial origins during the period leading up to World War I.[9] By the mid-1890s, garment workshops introduced limited division of labor in order to meet deadlines and keep pace with orders.[10] Around the same time, the Great Northern Telegraph Company of Denmark built telegraph lines in Imperial Russia, similar to their work in China during the Qing dynasty.[11]

With industrial origins dating prior to 1917, industrial workers in telecommunications and textiles alike played a notable role in the rise of the Mensheviks and the Bolsheviks, revolutionary torchbearers of the Communist revolution.[12] The "painful and disorienting conditions of the new industrial experience" and the "grievance about the circumstances under which they had been compelled to leave the village" influenced textile workers' belief that "soviet power was necessary in order to solve the economic crisis, not as an end in itself."[13]

After the founding of the Soviet Union in 1917, industrial workers' political significance in the Bolsheviks' response to internal and external pressures propelled the incorporation of *capital-intensive and defense sectors*, whether telecommunications or defense textiles, into the military industrial complex after the New Economic Policy during Stalinization and beyond. What became perceived of strategic value were critical raw materials, such as cotton, chemicals, and steel, for the defense infrastructure of the country. Over time these inputs' relationship to the vast

---

[8] See March (2007), 33–52, on the supranational aspirations of both Imperial Russia and Stalinism, which suppressed civic and ethnic based nationalism.

[9] See Ward (1990), 52–58.   [10] See Weinberg (1993), 42.

[11] See Great Northern Telegraph Company (1969).

[12] See Koenker (1981), Ward (1990), and Weinberg (1993).

[13] See Koenker (1981), 44–45, 253. Also, see "The Fate of a Textile Town," *Moscow Times* (October 31, 2001).

country's *natural resources* became associated with the safeguard and integrity of an imagined homeland. Military production during the World War I witnessed a sharp decline in textile production though some industrial centers refocused to produce military clothing. Lenin's New Economic Policy (NEP) reintroduced managers and specialists and combined market forces and state control, only to recentralize by the end of the 1920s. In early NEP, the textile industry was a lead industry, and wages rose to pre-war level by 1924. The Central Council of Trades Union committed to all-money wages, leaving implementation to the provinces, and the state assumed social services not previously provided.[14]

At the end, textile workers played an important role in the functioning and ultimately dismantling of the NEP. Wage-scale reforms, in 1927, adversely affected older and more disciplined, and skilled workers, leading to "difficulties in the social order" and strikes.[15] Textile workers demanded material improvements and participation in enterprise administration; these demands departed from priorities in centralized planning and production.[16] In the milieu of motivations among new and old stakeholders (workers, functionaries, and revolutionary elites), between 1928 and 1941, the dictatorial and mobilization tactics of Stalin's "revolution from above," however, pacified textile workers, who maintained revolutionary commitments despite their resentments, and disrupted the working class of its cohesion and solidarity.[17]

9.1.1 "The Drive Not for Cotton But for Steel" and Fiber and Synthetic Textiles Designated as Defense

"The drive not for cotton but for steel," beginning with the 1st Five-Year Plan (1928–1932) increasingly distinguished defense textiles from the nondefense apparel subsector, which also played a key role in facilitating

---

[14] See Ward (1990), 158–159.   [15] See Kuromiya (1990), 104.
[16] Koenker (1981), 21. Ward (1990), 18–19 contends that the drift toward centralization was as much ideology as it was the center's inability to manage and coordinate the disparate stakeholders horizontally and up and down the supply chain from cotton to garments.
[17] Kuromiya (1990), 78–125, characterizes the "crisis of 'proletarian identity'" and Stalinist methods to shape it. The "ideology of class war" displaced bourgeois specialists (and the kulaks) and, along with the elimination of the prerevolutionary capitalist market economy, facilitated Stalinist industrialization.

industrialization.[18] Unlike China and India to this day, whereby chemical fiber is classified as technical textiles, Soviet planners managed the research and development and production of chemical fibers and synthetic rubber as basic chemical products. As shown in Chapter 11, this Russia-specific *sectoral organization of institutions* became significant when the Russia Federation designated petrochemicals, which are inputs in technical textiles, as a strategic natural resource for defense security.

By the 1930s and 1940s, Stalinist industrialization focused industrial policy and labor regulation on communications as one of the priority industries, which also included metal, iron and steel, chemicals, mining, oil, and transport.[19] During World War II, what constituted "defense" industry broadened to include not just armament plants, but also any sectors that supplied the military; fiber and synthetic textiles and rubber joined the list in the early 1940s.[20] The production of technical textiles became closely linked to Soviet industrialization. In demand but in short supply were quality manufactures of canvas and rubber protective garments, gloves, and footwear for foundries and metallurgical shops, iron and steel work, railway stoking and engine maintenance, and other jobs in extreme temperatures, such as chemical plants.

In a speech in 1946, Stalin emphasized that cotton, along with metals, fuel, and grains, was one of the bases of the postwar economy.[21] Though concentrated in Central Asia and the Caucasus, areas untouched by the war, cotton production had decreased during the war. Through increased material inputs and incentives for peasant farmers, cotton production grew considerably in the immediate post-war period and outstripped overall agricultural production. To fulfill targets set in the 4th Five-Year Plan, the state created the Ministry of Cotton Growing in 1949. By 1955, cotton cloth made up 85 percent of the textile industry.

The Soviet state sought to expand the textile industry by building new mills in West Siberia, North Caucasus, Uzbek, and other new republics; modernize with automatic looms and textile machinery; and provide more quality raw materials by developing cotton, flax, wool, and synthetic fiber.[22] The Ministry of the Chemical Industry operated state-owned chemical manufacturing enterprises and associated research institutes with equipment provided by the Ministry of Chemical and Petroleum Machine Building. The V.A. Kargin Polymer Research

---

[18] See Kuromiya (1990), 305.   [19] See Filtzer (1986), 146–147.
[20] See Filtzer (2002), 162, 211–212.   [21] See CIA (1956), 15.
[22] See Grigor'ev and Aksentsova (1960).

Institute in Nizhny Novgorod, today under the Russian Ministry of Industry and Trade, became established in 1955 to produce electro-insulating material for the development of the supersonic aircraft. The decisions (in 1958) on the progress of the chemical industry and "On Measures for Ensuring the Comprehensive Production of Cotton of 1959" adopted by the Central Plenary Committee of the Communist Party and planning bureaucracy of the USSR were designed to decrease "the lag behind some industrially-developed capitalist countries."[23] These developments in technical textiles contrast sharply with their post-Soviet decline until sector-specific state interventions in the 2010s, profiled in Chapter 11.

9.1.2 A Civilian Communications Infrastructure within the Soviet Defense Industrial Complex

From the early 1960s, the paramount focus on heavy industry for the military industrial complex shifted to incorporate more of an emphasis on consumer goods. After the atomic bomb in 1959 and Sputnik in 1957, the Soviet state under Nikita Khrushchev (1953–1964) in the 1950s and 1960s enacted de-Stalinization reforms and re-established political ties with the West. The World Festival of Youth and Students in 1957, the Kitchen Talks in 1959 at the American National Exhibition, and the International Exhibition of Consumer Goods in 1961 were cultural spectacles designed to spur internal and external changes. Khrushchev was determined to catch up to the Americans on milk, meat, and butter per person.

Separate from the military and dedicated networks, the Soviet Union sought to develop a civilian telecommunications infrastructure, which comprised city telephone exchanges, the rural telephone network, the long-distance telephone network and the telegraph network, radiofication (the Soviet system of wired broadcasts to home loud speakers), wireless radio and television, and the Soviet postal service.[24] During this time, the Soviet Union helped develop fiber optics, a collaboration with a foreign consortium of manufacturers, which included U.S. West, Japan's KDD, DBP Telekom, British Telecom, Italy's Societa Finanziaria Telefonia, and Australia's OTC.[25] Used mainly for military applications, the program aimed to provide domestic service and establish a high-capacity land-

---

[23] See Titov and Galanin (1960), 11.　　[24] See Lewis (1976).
[25] See Noam (1992), 288.

based link between Europe and Japan. The United States' prohibition of the export of sensitive technology to Russia ultimately aborted the plan. Implemented by the 23rd Party Congress as a mandate of the 1966–1970 Five-Year Plan, the Soviet telecommunications infrastructure operated under a Unified Automated System of Telecommunication (EASS). With the EASS system, the idea was for the Soviet leadership to maintain centralized control of the backbone infrastructure through an integrated switching and transmission facility considered the "primary network," which connected separate traffic networks for specialized functions, referred to as "secondary networks." In practice, EASS was underutilized, with telegraph, telephone, radio and TV distribution, and data transfer networks very rarely using common facilities, the satellite communications separate from the rest, and the telegraph systems partially integrated.[26] Antiquated equipment and procurement from a variety of foreign suppliers further exacerbated the gap between the vision and reality, resulting in *Minsviaz*, the telecommunications monopoly provider for civilian use, ignoring EASS.

The Soviet state security KGB and the military had their own separate, underutilized telephone, telegraph, and satellite networks. The military and dedicated networks used by government ministries and the Communist Party also tended to be more modern and efficient than civilian ones.[27] As an important consumer of input equipment manufactured by the Soviet military industrial complex and the telecommunications monopoly, *Minsviaz* depended on the defense industrial ministries. Because these ministries prioritized serving Soviet military and security services, the *Minsviaz's* weak bargaining position severely affected its ability to operate the other government and civilian networks.

The path "from Sputniks to panties" was anything but smooth as ministries competed for funding and government demand under Khrushchev to design and produce nukes and submarines.[28] Vast financial and physical resources were allocated to defense sectors located in resource-rich places in the USSR remote from the reach of invaders to produce equipment for battlefields and peacetime alike.[29] There were concentrated resources for war, but the Soviet government could not provide enough incentives for farms and plants to produce consumer goods. Khrushchev promised to listen to regional governors and created a party committee in industry and agriculture, but reformers felt

---

[26] See Campbell (1995).   [27] See Kelly, Salamon, and Grassman (1992).
[28] See Goldman (1963).   [29] See Gaddy (1996).

threatened by institutional reforms (such as term limits in 1961). The assassination of Lavrentiy Beria, the minister of national security under Stalin, orchestrated by Khrushchev's coup in 1953, had provided impetus for elites pursuing self-interest over reform.

Ultimately, during the leadership of Leonid Brezhnev, the fear that what occurred in 1968 in Prague Spring could happen in Russia put an end to economic liberalization, however poorly executed. On the one hand, the discovery of oil for extraction in the 1970s halted attempts at producing consumer goods and increased reliance on oil revenues for the import of consumer goods and inefficiencies in the labor market. On the other hand, also facilitated by loans from the U.S. government, the 1972 Grain Deal under Brezhnev, which purchased American wheat, feed grains and soybeans and was largely negotiated in secret with privately held companies, significantly scaled up trade relations with capitalist countries.[30]

"Those years under Brezhnev saw little incentives to change the old system. Russia had the oil economy to rely on to provide capital for import of consumer goods from the late 1960s into the 1980s. The political regime became much more oppressive and the five-year plans provided little information for micro-level operation. Failure was inevitable for Gorbachev as he did not have enough information on the economy due to succession of artificial plans," explained Andrei Yakovlev of the Higher School of Economics in Moscow.[31]

9.1.3 Sectoral Market Governance under *Perestroika* and the Collapse of Light Industries

In the 1980s, party leaders of the post-war generation, personified by Mikhail Gorbachev, sought to modernize the Soviet system in the context of geopolitical competition between the USSR and the United States. From 1985–1991, under Gorbachev, the Soviet leadership introduced liberal political and economic reforms, *glasnost* and *perestroika*, respectively. The USSR and the United States' renewed arms race and attempts at arms control cooperation to end the Afghan war, in addition to the massive loans that kept the Soviet economy afloat, influenced planned targets in sectors connected to the heavy and defense industries as well as transportation and communication.

---

[30] See "Soviet Grain Deal is Called a Coup," *New York Times* (September 29, 1972).
[31] Interview in Moscow on June 10, 2015.

Telecommunications was an important link between many of the issues up for reform, including pricing, research and development, the reweighing of civilian/military priorities, the attitude toward technology transfer, and Soviet relations with its allied nations.[32] At the start of *perestroika*, however, the Soviet telecommunications infrastructure was technologically outdated and did not adequately connect state branches and state and society. Nor did it meet the requirements of the USSR's superpower aspirations. In a 1985 meeting of the assembled *Minsviaz* leadership, Gorbachev related the unsatisfactory relationship between EASS and the secondary networks and sought to better integrate and fulfill different government branches' network requirements. By the end of the decade, however, the vision of converting to digital switching and transmission with economies of scale under the EASS system was never realized. The KGB's operation of several systems under different director- ates facilitated its attempted coup in 1991, during which Gorbachev was cut off.[33]

In parallel, *perestroika* decentralized planning in light industries and food production, introduced independent accounting at the enterprise level and subjected directors to election by their workers.[34] To modernize industry in order to compete with the United States, economic reforms incorporating market mechanisms, such as permitting new ownership structures, began to reorganize the role of the state in market coordination well before the collapse of the Soviet Union. Not perceived to constitute a strategic component of the Soviet military industrial com- plex, the textile industry was one of the first to undergo economic liberalization.

Notwithstanding market reform and the new economic realities, the *perceived strategic value* of technical textiles as an important input for industrialization and defense continued to shape the role of the state in market coordination and the nature of property rights distribution. Even while permitting new ownership structures and introducing market mech- anisms in supply chain coordination in apparel and clothing and more labor-intensive textile sectors, the five-year plans of the 1980s introduced a chemical investment program to increase national industrial production from the 1975 level of 6.9 percent to 8 percent by 2000. To support the industrial policy, the State Research Institute for Chemical Products (now State Research Institute of Organic Chemistry and Technology) was

---

[32] See Campbell (1995). [33] See Campbell (1995).
[34] See Ellman and Kontorovich (1998).

founded in 1985. The 12th Five-Year Plan (1986–1990), for example, favored investments in agro-industrial, fuel and power, and machine-building complexes.[35]

By the late 1980s, the system of self-financing and application of "market rationality" to modernize and restructure production and create a more flexible labor market, and the related stoppages and production cutbacks, greatly affected both labor-intensive and capital-intensive textile sectors.[36] The breakdown of the command system of supply-allocation led to a general contraction of output and shortages of materials and components throughout the industry. Moreover, large swaths of high-skilled workers left their jobs at state enterprises for cooperatives. Inflation and deepening shortages witnessed the predominantly female, low-skilled labor in light industries, such as textiles and apparel, leave the workforce entirely. The accelerating collapse of economic ties between enterprises, and shortages of labor, on the one hand, and of synthetic fibers, thread, wool, linen, leather, dyes, and other materials, on the other hand, reinforced each other.

The insolvency of the noncompetitive and inefficient, in addition to the dismantling of the centralized coordination of sectoral economic activity in the regions without prompt replacement, resulted in factory closures across regions in the textile industry. The devolution of planning led to a surge in wages while weakening the ministries' capacity to regulate production, leading to imbalances in supply and consumer demand and government receipts and expenditures. Gorbachev's removal of the Party from economic management under *glasnost*, in 1988, furthered weakened regulatory enforcement and inspired political pressures from below in the form of national protests in the Baltics and the Caucasus.[37]

By 1989, the textile industry suffered acute shortages due to the supply situation, further exacerbated by sale restrictions imposed by the republics. The Ministry of Light Industry attempted to sign bilateral agreements with other republics to barter raw materials for finished cloth in 1990. The demoted State Committee for Light Industry, which replaced the All-Union Ministry of Light Industry, with much of its regulatory capacity devolved to the republics, however, could not enforce them.[38] Gorbachev's presidential edict to guarantee supply contracts in 1991 at 1990 levels had no effect as the foundations of economic coordination between different government branches and industries crumbled further,

---

[35] See Ellman and Kontorovich (1998).   [36] See Filtzer (1994), 49–55.
[37] See Ellman and Kontorovich (1998), 22.   [38] See Filtzer (1994), 139.

and protectionism of the regions intensified. The Soviet leadership responded with crackdowns. However, such efforts to reintroduce central controls did not stop leaders in the republics from abandoning the Soviet leadership.[39]

Table 9.1 maps the evolution of the *perceived strategic value* of *national security* and *resource management* to internal and external pressures faced by state elites across significant moments of national political development. Analysis begins at the developmental origins of modern industry in our main composite sector cases.

9.2 POLITICAL CONTEXT OF NATIONAL SECURITY AND RESOURCE MANAGEMENT (1990–2000)

The driving *perceived strategic value orientation* prevalent during the introduction of competition and reorganization of administrative management, part and parcel of market reforms begun by Mikhail Gorbachev in the late-Soviet period and through the state centralization initiated by Vladimir Putin two decades later, are rooted in and reinforced during significant historical moments of political consolidation, as shown in Secton 9.1. Scholars, government officials, corporate executives and managers, and leaders of business and sector associations alike emphasize the impact of feudal Russia and Soviet-era thinking on the *perceived strategic value* in today's Russia of industrial sectors associated with *national defense* and *resource endowments*.[40] Also analyzed are the effects of *sectoral structures and organization of institutions* on the role of the state in market coordination and distribution of property rights.

After the founding of the Russian Federation in 1991, outside the most sensitive civilian/security overlaps, the Yeltsin years through the mid-1990s witnessed foreign direct investment and Western participation in military/industrial conversions and infrastructural modernization, including telecommunications mobile networks. "The term conversion was in vogue at the time inside military industry circles. During Soviet times, CNPO (Central Scientific Production Conglomerate) Vympel was one of the largest structures in the military-industrial complex charged with the creation of an anti-missile defense," explained Dimitry Zimin, founder of

---

[39] See Kotkin (2001) and Filtzer (1994), 138.
[40] Indepth interviews in Russia, Silicon Valley, and Washington, D.C. between 2010 and 2021.

TABLE 9.1. *Russia: Perceived strategic value and resource security nationalism (1850–1980s)*

Sectoral Origins and Beyond	Telecommunications 1890s First Telephone Network		Textiles 1890s First Mechanized Textiles	
Perceived Strategic Value	*External Pressures*	*Internal Pressures*	*External Pressures*	*Internal Pressures*
Defense Security	• World War I • German invasion of 1941 • World War II • Cold War geopolitics • Prague Spring (1968) • Fiber optics development with foreign nations and firms (1960s) • Renewed arms race with U.S. (1980s)	• Russian Revolution (1910s) • Calls for import substitution industrialization (1920s) • Assassination of Lavrentiy Beria/Khrushchev's coup (1953) • Sputnik (1957) • National network integration/ modernization (1980s) • Perestroika (1985) • KGB-led Coup (1991)	• Stalinist Industrialization • World War II • Cold War geopolitics • National protests in the Baltics and the Caucasus (late 1989/ 1990)	• Russian Revolution (1910s) • Central Council of Trades Union and All-Union Textile Syndicate (1920s) • Stalinist Industrialization • Famines (incl. 1946–1947) • Post-WWII industrialization • 4th Five-Year Plan (1945–1950) • 12th Five-Year Plan (1986–1990) • Perestroika (1985)

(continued)

TABLE 9.1. (*continued*)

Sectoral Origins and Beyond	Telecommunications 1890s First Telephone Network	Textiles 1890s First Mechanized Textiles
	• Kitchen Talks (1959) • 1972 Grain Deal • Cold War geopolitics • National protests in the Baltics and the Caucasus (late 1989/1990)	• Kitchen Talks (1959) • World War II • 1972 Grain Deal • Bilateral raw material bargains between Soviet republics (late 1980s)
Resource Assets	• "From Sputniks to panties" • Defense and dedicated networks in resource-rich oblasts[a] • Discovery of oil for extraction (1970s) • *Glasnost* (1985)	• "From Sputniks to panties" • Discovery of oil for extraction (1970s) • *Glasnost* (1985) • Edict on supply contracts (1991)

[a] Oblasts are administrative regions in Russia and the former Soviet Union.

mobile network operator VimpelCom, now VEON, one of Russia's largest privately owned mobile service providers.[41]

In contrast to telecommunications mobile services, however, "the Russian government never privatized fixed-line because it was traditionally viewed as a military/security issue," said Olga Bychkova of the European University of St. Petersburg.[42] The Russia Federation inherited the Unified Automated System of Telecommunication (EASS) under the control of the military, though one unified telecommunication fixed-line network running on the same cable never actually functioned as envisioned when it first was erected in the 1960s.

"Oil and gas were not considered a security issue at the founding of the Russian Federation. The government gave them away until it took them back. But the oil pipelines, a strategic military asset, operating on land still owned by the state, were always owned and produced by the state. Huge windfalls in profits and property rights over land and pipes make it easier for the state to retake oil and gas. At the end, no asset grabbing by the government took place in telecommunications like what took place in oil and gas. Regional fixed-line networks were already owned by the state, and compared to oil and gas, mobile profits aren't that huge," Bychkova explicated.

Nevertheless, how the introduction of competition and privatization of the various specialized and civilian networks unfolded reveals that even those rewarded with radio frequencies to run mobile networks without existing stakeholders were formerly closely connected to the military-industrial complex. "Mr. Zimin [of VimpelCom] built his company, the first to list on the New York Stock Exchange in the post-Soviet era in 1996, based on his relationship with decision-makers. Whether it was VimpleCom or Megafon, the founders needed connections because of the need to acquire licenses," elaborated Sasha Galitsky, a venture capitalist and IT entrepreneur who began his career as a Soviet space engineer.[43]

In the summer of 1998, a financial crisis afflicted Russia, followed by a marked economic downturn. Soon thereafter, in 1999, Russia experienced a period of political uncertainty with the December parliamentary elections and impending changes and replacement of Yeltsin. "After the 1998 crisis, new Russian elites began to think about Russia's future....

[41] See Zimin (2007), Chapter 5.   [42] Interview on June 17, 2015, in St. Petersburg.
[43] Interview on June 17, 2015 in Moscow. See Zimin (2007) on VimpelCom's run-ins with state authorities on gifts to officials and licensure and spectrum issues in the early 2000s, shortly after Putin's election. Also, see Sharafutdinova (2010) on crony capitalism and Gans-Morse (2017) on business demand for property protection.

Increase in oil prices provided incentives for different groups to catch up old rents produced by oil, leading to internal competition for control over important sources of rent," said Yakovlev.[44]

Vladimir Putin became the acting president in 1999, after Yeltsin's resignation, and then president in 2000, with the help of the father of privatization, Anatoly Chubais. Immediately, Putin set out to reconceptualize what must be done for Russia to achieve national development, including in science and technology.[45] After a decade of unregulated markets with corporate and state asset stripping, civil society and government bureaucracy alike supported Putin's call to consolidate state power.[46] Putin and the strange bedfellows that he assembled "recognized that 'weak state' constraints led to a serious failure to the country. They concluded it was best for them to restore the state, which became the basis for Putin's selectorate. Putin's rise to power would have been impossible without the complicity of elite groups who also wanted to restore the state," stated Yakovlev.[47]

"First generation oligarchs who sought policy influence collided with Putin. Second generation ones are less powerful and less targeted by the administration," explained Alexey Klaptsov, a director of a Moscow-based investment fund. In addition to the oligarchs outside of defense and natural resources sectors who have benefited from their patronage of Putin, political support for Putin has centered on those connected to the budget in the middle (pensioners, doctors, bureaucrats, and teachers). In the next two decades, decrees, laws, and regulations to control and manage the direction of foreign investment, nationalize companies, and clarify the role of state corporations enhanced the government's role in market governance, which varied by sector.

9.3 RISE OF RESOURCE SECURITY NATIONALISM AND SECTORAL VARIATION (2000–2020)

The political context of *national security* and *national resources* as paramount to *perceived strategic value* in the post-1991 period is shaped and reshaped by the external and internal pressures faced by state elites, as

---

[44] Interview on June 10, 2015, in Moscow.

[45] Interview with Irina Dezhina, Research Group on Science and Industrial Policy at Skolkovo Institute of Science and Technology, on June 11, 2015, in Moscow.

[46] Interview with Alexey Klaptsov, director, SPRING/Halcyon, on June 11, 2015, in Moscow. See Wengle (2015) on the centralizing role of the state in the liberalization and privatization of electricity.

[47] Interview with Andrei Yakovlev, professor at Higher School of Economics, on June 10, 2015, in Moscow.

TABLE 9.2. *Russia: Political context of national security and resource management (1980–2020)*

Perceived Strategic Value	External Pressures	Internal Pressures
National Security *Political Social Stability/ Regime Legitimacy* (1980–2000) *National Sovereignty* (2000–2020)	• Washington Consensus, the International Monetary Fund, and the World Bank (1990s) • Multilateral and nongovernmental organizations, Western governments, multinational corporations (1990s) • FDI and Western participation in military/ industrial conversions (1990s) • Oil price fluctuations (late 1990s, 2010s) • Asian financial crisis (1997–1999) • Color Revolutions (2000–2005) • Russo-Georgia War (2008) • Arab Spring (2010–2012) • Edward Snowden's revelation of the U.S. National Security Agency's PRISM program (2013) • Crimea annexation/ intervention in Ukraine (2014) • U.S. presidential election (2016) • Russian military-sponsored computer hacks/ intervention in U.S. elections (2016s and beyond)	• *Glasnost* and *perestroika* (1985–1991) • Imbalances in supply and demand, sale restrictions, and factory closures (late 1980s) • Breakdown of cross-oblast supply chain (late 1980s) • National protests in the Baltics and the Caucasus (1988) • KGB attempted coup (1991) • Collapse of the Soviet Union (1991) • Inflation and financial crisis (1992) • Loans for shares scheme (1996) • Reelection of Yeltsin (1996) • Financial crisis (1998–1999) • Political uncertainty (1999) • Resignation of Yeltsin (1999) • Election of Putin as president (2000–2008, 2012-current) • Putin as prime minister (2008–2012) • Political protests in response to legislative electoral irregularities (2011) • Demonstrations against fraud in presidential and regional elections (2012–2013) • "Safe Internet League" (2012)

(continued)

TABLE 9.2. *(continued)*

Perceived Strategic Value	External Pressures	Internal Pressures
Resource Management *Natural Resources* (2000–2020) *National Technology Base* (2010–2020)	• FDI and Western participation in military/industrial conversions (1990s) • Oil price fluctuations (late 1990s, 2010s) • Asian financial crisis (1997–1999) • Global financial crisis (2008) • Uncertainty of global oil demand (2010s) • Edward Snowden's revelation of the U.S. National Security Agency's PRISM program (2013) • Accession to the World Trade Organization (2012) • Crimea annexation/intervention in Ukraine (2014) • Western sanctions (post-Crimea/2014) • "Gray imports" and competition from China, Turkey, Central Asia, and CIS countries • Chinese investments in oil and petrochemicals (2010s) • COVID-19 global pandemic (2000-)	• Inflation and shortages of hard currency (early 1990s) • Acute shortages in raw materials and supply inputs (early 1990s) • Breakdown of supply links (early 1990s) • Loans for shares (1996) • Financial crisis (1998–1999) • Supplier debt and bank loan defaults and hostile takeovers by economic rivals (1998) • Cheap oil (2010s) • Election of Putin as president (2000–2008, 2012-) • Putin as prime minister (2008–2012) • Medvedev's modernization program, incorporating central control and market tools and actors • Depreciation of ruble (post-2014) • Sochi Olympics (2014)

shown in Table 9.2. The perceived strategic value of *resource security nationalism,* in the context of globalization, are reflected in the rules and regulations concerning the role of the state in market coordination and property rights arrangements affecting strategic and less strategic sectors from 1990 to 2020 (Table 9.3 and tables in the sectoral case chapters). Regulatory centralization began to take shape in the late 1990s and after

TABLE 9.3. *Russia's resource security nationalism: Law and political economy*

Globalization	National Security	Resource Management
• Liberalization, privatization, and stabilization of the Russian Federation (1991) • Russian Temporary Statue on Communications (1992) • Law on Foreign Investment of 1999 • Federal Law No. 57-FZ "On the Procedure of Foreign Investments in Economic Entities Strategically Important for National Defense and State Security" (2008, amendments 2011, 2013) • Medvedev's modernization program (2008–2012) • Accession to World Trade Organization (2012) • WTO Basic Telecommunications Agreement (2012) • "Open Door Policy" of automatic FDI approval up to 10% (Pre-2014 Crimea) • Speeches to Kremlin and Federal Security Service linking Crimea and Color Revolutions (2014–2015)	• SORM [System of Operational Investigatory Measures] (1996, various updates) • Information Security Doctrine (2000) • National Security Concept of 2000 • Law on Communications of 2004 • Concept for Long-term Socioeconomic Development of the Russian Federation (2007, 2012) • Federal Law No. 57-FZ "On the Procedure of Foreign Investments in Economic Entities Strategically Important for National Defense and State Security" (2008, amendments 2011, 2013) • Federal Law No. 174-FZ on the Promising Research Fund (2012) • "On information, information technologies and protection of information" No. 149-FZ (2006, 2012, various updates) and creation of "Internet Blacklists" • Speeches to Kremlin and Federal Security Service linking Crimea and Color Revolutions (2014–2015) • National Security Strategy (2015) • Anti-Terrorist Law (2016) • Initiatives to Control the Internet (2010s)	• National Security Concept of 2000 • Presidential decree on strategic enterprises and joint-stock companies (2004) • Long-Term Socioeconomic Development of the Russian Federation (2007, 2012) • Government Commission on Monitoring Foreign Investment (2008) • Federal Law No. 57-FZ "On the Procedure of Foreign Investments in Economic Entities Strategically Important for National Defense and State Security" (2008, amendments 2011, 2013) • National Security Strategy (2015) • "Sovereign Internet Law" (2019)

Putin's election, with effects beyond the telecommunications backbone infrastructure. Putin released, by presidential decree, the National Security Concept of 2000 and tasked the Center for Strategic Development, founded by German Gref, the Minister of Economics and Trade and one of the liberal reformers in Putin's first cabinet, to charter the "strategic vision" for Russia.

Telecommunications became designated as a strategic sector, along with the "defense-industrial complex" and national resource deposits, for national development.[48] The government introduced laws and regulations on communications and anti-terrorism, which intensified state control of information dissemination. In May 2008, the central state merged the telecommunications ministry with the agencies for the management of media and mass communications. Incidentally, the bureaucratic centralization took place a couple of months before Russian troops crossed the Georgia border in support of separatists in South Ossetia and Abkhazia. The Russo-Georgia War became the first in history in which military action and cyber and information warfare occurred simultaneously.

Shortly before the end of Putin's first presidency, he tasked Gref in 2007 to update the strategic plan. The resulting Concept for Long-Term Socioeconomic Development of the Russian Federation envisioned Russia as one among top-five world economies and a leader in technological innovation, global energy infrastructure, and global finance. "The Concept places Russia in an international context, where the rest of the world is treated either as a reference point or a vehicle for achieving its goals."[49] Even before the 2008 financial crisis forced the Concept's revision in 2012, the ministers of finance and economic development disagreed on the financial costs of actual implementation. The Concept was premised on a 6 percent annual compound economic growth rate; the reality was a low of -11 percent and high of 6 percent between 2007 and 2012.

During the 2008–2009 financial crisis, around the same time "liberal economies" nationalized struggling companies in critical sectors, such as the United State's bailout of automakers, Putin declared, "If things continue moving in this direction, we will be obliged to take steps to protect

---

[48] See decree No. 24 National Security Concept of The Russian Federation (January 10, 2000), Russia Ministry of Foreign Affairs.
[49] See Kuchins, Beavin, and Bryndza (2008).

our own interests."[50] Dmitry Medvedev, who was president-elect at the time, concurred: "In concrete situations the state should determine for itself what is necessary to keep and what needs to be freed and what should be returned so as to ensure economic stability."[51] The day before Putin stepped down as president in May 2008, he signed the Federal Law No. 57-FZ "On the Procedure of Foreign Investments in Economic Entities Strategically Important for National Defense and State Security" ("Strategic Enterprises Law").

Named as strategic were forty-five activities, which included cryptographic services, publishing and printing, radio and television broadcasting, and telecommunications, alongside natural resources, defense, energy, aircraft and aerospace industries, and critical infrastructure. Foreign investment was limited to less than 50 percent for foreign private investors and less than 25 percent for foreign state entities on all listed activities with the exception of "subsoil" mining activities, whereby the limits were less than 25 percent and 5 percent, respectively. Government approval must be obtained per "transaction" in the identified activities "of strategic importance to the country's defense and national security," and every time foreign investors acquired a 5 percent or greater interest in designated strategic companies, including those with the rights to natural resource deposits.[52]

That same year the establishment of the Government Commission on Monitoring Foreign Investment, which comprised of Medvedev and central-level ministers, prevented foreign investors from gaining control of lucrative assets and were expected to limit opportunities for corruption and arbitrary decision-making and at the same time limit the ability of Russian companies to sell their assets without government permission. "The government doesn't want FDI in even privately owned Russian businesses because it is easier to control them," said Klapstov.[53] The commission's enforcement of the Strategic Enterprises Law affected foreign investment in privately owned telecommunications operators of previously liberalized mobile services.

---

[50] See quote by President Putin in a press conference in Abu Dhabi, September 10, 2007, reported in "Russia's New Law on Foreign Investment in Strategic Sectors and the Role of State Corporations in the Russian Economy," Akin Gump Strauss, Hauer, and Feld (October 1, 2008).

[51] See "Interview Transcript: Dmitry Medvedev," *Financial Times* (March 24, 2008).

[52] See "The Law on Foreign Investments in Russian Strategic Companies," *Hogan Lovells* (2011).

[53] June 11, 2015 interview in Moscow with Klapstov.

9.3.1 Innovation for Innovation Sake: Medvedev's Modernization Program and WTO Accession

Initiated in the early Putin period and rolled out under Medvedev as the new president was the new Russian vision for "modernization." Medvedev's modernization program launched during the 2008 global financial crisis was touted as innovation for the sake of innovation and incorporated market tools, such as venture capital funds and public-private partnerships, which included the establishment of the Skolkovo Institute of Science and Technology in 2011.[54] The general mood among liberal reformers who supported Putin was for Russia to engage the global economy. Openness rather than protectionism was viewed as the best way for technological innovation, leading to Russia's World Trade Organization (WTO) entry in 2012.[55]

The 2011 update of the Strategic Enterprises Law retained telecommunications as a strategic sector and excluded a few banking activities to ensure Russia's WTO accession. The level of protectionism did not exceed what were already protected sectors, such as the 28 percent foreign investment ceiling in finance. Regulatory centralization and the multistep reorganization of fixed-line Rostelecom to centralize state ownership and management of an integrated backbone infrastructure empowered the control of information dissemination in the context of political opposition, as shown in Chapter 10. Moreover, State-funded venture capital firms invested in strategic high-tech areas, such as Rusnano in nanotechnology (see Chapter 11).

Putin issued several decrees, in 2012, on what he expected going forward. "By 2015, Russia will have in world publications a reach of 2.41 percent, debated among the scientific community...now around 1 percent. Universities pushed and obligated to increase this indicator becomes like a fetish," Irina Dezhina of the Skolkovo Institute of Science and Technology explained.[56] The need to strengthen advanced manufacturing, like that of the Germans and Americans, became urgent. Customize and localize became the first steps with the need to improve higher education expressed at highest levels.

---

[54] See Indukaev (2020).
[55] Interview with Natalya Ivanova, deputy director at the Institute of World Economy and International Relations of the Russian Academy of Sciences, in Moscow on June 10, 2015.
[56] Interview in Moscow with Dezhina on June 11, 2015.

9.3.2 Political Protests, Rising Oil Prices, and Reinforcement of Strategic Sectors in Post-WTO

In spite of Russia's WTO accession in 2012, economic liberalization halted in parallel to increases in oil prices in the 2010s. Moreover, political protests, beginning with those in December 2011 in response to legislative electoral irregularities and continued into 2012 and 2013 with demonstrations against fraud in presidential and regional elections alike, became the pretext for political retrenchment. Pro-government TV and news media reported mainly pro-Kremlin protests funded by the state and spread propaganda and misinformation via social media to counter dissent and opposition fomenting on the Internet. Moreover, during the December 2011 elections, prosecutors in Moscow accused GOLOS Association (Movement for Defense of Voters' Rights), the only Russia-based election watchdog organization independent of the Russian government, of conducting a negative campaign against an unnamed political party, believed to be United Russia, the ruling political party with Putin as the de facto head. Pro-Putin media further accused GOLOS of receiving funding from the United States Agency for International Development (USAID).

The Russian elite focused on confronting what were perceived as defense challenges. Even before the Crimean intervention, the Russian government passed Federal Law No. 174-FZ on the Promising Research Fund in 2012. The research and development (R&D) fund assumed the risk and finances of the development of "military, special, and dual-purpose technology." All the same, Russia fulfilled 50 percent of its WTO commitments until political issues surrounding Ukraine stopped the process, in addition to derailing Russia's engagement with the big seven OECD countries. "While the military-industrial complex sectors are declared strategic, prior to Crimea there was an 'Open Door Policy' to attract FDI even in strategic sectors, with approval required for investment of 10 percent or more," explained Nikita Lomagin, Rector and Professor of European University at St. Petersburg.[57]

9.3.3 Crimea Annexation, Western Sanctions, and National Technology Base as Resource Management

In speeches to the Kremlin in March 2014 and to the Federal Security Service in March 2015, Putin explicitly connected Russia's annexation of

[57] Interview with Lomagin on June 15, 2015, in St. Petersburg.

Crimea with the color revolutions and the Arab Spring, which, he reiterated, were engineered from the West, namely, the United States.[58] "Putin enjoys consensus at the highest level in the military, political, and market branches for his grand vision of what are imminent threats to Russia," said Lomagin. Ministries and agencies as well as Duma deputies, the Russian Orthodox Church, conservative political organizations and think tanks, and regional politicians supported political intervention in the Ukraine.[59]

Then Western sanctions against Russia after the annexation of Crimea led to the depreciation of the ruble in the post-2014 period. The National Security Strategy, approved on December 31, 2015, responded along the lines of the *perceived strategic value* orientation to underscore the development of "the defense industry complex as the motor for the modernization of industrial production" and "the creation of strategic reserves of mineral and raw-material resources."[60] The National Security Strategy specifically targets the agricultural-industrial complex; pharmaceutical industry; high-tech sectors, including space and nuclear energy; heavy machine building; aircraft manufacturing and instrument making; and the revival of electronic and light industries, shipbuilding, and machine tool manufacturing. It further calls for an import substitution strategy to reduce dependence on foreign technologies and industrial product.

In essence, the *perceived strategic value of resource management* extended to the national technology base and centralized the state's management of market actors. The textile case studies in Chapter 11 show that in the 2010s and beyond, directed financing to large, well-connected producers of geosynthetics and manmade fibers, which cheap oil and defense imperatives after Crimea help to sustain, characterizes the dominant pattern of market governance in more defense-oriented sectors of nonstrategic industries.[61] New rules and regulations concerning the business scope of telecommunications value-added service providers and

---

[58] See "Mediaforum nezavisimykh regional'nykh I mestnykh SMI [Forum of Independent Regional and Local Mass Media]," Prezident Rossii (April 24, 2014); "Obrashchenie Prezidenta Rossiiskoi Federatsii [Address of the President of the Russian Federation]," Prezident Rossii (March 18, 2014); "Security Council Meeting," Prezident Rossii (July 22, 2014); and "Zasedanie kollegii FSB [Meeting of the FSB Collegium]," Prezident Rossii (March 26, 2015).

[59] See Pallin (2017) and Lomagin (2012).

[60] SeeRussian Federation Presidential Edict 683 on December 31, 2015 approved the text of "The Russian Federation's National Security Strategy."

[61] See "Globalization Can Save Russia's Light Industry," IQ HSE IU (February 6, 2014).

consolidated state ownership and management of backbone infrastructure in Chapter 10 are also representative. Not to be outdone, charging forward toward a Russia-centric state-managed Internet (RuNet) is the proposal by Rostelecom, in early 2020, to establish a government-owned online ecosystem as the digital economy project of the thirteen state-centric National Projects, a political centerpiece of Putin's fourth term. The ecosystem aims to protect users from technologies, which "can significantly affect economic development and social stability and carry risks of...spreading fake news and negative influence from foreign organizations."

The proposed ecosystem includes the creation of state-run messengers, gaming services, browsers, and operating systems in addition to state-controlled content recommendation systems and speech and gesture recognition and virtual and augmented reality technology. Skepticism abounds in the still relatively liberal market environment of the IT/software sector (as shown in the IT/software case study in Chapter 10), where there are existing solutions developed by private Russian technology companies. "There's a high probability of a completely useless waste of funds," predicted Karen Kazaryan, Public Policy and Government Relations Analyst at the Russian Association for Electronic Communications.[62]

9.4 STRATEGIC VALUE FRAMEWORK AND SECTORAL PATTERNS OF MARKET GOVERNANCE

"What is valued deep within the Russian soil is this idea that individuals sacrifice for the nation. Bolsheviks came and gave national purpose. This is the continuity in Russian thinking. Goals are for the nation, not commercialization. People are willing to work for the nation even at the expense of efficiency," elaborated Fuad Aleskerov of the Higher School of Economics in Moscow.[63] This chapter has shown that *national security* and *resource management* are of paramount *perceived strategic value* and that state elites from the Soviet era to Putin's Russia responded to internal and external pressures to govern industrial sectors with different technological requirements and organization of institutions.

---

[62] See "Russia Proposes Internet Ecosystem to Protect Users From 'Foreign Influence'— Report," *Moscow Times* (February 6, 2020).
[63] Interview on June 9, 2015, in Moscow with Fuad Aleskerov, distinguished professor of mathematics, Higher School of Economics.

The next two chapters systematically examine regulatory and market developments in telecommunications and textiles in Russia to substantiate the analytical leverage of the Strategic Value Framework. How much of the economic and security nexus shaping market governance, today, is a legacy of the Soviet military-industrial complex, and how much of it is rooted in historical values born of internal and external pressures confronted by state elites across different regime types? The longitudinal case studies of the dominant patterns of market governance in telecommunications and textiles in Russia, today, sharpen our understanding of the intersubjectivity of the economic and security nexus. Moreover, as a hybrid political regime, the Russia-sector cases allow us to examine the relative weight of political institutions versus path-dependent sectoral institutions on market governance structures. The inclusion of the Russian cases also probes the role of international norms and organizations in shaping market governance.

Since Soviet collapse, the state has exercised *centralized governance* in telecommunications, perceived strategic for *national security* and *resource management*. The twists and turns of fixed-line liberalization and reregulation witnessed the federal government consolidating centralized ownership and management of civilian landlines under regional governance in addition to the dedicated landlines historically managed by the defense military complex. Centralized market coordination also presides over predominantly privately owned mobile and value-added service providers operating in fiercely competitive markets.

In contrast, various lower-level bureaucracies and non-sector-specific economywide rules regulate previously state-owned enterprises, privatized in the post-1992 period, in telecommunications equipment, which is perceived less strategic since the state already owns and manages backbone infrastructure. Information Technology (IT)/software, a sector not associated with defense security bureaucracies yet benefiting from former science and technology personnel of the Soviet military-industrial complex, has experienced *regulated governance*. Private enterprises and local governments coordinate markets regulated by economy-wide rules, and Russian software companies tap into outsourcing markets in the Commonwealth of Independent States (CIS) and Europe. In the face of perceived security threats from within and without after economic crises and conflicts with neighboring countries, however, the state has increasingly intervened to control the information infrastructure in IT/software and telecommunications.

Perceived not to be strategic for *national security* and *resource management*, the textile industry was among the first sectors to experience

TABLE 9.4. *Perceived strategic value and sectoral patterns of market governance: Russia*

Industrial Sector	Telecommunications	Textiles
Perceived Strategic Value	Strategic for *national security*, with defense orientation as military-industrial complex remains in the shadows, for information control in Putin era; strategic for search for national vision in post-1998 economic crisis, which consolidated Putin's power, strengthened in the aftermath of 2011 social protests and 2014 Crimea annexation	Strategic for *local and regional development* as local authorities gained economic control as early as the mid-1980s during *perestroika;* strategic for *resource management* are petrochemicals, raw material inputs for technical textiles, designated a "core asset" in the face of Western sanctions post-Crimea in the mid-2010s
Sectoral Structural Attributes	Capital intensive, complex interactive technology, producer-driven commodity chain	Labor intensive, linear technology, buyer-driven commodity chain
Country-specific Sectoral Organization of Institutions	During the Soviet Union, spatial geographic organization of institutions dictated locations of industrial and resource strength; and military and civilian telecommunications networks were centrally managed. In Russian Federation, dual use and infrastructural sectors remain state-owned and/or with strong state imprints, enabling information control of the Internet; devolution of state R&D organs led to private equipment makers and brain drain.	During the Soviet Union, spatial geographic organization of institutions dictated locations of industrial and resource strength; and separate subsector-specific ministries regulated textile sectors; these ministries centralized under Ministry of Atomic Energy and Industry during *perestroika.* In the post-Soviet era, the creation of the Ministry of Industry and Trade subsumed the atomic ministry; in the 2000s, separate departments regulate textiles and clothing and capital-intensive technical textiles.

(continued)

TABLE 9.4. *(continued)*

Industrial Sector	Telecommunications	Textiles
Dominant Patterns of Market Governance	*Centralized Governance* (Basic and Value-added Services) *Regulated Governance* (non-defense Telecoms Equipment)	*Private Governance* (Apparel and Clothing) *Decentralized Governance* (Technical Textiles)
Coordination Mechanisms		
Level of State Control	Central goals; central-level ministry and regulator	Local goals; local bureaucracies
Issue Scope	Sector-specific rules and regulations on market entry and business scope	Economy-wide rules and regulations on market entry and business scope
Distribution of Property Rights	Diverse and various ownership structures in mobile and value-added services and telecommunications equipment; state-ownership of fixed-line networks	Diverse and various ownership in clothing and apparel; subnational state-owned and partially privatized enterprises dominate in technical sectors, and limited FDI across sectors

decentralization under Gorbachev's *perestroika*. Mass privatization after the breakup of the Soviet Union further reenforced the *decentralized governance* pattern dominant in apparel and clothing. Apparel and clothing factories shut down or privatized to former managers only to languish with antiquated equipment. Today, Russian textile and garment manufacturers are outcompeted by illegal imports from China and other CIS countries. Industrial and technical textile sectors, which incorporate oil and petrochemicals and higher technological intensity, in accordance with the interacting strategic value and sectoral logics, experience state intervention from central and regional governments in response to political and economic pressures, such as oil boom and bust cycles and Western sanctions in post-Crimea annexation. The central government has designated petrochemicals a critical input for chemical fiber processing and provides fiscal incentives to develop technical textiles. Local governments have worked with local and national oligarchs to revive former factories and production lines, and courted foreign direct investment.

Table 9.4 summarizes the dominant sectoral patterns of market governance shaped by the interacting effects of Russia's *resource security nationalism* and sectoral structures and organization of institutions. It outlines how perceived strategic value and sectoral characteristics during significant moments of internal and external pressures shape coordination mechanisms and distribution of property rights in strategic and less strategic industries, represented by telecommunications (Chapter 10) and textiles (Chapter 11), respectively.

National Security and Infrastructure and Resource Sectors

Centralized Governance in Russian Telecommunications

The Strategic Value Framework's interacting strategic value and sectoral logics hypothesize that the higher the *perceived strategic value* of a sector, the more likely the state will intervene to coordinate markets and dictate the nature of property rights; and that *sectoral structures and organization of institutions* shape actual goals and the methods employed.[1] Having identified the origins and evolution of Russia's *perceived strategic value* orientation in the preceding chapter, the cross-time sectoral and subsectoral case studies, in this chapter, expose the *perceived strategic value* of defense origin infrastructural sectors, represented by telecommunications, for *national security* and *resource management*, and the path-dependent effects of the Soviet military industrial complex. After Soviet collapse, even as the state enacted mass privatization and macro-level liberalization, *centralized governance* by the Russian government characterized market coordination and the property rights arrangements in telecommunications.

Vladimir Putin's responses to internal and external pressures from democratic protests and economic crises to military interventions in Georgia and Ukraine have reinforced the dominant sectoral pattern of market governance in telecommunications. On the one hand, illustrated by company case studies, the federal government consolidated the regional ownership and management of civilian networks and the dedicated landlines (historically managed by the Soviet military) in one corporate entity. Centralized market coordination of the predominantly

---

[1] See Table 2.4 for sectoral structural attributes.

privately owned mobile and value-added service providers operating in fiercely competitive markets maintain the state control and manipulation of information for regime legitimacy and authoritarian rule. This has entailed state interventions in foreign equity ownership and content and traffic on the Russian Internet (known as the RuNet). On the other hand, the strategic value and sectoral logics at the subsectoral level shapes the more *decentralized governance* of telecommunications equipment and IT and software services. In the mid-2010s, however, state retrenchment of information infrastructure in the name of *resource security nationalism* threatens to reregulate previously liberalized sectors.

At the founding of the Russian Federation, foreign direct investment (FDI) surged in telecommunications. The new government sought to dismantle central planning and ownership and convert equipment production from military to commercial purposes. Today private domestic and foreign-invested mobile and value-added service providers serve competitive markets in Russia and the CIS (Commonwealth of Independent States). Yet, because the Soviet Union operated fixed-line networks for both civilian and defense use, the *perceived strategic value* of military sectors and the *existing sectoral organization of institutions* led the new country to retain ownership of the patchwork of regional landlines in spite of the massive privatization underway. The defense-industrial complex has also shaped how privately- and state-owned domestic equipment makers invested in defense-oriented technologies, such as satellite-based telecommunications, and the development of IT services staffed by former defense sector workers.

"National security is perceived as the red line and telecoms has a military, security side."[2] The Russian telecommunications case studies show the interactive effects of the strategic value and sectoral logics in the context of state elite decisions-makers' responses to economic and political crises in the aftermath of macro-level liberalization. Contemporary external and internal pressures include the loans for shares and global financial crises, democratic protests, and Russia's external interventions of neighboring countries as shown in Section 10.1. This laid the groundwork for *centralized governance*, whereby the state centralized regulatory enforcement to modernize and retain majority state ownership of wireline infrastructure and control information dissemination.

---

[2] Interview on June 15, 2015, in St. Petersburg with Nikita Lomagin, Rector and Professor of European University at St. Petersburg.

This has occurred in the name of *national security* and *resource management* in the context of fierce competition and variegated property rights arrangements.

Section 10.2 traces the two-decade process of liberalization and reregulation in fixed-line services, during which the state consolidated control of state-owned but regionally fragmented telecommunications networks. A sector-specific central ministry and presidential-level foreign investment monitoring agency next intervened to restrict the level and scope of foreign ownership in mobile services, as shown in Section 10.3. The section also analyzes the micro-management of content and data storage of value-added services operating the RuNet, which was designated a national security imperative by Putin.

Section 10.4 on non-defense telecommunications equipment shows that non-sector-specific economywide rules by the commerce ministry regulate private enterprises predisposed to Russia's traditional dominance in defense-oriented dual-use applications. The subsector examination of IT services, informed by the companies TerraLink and First Line Software, reveals an extensively liberalized context of *private governance* affected by state restrictions on data in post-Crimea annexation. The analytical leverage of differentiating the market coordination and ownership dimensions of market governance demonstrates the lack of rules and interventions concerning ownership structures does not adequately measure the Russian state's encroaching control of telecommunications in post-Soviet globalization and development. Rather, the Strategic Value Framework identifies when and how the Russian state has found other effective market coordination tools to achieve national security and resource management imperatives.

10.1 STRATEGIC VALUE AND SECTORAL LOGICS: CENTRALIZED GOVERNANCE IN TELECOMMUNICATIONS

The market transition launched by the founding of the Russian Federation introduced new state and non-state economic stakeholders to the economy and telecommunications was not unaffected. In response to the 1998 and 2008 economic crises, the 2011–2013 social protests, and the 2014 Crimea intervention, historically rooted *perceived strategic value* for *national security* and *resource management,* measures for which Russian telecommunications scores high, has influenced state goals and methods. *Sectoral structures and organization of institutions* further shape the actual extent and scope of the state in market coordination and distribution of property rights across subsectors. The *centralized governance* of Russian telecommunications today has sought to achieve infrastructural modernization, network integration, and the control of information. A supraministry regulates business operations and content provision of telecommunications basic and mobile services, and separate departments of the commerce ministry, that of defense and non-defense telecommunications equipment. The state owns and operates backbone infrastructure and oligarchs and FDI dominate mobile, value-added, and equipment sectors. Compared to other large developing countries, including China and India, Russia has scored far ahead in access to telephone lines (ground and cellular) (Figures 7.1 and 7.2) and individuals using the Internet (Figure 10.1), and later, in secure Internet servers (Figure 10.2).

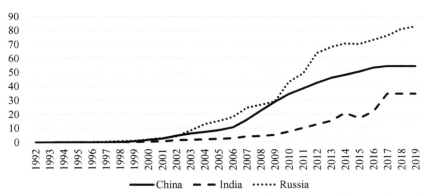

FIGURE 10.1. Individuals using the internet (% of population), China, India, and Russia (1992–2019)
Source: International Telecommunication Union (ITU) Statistics (2021).

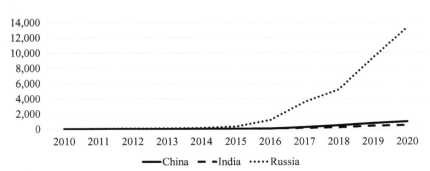

FIGURE 10.2. Secure internet servers (per 1 million people), China, India, and Russia (2010–2020)
Source: Netcraft (http://www.netcraft.com/) (2021).

10.1.1 State Ownership of Defense-Civilian Networks in Context of Macro-Level Liberalization

In the waning days of the Soviet Union, *perestroika* reforms merged the equipment and service ministries to modernize and expand telecommunications networks. In June 1991, following constitutional reform, the recently centralized telecommunications ministry, *Minsviaz,* corporatized the telecommunications monopoly and established the state-owned joint-stock company Sovtelekom to operate civilian fixed-line networks. The *Minsviaz* had operated an all-Union monopoly that extended across fifteen Soviet republics connected by the Unified Automated System of Telecommunication (EASS), set up in the 1960s, to integrate defense and civilian networks. In practice, EASS never realized seamless integration, as discussed in Chapter 9. After the founding of the Russian Federation in December 1991, the market reform program led by Russian and Western economists and international financial institutions separated postal services and equipment production from telecommunications and restructured the interregional, oblast-level, and local telecoms operators with the intention to corporatize and privatize them.

The State Property Committee of Russia established the state-owned enterprise Rostelecom, which took charge of long-distance and international connections. The state-owned telecommunications holding company Svyazinvest, established in 1994, held the assets of Rostelecom and those of regional networks.[3] Without the notice of foreign investors, however, Svyazinvest preserved the state's controlling ownership of the incumbent nationwide backbone operator and incumbent interregional and local carriers and permitted only non-controlling shares of the state-owned fixed-line networks to be sold for profit. Moreover, the *Minsviaz* liberalized market entry in bypass networks but did not issue new licenses for the crisscrossing wireline networks, which had served the military-industrial complex and the civilian population.[4]

---

[3] See presidential Decree No. 1989 "On Specific Features of State Management of the Public Switched Network in the Russian Federation" (October 10, 1994); Government Resolution No. 1297 (November 25, 1994); and Government Resolution No. 742 (July 24, 1995), Russian Federation Central Government.

[4] Interview on June 17, 2015, in St. Petersburg with Olga Bychkova, professor of the European University of St. Petersburg. Also, see Campbell (1995).

10.1.2 Weakened Regulatory Authority in the 1990s and Regional Monopolies in Mobile Services

The Russian Temporary Statue on Communications, in 1992, stipulated that a license was not required by *Minsviaz* for any departments not connected to the utility network and that the *Minsviaz* did not have a regulatory role in tariffs in specialized services markets, such as cellular connection and value-added services.[5] A decree further permitted any state or private enterprise to operate mobile services, a market in which there were no incumbents. The elimination of *Minsviaz's* authority in investment planning, tariff setting, and service operation left mobile network licensing the *Minsviaz's* main instrument for exerting control over industrial development.

Discretionary licensing initially favored regional state-owned incumbents at the expense of infrastructural modernization as new service providers and their foreign joint venture partners were confined to operating bypass networks or last mile/international connections. Partial privatization, which involved foreign investors, in 1994, enhanced the market power of incumbent carriers in fixed-line services. FDI mostly served as strategic investors without controlling shares. Aside from urban industrial centers, where FDI competed in international termination, the scope of foreign participation remained limited. Under these auspices, M-Bell, the joint venture between Moscow Local City Network and Bell Canada, operated the ISKRA network, which extended across the country and formerly served Communist Party Officials, to connect internationally.[6]

With the fixed-line networks in the hands of regional bureaucratic stakeholders, *Minsviaz* licensed privately invested interregional and regional mobile carriers. This occurred in parallel with the loans for shares scheme presided over by Anatoly Chubais in 1996, which, in addition to securing Yeltsin's re-election, enabled the banking oligarchs' accumulation of industrial holdings. The results were the establishment of regional monopolies in mobile services under the control of competing state-owned and nonstate oligarchic holdings. The Alfa Group and Sistema, two leading industrial groups led by banking oligarchs, and other private-capital firms invested in the fixed-line and mobile networks of major cities, international gateways, and value-added services.

---

[5] Interview with Bychkova (June 17, 2016). Also, see Campbell (1995), 207–228.
[6] See Kelly, Salamon, and Grassman (1992).

10.1.3 State Retrenchment in Telecommunications Regulation after Financial and Political Crises

Throughout the 1990s, taking advantage of the distribution of mobile frequencies, oligarchic groupings came to control new infrastructural development when they invested in mobile and value-added services, subsectors not already under state-controlled, partially privatized inter-regional fixed networks, and the incumbent local network operators. Near the end of the decade, however, when financial crisis shook up the oligarchy that had dominated Russian politics and economics, supplier debt and bank loan defaults led to hostile takeovers by economic rivals.

Ownership swaps and mergers and acquisitions notwithstanding, the 1998–1999 economic crisis did not immediately transform the market landscape in telecommunications.[7] With the oligarchic tycoons aggressively competing with one another in lobbying the Duma and providing direct services to members of the government for influence on politics, telecommunications policymaking remained haphazard under the weakened *Minsviaz*.[8] Investment and network planning, which are critical for an industry characterized by high asset specificity and complex interactive technology, puttered along slowly and fell in the hands of rival holding groups with more concern for increasing market share than network integration.[9]

If the 1998 financial crisis alone did not reshape the market landscape monopolized by a select group of oligarchs, the political transition from Yeltsin to Putin in 2000 did in the name of the financial crisis. The *perceived strategic value* of telecommunications as an important national economic asset in the post-1998 financial crisis interacted with the *sectoral structures and organization of institutions* and shaped how the state regained and reinforced centralized ownership of fixed-line networks and consolidated control over information dissemination.

10.2 FIXED-LINE SERVICES: NETWORK INTEGRATION AND INFRASTRUCTURE CONTROL VIA REGULATORY CENTRALIZATION AND STATE OWNERSHIP

The Putin era in the 2000s and beyond witnessed state retrenchment in telecommunications, consolidating state ownership and operations of the

---

[7] See Barnes (2003a) on the impact of the 1998 economic crisis on Russian politics.
[8] Nesvetailova (2005) on political dynamics of oligarchy.
[9] Yakubovich and Shekshnia (2012).

backbone infrastructure under one centralized company in ways that the EASS never achieved. The reorganization of state authority over the telecommunications infrastructure involved the corporate centralization of Svyazinvest and the subsequent merger of Svyazinvest and Rostelecom, mergers and acquisitions of regional networks, and the issuance of new rules and regulations to control information dissemination. Restrictions on FDI and the expanded regulatory purview of the telecommunications bureaucracy further consolidated state control of market entry and exit.

The twists and turns of centralized network integration began in 2001, with the mergers of local fixed-line operators. Seven regional incumbents under the OJSC Svyazinvest umbrella integrated the patchwork of inefficient, regional fixed-line networks, uniting seventeen territorial centers of long-distance communications and TV broadcast. Shortly thereafter, a 2004 presidential decree on strategic enterprises and joint-stock companies included telecommunications service providers under both state and oligarchic control. The Communications Law of 2004 further protected Rostelecom's monopoly in long-distance and the government's role in regulating telecoms ownership, radio frequencies, and IP telephony.[10] That same year, Putin merged the ministries of communications and transportation, only to separate them and consolidate state power over all forms of communication, including the post, under the Ministry of Communications and Mass Media. In 2006, Rostelecom took control of the Internet backbone infrastructure.

Under the auspices of the 2008 financial crisis, the government reorganized the Ministry of Communications and Mass Media and created the Ministry of Telecommunications and Mass Communications. The Strategic Enterprises Law of 2008 (No. 57-FZ), also discussed in Chapter 9, revised the Law on Foreign Investment of 1999 to strictly regulate foreign investment in forty-five strategic activities, which now included "transactions" in natural resources, defense, media, and natural monopolies, such as telecommunications, to safeguard Russian companies of "strategic importance for national defense and security."[11] The Svyazinvest Holding Company became fully nationalized after partial privatization of noncontrolling shares in the 1990s. The following year, in 2009, Rostelecom delisted from the New York Stock Exchange (NYSE) after its initial public offering over a decade

---

[10] See Alexander (2004).
[11] See "The Law on Foreign Investments in Russian Strategic Companies," *Hogan Lovells* (2011).

earlier.[12] Shortly before Russia's World Trade Organization (WTO) accession in 2012, Rostelecom listed on the Moscow Exchange.

In its WTO accession protocol, Russia agreed to implement the WTO Basic Telecommunications Agreement even as the 2011 update of the Strategic Enterprises Law of 2008 excluded cryptographic operations of banks, but retained telecommunications as a strategic sector.[13] After the WTO entry, Medvedev signed a decree in 2012 that reorganized Rostelecom through the takeover of Svyazinvest, merging interregional fixed operators with Rostelecom. Rostelecom continued to restructure to strengthen government control, increase efficiency, and expand into other market segments of telecommunications services. Before its full dissolution in 2013, Svyazinvest centralized landline networks in one company. That same year, TransTelekom, a subsidiary of state-owned Russian Railways and one of the largest networks in the world of fiber optical cables, also completed the corporate centralization of all regional subsidiaries.

Upon the state's consolidation of backbone infrastructure, Rostelecom entered other subsectors. The Ministry of Defense allocated the state-owned operator frequencies for the creation of fourth-generation wireless networks in 2011. The next year, the Rostelecom acquired Sky Link, which held GSM second-generation mobile licenses for 76 regions in Russia covering 90% of the population. In 2014, the company consolidated its role as one of Russia's top mobile service providers when it teamed with Tele2 Russia to provide nationwide services. Rostelecom transferred all its mobile assets to the joint venture, reaching 45 percent ownership. A year later, Rostelecom obtained full control over Globaltel, the exclusive operator of global satellite communications system Globalstar in Russia. The state intended to retain control of corporate governance; at the time, the Presidential Press Secretary Dmitry Peskov stated that the head of the Presidential Administration, Sergei Ivanov, would become the head of the Board of Directors.[14]

Figure 10.3 shows the increase in fixed-line subscriptions when the Communications Law of 2004 protected Rostelecom's monopoly position, and Rostelecom took control of Internet Service Providers (ISPs) in

---

[12] See "Delisting of Rostelecom's ADRs from the NYSE and Deregistration with the SEC," Rostelecom Press Release (November 11, 2009).
[13] See "A Legal Overview of Foreign Investment in Russia's Strategic Sectors," *Clifford Chance Briefing Note* (May 2014).
[14] See Pallin (2017), 23.

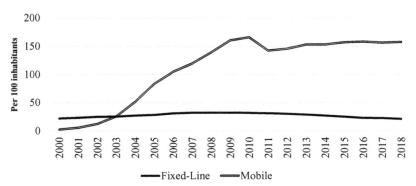

2006. All the same, though the reorganization of Svyazinvest integrated
the regional networks and the merger in 2013 with Rostelecom centralized network management, fixed-line growth has petered. During the
same time, Rostelecom has also invested into other market segments
and subsectors. Moreover, compared to China and India, countries which
have also held onto wireline infrastructure, Rostelecom leads in subscrip-
tion rate from 1990 (Figure 7.1).

10.3 MOBILE AND VALUE-ADDED SERVICES: CONTROL OF FOREIGN INVESTMENT AND RUNET IN 2010 AND BEYOND

In contrast to state-owned landlines, mobile and value-added services in
Russia – without existing state-owned incumbents in 1992 – remain
largely privately owned and running on modern networks. The Russian
government's relative openness toward private and foreign investment in
mobile and value-added services is unlike in China, where the government
retains ownership of all basic services and restricts the business scope and
ownership structures of VAS providers.[15] In a liberalized environment,
through the 1990s and the first decade of the 2000s, foreign capital of
various stripes invested in mobile service provision as partners of the
privatized cellular subsidiaries of the state-owned regional fixed-line networks and wholly privately owned mobile service providers, as illustrated
by the company cases. FDI dipped in the aftermath of the 1998 financial
crisis, but returned to pre-crisis level in 2000. Figure 10.1 shows that

[15] See Yakubovich and Shekshnia (2012).

mobile subscriptions per 100 inhabitants surpassed fixed-line in 2003. Later in 2012 and beyond as the *perceived strategic value* of *resource management* increased in importance under internal and external pressures, the Russian state enhanced its role in market coordination, including in controlling the Internet.

In the early days of the Russian Federation, the most successful mobile operators were the operators, privatized or independent to begin with, that obtained regional licenses and partnered with flexible foreign investors. Foreign equipment makers, cellular operators, or investment funds provided expertise, equipment, and financial resources. The active owners of the independent entities tended to be Russian, and they often partnered with government entities such as a research institute of the Russian military-industrial complex, which held minority stakes. The two largest mobile carriers Mobile TeleSystems (MTS) and Beeline were established in the more liberal regulatory environment with very different ownership structures.

Ranked first in Russia in 2019, MTS today operates in four countries. Founded as a joint venture between the Moscow City Telephone Network, German mobile carrier T-Mobile, and the German equipment manufacturer Siemens, MTS in 1994 became Moscow's first mobile service provider. In 1997, MTS expanded into other regions in Russia after obtaining regional licenses and in 2000 became listed on the New York Stock Exchange. By 2010, the company had expanded into branding handsets and becoming an Internet and cable TV provider. After launching Russia's first fourth-generation TD-LTE network in 2012, MTS is now owned and controlled by Sistema, the oligarch-owned holding company with interests in various sectors, including telecommunications, banking, and oil, which acquired the Moscow City Telephone Network. Following a trend of Russian companies delisting from stock exchanges abroad after the commencement of Western sanctions over Russian intervention in Ukraine, MTS launched a review to delist from NYSE in 2019. The decision also followed a 2016 settlement of a U.S. bribery case over its operations in Uzbekistan. In 2021, the company is dual listed on the NYSE and Moscow Exchange.

In the same year MTS came into operation in 1994, Beeline mobile services was also launched in Moscow by Dimitry Zimin (a scientist at the A.L. Mints Institute of Radio Engineering [RTI] charged with military/industrial conversion) and Augie K. Fabela II (a young American entrepreneur). Fabela had founded Beeline's parent company VimpelCom, now VEON, two years earlier in 1992.[16] That year, Zimin, in his fifties, invited the American family firm Plexis owned by Fabela to partner with him and other technical experts from RTI to develop cellular communications. Zimin zeroed in on mobile only after several false starts with satellite and cable television systems by KB Impulse, a small enterprise registered by the RTI within the USSR's framework of conversion programs. VimpelCom's rapid entry into the mobile market benefited from the loans for shares privatization scheme, which aided Yeltsin's reelection. The company became listed on the New York Stock Exchange in 1996 and through various mergers and acquisitions and divestments obtained fifth rank worldwide in 2011 with half of its revenue earned in Russia. VimpelCom switched to NASDEQ in 2013 after an agreement between the two rival main shareholders, Altimo of the Alfa Group, headed by Russian oligarch Mikhail Fridman, and Norwegian state-owned operator Telenor.

Altimo and Telenor agreed to increase the former's shares after the Russian government intervened under the Strategic Enterprises Law in 2012 to prevent Telenor from increasing its shares in VimpelCom's non-Russian incorporated holding company. The Russian government filed, in Russian court, an objection to Telenor's acquisition of shares, which would have increased the Norwegian state-owned operator's interests above the 25 percent maximum threshold mandated by Russian law.[17] Despite Russia's accession to the WTO happening around the same time, the enforcement of the Strategic Enterprises Law regarding a transaction between non-Russian entities shows the regulatory reach of the Russian Commission on Monitoring Foreign Investment, discussed in further detail below.

The VimpelCom intervention occurred two years after the commission in 2010 applied the Strategic Enterprises Law to prevent a joint venture between Altimo and the Swedish and Finnish joint venture company TeliaSonera. The aborted JV would have increased TeliaSonera's shares in MegaFon, the second largest mobile carrier in Russia. In that case, the Russian government argued that the new company would have allowed a foreign state-owned investor to gain effective control of

---

[16] Fabela exited Russia and VimpelCom shortly after the telecoms ministry obligated the company to free part of the frequency band for a competitor. See "Phone Farce in Russia," *Economist* (September 14, 2000).

[17] See "A Legal Overview of Foreign Investment in Russia's Strategic Sectors," *Clifford Chance Briefing Note* (May 2014).

Megafon. In doing so, the Russian government signaled that government approvals pertaining to the rules of the Strategic Enterprises Law should have preceded actual transactions. Beyond investment process and ownership interventions, *centralized governance* in telecommunications also pertained to formal and informal rules and actions to control business operations as they pertain to information dissemination on the RuNet.

10.3.1 "RuNet" (Russian Internet): Putin-Era Regulatory Centralization and Internet Policy a National Security Concern

The evolving *perceived strategic value* of the Internet for national security imperatives, in response to internal and external pressures, shapes the Russian government's centralized coordination of information control of the variegated property rights arrangements in Internet service provision. The *structural characteristics* of the Internet, as telecommunications value-added services that operate on backbone infrastructure, determine the actual details of the rules and regulations and state interventions employed in the name of national security. The year Putin became president in 2000, the state named the "RuNet," the segment of the Internet where the Russian language and Cyrillic letters are used predominantly, a national security concern. However, not until 2012, in response to civil society protests and conflicts in Crimea between Russia and Ukraine, viewed by Putin and his government to be politically destabilizing and tangible threats to national security, did the state redouble efforts to control telecommunications networks and manage information dissemination on the Internet with internally and externally focused intelligence services.[18] The "Sovereign Internet Law" of 2019 represents the culmination of the demarcation of a Russia-specific Internet.

As early as 1996, the Information Exchange Law, well before Putin's election, gave the state the authority to intervene in Internet architecture, flow, and access despite the low internet penetration rate at the time.[19] "Various updates allowed the government to use the SORM [System of Operational Investigatory Measures] to monitor and conduct search and surveillance of telephone and internet communications. Networks and producers are obligated to allow wiretapping due to national security,"

---

[18] See Deibert and Rohozinski (2010) and Greene and Robertson (2019) on different generations of increasing internet controls and Robertson (2010) on the politics of protests. See Diresta and Grossman (2019) on online dissemination pathways.

[19] See Alexander (2004).

explained Alexander Akhmataev, project director at Rostelecom.[20] In this regulatory context, the government-owned Relcom enjoyed a near monopoly of the value-added services market, followed by Demos and Russia On-line, in 1999. Five years later, five ISPs had control of 85 percent of the market, operating on cable infrastructure controlled by Russian Railways owned Transtelekom (TTK).

Shortly before Yeltsin stepped down as president, in 1999, SORM reform required the Federal Security Service (FSB) to obtain a post-collection court warrant to search records; however, when Putin became president in 2000, almost immediately he began to centralize in a more targeted manner the monitoring and surveilling of communications and in managing when and how information is received by users. The Information Security Doctrine in 2000 defined Internet policy as a national security concern and empowered the executive branch, while limiting individual rights in cases of security concerns. Moreover, a government order in 2000 eliminated the requirement that the FSB had to provide telecommunications and internet companies documentation on targets of interest prior to accessing information.

The Law on Communications of 2004 consolidated state power over all forms of communications into one supraministry, followed by the incorporation of the Russian Institute for Public Networks, created in 1992 to develop basic internet infrastructure, under the Ministry of Communications and Mass Media (*MinComSvyaz Rossii*). Reorganizations in 2008 and 2018 added issues areas under the ministry's purview, including digital development. In 2008, the *Roskomnadzor*, Russia's internet-oversight agency, was created under the *MinComSvyaz Rossii*, shortly before the Russo-Georgia War became the first in history in which military action and cyber and information warfare occurred simultaneously. By the civil society protests (during the 2011–2013 period) on claims against a flawed legislative election process, the Russian government had centralized control of communications infrastructure (as discussed in Section 10.2) and identified the control of information as an important mechanism for containing external security threats.

Upon returning to the presidency in 2012, Putin reinforced the state's multiprong direct and indirect efforts in network management and ownership of the most important infrastructure and websites.[21]

---

[20] Interview in Moscow on June 10, 2015. Also, interview with Klaptsov (June 15, 2015). More on SORM, see Maréchal (2017).

[21] See Pallin (2017).

An amendment to "On information, information technologies and protection of information" No. 149-FZ, first issued in 2006, and updated several times, permitted the government to create a registry of domain names with the URLs and network addresses of web pages that contain harmful internet content. The amendment was part of a bill initiated by conservative Duma deputy Elina Mizulina and the "Safe Internet League," backed by the Russian Orthodox Church, businessman Konstantin Malofeev, and retired *MinComSvyaz Rossii* Minister Igor Olegovich Shchyogolev, who had served as Putin's press secretary in the early 2000s.[22]

The "Internet blacklist," ostensibly designed to protect children from homosexuality, pedophilia, extremism, narcotics, and suicide, also blocked opposition-minded news and commentary on websites and blogs of opposition leaders. The self-regulating non-governmental organization that was proposed to implement and supervise the blacklist was never established, and the *Roskomnadzor* assumed implementation and supervision. At the time, Yuri Vdovin, vice-president of Citizens' Watch, a human rights organization based in Saint Petersburg, explained, "The government will start closing other sites—any democracy-oriented sites are at risk of being taken offline. It will be [an attack on] the freedom of speech on the Internet."[23]

10.3.2 External Security Threats and Rules on Storage and Micromanagement of Data and Content

The Freedom House rated the Internet in Russia "partly free" in a report released in 2014.[24] The semi-liberal environment, however, changed dramatically following Russia's intervention in Crimea in February and March that year during the invasion of Ukraine. In addition to hardware requirements for data surveillance and rules on internet content and traffic, new and revised laws began to micromanage data storage and management, affecting the business scope of mobile and value-added service providers, particularly ISPs. By mid-2014, the Russian government explicitly identified the Internet as a platform for foreign intelligence services to threaten Russia's security and sovereignty.

To the Russian Security Council in July 2014, Putin described the threat posed to Russia's sovereignty and connected the national security threats to Information Communications Technology (ICT): "Attempts

---

[22] See Greene and Robertson (2019), 41–51.
[23] See "Russia Internet Blacklist Law Takes Effect," *BBC World News* (November 1, 2012).
[24] See Freedom House (2014).

are clearly being made to destabilize the social and economic situation, to weaken Russia in one way or another or to strike at our weaker spots, and they will continue primarily to make us more agreeable in resolving international issues. So-called international competition mechanisms are being used as well (this applies to both politics and the economy); for this purpose, the special services' capabilities are used, along with modern ICT and dependent, puppet non-governmental organizations—so-called soft mechanisms."[25]

The tension between the role of the state, net neutrality, and national security became apparent when technology entrepreneur Ilya Vladimirovich Ponomarev, who had supported more laws regulating the "hotbed for cybercrime" in 2012, became the only member of the State Duma to vote against the annexation of Crimea.[26] At the time, Ponomarev, now in exile, withdrew from the mayoral race in Novosibirsk, Siberia after opposition consolidated to run against him and labeled him a "national traitor" and a "fifth columnist."

MinComSvyaz Rossii minister Nikolai Nikiforov prepared a report in March 2015 dedicated to the "sovereignty of the Russian Internet," approved by Deputy Prime Minister Arkadii Dvorkovich, to regulate the activities of private companies that operate critical communications infrastructure.[27] Shortly thereafter, the government enacted restrictions on the business scope of internet companies with the Federal Law on Localization of Personal Data released in 2015. Justifications for requiring all data pertaining to Russian citizens to be stored within Russia also included Edward Snowden's 2013 revelation of the U.S. National Security Agency's PRISM program, which tapped into American ICT companies' data centers to extract desired information.[28] Russia joined China, Vietnam, Indonesia, and Malaysia as one of the few countries in the world that required data operators, including companies with data storage abroad, to "record, systematize, accumulate, store, amend, update and retrieve" data using databases physically located in Russia.[29]

---

[25] See "Vladimir Putin Chaired a Security Council Meeting in the Kremlin," *Prezident Rossii* (July 22, 2014).

[26] See "Russian Duma Passes Internet Censorship Bill," *Wall Street Journal* (July 11, 2012) and "Odd Man Out When Vote was 445-1 on Crimea," *New York Times* (March 28, 2014) and "A Year Ago He was the Only Russian Politician to Vote Against Annexing Crimea. Now He's an Exile," *Washington Post* (March 23, 2015).

[27] See Pallin (2017).   [28] See Maréchal (2017).

[29] See "Clarifications Published on Russia's Personal Data Localization Law," *Duane Morris LLP* (September 7, 2015).

The data localization rules enforced by *Roskomnadzor* have also blocked the access of personal data obtained via the Internet in the conduct of business targeting Russian consumers.[30] Shortly after the localization rules came into force, in late 2015, Google shut down its development office in St. Petersburg and relocated staff to Switzerland, Germany, and the United States. In 2013, Eric Schmidt, the CEO of Google's parent company Alphabet, said he was, at the time, "worried that Russia was beginning to copy China in internet censorship."[31]

During the ongoing crises in Crimea and eastern Ukraine, yet another update to SORM required companies to install government-provided Deep Packet Inspection (DPI) capability to control the flow of traffic based on its origin, destination, file type (text, voice, multimedia), protocol (P2P, FTP, HTML, SMTP), or the content of itself.[32] The Alfa Group's Eco Telecom-managed Russian telecommunications equipment maker RDP.ru, 15 percent of which is owned by the state, manufactured the deep traffic filtering equipment. The European Court of Human Rights ruled in 2015 that the SORM violated Article 8 of the European Convention on Human Rights and implementation of DPI stalled.[33]

A year later, the "Anti-Terrorist Law," signed in 2016, substantially updated and revised the Federal Law No. 126-FZ "On Communications" and the Federal Law No.149-FZ on the management of recording and storage of the telecom service providers' customers and internet users' data and communications. Operators are required to store in Russia information on the receipt, transmission, delivery and/or processing of their customers' voice data, text messages, pictures, sounds, video messages, or other messages within three years of the date of receipt, transmission, delivery and/or processing. The Anti-Terrorist Law also increased the period of storage of the same information for internet users from six months to one year as required by the Federal Law of the Russian Federation No. 97-FZ of 2014.

---

[30] See "Legal and Practical Approaches to Meet Requirements for Localization of Personal Data," *Software Russia* (July 23, 2015).

[31] See "Google to Close Engineering Office in Russia as Internet Restrictions Bite," *Guardian* (December 12, 2014). Other FDI that exited include Adobe Systems and Intel Corporation.

[32] See Soldatov and Borogan (2015).

[33] See the European Court of Human Rights Judgment on Roman Zakharov v. Russia (Application no. 47143/06 (December 5, 2015)).

The law further requires service providers to hand over the information necessary to decode users' encrypted messages.[34]

10.3.3 User-level Control Mechanisms: Internet Curator, Propaganda Army, and "Blogger Law"

Notwithstanding the control mechanisms targeting market access, business scope, and data management, anti-Putin opposition incubated in cyberspace. Interactions on social media became a collective action channel for users to not only consume but also exchange information to coordinate protests.[35] In response, the state extended SORM to include social networking sites. Moreover, the Kremlin appointed a "curator" to counter the opposition and mobilize an echo-chamber following in order to shape and reframe how the RuNet characterizes the state's actions. Similar to China's approach in Chapter 4, the Russian government employed a propaganda army of paid online commenters not unlike China's fifty-cent army.[36] The updated Act of Information, in 2014, authorizes the blocking of any website without explanation.

Moreover, "the blogger law" requires anyone whose online presence draws 3000 or more daily readers to register, disclose personal information, and submit to the same already stringent regulations as mass media with *Roskomnadzor*. ISPs and the owners of social networks are required to provide information on the number of daily readers and visitors to a special state registry containing detailed information such as phone numbers and home addresses of bloggers. Liberal blogger and internet entrepreneur Anton Nosik explained, "It's about creating a situation where big brother is watching you. You are part of a list, you are being watched, being observed, you are being served notices and could even serve a criminal sentence if you choose to speak out."[37] While most

---

[34] See Victor Naumov, "Russian Federation: Russia's New Anti-Terrorist Law," *Mondaq* (July 22, 2016). Also, see Federal Law No. 374-FZ "On Amendments to Federal Law 'On Counteracting Terrorism' and to Certain Other Legal Acts of the Russian Federation with regard to Establishing of Additional Measures on Counteracting Terrorism and Ensuring Public Security."

[35] See Little (2016) on communication technology and protests; and Enikolopov, Makarin, and Petrova (2020) on the impact of VK, Russia's dominant social medial network on the 2011 protests.

[36] See "Russian Propaganda Is Taking Over Online Comment Boards," *Business Insider* (May 4, 2014) and "Russia's Online-Comment Propaganda Army," *Atlantic* (October 9, 2013).

[37] See "Russia Tightens Controls on Blogosphere," *Guardian* (July 31, 2014).

defendants are critics of the Kremlin's policies, especially on intervention in Ukraine, and receive prison terms, in 2016, the government fined Nosik under the law for extremism for a blog post on Syria.[38]

10.3.4 Safeguarding from "Western Threats": Internet Borders and Cyberwarfare

From the mid-2000s, the Russian government has framed the Internet as a creation of the West designed to subvert Russia's sovereignty. Mobilizing support for a secure "Russia-oriented Internet," Putin evoked Western infiltration in a television interview, "[Western intelligence agencies] are sitting online. [The internet] is their creation. And they hear, see and read everything that you are saying and they're collecting security information...But everything is possible in theory. So we must create a segment [of the Internet] which depends on nobody."[39] As analyzed above, *MinComSvyaz* minister Nikiforov's 2015 report led to the strengthening of the government's right to intervene on the management and storage of data under the auspices of national security.

This was the domestic political context for the hackers of the Russian military intelligence agency who broke into the servers of the Democratic National Committee and released damaging information about presidential candidate Hillary Clinton.[40] Then a series of further amendments to the "Law on Communication" and "On Information, Information Technologies, and Information Protection," popularly referred to as "the Sovereign Internet Law" and initiated by Duma deputies Ljudmila Bokowa, Andrei Klischas, and State Duma MP Andrei Lugowoi, passed the Putin-dominated Duma in 2019. The law reinforces the various mechanisms that were already managing the Internet within Russia's borders, further centralizes the management of telecommunication networks and cross border connections, and authorizes a Russian national Domain Name System (DNS) to create the RuNet.

---

[38] See "Russian Blogger Anton Nosik Convicted of Extremism," *BBC World News* (October 3, 2016).

[39] See "Russia's Great Firewall: Is It Meant to Keep Information in—or Out?" *Guardian* (April 28, 2019).

[40] See Mueller (2019) and Diresta and Grossman (2019). The actual delineation of the responsibilities of internally and externally focused intelligence agencies is unknown; however, the U.S. government has identified S.V.R., a spinoff from the Soviet-era K.G.B., as the Russian agency responsible for the DNC hacking, in addition to other hacks including of USAID to obtain information of human rights groups critical of Putin.

10.4 TELECOMMUNICATIONS EQUIPMENT: PRIVATIZATION OF SOVIET BUREAUCRACIES AND INDUSTRIAL UPGRADING VIA DIVESTMENT AND REGULATION

Perceived less strategic to immediate national security imperatives and associated with firmware which operate on top of state-owned backbone infrastructure, in the newly established Russian Federation in 1992, the State Property Committee separated equipment production from service provision when reorganizing the telecommunications monopoly Sovtelekom. Moreover, state reformers, with the assistance of government experts and senior businesspeople from OECD countries, resumed the conversion initiated under *perestroika* of defense plants to production of civilian telecommunications. Today, Russia regulates telecommunications equipment separately from service provision and information dissemination. Moreover, non-defense and dual-use telecommunications equipment in Russia are under the purview of the Ministry of Industry and Trade (*Minpromtorg*)'s Department of Electronic Industry. A separate Department of Defense Industry under *Minpromtorg* specializes in legal and methodological support of the licensed activities of the defense industrial complex. This varied from China, which merged the equipment and service ministries to consolidate state control in 1998, as shown in Chapter 4. It also differed from state-directed R&D in telecommunications equipment and a telecommunications regulator created in 1997 in India analyzed in Chapter 7.

The distribution of property rights in telecommunications equipment is variegated, from state-owned to privately owned, and varies by subsector. Foreign equipment makers (such as Ericcson, Alcatel, and Siemens) dominate infrastructural equipment, governed by service agreements with the telecom operators. Domestic producers as a function of comparative advantages rooted in the Soviet-era military-industrial complex cluster around satellite technologies. "Towers and fire pressure systems and shelters are Russian-supplied and installed, but base stations and multiplexes are foreign-made, which are more reliable and price competitive," quipped Rostelecom project director Alexander Akhmataev.[41] Telecommunications make up 10 percent of Russia's vast majority of technology imports in machinery and equipment.[42]

---

[41] Interview in Moscow on June 10, 2015.   [42] See Terebova (2017), 331.

Up until *perestroika*, the Soviet telecommunications infrastructure of the various central and local networks operated on antiquated switching equipment with technology, which dated to the 1880s. The EASS system, designed to integrate military, specialized, and civilian networks but failed in practice, relied on infrastructure built in the early twentieth century using Ericcson and Siemens equipment.[43] The Ministry of Communications Equipment Industry, the Ministry of the Electronics Industry, and the Ministry of the Radio Industry, all part of the defense industrial complex, prioritized military procurement.

In the 1960s, the Soviet Union helped develop fiber optics, used mainly for military applications, in collaboration with foreign manufacturers. The plan stalled when the United States prohibited the export of sensitive technology to Russia.[44] Outside of defense requirements, research and development at the *Minsviaz*'s two research institutes and network of educational institutions were limited.[45] *Minsviaz* relied on Eastern Europe, where it procured networking equipment for the modernization of the old crossbar exchanges.[46] In addition to interagency politics, the vast variety of suppliers and the increase in transmission capacity over time without modern switching equipment contributed to poor interconnection.

After the founding of the Russian Federation, military procurement was cut by two-thirds in January 1992. Defense-industrial ministries were subsumed under the Ministry of Industry and turned into the State Committee for Industrial Policy and sectoral committees of lesser status. As detailed in Section 10.1, cognizant of the importance of a central authority in converting existing manufacturing facilities from military to civilian use and in coordinating telecommunications development, even as post-Soviet reformers dismantled central planning, the reformers retained *Minsviazi*. The fast-paced economy-wide liberalization and privatization, however, weakened the ministry's ability to achieve its post-Soviet goals of commercializing manufacturing facilities and coordinating network development.

Until anti-foreign sentiments began to emerge in the aftermath of Russia's intervention in Crimea in 2014, the post-Soviet state did not focus too much funding or energy on the R&D of telecommunications equipment. "During Soviet times, the country didn't have major development in telecoms equipment because the Soviets used Siemens and Nokia

---

[43] Interview with Bychkova (June 17, 2015). Also see Noam (1992), 287.
[44] See Noam (1992), 288.   [45] See Campbell (1995) and Gaddy (1996).
[46] See Noam (1992), 274–289.

equipment dating back to pre-Soviet times. In the 1920s, there were brief calls for import-substitution industrialization. Questions about foreign equipment used in Russia were not raised again until after Crimea," explained Olga Bychkova of the European University of St. Petersburg.[47]

The 1992 Law of Conversion targeted military producers and searched for Western partners for them to manufacture microwave, satellite, and cellular radio-based communications equipment for the civilian sector.[48] Moreover, the Russian Temporary Statue on Communications separately regulated military and government networks from civilian networks, granting leeway for state-owned military communications entities to court and be courted by private interests. International organizations, such as the OCED and its Center for Cooperation with the European Economies in Transition, held military/industrial conversion "seminars."

One conference on such efforts took place in *Krasnoyarsk*, Siberia, a "closed city" in a region of high-tech military production under the USSR.[49] There, factories produced equipment for radio and satellite communications, dedicated military networks, and TV broadcasting. The military had accounted for 7.5 percent of the Net Material Product (Soviet measure similar to the GDP) and up to 47 percent of the government spending. Up for "sale" were a Radio-Technical Plant and the Scientific and Production Association for Applied Mechanics.[50] "Russia never was strong in widespread technology, always strong in high-level technology, but commercialization has never been a strong point in Russia. Russians created the horseshoe, video recording, and helicopter, but who knows that?"[51]

The science and technology personnel who departed bankrupted or ill-organized state institutions applied their defense expertise in dual-use telecommunications equipment.[52] Physicist Valentin Gapontsev founded IPG Photonics, a private producer of fiber optics lasers and amplifiers, in the basement of the Institute of Radio Engineering of the Academy of Sciences. "The Russian market was completely frozen, and the Western market did not demonstrate any opportunity for similar technologies.

[47] Interview on June 17, 2015, in St. Petersburg.   [48] See Gaddy (1996).

[49] During Leningrad Siege (1941–1944), security R&D moved to far-flung remote places such as Siberia and Vologda, which also disseminated knowledge across the USSR.

[50] See Kelly, Salamon, and Grassman (1992).

[51] Interview on June 9, 2015, in Moscow with Fuad Aleskerov, professor of mathematics, Higher School of Economics.

[52] Interview on June 17, 2015, in Moscow with Sasha Galitsky, partner and founder of Almaz Capital and former state engineer.

Our only chance was to introduce a new disruptive technology: High-power fiber lasers (powerful lasers in communications). In 1992, I began to focus all my limited resources in that direction," explained Gapontsev.[53] IPG shifted to vertical integration to produce pump diode during the early-2000 telecoms industry slowdown.

10.4.1 Deregulated Markets in Information Technology Services until Crimea Annexation

The Russian government has more loosely regulated Information Technology (IT) and software services. These are ICT sectors characterized by intangible assets difficult for the government to regulate and seize and to which former technocrats of the military industrial complex have flocked. The less tangible nature of IT and software assets despite its personnel origins in the defense sector have shaped the role of the state in market coordination and the dominant variegated ownership structures. Their evolving *perceived strategic value* for national security and national assets in the context of internal and external pressures, however, has influenced recent state interventions. "Historically the IT sector was part of the big arms development of the Soviet Union. Programmers from an importer-exporter of computer hardware and software controlled by the Ministry of Foreign Trade invented the computer game Tetris. *Perestroika* awarded, those involved in IT, the opportunity to become independent. When the company privatized, the game designer Alexey Pajitnov became an oligarch," said Sasha Galitsky, managing partner at Almaz Capital Partners and board member of the Skolkovo Foundation.[54] Galitsky himself used Chubais vouchers to establish a company, in the early 1990s, that operated with Sun Microsystems terminals. "Telecoms infrastructure remained connected to the state, but those who worked in defense in the equipment makers became part of the brain drain," Galitsky explained.

In the immediate post-Soviet era, privately owned and foreign-invested firms without the government's micromanagement entered the IT market, perceived by the new state as low in strategic value because of its intangible assets. "In IT, there are no fungible entities. The government doesn't have entities to pick up to control. Even 90 percent of software in oil and

---

[53] See Gapontsev (2007).
[54] Interview on June 17, 2015, in Moscow. Galitsky has also served on the board of mobile carrier MegaFon, and as an executive in the Soviet space sector.

gas are in foreign hands," explained Valentin Makarov, the director of Russoft, an Information Communications Technology industry association based in St. Petersburg.[55] In contrast, in China, software services are defined as telecoms value-added services, perceived strategic for national security and social and political stability. Chapter 4 delineates how though ownership structures are variegated, a supraministry strictly regulates market entry and business scope with China-specific standards.

Shortly after the fall of the Soviet Union, software designers began operations under the Database Law, which provided legal and privacy protection. The law protected software designers and set up a registration mechanism, comparable to the licensure of private dedicated satellite links in India around the same time, which jumpstarted the development of IT services analyzed in Chapter 7. The 1995 Information Law further emphasized that privacy interference requires court sanction. Registration and protections, combined with a relatively developed backbone infrastructure dating from the Soviet era, helped to sustain a burgeoning software services sector. In the Putin era, registration at the State Registration Authority and the State Statistical Committee and the compliance of myriad economy-wide tax and labor codes and welfare and social funds remain the non-sector-specific requirements.[56] Market coordination is decentralized, with local sector and business associations and local governments enforcing economy-wide rules.

Laws passed in the post-Crimea annexation period to control data and information under the auspices of national security and resource management, however, have restricted IT companies' business scope. These include rules on the localization of data storage and the Anti-Terrorist Law (signed in 2016) on the recording and storage of the telecom services' customers and internet users' data and communications as discussed in Section 10.3. Galitsky explained, "Telecoms development in the 1990s was very divided but now closely connected due to technological convergence," referring to the effects of ever-restrictive internet- and telecommunications-related laws on what had been a decentralized and liberalized IT industry regulated by economy-wide rules rather than sector-specific policies. Figure 10.4 shows by way of patent filings the rapid development of ICT populated by Science and Technology

---

[55] Interview with Makarov in St. Petersburg on June 15, 2015.
[56] Interview with Natalya Loseva, head of Public Relations and Marketing, and Tatiana Modeeva, managing partner, Acsour Accounting and HR Management, in St. Petersburg.

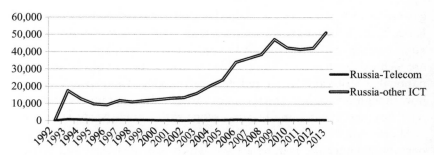

FIGURE 10.4. Russia patents: Telecommunication and other information communications technology (1992–2013)
Source: World Intellectual Property Organization (2015).

personnel with Soviet defense sector origins versus other areas of telecommunications.

10.4.2 Based in Russia, Incorporated Globally: Software Services in the Putin Era and Beyond

"It was easier to start a company than to find a market," quipped Nick Puntikov, CEO of First Line Software, a privately owned custom software services company headquartered in St. Petersburg and a member of Russoft.[57] Former engineers of the Academy of Sciences, who began their careers running government factories equipped with computers in the 1980s, founded First Line Software in 1995 when hyperinflation of exchange rates drastically reduced their monthly salaries. At the time, shortly after the first generation of Russian personal computers was assembled in the late 1980s, First Line began with contract work for international connections made through the founders' government positions. The company officially entered software outsourcing when the Star Group of Switzerland, a computational linguistics company operating in multiple industries, approached First Line to collaborate in their localization. Later, in 2000, First Line incorporated in the United States and opened an office in Cambridge, Massachusetts. "Only 30 percent of our clientele are Russian. The rest are Western clients. Our offices in Holland, Singapore, and the U.S. execute contracts in those countries. The closer we are to the international market, the less likely the political interference," said Puntikov.

[57] Interview with on June 16, 2015, at First Line in St. Petersburg.

The centralization of the state's role in market coordination after the 1998–1999 economic crisis, which preceded Putin's election, did not affect market developments in IT and software services in the same way it did fixed-line telecoms and even mobile and valued-added services. Two top Russian artificial intelligence software firms – ABBYY founded by Armenian-born David Yang and Cognitive Technologies founded by Olga Uskova, who comes from a family of Soviet programmers – came of age in this landscape beyond the shadows of oligarch corruption and state intervention.[58] "The comparably top-notch quality of Russia's IT services in AI is why we have a team of software developers in Moscow, and no requirement like China to configure Russia-specific codes," exclaimed the marketing director for a global medical device company.[59]

"After the 1998 financial crisis, you felt the government was on your side, not trying to make the situation worse," quipped Ron Lewin, founder and CEO of TerraLink, which provides integrated IT services in Russia and the CIS. TerraLink, founded in 1989 and registered as a holding company in Canada, began operations in Russia and the CIS in 1994 by providing software integration services. Armed with venture capital funding from Western investors, including leading angel investor Esther Tyson, TerraLink entered the liberalized IT market with relative ease and without too much competition.[60] "The corporate headquarters in Canada serves as the public face outside of Russia but does very little business. Most contracts stipulate Russia law, occasionally [the] Hague or Canada, but my business clients are mostly Russian companies," explained Lewin.

"We have never felt that we had to engage in shadowy activity. We were a legal Russian entity all along. The government couldn't touch the sector—it is not big nor interesting enough. Everything requires documentation and authorization and, once received, you are on your own. You are told what you are allowed to do instead of what you are not allowed to do. Military contracts are not allowed for non-Russian companies," explained Lewin. "IT did not become criminalized during the 'corporatization movement' of the 1990s. The brain is difficult to control....It has intangible assets difficult to control and buy."[61]

[58] See "State Companies Oblivious to R&D," *Moscow Times* (June 30, 2011).
[59] Interview on February 20, 2021 in Santa Clara, CA.
[60] Interview with Lewin (June 18, 2015).   [61] Interview with Galitsky (June 17, 2015).

Overtime, internal market competition mounted. "The lack of rule of law, corruption, all factors. The Russians compete differently—brazen, obvious favoritism abounds six months before tenders are announced, and bids are disqualified for unreasonable rationale. By the mid-2000s, companies close to the government sprung up overnight to receive government tenders they easily won. They were the only companies to meet the criteria set forth in the open bidding. They got into the IT business to partake in government projects with big budgets, such as the operation of elections, pocket integrator."

The government consolidated state supervision of ICT and media in one supraministry in 2008. Reregulation, such as amendments in 2012 to the Criminal Code on establishing liability for fraud with respect to computer data and the 2015 federal law on localization of personalized data, sharpened the deliberate orientation of the state. The 2014 Crimea crisis further strengthened the government's resolve to intervene at the sector and firm levels if national security imperatives relating to computer data are at stake. "In 2015 government and business interests are not aligned. This is practically the first time since being here [in 1990] that I feel this way," Lewin professed.

Russian privately owned First Line experienced the change differently. "The situation has changed since 2000 in that the government knows us now, with Russoft lobbying the government for support, such as a stable taxation system. Now the government courts us with regards to export support, which didn't exist before when the industry was built from scratch. This isn't import substitution. We have avoided the imagined danger of using foreign software, and we do not fear the government will grab our assets," explained Puntikov. "As Russia moves toward isolation, however, brain drain will become a problem. Recently, Intel announced it is closing its office opened in St. Petersburg, downsizing and leaving businesses in part because of geopolitics," continued Puntikov. First Line's top competitor, Luxoft, a digital strategy and software company established in 2000, moved its headquarters to Switzerland in 2014 after military intervention in Ukraine, then to the United States, where a Hewlett Packet spin-off DXC Technology acquired it in 2019.

At least immediately, "the effects of the sanctions are mainly in prospective clients that disappeared when Ukraine developed. We have also encountered times when left off of outsourcing lists. Most work is virtual, so existing clients don't have to be onsite even if we interact daily like with Dell. First Line's challenge is to convince experienced software

TABLE 10.1. *Russia: Laws, rules, and regulations governing telecoms subsectors*

Market Coordination	Property Rights Arrangements
Telecommunications Writ-Large	

Market Coordination

- Liberalization of tariffs for local and domestic long-distance service (1992)
- Russian Temporary Statue on Communications (early 1990s) (liberalization of entry and ownership in gateway interconnections and mobile services)
- Elimination of investment planning, tariff setting, and service operation of the telecommunications ministry (early 1990s)
- National Security Concept of 2000
- Center for Strategic Development
- Communications Law of 2004 (Rostelecom monopoly on long-distance; government regulation of ownership, radio frequencies, and IP telephony)
- Law on Communications (2004)
- Creation of supraministry, Ministry of Communications and Mass Media, including posts (2004)
- Laws and regulations on communications and anti-terrorism
- Merger of bureaucracies in telecommunications and media and mass communications (2008)
- Ministry of Telecommunications and Mass Communications (2008)
- Long-Term Socioeconomic Development of the Russian Federation
- Federal Law No. 57-FZ "On the Procedure of Foreign Investments in Economic Entities Strategically Important for National Defense and State Security" (2008, amendments 2011, 2013) – "Strategic Enterprises Law"
- Ministry of Digital Development, Communications, and Mass Media (2018)

Property Rights Arrangements

- Reorganization of state-owned monopoly Sovtelekom, establishment of Rostelecom, and separation of equipment production from service provision (1992)
- State-owned telecommunications holding company Svyazinvest established in 1994
- Russian Temporary Statue on Communications (early 1990s) (liberalization of entry and ownership in gateway interconnections and mobile services, including FDI)
- Presidential decree on strategic enterprises and joint-stock companies (2004)
- Federal Law No. 57-FZ "On the Procedure of Foreign Investments in Economic Entities Strategically Important for National Defense and State Security" (2008, amendments 2011, 2013)
- State-owned fixed-line, ISP, and railway networks (2013)
- Delisting of Russian mobile service providers from international stock exchanges following Crimea intervention

(continued)

TABLE 10.1. (*continued*)

Market Coordination	Property Rights Arrangements

Telecommunications Fixed-Line Services

• Liberalization of tariffs for local and domestic long-distance service (1992) • Russian Temporary Statue on Communications (early 1990s) (liberalization of entry and ownership in gateway interconnections and mobile services) • Russian Institute for Public Networks (Internet development) (1992) • Communications Law of 2004 (Rostelecom monopoly on long-distance; government regulation of ownership, radio frequencies, and IP telephony)	• Reorganization of state-owned monopoly Sovtelekom, which was corporatized under *perestroika*, and establishment of Rostelecom, which took charge of long-distance and international connections, by State Property Committee of Russia (1992) • Partial privatization of previously specialized non-civilian networks (1990s) • FDI mostly strategic investors without controlling shares (1990s) • Merger of fixed-line operators created regional incumbents (2001) • Rostelecom took control of ISP backbone (2006) • Rostelecom delisted from the New York Stock Exchange (2009) • Rostelecom listed on the Moscow Exchange (2011) • Multi-step reorganization of Rostelecom to consolidate state control of backbone infrastructure, which included integration of regional networks and merger with state-owned holding company Svyazinvest before its dissolution (2011–2013) • Corporate centralization of regional subsidiaries of TransTelekom, the world's largest network of fiber optics • Rostelecom entered mobile and satellite services (2014 and beyond)

Telecommunications Mobile and Value-Added Services

• Russian Temporary Statue on Communications (early 1990s) (liberalization of entry and ownership in gateway interconnections and mobile services)	• Russian Temporary Statue on Communications (early 1990s) (liberalization of entry and ownership in gateway interconnections and mobile services, including FDI)

Market Coordination	Property Rights Arrangements
• Information Law (1995) liberalization of state information	• Establishment of regional mobile monopolies via Loans for Shares Scheme (1996)
• Communications Law (1996) privacy guarantees	• First mobile service provider MTS established as a joint venture between Moscow City, T-Mobile, and Siemens (1994)
• Information Exchange Law (1996) sanction for state interference in Internet	
• SORM [System of Operational Investigatory Measures] (1996, various updates) – government provided hardware to monitor user communications	• Judicial interventions regarding foreign equity level under Strategic Enterprises Law (2010 and beyond)
• Information Security Doctrine (2000)	
• "On information, information technologies and protection of information" No. 149-FZ (2006, 2012, various updates) creation of "Internet Blacklists"	
• *Roskomnadzor* (Internet Oversight Agency) (2008)	
• Federal Law of the Russian Federation No. 97-FZ (2014) data storage	
• Minister of Communications report targeting private companies in critical information infrastructure	
• "The Blogger Law" – revised Information Act (2014)	
• Federal Law on Localization of Personal Data (2015)	
• Deep Packet Inspection Installation (2015)	
• Anti-Terrorist Law (2016)	
• 13 National Projects (2020)	
• "Sovereign Internet Law" (2019)	

Telecommunications Equipment

• Law of Conversion of 1992	• Separation from telecommunications monopoly and corporatization of equipment production by State Property Committee of Russia (1992)
• Department of Electronic Industry, Ministry of Industry and Trade (Minpromtorg) for non-defense and dual use	

(*continued*)

TABLE 10.1. (*continued*)

Market Coordination	Property Rights Arrangements
• Department of Defense Industry, Minpromtorg, for defense equipment • Digital Economy Project of 13 National Projects (2020)	• Liberalization of market entry to private and foreign investment (1992)

Information Technology and Software Services

• Database Law (1992) liberalization of IT and software services by • State Registration Authority • State Statistical Committee • Tax and labor codes and welfare and social funds • Criminal Code (2015) establishment of liability for fraud in computer data • Federal law on localization of personalized data (2015) • Rules on localization of data storage (2014) • Anti-Terrorist Law (2016)	• Liberalization of market entry to private and foreign investment (1992)

programmers to leave Russia to move closer to clients," said Alexander Pozdniakov, Chief Operation Officer of First Line.[62] Moreover, other multinationals, such as the U.S. company Dell EMC, found market opportunities in data storage and processing shortly after the announcement of the data localization rules. Dell EMC collaborated with St. Petersburg State Polytechnic University to establish the Polytechnik-EMC within the Institute for Information Technology and Management.[63] Smaller foreign companies from biomedical devices to

---

[62] Interview on June 16, 2015, at First Line in St. Petersburg. See also "Intel Open Russian Development Center, Says Report," *EE Times* (July 23, 2004) and "Closure of the Center in St. Petersburg," *TA Advisor Government Business IT.*

[63] See "SPbSPU and EMC Corporation Will Develop IT-education in Saint-Petersburg" and "Polytechnik-EMC Opens in St. Petersburg," press statements for St. Petersburg State Polytechnic University and EMC/Dell released in February 2014.

TABLE 10.2. *Russia telecommunications subsectors: Strategic value, market governance, and development*

Centralized Governance	Dominant Coordination Mechanisms	Dominant Distribution of Property Rights	Development Outcomes
High Strategic Value Infrastructure Integration and Management	**Basic Services** Centralized, sector-specific regulation of service provision and information dissemination by supraministry; ban on private ownership; restrictions on private investment; and state-led restructuring and network integration	**Fixed-line Services** State-owned fixed-line network and internet infrastructure centralized under one national fixed-line monopoly	**Fixed-line Services** Inefficient patchwork of wireline networks undergoing restructuring and modernization under Putin-era centralization of regional networks into one fixed-line incumbent
High Strategic Value Control of Foreign Investment and Information Dissemination	**Mobile and Valued-added Services** Liberal rules on market entry and strict rules on foreign investment level and business scope; strict rules on surveillance hardware and content, storage, and management of data by mobile and VAS providers, including Internet Service Providers	**Mobile and Valued-added Services** Variegated ownership types, including private and foreign-invested service providers; foreign private investors restricted to <50% stakes and foreign government investors to <25% stakes	**Mobile and Value-added Services** Regional monopolies controlled by oligarchic industrial groupings; market share into CIS and European markets
Low Strategic Value Economywide Social Welfare and Data Control	**Equipment and ICT** Non-sector-specific regulation by commerce ministry of non-defense equipment with liberal rules on entry and business scope; IT/software affected by hardware and data management rules	**Equipment and ICT** Variegated ownership types, including partially state-owned, Soviet-era defense-originated equipment makers	**Equipment and ICT** Less competitive terminal equipment makers applying defense R&D; globally competitive ICT and software outsourcing services

semiconductor networking have also retained their IT/software offices in Moscow and Nizgny Novgorod, to name a few places.[64]

Table 10.1 shows temporal and subsectoral variation in laws and regulations governing telecommunications, as analyzed in this chapter. Table 10.2 maps dominant patterns of market governance structures and development outcomes in telecommunications.

---

[64] Interviews on January 31, 2021, with director of engineering of a global semiconductor firm in San Jose, California; and on February 20, 2021 in Mountain View, with marketing director of a global medical device company.

11

Regional Development and Labor-Intensive Sectors

Private Governance in Russian Textiles

The Strategic Value Framework illuminates the lasting impacts of the state's *perceived strategic value* orientation toward an industrial sector, predicting that the higher the perceived strategic value, the more likely the state will intervene in market coordination and dominant property rights arrangements. *Sectoral structures and organization of institutions* filter the relative influences of perceived strategic value in response to internal and external pressures and shape the governance details.[1] The previous two chapters show how Russia's perceived internal and external threats, relative resource endowments, and the institutional legacies of the Soviet defense complex have oriented state elites toward *resource security nationalism*. Interactive strategic value and sectoral logics shape the centralized market coordination and state ownership and intervention in corporate governance of capital-intensive sectors with application for national security and high contribution to infrastructural resources.

In contrast, *perestroika*-era liberalization and mass privatization in the immediate aftermath of Soviet collapse decentralized market governance to regional governments and private economic actors those labor-intensive and consumer-oriented, light industries, such as textiles, perceived less strategic for national defense and resource management. This chapter's cross-time sectoral case studies, illustrated by company cases, show the development of the textile industry after the collapse of the Soviet Union has remained largely out of the spotlight of neoliberal reforms and is eschewed by international organizations and international

---

[1] See Table 2.4 for sectoral structural attributes.

investors. In the interim years, the domestic manufacturing of apparel and clothing has lagged behind the rest of the economy, with antiquated machinery and production processes and limited market share domestically and globally.

The lower perceived strategic value of textiles and sectoral institutional arrangements, such as the breakdown of Soviet era supply links relied on by textile enterprises, have shaped how local and regional state authorities enforce economywide rules and variegated market players respond to business conditions, as shown in Section 11.1. In the context of *private governance*, local companies struggle to stay afloat and periodic subnational interventions react to economic and political crises affecting the employment imperative and other local interests, on the one hand. The varied experiences of Vologda Textiles and BTK Group presented in Section 11.2 are characterized by local government and regional oligarchic interventions in the context of competition from foreign legal and illegal imports and limited national support.

On the other hand, Section 11.3 shows how local governments and the central state promote well-connected apparel producers of defense clothing and capital-intensive, value-added technical textiles containing oil and petrochemical inputs designated strategic resources in the aftermath of the Crimea annexation in the mid-2010s. Thus, technical textiles, identified by the state in the 2000s as outputs of strategic petrochemical assets and potentially lucrative applications of chemistry and physics, encounter *decentralized governance*. A mix of central state and local government-coordinated regional and national fiscal and investment policies, at relative degrees of state capacity, has incentivized and subsidized locally powerful and predominantly private firms. Central intervention also occurs during phases of economic and geopolitical instability. Section 11.4 shows the persistent effects of spatial geographic organization of institutions dating to the Soviet era, in addition to recent public–private initiatives in the Putin era, on textile trade and distribution.

11.1 STRATEGIC VALUE AND SECTORAL LOGICS: PRIVATE GOVERNANCE IN TEXTILES

Today, Russia's clothing market is the ninth largest in the world at close to $30 billion annually; however, imported goods account for over 80 percent of the total market, with 60 percent of apparel imports originating from China and South Asia.[2] "Russians consume luxury brand names in fashion and in casual sports apparel at a very high rate, with imports from varieties of sources. A great deal from China and illegal imports from Western nations," explained Guy Carpenter, a global textile consultant based in North Carolina in the United States who has traversed the former USSR since the waning days of *perestroika*.[3] "Russians will say they can make similar goods as well. True that they can produce quality, but not very much of it," continued Carpenter.

Today the Russian textile industry is regulated by *private governance*, characterized by mixed local and central government enforcement of economy-wide regulations without adequate resources and enterprises of various ownership structures, which range from privately owned by former Soviet managers and workers to oligarch-held holding companies and local state government-owned enterprises. The industry's low perceived strategic value for national security and resource management imperatives and path-dependent sectoral institutional arrangements dating to the period immediately before the breakdown of the Soviet Union shape the extent and scope of state control of market coordination and distribution of property rights, which vary by subsector.

In the immediate breakdown of the Soviet Union in 1991, similar to the *perestroika* policies in the previous decade, the State Committee for Private Property Management led by Anatoly Chubais first targeted light industries for privatization and deregulation, from prices to supply chain coordination. Unlike in the landline telecommunications networks held onto by the state analyzed in Chapter 10, the privatization of state-owned textile enterprises in industrial clusters created by the Soviet supply chain installed many Soviet-era managers as new owners.[4] Almost from the start, the managers' ability to assert complete control over the production process and retain their managerial authority was compromised. Price liberalization of raw materials put strain on the textile supply chain, which Soviet federalism erected and Gorbachev reforms began to dismantle but did not replace as discussed in Chapter 9. Moreover, a shortage of hard currency made sources of foreign raw materials, including synthetic fiber, unattainable. Suppliers were unwilling to sign or fulfill contracts unless on a barter basis or at vastly higher prices. The price of thread costs

---

[2] See McKinsey FashionScope (2020) and FashionUnited.com accessed at https://fashionunited.ru/statistics/fashion-industry-statistics-russia/, respectively.
[3] Interview on May 27, 2015.   [4] See Pennar (1992).

less than cotton, which is the raw material.[5] Shortened hours and temporary closedowns became the norm, and unemployment soared.

"Under the Communists, cotton was grown in one area and bartered to another area. Kazakhstan cotton traded to northern Romania to be spun into yarn and then transported to western Romania to be knit and woven into fabric," said Carpenter.[6] "Factories came to a stop when the Berlin Wall fell. Managers were eager to fill orders, but it would take them weeks to study the requirements while waiting to no avail for supply materials to come in." The vicious cycle of acute shortages in raw materials and fabrics and apparels produced by domestic mills also affected upstream defense production of the textile machinery.[7] The company case studies show the shortage of supplies created by the Soviet breakdown continues to afflict labor- and capital-intensive textiles today, further exacerbated by the economic and political crises of the past three decades.

It soon became clear that the general economic woes, the breakdown of the Soviet supply links, and the absence of an institutional infrastructure to support a market system would soon lead to the near collapse of the textile industry. Between 1990 and 1994, textile production dropped by nearly 80 percent, becoming one of the most severely affected segments of manufacturing.

Afterwards, textile production stagnated at about 20% of the 1990-level until 1999, after the 1998 financial crisis.[8] The 1998 financial crisis, which saw the Russian government devalue the ruble and default on its debt, adversely affected a textile industry already struggling to survive. Local governments, out of desperation of limited options to sustain local economic development and retain employment, intervened at the company level. Many struggling enterprises, initially privatized to former state managers, came under the ownership of holding companies of local and regional oligarchs.

During times of economic crisis, some companies, which were privatized in the early 1990s, reverted back to state ownership. Continued reliance on Soviet-era practices, such as output targets, and limited resources, however, prevented effective restructuring and undermined

---

[5] See Filtzer (1994), 140. [6] Interview on May 27, 2015.
[7] See Gaddy (1996), 104–107.
[8] See Hanzl and Havlik (2003). In labor productivity, price, quality, and trade with the European Union the Russian textile industry ranked comparatively far below the rest of Central Eastern Europe, whereby textiles have played a relatively important role in those economies.

operations between managers and the new owners.[9] Moreover, limited interest from domestic and international investors further influenced the enterprises' inability to rebound. The reorganized companies were often left without funds, limited knowhow, and antiquated equipment to compete with cheap imports from China and South Asia in the low-end segments and American and European brands in the high-end segments.

As local governments and company stakeholders grappled with limited options to revive struggling textile enterprises in the context of economic crises and foreign competition in a liberalized environment, the central state was much more willing to exercise limited resources and capacity to affect industrial development in the technical sectors and to aid well-connected regional oligarchs. Ideologically disparate political actors prioritized the development of technical textiles in ways not dissimilar from the height of *perestroika* a decade before Soviet collapse, as shown in Chapter 9, when the five-year plans of the 1980s identified technical textiles as strategic for national security even while clothing and apparel underwent deregulation and industrial and enterprise restructuring. In addition to their geostrategic importance in the Putin era, the structural attributes of subsectors, such as the petrochemical inputs of synesthetic fiber, have shaped market governance and development.

11.2 APPAREL AND CLOTHING: LOCAL INDUSTRIAL DEVELOPMENT VIA LOCAL STATE INTERVENTIONS AND CENTRAL SUBSIDIES OF REGIONAL OLIGARCHS

The manufacturing and trade of clothing and apparel and textiles falls under the Ministry of Industry and Trade (Minpromtorg)'s Department of Light Industry and Forestry Complex created in the mid-2010s. The precise role of the decentralized state in market coordination and the dominant composition of ownership structures (and their developmental impacts) of *private governance* in Russian textiles vary by region and company. Linen producer Vologda Textiles, a merger of two state-owned companies managed by a private company, in the city of Krasavino in Vologda oblast typifies the experiences of textile enterprises struggling economically in an otherwise vibrant region teeming with Russian and foreign investment.[10]

---

[9] See Morrison (2005).
[10] Interviews in June and July, 2015, with managers of the Department of Economic Development of the Vologda government and current and former management of Kras and Vologda Textiles.

Originally state-owned during the Soviet era, after privatization in the early 1990s, the two companies struggled with cash flow due to high interest rates and the elevated costs of raw materials and energy. In those days, the companies produced cloth from raw materials purchased by European and American buyers. After the 1998 financial crisis, the private companies managed by workers went bankrupt, and the local government became a major shareholder in each company, in 2000. The two companies continued to operate separately, until 2008, when the global financial crisis hit. The Vologda government merged the two companies during the 2008 crisis. The local government entrusted management to a private company and, after operating as a merged company under private management for several years, Vologda Textiles declared bankruptcy. Production ceased in 2015, after which the local government assisted the company to pay the salaries of specialized workers and became involved in negotiating with potential investors.

The local government intervened several times, to become a shareholder, to reorganize the companies, and to subsidize its welfare functions in a limited capacity due to the significant contribution of Vologda Textiles to the local economy. During the Soviet era, both companies generated 30 percent of general government tax income for the city. The figure fell to 2–3 percent, when the combined company declared bankruptcy in 2015. Employment also fell to 500 people from 4,000 during the Soviet era. Moreover, the companies once exported to the Netherlands, Italy, and Slovenia with buyers and distributors from all over Europe. "In recent years, Europeans no longer pay for the raw materials, and foreign investors have shown very little interest. In April 2015, an Indian company expressed interest but has not acted," explained Kolesov Vasilii, formerly the general manager of Kras, one of the companies, now retained as a consultant.[11] In hopes of restarting production, Vasilii has traveled to Los Angeles to meet with prospective buyers.

Notwithstanding limited local government interventions, "our experience shows it doesn't matter who are the shareholders if they are unwilling to replace outdated equipment, which damages the cloth, and pay for expensive raw materials," expounded Vasilii. "Kras, one of the SOEs founded as a private company in 1851, survived through wars to become the brand of the region. When the companies merged, Kras hadn't technologically upgraded since 1985. Some of the Swiss machines still in use in 2015 dated back to the 1950s and 1970s," he said.

---

[11] Interviews on July 8 and July 13, 2015, with Kolesov Vasilii, OAO Vologda Textiles.

"These problems are faced in all regions, not just in Vologda," Vasilii further explained. Vologda's famous lace handicraft producers are on their last legs, and the fate of a sewing factory rests on the continued partnership with a longtime German client. The woes suffered by Vologda Textiles are representative of the Russian textile industry, which remains in shambles. Between 1998 and 2010, Russian textile exports, already miniscule compared to the rest of the economy, fell 80 percent (from 1 percent to less than 0.2 percent of total exports).[12] In 2007, Russia imported five times more textiles than it exported, making it barely a textile-producing country.[13] The official imports do not capture the nonofficially sanctioned "gray market" imports, estimated at 48 percent of the textile market, mostly imports from China, Turkey, and the Commonwealth of Independent States (CIS) countries due to transshipping and relabeling. In 2018, though Russia's apparel market ranked ninth globally, domestic production made up less than 20 percent of consumption, with about 650 large and medium enterprises and 4,000 small companies.[14]

11.2.1 Firm-Level Variation on Impacts of Central Interventions After Crimea Annexation

Geopolitical concerns after Russia's annexation of Crimea have shaped central-level attention to the woes of the apparel and clothing industry. Vastly different experiences of apparel and clothing manufacturers, however, reveal the enterprise-level variation in economic benefits of the "national" strategy. The relative impacts of *perceived strategic value* and *sectoral structures and organization of institutions* on the role of the state in market coordination and property rights distribution are especially apparent. In 2014, Putin and Dmitry Medvedev toured Vologda Textiles, at the brink of bankruptcy, and stayed for "a planning meeting" during a country-wide textile meeting organized by the central and regional governments. Tax adjustments, such as a tariff freeze on inputs, and downstream and upstream solutions, such as a medium-term

---

[12] See OECD trade and industry data for 2011, accessed in 2018.
[13] See International Trade Commission (2010).
[14] See "FashionNet: Russia's Bid to Launch its Fashion Industry," *Forbes* (February 14, 2018) for the former figure and for the latter, see "Russia to Provide Financial Support to Domestic Textile Industry," *Fashionating World* (May 6, 2016). Also, see "Crisis in Russian Clothing Sector Creates Opportunities for Southeast Asian Exporters," *Russia Beyond* (February 26, 2021).

plan to subsidize linen production by seed purchase for agriculture and state procurement of linen for uniforms, respectively, were discussed as prospective market and nonmarket mechanisms. Shortly after the meeting and after Russia annexed Crimea, the Russian government banned textile imports in military uniforms, leisurewear, underwear, bedclothes, hats, socks, pillows, and shoes.

Two years later, the "Strategy of Development of Textile and Light Industry in the Russian Federation" aimed to achieve 50 percent of domestic production for the internal market by 2025.[15] Then in 2018, in a bid to promote a Russian fashion industry, a public–private initiative between business associations and government-affiliated think tanks proposed the ambitious goal of 70 percent by 2035.[16] According to the all-Russian Union of Entrepreneurs of Textile and Light Industry (Souzlegprom), the light industry development strategy "provides state support for textile and garments manufacturers, including modernization of technological base and enhancing their competitiveness, among other measures." Incorporated are some of the methods discussed with high-level official fanfare at the meeting, in 2014, inside Vologda Textiles. However, the company has not benefited from the promised support.

In contrast to Vologda Textiles' experience, the BTK Group, a manufacturer of men's apparel based in the financial and industrial capital of St. Petersburg, Russia's second largest city, formed in 2007 as a merger of two of Russia's largest apparel manufacturers, one founded in 1906 and the other in 1945. BTK became, in 2012, an exclusive supplier of military uniforms and was officially added by the Ministry of Industry and Trade to the Consolidated Register of Defense Contractors in 2014 when the government banned military apparel imports. The distinction secured a $1.5 billion contract with the Ministry of Defense. In 2015, BTK made the list of 199 enterprises, which the Russian government would consider first in its anti-crisis measures. "The government support reaches only large factories and is limited to placing government orders mostly for defense and industrial uniforms," explained Anna Lebsak-Kleimans of the New York-based CEO Fashion Consulting Group.[17]

---

[15] See "Russia to Provide Financial Support to Domestic Textile Industry," *Fashionating World* (May 6, 2016).
[16] See "FashionNet: Russia's Bid to Launch Its Fashion Industry," *Forbes* (February 14, 2018).
[17] See "Crisis in Russian Clothing Sector Creates Opportunities for Southeast Asian Exporters," *Russia Beyond* (June 9, 2015).

Personal connections to Putin also help. Taimuraz Bolloev, the billionaire oligarch owner of BTK, is formerly the head of breweries in St. Petersburg and served on the Sochi Olympics committee. The special treatment received by BTK in the government's enforcement of its light industry strategy has empowered BTK to expand its holdings in the Soviet Shahtinskii silk and cotton mill, one of the largest producers of textile products in Europe during the 1970s and 1980s, in the Rostov oblast, southeast of St. Petersburg.[18] The complex of modern equipment infrastructure imported from northern and Western Europe, before the 2014 EU sanctions, included a sewing factory, finished goods warehouses and auxiliary engineering shops, and the production capacity for nonwovens fabrics with "smart" properties from synthetic fibers in addition to the production of synthetic fibers and heat retainers.

11.3 INDUSTRIAL AND TECHNICAL TEXTILES: NATIONAL TECHNOLOGY BASE AND DEFENSE INDUSTRY INPUTS VIA CENTRAL INVESTMENTS AND INDUSTRIAL POLICY

"The clothing and apparel industry is almost dead, further crippled by the active shadow economy of gray business. Technical textiles, in contrast, draws in FDI for modernization and helps sustain the military-industrial complex with aviation and space industry applications," explicated Natalya Ivanova, deputy director of the Institute of World Economy and International Relations of the Russian Academy of Sciences.[19] A recipient of special treatment as a large private enterprise owned by a politically connected entrepreneur with connections to Putin, BTK, nonetheless, operated within the dominant pattern of *private governance* in clothing and apparel. BTK's foray into capital-intensive industrial and technical textiles, in the mid-2010s and beyond, exposes billionaire oligarch Bolloev and BTK to the higher extent and scope of central state and local government control in the *decentralized governance* characteristic of market coordination and distribution of property rights arrangements in the technical sectors. These are textile sectors that supply and have applications for medicine, materials processing, construction, oil and gas, rail, telecommunications, shipbuilding, and automobiles, to name some.

---

[18] See "BTK Holding to Establish One of Russia's Largest Technical Textiles Plants," *Innovation in Textiles* (October 22, 2014).
[19] Interview on June 10, 2015 in Moscow.

In the context of economy-wide market reforms, the federal and local governments have intervened *proactively and reactively* in response to internal and external pressures to coordinate industrial development with import substitution policies in technical textiles. They do so at the behest of nonstate stakeholders, such as sector and business associations and dominant enterprises, for deliberate local government and central state interventions during crisis moments and because technical textiles are perceived strategic as critical material inputs in defense and nondefense industries of the national economy.

After the founding of the Russian Federation, along with regional governments and related universities and research bureaucracies, the Department of Chemical Technology and Bioengineering Technologies and the Department of the Defense Industry of the Ministry of Industry and Trade regulate industrial and market development with economy-wide and sector-specific rules. The dominant distribution of property rights consists of privately owned and state-invested enterprises operating in industrial facilities, which date as far back as the Tsarist period. Many enterprises began production under the purview of the USSR's military-industrial complex of advanced chemistry and other related heavy industries, as analyzed in Chapter 9.

Notwithstanding these interventions, not unlike in apparel and textiles, foreign producers dominate the domestic market for technical textiles.[20] "Chemical fiber processing collapsed after the 1998 economic crisis and was never restored. The regional monopoly of raw materials further exacerbated the sector's woes. Few plants exist, and they are cross-subsidized as part of the military sector," explained Evgeny Belov, the head of Engineering and Technology for Bayer Russia and CIS.[21] The Russian Union of Entrepreneurs of Textile and Light Industry estimates that domestic technical textiles meet only 15–17 percent of domestic consumption. The situation further downstream is similar: The share of imports of synthetic fibers and yarns in the domestic market was estimated at about 71 percent.[22] In 2016, the Russian technical textiles industry ranked 54 out of 70 countries, compared to number three-ranked China and India (which was numbered 17 in the list). Three years

---

[20] See "New Projects to Create Growth Conditions for Russian Technical Textiles," *Innovation in Textiles* (April 8, 2015).
[21] Interview in Moscow on June 11, 2015.
[22] See "New Projects to Create Growth Conditions for Russian Technical Textiles," *Innovation in Textiles* (April 8, 2015).

later, Russia produced only 1 percent of the world's petrochemical supplies despite ample oil and gas resources.[23]

11.3.1 Post-1998 Financial Crisis and 2014 Western Sanctions: State Interventions & Petrochemicals as Strategic Resource Assets

The experience of petrochemical producer SIBUR is representative of the more intentional role of the state in market coordination and ownership in technical textiles because of the higher *perceived strategic value* and *sectoral structures and organization of institutions*. Russia's reliance on its oil production and the post-Putin regulatory centralization and nationalization of the oil sector are important factors. The Presidential Administration and the Ministry of Energy develop policy over related activities implemented by the Ministry of Industry and Trade's Department of Chemical Technology and Bioengineering Technologies.

At the height of macroprivatization and liberalization in 1995, the Russian government founded SIBUR. Headquartered in Moscow with production sites all over the country, SIBUR became vertically integrated in 1998. At that time, during the Russian economic crisis when many state-owned companies liquidated and the government held onto only the most strategic assets, SIBUR acquired over sixty companies for a full production chain from the processing of raw materials to the manufacturing of finished goods. In 2001, a then privately held Gazprom, the corporation created from the Soviet Ministry of Gas Industry, acquired a 51 percent stake. SIBUR became state-owned again when the Putin government renationalized Gazprom in 2005. Gazprom divested SIBUR, in 2008, after deciding that petrochemicals are non-core assets.

Patents related to chemicals and technical textiles sharply increased shortly before the steep falls during and after the 1998 and 2008 financial crises (Figure 11.1). All the same, production of chemical fibers and threads steadily declined from 2000 to the end of the decade (Table 11.1). Moreover, Russian exports of medium high-tech goods, under which chemical fiber and threads fall, remained relatively flat between the late 1990s and through 2014; this is also true for low-tech goods, which include apparel textile products (Figure 11.2). The inverse is true of imports of these categories of goods (Figure 11.3).

---

[23] See "Russia Embarks on Petchems Push," *Petroleum Economist* (July 26, 2019).

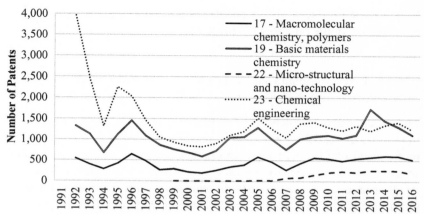

FIGURE 11.1. Russia patents: Chemical materials, fiber processing, and nanotechnology (1991–2016)
Source: World Intellectual Property Organization (2019).

As a private company, in 2011, SIBUR divested its tire and mineral fertilizer businesses to focus on investing in the production of polymers, a critical input for high-tech materials. In a 50–50 joint venture with Belgian Solvay Group near Kstovo, in the Nizhniy Novgorod region, SIBUR established RusVinyl. RusVinyl, the largest integrated polyvinyl chloride (PVC) plant in Europe, has received 12.5-year financing from Russian and international banks, including HSBC, Sberbank, and the European Bank for Reconstruction and Development.[24] At the time, the Nizhniy Novgorod regional government designated RusVinyl a priority project. RusVinyl also benefited from becoming a key investment of the "State Plan for Development of the Oil and Petrochemical Industries." Moreover, the Ministry of Industry and Trade incorporated RusVinyl into the long-term State Program-2035 for the strategic development of the petrochemical industry.[25]

Western sanctions imposed on Russia, in 2014, after the intervention in Crimea intensified and emboldened domestic industry calls for protectionism and promotion of indigenous industry. The Russian Association of Textile and Textile Producers advocated for a ban on imports from sanctioning countries and the enforcement of illegal imports from China,

[24] See "RusVinyl: SIBUR and Solvay's Market Risk First," *Project Finance and Infrastructure Finance* (June 2011).
[25] See "«RusVinyl» Finalizes the EUR750 Million Project Financing Agreement," SIBUR Press Release (June 17, 2011).

TABLE 11.1. *Russia: Production of chemical fibers and thread (in thousands of tons)*

Product Types	2000	2001	2002	2003	2004	2005	2006	2007	2008	2009
Synthetic fibers and threads	105	115	106	127	122	119	116	111	102	86.12
Fibers	18.4	21.9	25.6	38.8	42.1	36.7	40.4	42.9	45.5	45.14
Textile fibers	18.3	18.4	14.3	14	12.1	11.3	11.9	13.3	13	8.25
Thread for cord fabric and industrial items, film fibers	68.2	74.9	65.9	74.4	68	70.8	62.6	54.4	43.5	32.73
Man-Made fibers and thread	59.1	42.9	53.3	59.9	65.3	38.5	38.4	36.3	20.5	18.88
Fibers	35	32.3	42.7	50.3	58.1	37.5	37.5	35.6	20.5	18.85
Textile fibers	22.6	10.6	10.6	9.6	7.2	1	1	0.7	0.03	0.03
Thread for cord fabric and industrial items, film fibers	1.5								0.009	
Total chemical fibers and thread	164.1	157.9	159.3	186.9	187.3	157.5	154.4	147.3	122.5	105

Source: Zotikova and Zotikov (2010).

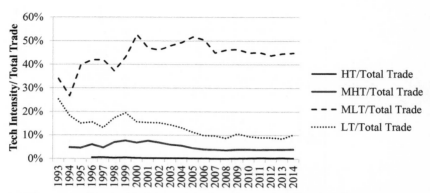

FIGURE 11.2. Russia: Tech intensity of exports as % of total trade (1993–2014)
Source: World Intellectual Property Organization (2017) with OECD Tech Intensity Definition.

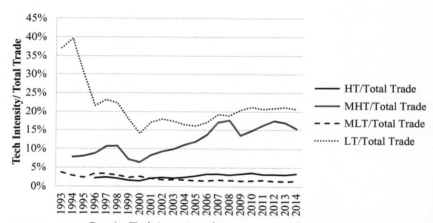

FIGURE 11.3. Russia: Tech intensity of imports as % of total trade (1993–2014)
Source: World Intellectual Property Organization (2017) with OECD Tech Intensity Definition.

Kazakhstan, and Kyrgyzstan.[26] Prime Minister Medvedev during a meeting in Ivanovo, on October 13, 2014, acknowledged, "Clearly, the situation is complicated, especially so because this industry has been in marked decline for decades. The situation has improved in certain segments, remained unchanged in others, and further worsened in still others. The number of workers in the sector is shrinking and now stands at 270,000, down from 400,000 seven to eight years ago. This is not entirely a bad thing, as it's also a sign of modern labor practices in the

---

[26] See "BTK Holding to Establish One of Russia's Largest Technical Textiles Plant," *Innovation in Textiles* (October 22, 2014).

industry. There are objective causes, including obsolete manufacturing facilities, dependence on imports of raw materials and, of course, tough competition."[27]

He continued, "Nevertheless, the industry still must be developed, and we can follow the example of a number of countries that managed to convert such factories into modern, efficient production facilities. The industry has plenty of room to grow, and the demand for textile will always be there. At nearly three trillion rubles, the retail market for light industry is the largest among all non-food product markets. These can be profitable businesses that are good for the country's budget. Soon thereafter, the government designated domestic production of synthetic fabrics a major pillar of the "Strategy of Development of Textile and Light Industry in the Russian Federation" released in 2016.[28] The Russian government aspired to increase the domestic production share to 80 percent of the local market by 2020.

In the late 2010s, amid uncertain prospects for global oil demand and fast-growth in the sector, in addition to Western sanctions after intervention in Crimea, the Russian government came to view petrochemicals as a strategic replacement of the reliance on crude oil.[29] The sanctions resulted in restrictions for supplies of various technologies, equipment, and raw materials.[30] Petrochemical products such as olefins, polyolefins, plastics, and elastomers are raw materials critical for domestic manufacturing, which the State Plan for Development of the Oil and Petrochemical Industries promotes with subsidies and a favorable tax regime.

To shift away from oil dependency, in 2015, the Center for Design, Manufacturing, and Materials became established at the Skolkovo Institute of Science and Technology.[31] Prioritized were the production of synthetic fabrics for road construction, defense, and aerospace. The state planned up to 13,000 kilometers of new roads by 2020, increasing

---

[27] See "Russia to Boost Textile Industry," *India Textile Journal* (November 30, 2014).

[28] See "Russia's Technical Textiles Industry Faces Raw Materials Shortage," *CCF Group Industry News* (April 19, 2019).

[29] See "Russia Embarks on Petchems Push," *Petroleum Economist* (July 26, 2019) and "Russia Eyes Petrochemicals as Answer to Crude Oil Reliance," *Reuters* (May 18, 2018).

[30] See "Europe: Russian Petrochemicals Industry on the Verge of Large-scale Growth," *Hydrocarbon Processing* (March 2019).

[31] The Skolkovo Institute established, in 2011, is a $300 million multi-year partnership between the Russian government and the Massachusetts Institute of Technology established. Interview with Irina Dezhina, Research Group on Science and Industrial Policy at Skolkovo Institute of Science and Technology, on June 11, 2015, in Moscow.

from 45 to 80 square meters of geosynthetic grids annually. The government planned to invest in SIBUR, one of the world's largest petrochemical companies, which announced a focus on geosynthetics. Moreover, the government designated up to $300 million in 2016 and 2017 toward developing the technical textiles industry, mainly to cover interest on Russian banks' loans to producers for equipment upgrading and acceleration of research and development.

The military budget, which reached a record high in 2016, also earmarked investments for the production of technical textiles and nonwovens for the national army. According to Andrei Razbrodin, president of Soyuzlegprom, the Russian Association of Textile and Light Industry Producers, "The Russian defense industry consumes about 30 percent of the technical textiles and nonwovens produced in Russia." Igor Komarov, then Director General of the State Corporation for Space Activities (Roskosmos), said, "The demand for technical textiles will be driven by ongoing plans to build the sixth generation for the Russian Air Force."[32]

In December 2016, the privately owned SIBUR sold a 10 percent stake to the Silk Road Fund, a Chinese government-backed investment fund.[33] The collaboration with the Silk Road Fund resulted in a distribution agreement with the Chinese state-owned Sinopec for ZapSibNeftekhim, SIBUR's new state-of-the-art value-added complex, funded in part by the State Plan for Development of the Oil and Petrochemical Industries, to supply polyethylene, a material input for technical textiles. China has also invested in the expansion of indigenous production of ethylene in the context of *decentralized governance*, as shown in Chapter 5. New competition, in addition to the polyethylene products being caught up in the U.S.-China trade war and the 2020 coronavirus outbreak, slowed demand and created production bottlenecks, respectively.[34] In February 2020, SIBUR delayed the public listing of 10–15 percent of its assets on the Moscow Stock Exchange.

---

[32] See "Advanced Textiles in Russia," *Industrial Fabrics Association International* (October 1, 2016).

[33] See "Silk Road Fund, a Chinese Investment Fund," SIBUR Press Release (December 14, 2016).

[34] See "China Section 301-Tariff Actions and Exclusion Process," United States Trade Representative. Accessed on November 24, 2020 at https://ustr.gov/issue-areas/enforcement/section-301-investigations/tariff-actions. Also, see "Road to IPO for Russia's Biggest Petrochemical Company Is Blocked by Trade Wars and Coronavirus," *Barrons* (February 24, 2020).

11.3.2 The Role of Subnational Governments and Public–Private Initiatives

The central government's sector-specific efforts in state procurement, input subsidies, and investment have led regional governments and private enterprises to plan for industry expansion. Promises of government subsidies for the purchase of raw materials and guaranteed demand as a registered and exclusive supplier of military wear propelled BTK's expansion into technical textiles with the Rostov-based production facility. Also, in 2014, the state-backed National Investment and Finance Corporation (NIFC) invested in the establishment of an industrial cluster for the production of textile and technical textile products in the Ryazan region outside of Moscow.[35] Similar to BTK, the cluster builds on an existing industrial base of Korablinsky, a local spinning and weaving factory established in 1962 and one of Russia's oldest textile producers.

Industrial and central calls for self-sufficiency also accelerated the development of a large-scale production of PET and polyester fibers complex in the Ivanovo region as part of the "Production of polyester textile fibers from polyether and processing in Ivanovo" plan.[36] Paul Konkov, the Ivanovo governor, said in 2016, "In the future, it will provide the creation of a complex of new textile plants, specializing in the production of innovative import substitution products for special and technical purposes with the use of polyester fibers and yarns." Plans halted in 2019, when state guarantees could not be secured after investment documentation for the project had already been completed and sent to Vnesheconombank, one of Russia's largest banks, for consideration.[37]

Despite central and regional governments' calls for self-sufficiency and import-substitution, with the exceptions of large companies owned by favored oligarchs, industrial and technical textiles will remain of secondary importance to the developmental goals of the Russian government. With limited financial resources and industrial coordination, the sector

---

[35] See "Investment Days of Ryazan Region Resulted in 5 Agreements Worth $125 million," *Invest in Regions* (October 9, 2014). Accessed July 25, 2019: www.investinregions.ru/de/news/Ryazan-investment-days-12-billion/.

[36] See "Synthetic Fiber Factory to Appear in Russia's Ivanovo Region," *Pravda* (October 12, 2012).

[37] See "New Projects to Create Growth Conditions for Russian Technical Textiles," *Innovation in Textiles* (April 8, 2015) and "Russia's Technical Textiles Industry Faces Raw Materials Shortage," *CCF Group Industry News* (April 19, 2019).

will continue to grapple with high product costs, low product quality, and limited market share.[38]

11.3.3 Not Quite Import Substitution: Industrial Policy and Investment in Deregulated Environment

With Russia's existing petrochemicals capacities already competitive in the global market in tailored, supply chain products, the State Plan for Development of the Oil and Petrochemical Industries may fall short of industrial upgrading. Bayer's Belov explained, "There are few cases of investment at the synthesis level, and they succeed because of knowhow and technology brought in by FDI. Only a few big Russian companies are able to push projects through that are above $1 billion. There is a huge distance between leaders like SIBUR and Rosneft and their followers." Dmitry Konov, the Chairman of SIBUR's Management Board, also maintained that "the main difficulty is related to the capital intensity of industry projects," which "will require significant incentives from the government," such as Saudi Arabia's regulated pricing and raw material discounts, which Russia is unable to provide.[39]

Started in 2007 by Anatoly Chubais, one of the architects of Russia's privatization process, the central government-owned venture capital fund Rusnano has invested in commercializing developments in the application of nanotechnology in synthetic fiber processing. Dmitry Medvedev incorporated Rusnano, designed to foster public–private partnerships, as part of his modernization initiatives.[40] Rusnano led global nanoscience research investment through the 2010s; however, the government's venture capital (VC) efforts have yet to produce an increase in significant publications or any visible breakthroughs in technology (Figure 11.1).[41] All the same, the number of patents filed in microstructural and nanotechnology increased after 2007 and fell in numbers after Western sanctions in response to Russia's annexation of Crimea. Notable also is the increase in patents in macromolecular chemistry and polymers (fiber processing) and basic materials chemistry after the release of the 2011 State Plan for the development of petrochemicals.

---

[38] See Terebova (2017) on challenges faced with import substitution in Russia's regions.
[39] See "Europe: Russian Petrochemicals Industry on the Verge of Large-scale Growth," *Hydrocarbon Processing* (March 2019).
[40] Interview with Dmitry Akhanov at Rusnano USA in Menlo Park, California on August 8, 2011.
[41] See Balzer and Askonas (2016).

Russia witnessed a 75 percent fall in foreign VC investments after the start of Western sanctions; thus in 2017, the Russian government announced a "coercion to innovations" initiative to direct large state-owned companies to set up corporate VC funds to help startups. So far few except for the very largest leading SOEs have funds, including Rostelecom, Roscosmos, Gazprom, United Shipbuilding Corporation, State Atomic Energy Corporation, and Skolkovo. The centralized administration of investment is not expected to change "how state-owned companies gain advantage through having access to administrative resources, government subsidies, and government defense contracts."[42]

11.4 TEXTILE TRADE AND DISTRIBUTION: INDUSTRIAL DEVELOPMENT VIA PUBLIC–PRIVATE INITIATIVES AND MARKET-BASED IMPORT SUBSTITUTION STRATEGY

At nearly $30 billion a year, Russia's domestic market in apparel and clothing is the ninth largest in the world. In the context of fully liberalized markets yet limited industrial capacity and small production volume, imported goods account for over 80 percent of the total market. In recent years, 60 percent of apparel imports originate from China and South Asian countries.[43] Trade and retail in apparel and textiles are dominated by domestic retail of mono-brands in the economy segment and foreign-invested multi-brand retailers in the luxury segment. Discounters, convenience channels, and informal retail – such as informal stalls in open-air markets – operated by Russians dominate the economy segment. In the upmarket, dominated by imports, are hypermarkets that anchor shopping malls or are located in outskirts of cities. Foreign-invested chains are among top players. Supermarkets and cash-and-carry stores also have among them foreign investors.

Notwithstanding the dominance of foreign imports in apparel and textile retail, large oligarchic-owned retailers include Bosco di Ciliegi Group of Companies by Mikhail Kusnirovich. Kusnirovich founded Bosco in the early days of the Russian Federation after he first landed in Bologna, Italy, home to the world's top fashion designers, in 1989, to help import equipment for an amusement park in Moscow's famed Gorky Park during the last days of *perestroika*. Kusnirovich signed licensing

---

[42] See Dezhina (2018), 20.
[43] *McKinsey FashionScope* (2020), reported by FashionUnited, accessed at https:// fashionunited.ru/statistics/fashion-industry-statistics-russia/.

agreements with Armani, Etro, Gucci, and other luxury brands to sell clothing in self-owned stores he managed and staffed. Eventually he amassed interests in shopping malls, megastores, and a variety of brands in fashion. His sportwear and lifestyle brands began outfitting Russian Olympians in 1992, and the company dressed Putin and the entire Russian Olympics delegation of 18,000 for the Sochi Olympics in 2014.[44] The teams of Spain, Serbia, and Ukraine have also worn Bosco uniforms.

Bosco di Ciliegi Group and Kusnirovich have gained a reputation for his loud colors and flashy designs. For example, according to Kusnirovich, the florid colors of the 2014 Olympic uniforms were purposely a "break from the past" of the "dark colors, grays, and blacks." It was also speculated that the "rainbow style," as Bosco's design director Igor Kazakov described it, flaunted the 2013 government ban against the distribution of gay "propaganda" to children, which human rights activists assert endangers LGBT youth by denying them access to affirming education and support services.[45]

Over the years, the Ministry of Industry and Trade has sought to promote Russia as a destination for contract manufacturing. As detailed in the subsector case studies, however, the slow and protracted development of the Russian textile industry lacks the production capacity and the industrial modernization necessary to supply domestic consumption, much less global markets. Thus, in recent years, industrial associations, such as the National Fashion Council and Russian Outdoor, in conjunction with state-affiliated think tanks, such as the National Technology Initiative, Agency for Strategic Initiative, and the Skolkovo Foundation, have collaborated with large retail conglomerates, including Bosco di Ciliegi Group, in public–private programs to achieve 70 percent domestic apparel coverage by 2035.

The FashionNet, for example, launched in 2018, promotes emerging domestic brands with production capacity based in Moscow, St. Petersburg, Ivanovo, and Kaliningrad, Russia's westernmost commercial port. "The FashionNet market goes far beyond the light industry because it includes many related things, including logistic infrastructure, electronic commerce, support of small businesses and young designers, companies

---

[44] See "For Sochi Games, Russians Trade Dour for Dazzling," *New York Times* (February 8, 2014).

[45] See "No Support Russia's 'Gay Propaganda' Law Imperils LGBT Youth," Human Rights Watch (December 11, 2018).

TABLE 11.2. *Russia: Laws, rules, and regulations governing textile subsectors*

Market Coordination	Property Rights Arrangements
Textiles Writ-Large	
• Ministry of Industry and Trade • State Committee for Private Property Management (GKI) (1992) privatization, deregulation on prices, and supply chain coordination • Strategy of Development of Textile and Light Industry in the Russian Federation (2016) • Russian Association of Textile and Light Industry Producers • Russian Association of Textile and Textile Producers • Russian Union of Entrepreneurs of Textile & Light Industry	• State Committee for Private Property Management (GKI) (1992) privatization
Apparel and Clothing	
• Ban of imports in military use (2014) • Strategy of Development of Textile and Light Industry in the Russian Federation (2016)	• Limited local government re-nationalization during economic crises
Nonwovens and Industrial Textiles (including Chemical Fiber and Geosynthetics)	
• Ministry of Industry and Trade's Department of Chemical Technology and Bioengineering Technologies • Ministry of Energy's Department of the Defense Industry • State Plan for Development of the Oil and Petrochemical Industries (2011, 2019) • Nizhniy Novgorod State Program-2015 by Ministry of Industry and Trade (2011) • National Investment and Finance Corporation (NIFC) industrial cluster (2014) • Center for Design, Manufacturing, and Materials established, Skolkovo	• Nationalization of the oil sector • Founding of SIBUR (1995) • SIBUR vertical integration via M&As raw materials processing to finished goods manufacturing (1998) • Gazprom acquisition of 51% of SIBUR (2001) • Nationalization of Gazprom (2005) • Establishment and corporatization of state-owned venture capital fund Rusnano (2007) • State divestment of SIBUR (2008) • SIBUR divested businesses to focus on chemical fiber/polymer production (2011)

(*continued*)

TABLE 11.2. *(continued)*

Market Coordination	Property Rights Arrangements
Institute of Science and Technology (2015)	• Privately owned RusVinyl, SIBUR's 50–50 joint venture with Belgian Solvay Group (2011)
• Russian Association of Textile and Light Industry Producers	• National Investment and Finance Corporation (2014)
• Russian Association of Textile and Textile Producers	
• State Corporation for Space Activities	
• Presidential Administration	
• Designation as major pillar of Strategy of Development of Textile and Light Industry (2016)	
• Prioritization of production of synthetic fabrics for road construction, defense, and aerospace and domestic investment in roads (2016)	
• Pledge of $300 million in 2016 and 2017 for modernization by federal government (2016)	
• Proposed Investment in SIBUR in geosynthetics (2016)	
• Expanded military budget, including in 6th generation airforce	
• "Coercion to innovations" VC funds of SOEs for startups (2017)	

Textile Trade and Distribution

- National Fashion Council
- Russian Outdoor
- FashionNet
- Russian Export Center
- Strategy of Development of Textile and Light Industry in the Russian Federation (2016)
- Tariff-free regime to import textiles and accessories without taxation for exportable textile and clothing products
- Tariff regime for technical textiles raw materials imports

...strategic value, market governance, and development

Private Governance	Dominant Coordination Mechanisms	Dominant Distribution of Property Rights	Development Outcomes
Low Strategic Value **Local Employment and Development**	**Apparel and Clothing** Decentralized enforcement of economy-wide regulation; regional government and enterprise-level market coordination	**Apparel and Clothing** Variegated market players; limited foreign investment	**Apparel and Clothing** Limited capacity and small volume in domestic production; trade boom for foreign producers and investors in "black and gray" imports, counterfeit products, and high-end retail
Medium Strategic Value **Industrial Development and Import Substitution**	**Industrial and Technical Textiles** Central and local bureaucracies and goals coordinate markets; economy-wide rules and sector-specific central-level investment subsidies and fiscal incentives in chemical fiber processing and synthetic fabrics	**Industrial and Technical Textiles** Subnational state-owned and partially privatized enterprises and FDI in joint ventures	**Industrial and Technical Textiles** Large state and regional oligarchic-owned enterprises main beneficiaries of import-substitution industrialization investments and fiscal incentives; ranked far behind China and India in capacity with FDI dominant in domestic production and imports
Medium Strategic Value **Market-based Import Substitution**	**Trade and Distribution** Liberalized market entry and business scope in trade and retail distribution; public–private initiatives on branding in apparel and clothing as "market-based import-substitution industrialization"; raw materials tariffs regime for technical sectors	**Trade and Distribution** Dominant Russian single brand retailers in economy segments and multinational multi-brand marketers in high-end segments, with exception of few oligarchic-owned apparel and textile companies.	**Trade and Distribution** Top ten retail market in the world in textiles and clothing, yet Russian domestic capacity across sectors fulfills less than one fifth of the market

that already can directly enter the world markets without becoming major players but staying small and medium ones. These are new technologies related not only to materials and fabrics but also to portable devices and electronics," stressed Oleg Fomichev, the Deputy Minister of Economic Development of the Russian Federation.[46]

Moreover, the Russian Fashion Fund of the National Fashion Council, started in 2019, streamlines complex production and distribution services for Russian designers. Not to be outdone, a tariff-free regime negotiated between the Russian Export Center and the Ministry of Industry and Trade enables Russian clothing manufacturers to import textiles and accessories without taxation for exportable products. Such public–private initiatives focused on textile trade and distribution, coupled with the targeted investments and tariffs regime for the manufacturing of petrochemical products in technical textiles, with the goal of achieving similar domestic market coverage, represent the "market-based import-substitution industrialization" policy in the liberalized and privatized Russian textile industry. This aim to actively replace foreign imports by engaging liberalized domestic industry departs from the "import-substitution-cum-FDI strategy" pursued by the Chinese government to actively court FDI to strategically develop the national technology base, examined in the China chapters (Chapters 3–5).

Since the days of the Soviet Union, the textile industry is perceived to be of low strategic value for national security; however, in the face of competitive pressures from China and geopolitical pressures in the post-Crimea era, the domestic industry's variegated market stakeholders have reframed textiles to represent national assets worthy of government concern. A viral promotion video on the Russian Internet for a textiles producer in Cheboksary on the Volga river, both parodies and captures such sentiments. Set to techno music with a 1990s aesthetic, the video contains such lyrical lines as "Gucci is made in China. This is made at home" and "winter leggings from the Republic of Chuvashia" (which experiences subzero Russian frost).[47] Table 11.2 shows temporal and subsectoral variation in laws and regulations governing textiles, as analyzed in this chapter. Table 11.3 maps dominant patterns of market governance structures and development outcomes in textiles.

---

[46] See "FashionNet: Russia's Bid to Launch Its Fashion Industry," *Forbes* (February 14, 2018).
[47] See "Kremlin Does Couture: Russia Creates the Fashion Fund," *Forbes* (June 28, 2019).

PART III

NATIONAL CONFIGURATIONS
OF SECTORAL MODELS

Development, New Capitalisms, and Future of Global Conflict and Cooperation

The book has introduced a new model for understanding the nature and scope of market governance in the developing world in the context of economic internationalization. The Strategic Value Framework contends that state elite decision-makers, socialized over time with particular values and identities borne of significant phases of institutionalization, respond to internal domestic and external pressures to globalize with fundamentally divergent market governance structures, which vary by country and by sector (within a country). In addition to the multidimensionality of state goals as a function of the *perceived strategic value* of state elites, the theoretical framework draws attention to the profound impacts of *sectoral structures and organization of institutions* as a mediation for the relationship between globalization and development.

The unifying theoretical framework has uncovered what market governance structures in the most politically and economically important countries in the developing world look like and how and why their practices depart from each other and their counterparts elsewhere in the world. Controlling for country size, geopolitical significance, and the timing of industrialization, the book's historical process-tracing from sectoral origins in Chapters 3, 6, and 9, on China, India, and Russia, respectively, identifies the origins and transformation of perceived strategic value and how state elites have responded to earlier episodes of national consolidation. From there, the intranational comparative sector case studies (telecommunications and textiles and their subsectors), focusing analysis in 1990 and beyond, of Chapters 4–5 (China), 7–8 (India), and 10–11 (Russia) delineate the national sector-specific patterns of market governance. They uncover how within the same political system (governed politically by democracy or authoritarianism), sectoral structures and organization of institutions interact with value-bounded rationality to shape the role of the state in market coordination and the dominant distribution of property rights arrangements.

The emergent *national configurations of sectoral models* redefine the existing models of development and varieties of capitalism on the interactions between company-level and national-level characteristics and hierarchical state-business relations. The book's multilevel comparative case research design empowers the finding that regime type reinforces or incrementally affects the perceived strategic value orientation but does not on its own explain or alter dominant patterns of resulting new capitalisms. Rather, the sector-specific dynamics emanating nation-specific sectoral pathways to development uncover how national imperatives rooted in perceived strategic value and sectoral structures and organization of institutions interact and shape how multinational and domestic companies alike experience the emergent institutional foundations of capitalism as discussed in Section 12.1 of this chapter.

The remaining of the chapter discusses the case-specific findings, including developmental outcomes and international relations, of the *national configurations of sectoral models*. Section 12.2 documents how *techno-security developmentalism* in China has shaped the *bifurcated capitalism*, which maps at the sectoral level from consumer electronics to fintech. Likewise, the perceived strategic value orientation of *neoliberal self-reliance* in India is personified in the rise of Modi and the *bifurcated liberalism* undergirding India's response to "the China factor" and ravages of COVID-19, as Section 12.3 shows. Section 12.4 contends *resource security nationalism* has shaped the rise of *bifurcated oligarchy* in Putin's Russia as state actions embolden the business of misinformation and subsidize defense-oriented textiles. Analysis of China's, India's, and Russia's varying initial responses to the COVID-19 global pandemic shows that the transborder shock, which has affected all three countries under study, has not fundamentally disrupted the national sector-specific pathways to globalization and development. Finally, Section 12.5 underscores that the interacting strategic value and sectoral logics have shaped pressing challenges of global conflict and cooperation from trade and tech wars to the global pandemic.

12.1 NATIONAL CONFIGURATIONS OF SECTORAL MODELS AND VARIETIES OF CAPITALISM

The prevailing literature on varieties of capitalism contends that different types of capitalisms are founded on production regimes defined by strategic interaction between firms, employees, and shareholders in the greater role imparted to the state.[1] On the one hand, the literature identifies dominant national models – liberal market versus coordinated market economies (LME vs. CME), based on findings from rich democracies – and contends that CMEs produce incremental innovation and LMEs generate radical innovation.[2] On the other hand, VOC studies on the developing world, such as Ben Ross Schneider's work on Latin America, which identifies distinct economic units in the form of multinationals and dominant family business groups characterized by hierarchal and oligopolistic control, show how different path dependencies have created its own competitive advantages.[3]

Focusing on understanding the varying institutional contexts underlying state-market interactions in developing countries undergoing global economic integration, the book's findings show that dominant patterns of market governance at the sectoral level are where varieties of capitalism (VOC) manifest. To begin with, the book extends the VOC literature by showing that firm-level behaviors are structured by national sector-specific patterns of market governance. The illustrative company cases supporting the main country and sectoral case studies expose the impacts of sectoral structures and organization of institutions (including types and hierarchies of state-market relationships at the sectoral level) interacting with state imperatives responding to real and perceived internal and external pressures. Distinct political economic units operate at the sectoral level, uncovering dominant distribution of property rights, in addition to the role of the state in market coordination. Variegated economic actors (determining levels of trade, investment, R&D, and productivity) and institutional ties to the state at the sectoral level link the allocation and distribution of resources among them.

The extent and scope of state control in market coordination in a sector is just as important, if not more so, than actual ownership arrangements, in mediating the relationship between globalization and

---

[1] See Hall and Soskice (2001), Thelen (2004, 2014), Streeck and Thelen (2005), and Fioretos (2011) for the advanced industrialized world.

[2] Vogel (2018) illuminates the role the state can play in market governance to achieve economic development and social equity; and Michael (2020) characterizes the paradoxes, compromises, and innovations of the hybridity of "public capitalism."

[3] Schneider (2013) focuses on the attributes of the firm and their connections to labor in understanding Latin American capitalism. Jackson and Deeg (2019) exhort business studies to focus more on the institutional context in order to better understand the role of firms in institutional change.

development. This is where regime type, at times, reinforces and, at times, incrementally influences the perceived strategic value driving the extent and scope of state control. However, the book's comparative and longitudinal country and sectoral case studies show that the regime type, by itself, does not alter dominant patterns of market governance.

China's authoritarian regime has buttressed the country's dominant sectoral patterns while India's vibrant democracy has forced the country's political parties to reinterpret historically rooted values in response to internal and external pressures. All the same, the comparative sector cases in China in Chapters 3–5 show that even within the same regime type, divergent sectoral patterns of market governance coexist as a function of interacting perceived strategic value and sectoral characteristics. What is more, these dominant sectoral patterns have facilitated the state's prioritization of state capacity and resources to enhance authoritarian control. Likewise, in India, reported in Chapters 6–8, elected leaders are forced to not just frame but substantively tailor their policies and strategies to state imperatives arising from existing but evolving values and institutions, which have stayed resilient.

Secondly, the Strategic Value Framework's emphasis on value-bounded rationality that is politically driven and historically rooted, in response to economic and political pressures rather than solely on ideas of how the economy functions, extends the VOC literature on the factors which drive institutional formation and change. Scholars of the advanced industrialized world have argued that different approaches toward economic liberalism are based on ideational variation about the role of the state in the economy.[4] The book's country-sector case studies show that institutional development is shaped (first and foremost) by national goals motivated by state elite insecurities and aspirations exhibited at the sectoral level birthed during significant moments of internal and external pressures. From there, sectoral structures and organization of institutions mediate those effects. The institutional foundations of capitalism emergent today, thus, require explicating how perceived strategic value interacts with sectoral specificities and country-specific institutional arrangements.

During the Cold War, disclosed in Chapter 10, the Soviet military industrial complex networked civilian and military telecommunications with regionally based wireline infrastructure. While basic telecommunications

---

[4] See Deane (1978), Hall (1989), and Vail (2018) on the power of economic ideas.

services were deregulated after the fall of the Soviet Union, the wireline infrastructure was never officially privatized. Rather, value attachments to what is perceived as defense infrastructure and the already regionally based carriers shaped the modernization of and later, the centralization of the telecommunications infrastructure under Putin's authoritarian rule. The establishment of the corporatized state-owned backbone infrastructure has enabled the aggrandization of Russian state power over information dissemination. This is a clear demonstration of the dominant nation-specific sectoral patterns of market governance undergirding capitalistic power in spite of the conventional wisdom of either neoliberal or oligarchic dominance of the Russian economy in the post-Cold War period.

Thirdly, an existing thread of the VOC literature suggests a strong relationship between the institutional complementarities and developmental outcomes.[5] This book shows precisely because of path-dependent national and intranational sectoral trajectories that incrementally transform and vary as a function of technological advances and sectoral structural attributes and the role of the state motivated by strategic value orientations, the emergent varieties of capitalism are simultaneously less dependent and more dependent on comparative advantages and disadvantages shaped by national structures than existing literature would suggest. On the one hand, China can strategically utilize the foreign direct investment (FDI) in both capital-intensive and labor-intensive sectors by adopting diametrically different market governance structures (Chapter 3–5). On the other hand, the existing sectoral organization of institutions across textile subsectors are low tech and small-scale in India. That reality coupled with the value placed on them in the nationalist imagination complicate the Indian government's shifting priorities to mobilize technological upgrading, as shown in Chapter 8.

12.1.1 Research Design, Alternative Explanations, and New Research Program

The book's multilevel comparative case (country, time, sector and subsector, and company) research design facilitates parallel demonstrations of the Strategic Value Framework, in addition to contributing to the

---

[5] See Jackson and Deeg (2008a, 2008b) review the VOC literature, and Schneider and Paunescu (2012) test their continued salience.

conceptualization and refinement of the theoretical model. The research design also examines alternative explanations. To begin with, the selection of China, India, and Russia and sectors and subsectors within them control for country size, geopolitical significance, timing of industrialization, and imperial or colonial past. Moreover, the variation on regime type (China, India) and transition between regime types (Russia) built into the cross-time and cross-national sector case studies permits the examination of the relative importance of democracy versus authoritarianism.

Importantly, the effects and limits of open economy politics are demonstrated by sectoral and subsectoral variation. The cross-time variation in all the cases shows the relative effects of path-dependent sectoral institutions within country and across national contexts regardless of regime type. Not to be outdone, the subsectoral analysis increases the number of cases, demonstrates the leverage of the theoretical framework, and shows the uneven effects of sectoral coalitional interests and existing organization of institutions in explaining sectoral patterns of market governance. Additional studies that seek to explain intranational sectoral variation and the relative impacts of sectoral structural and institutional characteristics would be welcomed. Such micro-level studies taking a macro-micro approach would provide empirical nuance to our understanding of the nature of regulation and governance as well as explicate intranational variation, raising theoretical questions about the relative importance of national, geographical, sectoral, and firm-level attributes. Macro perspectives provide a good starting point of inquiry, and microlevel comparative sectoral analysis helps to adjudicate between competing views of twenty-first century market governance in the developing world in the context of global economic integration.

The multilevel comparative sectoral approach identifies *national configurations of sectoral models* of globalization and development, in addition to uncover rich case-specific findings. Table 12.1 encapsulates the conceptual and analytical leverage of the Strategic Value Framework and market governance typology for the case specific findings in the 1990s and beyond. Highlighted are the perceived strategic value orientations and sectoral structures and country-specific sectoral organization of institutions shaping the national and intracountry sectoral variations identified in the book. Presented in the rest of the conclusion chapter are the case-specific new capitalisms and development outcomes and applicability to other sectors in the respective economies. Analyzed also are implications for geopolitics and geoeconomics and the COVID-19 global pandemic.

TABLE 12.1. *National configurations of sectoral models and new capitalisms*

Variables and Concepts	Cases and Findings					
Country	China		India		Russia	
National Configurations of Sectoral Models and New Capitalisms	*Techno-Security Developmentalism*		*Neoliberal Self-Reliance*		*Resource Security Nationalism*	
	Bifurcated Capitalism		Bifurcated Liberalism		Bifurcated Oligarchy	
Global Economic Integration	1990s and Beyond		1990s and Beyond		1990s and Beyond	
Regime Type	Authoritarianism		Democracy		Semi-Authoritarianism	
Sector	Telecoms	Textiles	Telecoms	Textiles	Telecoms	Textiles
Perceived Strategic Value	National Security and National Technology Base	Political Stability and Local Goals	Economic Stability and Globalization	Political Legitimacy and Economic Development	National Security and Resource Management	Local and Regional Development
Country-specific Sectoral Organization	Post-Tiananmen Legacy	Reform-Era Decentralization	Pro-Liberalization Business	Labor-intensive Small-scale Industry	Soviet era Military Industrial Complex	*Perestroika* Legacy
Market Governance	Centralized Governance	Decentralized and Private Governance	Regulated Governance	Centralized and Decentralized Governance	Centralized Governance	Decentralized and Private Governance

12.2 TECHNO-SECURITY DEVELOPMENTALISM
AND BIFURCATED CAPITALISM IN XI'S CHINA

The dominant sectoral patterns of market governance in China, today, presented in their full complexity in Chapters 3–5 show that nearly forty-five years since the Open Door Policy in December 1978, the Chinese political economic system has neither transitioned in a unilinear manner toward Western-style capitalism, nor in the direction of straightforward state capitalism that employs industrial policies in the traditional sense. The distinct patterns of market coordination and the distribution of property rights arrangements dominant in the strategic and less strategic sectors and subsectors, as exemplified by the regulatory and development trajectories of telecommunications and textiles and their subsectors, replay across the Chinese economy. In the context of global market and ideological pressures, decentralization, and the proliferation of old and new interests, *bifurcated capitalism* shaped by *techno-security developmentalism* has emerged in the nearly forty-five years of the reform era.

This Chinese-style capitalism maximizes the gains and minimizes the costs of global economic integration and increases state authority and capacity in controlling infrastructural assets perceived strategic to the state and in structuring market entry and sectoral developments at home and abroad. China has introduced market competition, including foreign investment, and exercised subsequent regulatory actions to limit or empower the influence of state and private market actors according to the perceived strategic value of industrial sectors for application for national security greatly defined and contribution to the national technology base. Tracing historically from sectoral origins, Chapter 3 shows the origins and evolution of the strategic value orientation of state elites across political regimes as they responded to internal and external pressures, and interactions with structural and institutional sectoral attributes.

By the mid-2000s, prior to Xi Jinping becoming paramount leader, the dominant sectoral patterns of market governance that focused on imperatives of national security and the national technology base greatly defined have achieved dividends. In telecommunication, the representative case of a strategic industry, the state owns telecommunications infrastructure and the state-owned carriers partner with global operators to tap developing country markets as part of China's Belt and Road, outbound FDI, and foreign-aid activities. As shown in Chapter 4, domestic privately owned and state-controlled value-added service (VAS) providers dominate internal markets and have gained market share globally. In textiles, the representative less strategic sector analyzed in Chapter 5, with world-class export production and global market dominance in contract manufacturing, Chinese apparel and clothing manufacturers adopt Information Communications Technology (ICT) applications and artificial intelligence. Moreover, there are increasingly Chinese global market players in chemical fiber processing, high performance fiber, and high-tech non-wovens; however, a proliferation of market players also operate in high-polluting segments.

With developmental headways across industrial sectors, the state's deliberate role in market governance increasingly involves global business acquisitions in addition to the continued strategic utilization of FDI. "The state has begun to stop accommodating runaway FDI in open sectors. The government aims to use FDI as a strategic tool for territorial development. Chinese firms still lack the best technology, so the state will still look to FDI for tech transfers and infrastructural development. It has used and will continue to use FDI to build the national market and create regulatory institutions to integrate the country to achieve developmental goals," elaborated a venture capitalist who has observed FDI patterns in addition to multiple rounds of reregulation before and after China's WTO accession.[6]

Since 2012, Xi Jinping has continued to use markets and the party-state to guide strategic industries and issue areas.[7] The Third Plenum of the 18th National Congress of the CCP, in 2013, stated what China had been doing all along: "Opening up" to maximize the benefits of globalization and doubling down on maintaining internal security to minimize the costs on its authoritarian regime. Made in China 2025 and the 13th Five-Year Plan, which target nanotechnology and artificial intelligence applications in textiles, for example, specify central-level coordination and research and development (R&D) funding in sectors and issue areas, which have national security applications and contribute to the national technology base.

Whether it is in electronic commerce and semiconductors in ICT, as shown in Chapter 4, or high-tech synthetic fibers in technical textiles examined in Chapter 5, through regulation according to interacting strategic value and sectoral logics, the central government sanctions and sponsors state-owned and state-controlled enterprises through direct

---

[6] Interview on October 10, 2005 in Beijing, with venture capitalist at Walden International.
[7] "China's Pledge of Big Reforms Cements Era of Market Forces," *Financial Times* (November 12, 2013).

interventions in equity ownership, corporate governance, and R&D. Communist party and State Council groups on cybersecurity, oil and gas line security, and the management of nongovernmental organizations further govern strategic sectors. Government policies, such as debt relief, low interest loans, and discretionary calibration of financial rules cushion the macroeconomy during ecomomic crises.

In addition to telecommunications and technical textiles, from financial technology and green technology to autonomous vehicles, which score high on economic and political measures of perceived strategic value, the dominant pattern of *centralized governance* holds. To maintain central control of the national money supply, exchange rate, and other macroeconomic tools, the state centralizes supervision of financial services along subsectoral lines due to competing bureaucratic interests, retains ownership and management of the Big Four banks, and restricts FDI to minority foreign equity investment. Parallel to the less restrictive regulation of telecommunications value-added services, the state permits private and foreign market entry in select subsectors of financial services using public–private joint venture arrangements to develop indigenous capacity and retain supervision of financial and human resources. Regulatory actions in anti-trust, exemplified in the 2020 and 2021 crackdowns on the firm size and business scope of the platform economy operating at the intersection of financial and communications infrastructures, IPR enforcement, standards-setting, and state sector reforms through mixed ownership structures and anti-corruption campaigns further reveal that Xi Jinping has fortified *techno-security developmentalism.*

Industrial sectors, which score low on the economic and political measures of perceived strategic value, from consumer electronics and foodstuffs to paper and textiles, in contrast, are characterized by *decentralized governance.* Economic decision-making in these less strategic sectors in China is decentralized to subnational geographical state authorities and variegated property rights arrangements coexist without central state intervention. Domestic and foreign businesses, alike, are only required to register for market entry, and the high number of domestic private players and the political and economic interests of local authorities, in addition to sectoral structural specificities, determine policies.

Local governments and firms are on their own to attract domestic and foreign investment in industries that fall outside of any national security or technology-related sensitivities. They do so through fiscal incentives and low-cost labor and production, with social and environmental consequences. For example, deregulation and the decentralization of regulatory enforcement in less capital-intensive and less value-added industries, many in high-polluting sectors, perpetuate such actions as delays in grid connection and the curtailment of transmission by local governments and operators motivated by interests outside the strict boundaries of the state's perceived strategic value orientation. These actions have favored environmentally unfriendly coal-fired power and coal-to-chemical plants even as China promotes green technology and rushes to install wind infrastructure.[8]

12.2.1 The Strategic Value Logic of China's National Sector-specific Responses to the COVID-19 Pandemic

Techno-security developmentalism interacting with sectoral characteristics shaped the ways in which central state leaders moved to shut down Wuhan and the country at the onset of the COVID-19 pandemic yet retained manufacturing capacity in strategic sectors associated with national security and the national technology base. In the context of China's swift lockdown and flattening of the death rate and targeted actions to cushion the stock market and the domestic economy, the Chinese government has not departed from the Made in China 2025 industrial policy of focusing on indigenous technological development, including high-tech materials and technical textiles. The Chinese government's attempts to control narratives on the country's response to the coronavirus also maps with the extent and scope of the state's role in market governance of sectors and issue areas deemed of strategic value to the state.

While the rest of the economy halted in February 2020, Changxin Memory Technologies (based in greater Wuhan) and Fujian Jinhua Integrated Circuit Company, both Chinese homegrown chip manufacturers on the United States' export control blacklist, along with other fabs producing DRAM or NAND memory chips with special licenses from the Ministry of Industry and Information Technology, continued to operate without disruption, as discussed in Chapter 4. Likewise, despite a national ban on domestic transportation of goods during the national

---

[8] See "Irrational Coal Plants May Hamper China's Climate Change Efforts," *New York Times* (February 7, 2017) and "Why Is China Suddenly Leading the Climate Change Effort? It's a Business Decision," *Washington Post* (June 23, 2017). Hsueh (2021) applies the interacting strategic value and sectoral logics to examine the growth and overexpasion of real estate development in China.

lockdown, special reserved carriages of highspeed rail in Wuhan continued to shuttle engineers and other staff to relieve the around 300 engineers who had been working on rotating shifts at state-owned Yangtze Memory Technologies.[9]

As the Chinese economy experienced its first contraction since 1976, the central government also moved quickly to focus on targeted measures at the sectoral level to relieve financial stresses building on companies and their bank creditors.[10] Estimated at about 1 percent of GDP, these sector-specific measures included reductions in the social insurance payments required of employers, lower electricity fees, and fiscal/Value Added Tax waivers. China's aviation regulator also announced a subsidy for domestic and international airlines. Moreover, after Xi implored local officials to refocus on the economy during a teleconference opened to county governments and top-party cadres, seven provinces announced investment projects worth Rmb 25 trillon ($380 billion), with 14 percent of that amount to be spent in 2020.[11]

Recalibrated rules on capital investment permitted companies to quickly raise capital by privately placing shares with investors at a discount of up to 20 percent of their trading price.[12] Investors were also permitted to sell the shares after six months, down from twelve months, and companies were allowed to list on ChiNext, a Nasdaq-style index for startups, without needing to meet profitability and debt ratio requirements. With COVID-19 spreading around the world and slowing down economies, governments from Australia and Germany to India responded to a spike in Chinese outbound mergers and acquisitions and investment by tightening rules on FDI.[13] Global acquisitions or "hostile takeovers by Chinese companies during the crisis" included state-owned VC China

---

[9] See "China Memory Production Unaffected by Coronavirus," *Evertiq* (February 3, 2020). Also, see "China-based Memory Fabs Continue Normal Operations Currently as Wuhan Coronavirus Has Yet to Impair Global Memory Supply," *TrendForce Report* (February 3, 2020).

[10] See "Coronavirus Could End China's Decades-Long Economic Growth Streak," *New York Times* (March 16, 2020).

[11] See "China's Xi Jinping Sounds Alarm Over Virus Outbreak at Party's Doorstep," *Bloomberg* (February 24, 2020).

[12] See "Coronavirus Prompts Boom in Risky China Share Placements," *Financial Times* (March 10, 2020).

[13] See "China's Acquisitions and Investments in Foreign Firms Amid COVID-19 Raise Eyebrows," GlobalData (May 5, 2020). Also, see Chapter 7 on India's response to Chinese FDI.

Reform Fund's ultimately unsuccessful attempt to purchase the British smartphone chipmaker Imagination.[14]

Importantly, amid fears of shortages of face masks and other medical supplies, top Chinese leadership, facing an image problem after initial delay in announcing the outbreak, zeroed in on such "strategic resources," both for internal use as well as for its global campaign to reframe the Chinese government's handling of the origins and spread of COVID-19. Already a major producer of surgical masks, filter products of nonwoven textiles analyzed in Chapter 5, and N95 respirators globally, China increased production ten-fold after the coronavirus outbreak.[15] This further included active pharmaceutical ingredients for antibiotics critical for addressing emerging secondary infections, of which China is also a leading producer.[16] Additionally, almost immediately China began to donate masks, respirators, protective suits, test kits, and ventilators to Europe, the United States, and developing countries like Iran and others in Africa.[17]

At the same time, just as companies and countries around the world raced to develop a vaccine, in order to control information dissemination surrounding the origins of the coronavirus, the State Council and the Academy of Sciences imposed restrictions on academic publications on the origins of the novel coronavirus on the grounds of ensuring "biosecurity."[18] The new restrictions managing basic research by academic researchers, disseminated by the Ministry of Education, follow reports of U.S. State Department cables warning of lax security measures after visits to the Wuhan Institute of Virology (designated a highest level-4 international bioresearch safety lab) and the nearby Wuhan Center for Disease Control and Prevention (a less secure level 2) in early 2018.[19] In mid-2021, scientists around the world and the Biden Administration

---

[14] See "US Probes Imagination Owner after Attempted Boardroom Takeover," *Telegraph* (April 11, 2020).

[15] See "The Global Mask Shortage May Get Much Worse," *Bloomberg* (March 10, 2020).

[16] See USCC (2019), 248.

[17] See "China Sends Doctors and Masks Overseas as Domestic Coronavirus Infections Drop," *The Guardian* (March 18, 2020); and "How Beijing Reframed the Coronavirus Response Narrative," *Financial Times* (March 16, 2020).

[18] See State Council Notice on the Strengthening of the Management of Publications of Scientific Papers Related to the New Coronary Pneumonia Epidemic (March 25, 2020)," as published before taken down by Fudan University College of Information Science and Engineering and China University of Geoscience in Wuhan.

[19] See "State Department Cables Warned of Safety Issues at Wuhan Lab Studying Bat Coronaviruses," *Washington Post* (April 14, 2020).

pressed for an independent investigation on whether the virus leaked from a lab after a WHO report based solely on Chinese government data dismissed that transmission possibility.[20]

12.3 NEOLIBERAL SELF-RELIANCE AND BIFURCATED LIBERALISM IN MODI'S INDIA

The Strategic Value Framework also sheds light on the nonlinear and multidimensional nature of democratic India's Big Bang Liberalization. The addition of a democracy to the study's research design shows that despite electoral pressures, historically rooted political values and sectoral institutions have remained resilient. Political parties swayed by electoral imperatives have reinterpreted value-laden state goals in the context of internal and external pressures without fundamentally changing them. By tracing regulatory and development trajectories at the sector and subsector, the book's micro-macro approach uncovers path dependency and policy feedbacks as a function of the perceived strategic value of *neoliberal self-reliance* grounded in post-Independence legacies and state responses to economic and political crises and impacts of sectoral organization of institutions. The India-sector case studies in Chapters 6–8 laid bare the interactive effects of the nationalist imagination à la Gandhian *swadeshiism* and Nehruvian techno-nationalism and sectoral organization of institutions, and an international liberalizing coalition during critical junctures of political and economic vulnerabilities in the 1980s and beyond.

As the Indian state introduced market competition internally in the 1980s and liberalized to external forces in the 1990s, *bifurcated liberalism* has characterized the dominant sectoral patterns of market governance, which undergirds Indian style capitalism. On the one hand, value-added, capital-intensive sectors with connections to a liberalizing transnational network, such as telecommunications, delineated in Chapter 7, are governed by *regulated governance*. The federal state regulates enterprises with variegated property rights arrangements in the context of far-reaching economic liberalization. The state's role in market coordination in telecommunications is represented by an independent regulator overseeing few entrenched bureaucratic and market stakeholders tied to post-Independence values and institutions. However, this varies by subsector;

---

[20] See "Biden Calls for U.S. Intelligence Agencies to 'Redouble' Investigative Efforts Into the Origins of the Virus," *New York Times* (May 26, 2021).

centralized market coordination and public sector enterprises govern a fixed-line network and telecommunications manufacturing. There are telecommunications infrastructure in the most rural areas and significant consumer choice in fixed-line and mobile and value-added services, with the latter service providers operating in global markets.

Existing stakeholders of technological bureaucracies founded during the Nehru era focus to this day on producing communications equipment for the national backbone infrastructure. Slow to enter mobile markets, however, domestic equipment makers face Chinese competition and the increasing reach of Chinese FDI in next-generation technologies and start-ups. Detailed in Chapter 7, technological convergence may aid India's leapfrogging into next-generation technology; software integration of global vendors' component solutions for the fifth-generation technology standard, for example, enables telecommunications service providers to avoid Chinese vendors, such as Huawei and H3C.

On the other hand, Chapter 8 shows that the *perceived strategic value* of India's labor-intensive, small-scale industry, represented by textiles, for political legitimacy and economic development, determines the more interventionalist role of the state in cushioning India's predominantly rural industry and small and medium enterprises from the effects of market competition. All the same, *national self-reliance* joined *neoliberal development*, a function of government responses to economic and political pressures beginning in the late 1970s and early 1980s, shape the details of export-oriented industrialization (EOI). Manmohan Singh's coalition government launched such EOI strategies in the 2000s, which Narendra Modi of the Hindu nationalist Bharatiya Janata Party has continued. The *centralized governance* of existing formal and informal protections and stakeholder interests in market segments and subsectors, such as handlooms and power looms, associated with the Indian nationalist imagination, coexists with subsidies and fiscal incentives to promote technological upgrading in technical textiles and large-scale mills as well as the introduction of foreign competition in internal retail and distribution.

This dominant sectoral pattern of market governance in sectors perceived strategic for the nationalist imagination has resulted, in general, to weak domestic industrial development and upgrading and low foreign entry/market penetration. Today low-tech, highly polluting handlooms and power looms engage in weaving and fiber processing, respectively. Moreover, vertically integrated large-scale mills and garment manufacturers have reach in global niche markets in apparel and clothing but domestic technical textiles, dominated by small-scale power looms, produce less technologically intensive commodities and have low global market penetration.

Perceived strategic value and structural and India-specific sectoral attributes also explicate the dominant pattern of market governance in sectors characterized by complex interactive technology *and* low asset specificity and local learning, such as pharmaceuticals. Similar to Indian textiles, the existing sectoral organization of institutions is proliferated by small-scale enterprises and legislation enacted in the 1970s, which barred medical products from being patented in the large developing country with mass poverty in line with Gandhian *Swadeshi's* emphasis on the national collective and rural self-sufficiency. In contrast to expectations of macroliberalization, the Department of Pharmaceuticals moved from the Ministry of Industry to a sector-specific ministry at the onset of Big Bang Liberalization and large companies control the majority of the Indian pharmaceutical market today. India participates in the Trade-Related Aspects of Intellectual Property Rights agreement and permits 100 percent FDI; nevertheless, multinational corporations, which focus on productions from high-end patents, serve only 12 percent of the market.[21] Elaborated below, the sectoral pattern of market governance of pharmasecuticals in India contributed to shaping the country's initial responses to the COVID-19 pandemic.

The election of Modi, in 2014, has not altered the *bifurcated liberalism* of the dominant sectoral patterns of market governance and related developmental effects. To begin with, the Modi government's seemingly contradictory economic policies validate the *neoliberal self-reliance* perceived strategic value orientation embodied in the modern textile mills versus the unorganized and small-scale handlooms and power looms. Modi has evoked Gandhi and the collective self-reliance signified by cotton textiles. In the Independence celebration in 2017, he declared, "There was Mohandas Karamchand Gandhi, who empowered his countrymen to weave the fabric of independence with cotton and spinning wheel."[22] Retaining protections for handlooms, the textile ministry announced a subsidy of $901 million on National Handloom Day that

---

[21] Sinha (2016) contends that "woodwork reformers" in a state-capital alliance shaped the development of Indian pharmaceuticals.

[22] See "Full Transcript of Indian Prime Minister Narendra Modi's Independence Day Speech," accessed on August 27, 2017 at http://time.com/4901564/narendra-modi-india-70-independence-day-speech/.

year and created an Indian Handloom Brand and pan-India Handloom Program for Weavers.

All the same, the elimination of high demonetization notes in 2016 has slowed domestic demand and affected cash-based small-scale, downstream and upstream sectors (cotton farms and gin, handlooms and power looms, nonmechanized garment finishing, and wholesale and retail trade). Moreover, the Goods and Services Tax (GST), which consolidates various direct and indirect taxes, streamlining the tax structure, benefits mainly large corporations. The uneven implementation of GST due to a liquidity crisis has led to the unsustainability of small-scale textile producers and unorganized sectors dominant in textiles. The government has not reimbursed textile producers for the 5 percent tax on output in the two-and-a-half years since GST went into effect. This has forced many firms to shut down or scale down on production.

Economic policies designed to boost domestic production, such as Made in India, Skill India, and Startup India, have had uneven effects. Made in India's provisions on intellectual property rights will likely have short-run benefits for technical textiles and capital-intensive producers and foreign-invested apparel and clothing retailers.[23] A domestic content policy governs the increasingly liberal environment for FDI in retail trade, and special incentives promote textile exports. Made In India also features a local content policy of 75 percent in drugs for local use and 10 percent in exports whereby large dominant Indian drug companies are not incentivized to produce for the domestic population. Despite the Indian government's own export restrictions on COVID-19 vaccines manufactured by the world's largest contract producer of vaccines in the country, less than 3 percent of the population is vaccinated when the deadly second surge hit in spring 2021.[24]

12.3.1 The Strategic Value Logic of India's National Sector-specific Responses to the COVID-19 Pandemic

In late March 2020, when countries around the world – particularly Italy and Iran – were hit badly by the coronavirus, India had yet to face a major crisis; the worst effects were to come a year later. Interacting strategic

---

[23] Data on technology-specific patent publications by the World Intellectual Property Organization show a significant increase in the number of patents filed in 2015 versus 2014, for example.

[24] See "India's Coronavirus Surge Creates Vaccine Supply Turmoil Far Beyond Its Borders," *Washington Post* (April 30, 2021).

value and institutional logics elucidate why when India first went into strict lockdown for 68 days, the country only had 519 cases and nine deaths, and how the state's initial responses resulted in a second, exponentially more deadly, major surge in March 2021, resulting in a total death toll of over 200,000 by mid-May 2021.

To begin with, existing sectoral organization of institutions oriented around mom-and-pop clinics and hospital chains, on the one hand, and a predominantly private pharmaceutical industry producing generic drugs, on the other hand, unevenly implemented testing. The wide distribution of antibiotics in this institutional context treated as well as exacerbated secondary infections tied to the effects of COVID-19.[25] From the very beginning, the actual extent and scope of the COVID crisis, unfortunately, was obscured by the perceived strategic value of the development of the pharmaceutical industry as a signal of India's modernization. The embeddedness of the sector's business class in politics and government further blurred the boundaries between regulatory institutions and the state. The Department of Pharmaceuticals and the Drug Controller General of India swiftly "granted approval to the Indian Council of Medical Research to use a combination of lopinavir and ritonavir in the event of the coronavirus disease."[26]

The National Pharmaceutical Pricing Authority, along with the Drugs Controller General of India, became tasked with monitoring the supply of active pharmaceutical ingredients (APIs) and checking illegal hoarding. The Directorate General of Foreign Trade restricted the export of APIs only to lift restrictions soon after. Meanwhile, the country's well-connected largest pharmaceuticals Serum and Bharat Biotech were approved to produce a homegrown Covaxin vaccine and AstraZeneca for export, respectively. The Ministry of Corporate Affairs' designation of COVID-19 spending by businesses as corporate social responsibility (CSR) activity under the Companies Law of 2013 (as discussed in Chapter 6) further reveals the seeming contradiction of the political weight of the business class and India's aggressive interventions.[27]

---

[25] See "India Scrambles to Escape a Coronavirus Crisis. So Far, It's Working," *New York Times* (March 17, 202) and "India Shows That Developing a Coronavirus Treatment Isn't Enough," *Atlantic* (March 16, 2020).

[26] See "Coronavirus in India: How the COVID-19 Could Impact the Fast-growing Economy," *Pharmaceutical Technology* (March 19, 2020).

[27] See the Ministry of Corporate Affairs General Circular No. 10/2020. Also, see "Corporate Affairs Ministry to Count Funds Spent to Tackle COVID-19 under CSR Activity," *Economic Times* (March 23, 2020).

The national lockdown in late spring 2020 had disproportionately affected migrants working for small-scale vendors and enterprises in the informal and unorganized sectors. Unable to work, cutoff from daily income, and with next to zero access to healthcare, many migrants were left homeless and with nowhere to go.[28] Protesters around the country, such as in Delhi and Surat, Gujarat, demanded the government transport them back to their hometowns and villages. Instead, protesters were met by police with their sticks to disperse them.

A year later, during a second, more deadly surge, the government halted vaccine export in April 2021 when multiple variants of the coronavirus ravaged cities and rural areas, propelling India to the second highest number of deaths after the United States. Unwilling to face political opposition during local elections, Modi went without a mask at political rallies and allowed a Hindu festival with millions of worshippers to take place.[29] Despite the worst approval ratings since becoming prime minister, Modi's popularity remains higher than any other politician.[30] No matter, in mid-2021, recently released rules on data management forced Facebook, Instagram, and Twitter to takedown social media posts critical of the government's response to the pandemic claiming they incite panic and could hinder government response.[31] With India falling short on vaccines the government reached an agreement, in May 2021, to obtain Spunik V, funded by the Russian government.

12.4 RESOURCE SECURITY NATIONALISM AND BIFURCATED OLIGARCHY IN PUTIN'S RUSSIA

The addition of market-transitioning and semi-authoritarian Russia to the research design shows that a strong, centralized state (particularly ones with autocratic leaders) are more capable of achieving state imperatives be they national security or resource management. All the same, the Russia-sector cases show that path dependent sectoral organization of institutions (before and after Soviet collapse) have effects, in addition to sectoral

---

[28] See "Coronavirus in India: Desperate Migrant Workers Trapped in Lockdown," *BBC* (April 22, 2020).

[29] See "India's COVID-19 Crisis Shakes Modi's Image of Strength," *New York Times* (May 1, 2021).

[30] See "PM Modi's Rating Falls to New Low as India Reels from COVID-19," *Reuters* (May 19, 2021).

[31] See "WhatsApp Sues India's Government to Stop New Internet Rules," *New York Times* (May 25, 2021).

technological attributes. Similar to those in China and India, the Russian telecommunications and textile sectors and subsectors presented in Chapters 9–11 have experienced macrolevel liberalization and microsectoral variation in market governance. Soviet-era value-laden and institutional legacies underscore the significance of sectors with application for *national security* and contribution to *resource management*. Putin's responses to political and economic reverberations since the late 1990s have reinforced the *resource security nationalism* shaping the *bifurcated oligarchy* of the dominant sectoral patterns of market governance in today's Russia.

Chapter 10 shows the reinforced *centralized governance* of state owned fixed-line telecommunications networks with Soviet defense complex origins. This contrasts with the variegated owners, which operate and manage globally competitive mobile carriers and value-added service providers. Regional monopolies in mobile and VAS services controlled by oligarchic industrial groupings enjoy market share in the Commonwealth of Independent States (CIS) and Europe. State ownership of backbone infrastructure and the impulse under Putin to designate telecommunications a strategic industry, however, govern the information dissemination of privately owned mobile and value-added services with centralized regulation on market entry, business scope, and investment level. The various updates to the Strategic Enterprises Law, first promulgated in 2008 after the global financial crisis and amended after the annexation of Crimea in 2014, regulate business operations and information dissemination in the name of national sovereignty and resource management.

The new prime minister and former chief of the Federal Tax Service, Mikhail Mishustin, appointed in January 2020, is charged with implementing a state-owned and government-managed digitized ecosystem to conduct surveillance. The national projects' digitalization plans also emphasize indigenous capacity in producing telecommunications equipment and the requirement that phone manufacturers pre-install Russian software. As the director of the Federal Tax Service, between 2010 and 2019, Mishustin implemented individual tax numbers and digital signatures. He also enforced new rules, which required retail establishments to employ an online cash register that automatically transmits real-time transaction data to tax authorities and submits all business-to-business invoices. Artificial intelligence technologies are then used to identify persons suspected of tax evasion.[32]

[32] See "Russia's New Prime Minister Augurs Techno Authoritarianism," *Foreign Policy* (January 20, 2020) and "IMF Staff Concludes Visit to Russia," International Monetary Fund Press Release No. 19/425 (November 20, 2019).

Mishustin also previously headed the committee on digitization in the Organization for Economic Cooperation and Development's Forum for Tax Administration.

These developments in the centralized governance of telecommunications are grounded in responding to perceived internal and external security threats, namely civil society protests, and the U.S. and European economic sanctions in response to Russian intervention in Ukraine and opposition against Russia's human rights violations and involvement in global cyberattacks. This contrasts with the deregulated and more *decentralized governance* of Information Technology and software services, characterized by the "intangible" structural sectoral attributes of the predominantly private and small and medium enterprise owners, many of which hail from the Soviet science and technology bureaucracies dismantled or privatized after communist collapse, as analyzed in Chapter 10.

Private governance, characterized by interactions between decentralized authorities with low state capacity and variegated private corporate actors, prevail in labor-intensive, less value-added industries, such as textiles, perceived less strategic for *resource security nationalism*. The path-dependent effects of *perestroika* and the economy-wide dismantling of central and regional state institutions and privatization following the collapse of the Soviet Union further shape the stunted and languishing growth and development of domestic textiles, analyzed in Chapter 11. Local and regional governments have regulatory authority; however, their effectiveness is limited, particularly of large enterprises owned by oligarchs in the less strategic sectors in which decentralized authorities are tasked to enforce economywide rules. The limited industrial capacity and small volume in domestic production have resulted in a trade boom for foreign apparel and textile producers and investors in "black and gray" imports, counterfeit products, and high-end retail, making Russia a top ten market globally.

The dominant pattern of market governance of less strategic industries for *resource security nationalism* in Russia is unlike the fate of labor-intensive, less value-added industries considered less strategic for *techno-security developmentalisn* in China. Distinct from the demoralized and dejected local market and local government stakeholders of the Russian nondefense, non-resource sectors, decentralization and the active engagement of the global economy in China have empowered local governments and private and foreign-invested economic actors to develop industry in the absence of state intervention. Similar to China, however, is that textiles and other labor-intensive sectors in Russia are perceived strategic by local governments because of their importance for local employment. Because of the Communist legacy that cities avoid dismissing employees, cities have subsidized important local companies to ensure jobs yet impart limited resources and state capacity for industrialization.

Notwithstanding the industrial decay of apparel and clothing in Russia, the perceived strategic value of petrochemical inputs for national security applications and resource management of technical textiles determines the deliberate orientation of the market and nonmarket interventions by central and local governments to promote import substitution industrialization. Public–private initiatives, such as the "coercion to innovation" to increase investments, have proliferated since global capital slowdowns after the imposition of Western sanctions in response to Russia's annexation of Crimea. Large state and regional oligarchic-owned enterprises are the main beneficiaries of such attempts at import-substitution in strategic subsectors of decentralized and deregulated industries.

12.4.1 The Strategic Value Logic of Russia's National Sector-specific Responses to the COVID-19 Pandemic

The Gamaleya Research Institute in Moscow in collaboration with the 48th Central Research Institute of the Ministry of Defense and the Vector Institute of the Rospotrebnadzor developed the COVID-19 vaccine Spunik V.[33] Scientists have questioned the Russian government-developed Spunik V vaccine's efficacy and the Central European and Baltic governments characterize geopolitical motives behind what they call a "Sputnik diplomatic offensive" amidst a disinformation campaign about western-produced vaccines.[34] A report by the European Union's European External Action Service (EEAS) alleged the misinformation campaign targeted "the West to worsen the impact of the coronavirus, generate panic, and sow distrust."[35]

---

[33] *Rospotrebnadzor*, the Russian Federal Service for Surveillance on Consumer Rights Protection and Human Wellbeing, oversees the formulation, enforcement, and monitoring of state policy and legislation on consumer rights and sanitary and epidemiological guidelines and hygienic norms.

[34] See "Doubts Mount About Efficacy of Russia's Sputnik Vaccine," *Voice of America* (May 17, 2021).

[35] See "Russia Deploying Coronavirus Disinformation to Sow Panic in West, EU Document Says," *Reuters* (March 18, 2020).

Nevertheless, how Vektor, a state virology and biotechnology center in Novosibirsk, Siberia joined the effort to develop a vaccine after first becoming the only lab in the country with the authority to test for COVID-19 in the early days of the virus reflects the Soviet geographical organization of industrial assets discussed in Chapters 9–11 and applied to understanding sectoral variation in market governance. Similarly, a function of the legacies of Soviet organization of institutions, 10 percent of the country's population experienced virus clusters in what were formerly company towns in the Soviet Union.

The interacting strategic value and sectoral logics of the *bifurcated oligarchy* of Russian-style capitalism, identified in this book, would explain what Natalia Zubarevich, head of regional studies at Moscow's Independent Institute for Social Policy, has described is the responses of Russia's oligarchs operating in the regions: "[they] understand that public discontent is growing, and they are making a down payment.... They need to take care of the goose that lays the golden eggs." They were among the first proponents of instituting regional lockdowns, contributed to buying medical equipment and protective gear and building hospitals. They pledged more than $300 million to help with the pandemic as the Russian government increased spending on health and economic programs in response to COVID-19 and a historical crash in oil prices. Their contributions bolstered and outpaced in timing government spending.[36]

Among those who have contributed to Russia's COVID-19 responses are billionaires close to Putin who own assets in telecommunications and geosynthetics in technical textiles. The telecommunication industry's Alfa Group, whose co-owners include billionaire Mikhail Fridman; Mail.ru Group, owned by Alisher Usmanov; and Sistema Group, owned by Vladimir Evtushenkov, have donated 1–2 billion rubles each to the government's anti-coronavirus committee, small and medium-sized businesses, hospitals and doctors, and efforts to develop test kits. Gennady Timchenko, whose holdings include gas producer Novatek and petrochemicals manufacturer SIBUR Holding PJSC, also pledged more than 1 billion rubles. Victor Vekselberg of the Renova Group, with assets in telecommunications and petrochemicals, has also donated express test kits and hot meals to older peoples in regions where he holds assets.

---

[36] See "Coronavirus Tests Fly by Private Jet as Russian Tycoons Help," *Bloomberg* (April 22, 2020).

12.5 SECTORAL INSERTION INTO GLOBAL ECONOMY
AND WITHER THE LIBERAL INTERNATIONAL ORDER

The *national configurations of sectoral models* identified in this study are being felt in the global economy as well as in other areas of global conflict and cooperation. This section examines the macro-global effects of the micro-institutional foundations unveiled by the book's multilevel comparative case research design. Doing so sheds light on the future of the Liberal International Order. Susan Hyde and Elizabeth Saunders have identified the malleable constraints, in which "all governments have an institutionally defined default level of domestic audience constraint that is generally higher in democracies, but leaders maintain some agency within these institutions and can strategically increase their exposure to or insulation from this constraint," making regime type an important differentiator in global politics.[37] Indeed the Trump administration responded to China's global economic integration with the U.S.-China trade war, which ultimately faced cross-sector political opposition in the United States. The Biden Administration in November 2021 also faced a cross-sector appeal to "ensure full implementation of the Phase One Agreement," which addresses long-standing market access barriers, "reduce harmful Section 301 tariffs and broaden the tariff exclusion process," and strengthen "U.S. relations with other key trading partners with shared interests.[38]

The complex interdependence created by the dominant sectoral patterns of market governance as a function of interacting strategic value and sectoral logics illuminates the cross-sector alliance responding to the ongoing trade war, and why decoupling from the Chinese economy may prove intractable without multilateral solutions.[39] Global political economic developments since the onset of the COVID-19 global pandemic is another case study of how regime type alone proves insufficient in explicating national sectoral responses to a phenomenon which has affected the world. Markets and consumers from Asia to Europe felt the effects of

---

[37] See Hyde and Saunders (2020).
[38] "Industry Letter to Secretary Yellen and Ambassador Tai," U.S.-China Business Council, American Chemistry Council, American Feed Industry Association, American Soybean Association, Advanced Medical Technology Association, and American Apparel & Footwear Association (November 12, 2021).
[39] See "Over 600 U.S. Companies Urge Trump to Resolve Trade Dispute with China: Letter," *Reuters* (June 13, 2019). Also interviews in Silicon Valley in 2020 and 2021, with engineering and marketing directors U.S. based companies in semiconductor and medical equipment industries.

lockdowns and subsequent social distancing mandates as the pandemic quickly spread.[40] Global trade in goods, already slowed, remained weak, and Chinese bond yields were at a four-year low.[41] Initial production slowdown in China, delaying necessary inputs, led American and European companies to rely on production networks elsewhere. By mid-2020, the outbreak proliferated and slowed economies around the world, including the United States; however, Chinese factories returned to full production, and with the exception of certain products in telecommunications blocked by import and export restrictions in the United States on national security grounds by the Trump administration, global supply chain networks resumed.[42]

As discussed in Section 12.2, Chinese state-sponsored high-tech enterprises in strategic sectors, such as semiconductors, never ceased operations. Their development within the dominant patterns of market governance of China's strategic sectors, detailed in Chapters 3 and 4, combined with how the coronavirus outbreak has focused attention on the country's increasing dominance up and down the supply chain in pharmaceuticals, raise questions about whether China would use its monopoly over the production of high-tech goods and antibiotics as foreign policy tools at its disposal.[43] The pandemic has also enumerated the Indian pharmaceutical industry's reliance on China for active pharmaceutical ingredients and key starting materials, 85 percent of which are manufactured in Hubei Province, the epicenter of COVID-19. While China and India together are home to 31 percent of all the U.S.-registered drug chemical facilities, the United States relies on China for finished products, including for 80 percent of the U.S. supply of antibiotics.[44]

---

[40] See "A Global Outbreak Is Fueling the Backlash to Globalization," *New York Times* (March 5, 2020) and "Wall Street Plunges with Global Markets in Turmoil," *New York Times* (March 18, 2020).

[41] See "Global Goods Trade Already Slow; Coronavirus Will Likely Make It Worse, WTO says," *Los Angeles Times* (February 17, 2020) and "Chinese Bond Yields Touch Four-year Low as Economy Sputters," *Financial Times* (February 19, 2020).

[42] See "Three Things That the Trade War with China Won't Change," *Washington Post* (January 3, 2019) and "Huawei Is Winning the Argument in Europe, as the U.S. Fumbles to Develop Alternatives," *New York Times* (February 17, 2020). See "Blindsided on the Supply Side," *Foreign Policy* (March 4, 2020) and "Coronavirus Wreaks Havoc on Retail Supply Chains Globally, Even as China's Factories Come Back Online," *CNBC* (March 16, 2020).

[43] Also, see "Is America's Antibiotic Supply at Risk?," *Wire China* (April 12, 2020).

[44] According to the U.S. Department of Commerce, China accounted for 95% of U.S. imports of ibuprofen, 91% of U.S. imports of hydrocortisone, 70% of U.S. imports of acetaminophen, 40%–45% of U.S. imports of penicillin, and 40% of U.S. imports of

In the context of relaxed capital rules in China to cushion a stock market down-spiral and increase liquidity and market power of firms during COVID-19, countries around the world, including India, France, Germany, and the Netherlands, raised concerns about key global market acquisitions by Chinese companies.[45] In late April 2020, without naming China, the Indian government revised FDI rules to require government approval of investment flowing from any country that shares "land border" with India. Discussed in Chapter 7, this requirement, also applicable to the transfer of ownership of existing or future FDI, previously covered only FDI from Pakistan and Bangladesh.[46]

Moreover, regulators in member countries of the European Union have requested the European Commission (EC) for permission to intervene in deals where non-EU government-backed companies distort competition. Under current rules, European states can stop Chinese takeovers only through acting as market participants with stakes by buying up shares of companies. A Dutch proposal envisioned the EC stopping these companies from buying EU competitors at inflated prices or undercutting them with artificially low-selling prices. The proposal also granted the EC the power to demand greater transparency in foreign companies' accounts.[47] All the same, at the end of December 2020, the EU and China struck a trade deal that proposed to roll back investment restrictions in Europe and China when ratified by member countries.[48]

China's concessions on labor and climate change rules proved pivotal in negotiations, despite pleas by the advisers of (the then U.S. president elect) Joseph Biden to hold off until the new administration and European partners could discuss common concerns. Many in the European Parliament have opposed ratification, however, because of crackdowns in Hong Kong and the forced labor and mass internment of Uighurs and other Muslims in Xinjiang. The Chinese government, for its part, views the EU-China Investment Agreement as showing that it does not face

---

heparin. Also, see "Coronavirus Exposes the Weak Links in the Pharma Supply Chain," *PharmaLetter* (March 17, 2020).

[45] See "To Avoid Hostile Takeovers Amid COVID-19, India Mandates Approvals on Chinese Investments," *Tech Crunch* (April 18, 2020).

[46] See Government of India Ministry of Commerce & Industry Department for Promotion of Industry and Internal Trade FDI Policy Section Press Note No. 3 (2020 Series).

[47] See "Vestager Urges Stakebuilding to Block Chinese Takeovers: EU Competition Chief Warns Pandemic Has Made Companies Vulnerable to Foreign Bids," *Financial Times* (April 12, 2020).

[48] See "China and E.U. Leaders Strike Investment Deal, but Political Hurdles Await," *New York Times* (December 30, 2020)

diplomatic isolation despite human rights violations and continued show-casing of military aggression toward Taiwan.[49] Moreover, the agreement may make it more difficult for the United States to formulate an allied strategy against China's trade and market practices.

The sectoral variation in dominant patterns of market governance uncovered in this book shows that the macronational and microsectoral analysis of the Strategic Value Framework would have enabled a more refined and nuanced strategy in confronting China's *techno-security developmentalism* and identifying potential problems in the operations and consequences of the authoritarian regime's *bifurcated capitalism.* China's gaining strength in frontier technological areas, such as artificial intelligence and green technology, in the tech war, and China's outward investments in infrastructure in the Belt and Road countries and in Africa and Latin America in exchange for critical resource inputs and diplomatic relations can also be examined through the Strategic Value Framework and multilevel comparative sectoral analysis.[50] A burgeoning literature examines China's outward globalization identifying the role of Chinese subnational governments in BRI projects and impacts of Chinese loans at the project level on the public finances of recipient countries.[51]

The Strategic Value Framework also illuminates the details of China's aggressiveness in the country's claim over Taiwan. China's ownership of telecommunications infrastructure and its strict regulation of the value-added services operating on top of it and related property rights arrange-ments have played a prominent role in the ongoing misinformation war-fare and news media takeovers in Taiwan. Their effects have met limited success from the civil society opposition of the Cross-Strait Agreement on Trade in Services in 2014, which launched Taiwan's Sunflower Movement, to the 2016 and 2020 democratic elections of President Tsai Ing-wen against pro-China candidates.[52] The cross-strait trade agree-ment, which civil society mobilization successfully blocked, proposed the liberalization of entry in Taiwanese services dominated by small and

---

[49] See Chapter 5 on the global response to forced labor in cotton and textile production in Xinjiang and the Anti-Foreign Sanctions Law promulgated in June 2021, which gives the state broad powers to seize assets from – and deny vias to – those individuals and entities from countries that have implemented sanctions against China for human rights violations.

[50] See Frick and Hsueh (2021) on Chinese outward FDI.

[51] See Ye (2020) on BRI. See Wise (2020) and Kaplan (2021) on China in Latin America.

[52] See "Taiwan Kicked Out Its Ruling Party for Getting Too Close to Mainland China. Here's What Comes Next," *Washington Post* (February 1, 2016).

medium enterprises yet offered limited liberalization of a few sectors of the Chinese economy in unattractive locales no different from the restricted markets available to other FDI. Such terms of the trade agreement fueled Taiwanese fears of the deliberate encroachment of Taiwan's communications infrastructure and vibrant services markets.[53]

Significantly, the analytical leverage of value-bounded rationality and sectoral analysis also sheds light on Russia's external relations. In the lead-up to the U.S. presidential elections in 2016, hackers in the Russian foreign intelligence service broke into the servers of the Democratic National Committee in the United States and released damaging information about Hillary Clinton.[54] This occurred in the context of deliberate regulatory actions and the various mechanisms already in place, including information manipulation and curation and the requirement of surveillance-equipment installation and government ownership and management of backbone infrastructure, which control information flow on the Internet. The direction and scope of Putin's centralization efforts in telecommunications services rests on the perceived danger "that NATO will disconnect Russia from the network, which is why the country needs an independent digital infrastructure for an autonomous Internet."[55] "[Western intelligence agencies] are sitting online. [The Internet] is their creation. And they hear, see and read everything that you are saying and they're collecting security information.... . But everything is possible in theory. So we must create a segment [of the Internet] which depends on nobody."

Developments in Russia make clear that the economic-security nexus and how it drives national decision-making at the sector level is particularly apparent in authoritarian regimes. The promulgation of the "Sovereign Internet Law" of 2019 after the Russian hacking attacks on the Pentagon, White House email system, and the Democratic National Committee and the spread of disinformation and propaganda during the 2016 U.S. elections can then be understood in the interacting strategic value and sectoral logics of Russia's *resource security nationalism* and resulting *bifurcated oligarchy*, which have enabled its implementation. Other cyberattacks have included a breach of at least seven U.S. government agencies and hundreds of large American companies in an operation

---

[53] See Hsueh (2014).
[54] See Mueller (2019) and Diresta and Grossman (2019). The actual delineation of responsibilities of internally and externally focused intelligence agencies is unknown.
[55] See "Is Russia Leaving the Global Internet?," *Russland* (November 2, 2019).

called "SolarWind" and the hacking of the United States Agency for International Development's email system to access information about human rights organizations and other groups critical of Putin.[56]

What does this mean for the future of the Liberal International Order? That India is a democracy means that a D-10 (G-7 democracies plus Australia, India, and South Korea) as envisioned by some is possible whereas Russia and China are potential opponents of the Liberal International Order. The Strategic Value Framework and multilevel comparative sectoral analysis have ascertained, unlike in China and Russia, perceived national security concerns do not pervade economic policymaking on how markets are governed in India unless politically expedient.

The Modi-led government, since 2014, defines national security as aimed at the details of confronting territorial disputes with neighboring countries, such as China and Pakistan, without relation to economic or industrial policy.[57] The ban on FDI from India's neighboring countries in the aftermath of border disputes between China and India is representative. Concerns about Chinese investment and acquisitions in high-tech sectors have raised the ante on Chinese FDI but have not led to a general clampdown on market entry and business in the context of the *neoliberal self-reliance* of India's *bifurcated liberalism*.

This does not mean that China and Russia cannot be balanced and that "a degree of acquiescence and acceptance from China" is not possible.[58] The Strategic Value Framework, which has identified national secctor-specific patterns of market governance, sheds light on the possibilities of forging of sector and issue-focused coalitions on individual problems even with authoritarian governments. The *national configurations of sectoral models* shed light on those critical details of the future of global conflict and cooperation.

---

[56] See "Russia Appears to Carry Out Hack Through System Used by U.S. Aid Agency," *New York Times* (May 28, 2021). The Chinese government, for its part, has also permitted and faciliated such cyberattacks as breaching Microsoft email systems and stealing sensitive and secret information around the world including research related to autonomous vehicles, genetic-sequencing technology, and infectious diseases. "U.S. Accuses China of Hacking Microsoft," *New York Times* (July 19, 2021).

[57] See Gokhale (2017).   [58] See Campbell and Doshi (2021).

Bibliography

Abdelal, Rawi. 2001. *National Purpose in the World Economy: Post-Soviet States in Comparative Perspective*. Ithaca: Cornell University Press.

Acemoglu, Daron, and James Robinson. 2006. *Economic Origins of Dictatorship and Democracy*. New York: Cambridge University Press.

2012. *Why Nations Fail: The Origins of Power, Prosperity, and Poverty*. New York: Crown Books.

Addis, Caren. 1999. *Taking the Wheel: Auto Parts Firms and the Political Economy of Industrialization in Brazil*. University Park: The Pennsylvania State University Press.

Aggarwal, Vinod. 1985. *Liberal Protectionism*. Berkeley: University of California Press.

Ahmed, Sadiq, and Ashutosh Varshney. 2012. "Battles Half Won: Political Economy of India's Growth and Economic Policy Since Independence." In *The Oxford Handbook of the Indian Economy*, edited by Chetan Ghate, 1–61. Oxford: Oxford University Press.

Alexander, Marcus. 2004. "The Internet and Democratization: The Development of Russian Internet Policy." *Demokratizatsiya* 12(4): 607–627.

Amsden, Alice. 1989. *Asia's Next Giant: South Korea and Late Industrialization*. New York: Oxford University Press.

Andrews, Matt, Lant Pritchett, and Michael Woolcock. 2017. *Building State Capability: Evidence, Analysis, Action*. Oxford: Oxford University Press.

Ang, Yuen Yuen. 2016. *How China Escaped the Poverty Trap*. Ithaca: Cornell University Press.

2020. *China's Gilded Age: The Paradox of Economic Boom and Vast Corruption*. Cambridge: Cambridge University Press.

Ang, Yuen Yuen, and Nan Jia. 2014. "Perverse Complementarity: Political Connections and the Use of Courts Among Private Firms in China." *The Journal of Politics* 76(2): 318–332.

Ansell, Ben, and David Samuels. 2010. "Inequality and Democratization: A Contrarian Approach." *Comparative Political Studies* 43(12): 1543–1574.

Appel, Hilary, and Mitchell A. Orenstein. 2018. *From Triumph to Crisis: Neoliberal Economic Reform in Post-Communist Countries*. Cambridge: Cambridge University Press.

Arnold, Caroline. 2011. "Cotton Textile Production in Colonial India." *World History* 15: 654–656.

Aslund, Anders. 1995. *How Russia Became a Market Economy*. Washington: Brookings Institution.

2019. *Russia's Crony Capitalism: The Path from Market Economy to Kleptocracy*. New Haven: Yale University Press.

Baark, Erik. 1997. *Lightning Wires: The Telegraph and China's Technological Modernization, 1860–1890*. Westport: Greenwood Press.

Babb, Sarah. 2013. "The Washington Consensus as Transnational Policy Paradigm: Its Origins, Trajectory and Likely Successor." *Review of International Political Economy* 20(2): 1–30.

Bagchi, Jayanta. 2004. *Indian Textile Industry: Liberalization and World Market*. New Delhi: Samskriti.

Balzer, Harley, and Jon Askonas. 2016. "The Triple Helix After Communism: Russia and China Compared." *Triple Helix* 3(1): 3–31.

Ban, Cornel, and Mark Blyth. 2013. "The BRICs and the Washington Consensus: An Introduction." *Review of International Political Economy* 20(2): 241–255.

Bardhan, Pranab. 2010. *Awakening Giants, Feet of Clay: Assessing the Economic Rise of China and India*. Princeton: Princeton University Press.

Barnes, Andrew. 2003a. "Russia's New Business Group and State Power." *Post-Soviet Affairs* 19(2): 154–196.

2003b. "What Do We Know Now? Post-Communist Economic Reform through a Russian Lens." *Comparative Politics* 35(4): 477–497.

2006. *Owning Russia: The Struggle Over Factories, Farms, and Power*. Ithaca: Cornell University Press.

Barnes, Jeb, and Nicholas Weller. 2017. "Case Studies and Analytic Transparency in Causal-Oriented Mixed-Methods Research." *PS: Political Science & Politics* 50(4): 1019–1022.

Bartley, Tim. 2018. *Rules Without Rights: Land, Labor, and Private Authority in the Global Economy*. Oxford: Oxford University Press.

Bassett, Ross Knox. 2017. *The Technological Indian*. Cambridge: Harvard University Press.

Baum, Matthew A., and David A. Lake. 2003. "The Political Economy of Growth: Democracy and Human Capital." *American Journal of Political Science* 47(2): 333–334.

Bendor, Jonathan. 2010. *Bounded Rationality and Politics*. Berkeley: University of California Press.

Bergère, Marie-Claire. 1990. *The Golden Age of the Chinese Bourgeoisie, 1911–1937*, translated by Janet Lloyd. Cambridge: Cambridge University Press.

Bianco, Lucien. 1971. *The Origins of the Chinese Revolution*. Stanford: Stanford University Press.

Bizzarro, Fernando, John Gerring, Carl Henrik Knutsen, Allen Hicken, Michael Bernhard, Svend-Erik Skaaning, Michael Coppedge, and Staffan I. Lindberg.

2018. "Party Strength and Economic Growth." *World Politics* 70(2): 275–320.

Blecher, Marc J., and Vivienne Shue. 1996. *Tethered Deer: Government and Economy in a Chinese County*. Stanford: Stanford University Press.

2001. "Into Leather: State-Led Development and the Private Sector in Xinji." *The China Quarterly* 166: 368–393.

Boix, Charles. 2003. *Democracy and Redistribution*. New York: Cambridge University Press.

Boone, Peter, and Denis Rodionov. 2001. *Rent Seeking in Russia and the CIS*. Warburg: Brunswick UBS.

Brandt, Loren, and Thomas Rawski, eds. 2019. *Policy, Regulation and Innovation in China's Electricity and Telecom Industries*. Cambridge: Cambridge University Press.

Breznitz, Dan. 2007. *Innovation and the State: Political Choice and Strategies for Growth in Israel, Taiwan, and Ireland*. New Haven: Yale University Press.

Brooks, Sarah M., and Marcus J. Kurtz. 2012. "Paths to Financial Policy Diffusion: Statist Legacies in Latin America's Globalization." *International Organization* 66(1): 95–128.

Bush, Richard. 1982. *The Politics of Cotton Textiles in Kuomintang China, 1927–1937*. New York and London: Garland Publishing Co.

Bussell, Jennifer. 2012. *Corruption and Reform in India: Public Services in the Digital Age*. Cambridge: Cambridge University Press.

Cammett, Melani. 2007. *Globalization and Business Politics in Arab North Africa: A Comparative Perspective*. Cambridge: Cambridge University Press.

Campbell, John L., and Leon N. Lindberg. 1990. "Property Rights and the Organization of Economic Activity by the State." *American Sociological Review* 55(5): 634–647.

Campbell, John L., J. Rogers Hollingsworth, and Leon N., Lindberg, eds. 1991. *Governance of the American Economy*. New York: Cambridge University Press.

Campbell, Kurt, and Rosh Doshi. 2021. "How America Can Shore Up Asian Order: A Strategy for Restoring Balance and Legitimacy." *Foreign Affairs* (January 12).

Campbell, Robert W. 1995. *Soviet and Post-Soviet Telecommunications: An Industry Under Reform*. Boulder: Westview Press.

Cao, Xun, Genia Kostka, and Xu Xu. 2020. "Information Asymmetry and Public Support for Social Credit Systems in China." Paper Presented at the Annual Meeting of the American Political Science Association, Washington, DC.

Carney, Richard. 2015. "The Stabilizing State: State Capitalism as a Response to Financial Globalization in One-Party Regimes." *Review of International Political Economy* 22(4): 838–873.

Central Intelligence Agency. 1956. "Current Support Memorandum: Re-Equipment of Soviet Textile Industry." *Office of Research and Reports*. CIA Historical Review Program Release.

Chakravartty, Paula. 2004. "Telecom, National Development, and the Indian State: A Post-Colonial Critique." *Media. Culture & Society* 26(2): 227–249.

Chakravorty, Sanjoy. 2019. *The Truth About Us: The Politics of Information from Manu to Modi*. Gurugram: Hachette India.

Chan, Wellington K. K. 1980. "Government, Merchants, and Industry to 1911." In *The Cambridge History of China*, edited by John K. Fairbank and Kwang-Ching Liu, 416–462. Cambridge: Cambridge University Press.

Chandavarkar, Rajnarayan. 2003. *The Origins of Industrial Capitalism in India: Business Strategies and the Working Class in Bombay, 1900–1940*. Cambridge: Cambridge University Press.

　2009. *History, Culture and the Indian City*. Cambridge: Cambridge University Press.

Chao, Kang. 1977. *The Development of Cotton Textile Production in China*. Harvard East Asian Monographs. Cambridge: Harvard University Press.

Charnysh, Volha, Christopher Lucas, and Prerna Singh. 2015. "The Ties That Bind: National Identity Salience and Pro-Social Behavior Toward the Ethnic Other." *Comparative Political Studies* 48(3): 267–300.

Chaudhry, Kiren Aziz. 1993. "The Myths of the Market and the Common History of Late Developers." *Politics & Society* 21(3): 245–274.

　1997. *The Price of Wealth: Economies and Institutions in the Middle East*. Ithaca: Cornell University Press.

Chen, Cheng. 2016. *The Return of Ideology: The Search for Regime Identities in Post-Communist Russia and China*. Ann Arbor: University of Michigan Press.

Chen, Lin. 2005. "Warning—being Totally Foreign-funded: Deep Thinking on the Trend of Being Totally Foreign-funded in Utilizing Foreign Investment." *Intertrade* 282(6), 44–48. (In Chinese)

Chen, Ling. 2018. *Manipulating Globalization: The Influence of Bureaucrats on Business in China*. Stanford: Stanford University Press.

Cheng, Tun-jen, and Stephan Haggard. 1987. "State and Foreign Capital in the East Asian NICs." In *The Political Economy of the New Asian Industrialism*, edited by Frederic C. Deyo, 84–135. Ithaca: Cornell University Press.

Chhibber, Pradeep K. 1997. "Who Voted for the Bharatia Janata Party." *British Journal of Political Science* 27(4), 631–639.

Chhibber, Pradeep K., and Rahul Verma. 2018. *Ideology and Identity: The Changing Party Systems of India*. Oxford: Oxford University Press.

Chowdary, T.H. 1998. "Politics and Economics of Telecom Liberalization in India." *Telecommunications Policy* 22(1): 9–22.

Christensen, Thomas. 2003. "China." In *Strategic Asia, 2002–03: Asian Aftershocks*, edited by Richard Ellings and Aaron Friedberg. Seattle: National Bureau of Asian Research, 51–94.

Clague, Christopher, Philip Keefer, Stephen Knack, and Olson Mancur. 1996. "Property and Contract Rights in Autocracies and Democracies." *Journal of Economic Growth* 1(2): 243–276.

Clarke, Donald, Peter Murrell, and Susan Whiting. 2006. "The Role of Law in China's Economic Development." Working Paper No. 187. George Washington University Law School.

Collier, David, Henry Brady, and Jason Seawright. 2004. "Sources of Leverage in Causal Inference: Toward an Alternative View of Methodology." In *Rethinking Social Inquiry: Diverse Tools and Shared Standards*, edited by Henry Brady and David Collier, 229–266. New York: Rowman & Littlefield Publishers.

Collier, Ruth B., and David Collier. 1991. *Shaping the Political Arena*. Princeton: Princeton University Press.

Dallas, Mark. 2014. "Manufacturing Paradoxes: Foreign Ownership, Governance, and Value Chains in China's Light Industries." *World Development* 57: 47–62.

Dasgupta, Aditya. 2018. "Technological Change and Political Turnover: The Democratizing Effects of the Green Revolution in India." *American Political Science Review* 112(4): 918–938.

Deane, Phyllis. 1978. *The Evolution of Economic Ideas*. Cambridge: Cambridge University Press.

Deeg, Richard, and Mary O'Sullivan. 2009. "Political Economy of Global Finance Capital." *World Politics* 61(4): 731–763.

Desai, Anand. 1999. *The Economics and Politics of Transition to an Open Market Economy: India*. Paris: OECD Development Center.

Desai, Ashok. 2006. *India's Telecommunications Industry*. New Delhi: SAGE Publications.

Deibert, Ronald, and Rafal Rohozinski. 2010. "Control and Subversion in Russian Cyberspace." In *Access Controlled: The Shaping of Power, Rights, and Rule in Cyberspace*, edited by Ronald Deibert, John Palfrey, Rafal Rohozinski, and Jonathan Zittrain, 16–20. Cambridge: MIT Press.

Dezhina, Irina. 2018. "Science and Innovations in Russia 2017." https://ssrn.com/abstract=3211916

Diresta, Renée and Shelby Grossman. 2019. "Potemkin Pages & Personas: Assessing GRU Online Operations, 2014–2019." White Paper. Stanford Cyber Policy Center Internet Observatory.

Dimitrov, Martin, ed. 2013. *Why Communism Did Not Collapse: Understanding Authoritarian Regime Resilience in Asia and Europe*. Cambridge: Cambridge University Press.

Donaldson, John. 2011. *Small Works: Poverty and Economic Development in Southwestern China*. Ithaca: Cornell University Press.

Doner, Richard. 1991. "Approaches to the Politics of Economic Growth in Southeast Asia." *The Journal of Asian Studies* 50(4): 818–849.

2009. *The Politics of Uneven Development: Thailand's Economic Growth in Comparative Perspective*. Ithaca: Cambridge University Press.

Doner, Richard, Bryan Ritchie, and Dan Slater. 2005. "Systemic Vulnerability and the Origins of Developmental States: Northeast and Southeast Asia in Comparative Perspective." *International Organization* 59(2): 327–361.

Doner, Richard, Greg Noble, and John Ravenhill. 2007. "Industrial Competitiveness of the Auto Parts Industries in Four Large Asian Countries: The Role of Government Policy in a Challenging International Environment." Working Paper. World Bank Policy Research.

2020. *The Political Economy of Automotive Industrialization in East Asia*. New York: Oxford University Press.

Doner, Richard, and Ben Ross Schneider. 2016. "The Middle-Income Trap: More Politics Than Economics." *World Politics* 68(4): 608–644.

2020. "Technical Education in the Middle-Income Trap: Building Coalitions for Skill Formation." *The Journal of Development Studies* 56(4): 680–697.

Doucouliagos, Hristos, and Mehmet Ali Ulubasoglu. 2008. "Democracy and Economic Growth: A Meta-Analysis." *American Journal of Political Science* 52(1): 61–83.

D'Souza, Errol. 2012. "The WTO and the Politics of Reform in India's Textile Sector: From Inefficient Redistribution to Industrial Upgradation." Paper Prepared for Research Project on Linking the WTO to the Poverty-Reduction Agenda. United Kingdom: Department for International Development.

Dunning, Thad. 2008. *Crude Democracy: Natural Resource Wealth and Political Regimes.* Cambridge: Cambridge University Press.

Eaton, Sarah. 2015. *The Advance of the State in Contemporary China: State-Market Relations in the Reform Era.* New York: Cambridge University Press.

Ekiert, Grzegorz, and Stephen E. Hanson. 2003. *Capitalism and Democracy in Central and Eastern Europe: Assessing the Legacy of Communist Rule.* Cambridge: Cambridge University Press.

Ellman, Michael, and Vladimir Kontorovich, eds. 1998. *The Destruction of the Soviet Economic System: An Insiders' History.* Armonk: M. E. Sharpe.

Enikolopov, Ruben, Alexey Makarin, and Maria Petrova. 2020. "Social Media and Protest Participation: Evidence from Russia." *Econometrica* 88(4): 1479–1514.

Etchemendy, Sebastián. 2011. *Models of Economic Liberalization Business, Workers, and Compensation in Latin America, Spain, and Portugal.* Cambridge: Cambridge University Press.

European Court of Human Rights. 2015. "Judgment on Roman Zakharov v. Russia [Application Number 47143/06] (December 5, 2015).

Evans, Allison and Rudra Sil. 2020. "The Dynamics of Labor Militancy in the Extractive Sector: Kazakhstan's Oilfields and South Africa's Platinum Mines in Comparative Perspective." *Comparative Political Studies* 53(6): 992–1024.

Evans, Peter. 1987. "Class, State, and Dependence in East Asia: Lessons for Latin Americanists." In *The Political Economy of the New East Asian Industrialization,* edited by Frederic C. Deyo, 203–226. Ithaca: Cornell University Press.

 1995. *Embedded Autonomy: States and Industrial Transformation.* Princeton: Princeton University Press.

Falleti, Tulia G., and Julia F. Lynch. 2009. "Context and Causal Mechanisms in Political Analysis." *Comparative Political Studies* 42(9): 1143–1166.

Farrell, Henry, and Abraham Newman. 2014. "Domestic Institutions Beyond the Nation State: Charting the New Interdependence Approach." *World Politics* 66(2): 331–362.

Fewsmith, Joseph. 2001. "The Political and Social Implications of China's Accession to the WTO." *The China Quarterly* 167: 573–591.

Filtzer, Donald. 1986. *Soviet Workers and Stalinist Industrialization: The Formation of Modern Soviet Production Relations, 1928–1941.* Dover: Pluto Press.

 1994. *Soviet Workers and the Collapse of Perestroika: The Soviet Labor Process and Gorbachev's Reforms, 1985–1991.* Cambridge: Cambridge University Press.

2002. *Soviet Workers and Late Stalinism: Labor and the Restoration of the Stalinist System after World War II*. Cambridge: Cambridge University Press.

Finanane, Antonia. 2008. *Changing Clothes in China: Fashion, History, Nation*. New York: Columbia University Press.

Fioretos, Orfeo. 2011. *Creative Reconstructions: Multilateralism and European Varieties of Capitalism after 1950*. Ithaca: Cornell University Press.

Fish, M. Steven. 2005. *Democracy Derailed: The Failure of Open Politics*. Cambridge: Cambridge University Press.

Frankel, Francine R. 2004. *India's Political Economy 1947–2004*. New Delhi: Oxford University Press.

Frazier, Mark W. 2019. *The Power of Place: Contentious Politics in Twentieth-Century Shanghai and Bombay*. Cambridge: Cambridge University Press.

Frick, James, and Roselyn Hsueh. 2021. "OFDI: A Chinese Foreign Policy Tool." Paper Presented at the 2021 Annual Convention of the International Studies Association.

Frieden, Jeffrey. 1991. "Invested Interests: The Politics of National Economic Policies in a World of Global Finance." *International Organization* 45(4): 425–451.

Frieden, Jeffrey, and Ronald Rogowski. 1996. "The Impact of International Economy on Domestic Politics: An Analytical Overview." In *Internationalization and Domestic Politics*, edited by Robert O. Keohane and Helen V. Milner, 25–47. Cambridge: Cambridge University Press.

Fu, Diane. 2017. "Disguised Collective Action in China." *Comparative Political Studies* 50(4): 499–527.

Fuller, Douglas. 2016. *Paper Tigers, Hidden Dragons: Firms and the Political Economy of China's Technological Development*. New York: Oxford University Press.

Fürst, Kathinka. 2016. Regulating Through Leverage: Civil Regulation in China. Doctoral Dissertation, Universiteit van Amsterdam.

Gaddy, Clifford. 1996. *The Price of the Past: Russia's Struggle with the Legacy of a Militarized Economy*. Washington: Brookings Institution.

Gandhi, M.K. 1958. *Collected Works of Mahatma Gandhi*. New Delhi: Publications Division Government of India.

1960. *Village Industries*. Ahmedabad: Navajivan Publishing House.

Gallagher, Mary. 2005. *Contagious Capitalism. Globalization and the Politics of Labor in China*. Princeton: Princeton University Press.

2013. "Capturing Meaning and Confronting Measurement." In *Interview Research in Political Science*, edited by Layna Mosley, 181–195. Ithaca: Cornell University Press.

2017. *Authoritarian Legality in China: Law, Workers, and the State*. Cambridge: Cambridge University Press.

Gans-Morse, Jordon. 2017. *Property Rights in Post-Soviet Russia: Violence, Corruption, and the Demand for Law*. Cambridge: Cambridge University Press.

Gapontsev, Valentin. 2007. "Independent Thinker." *International Society of Optics and Photonics* 2(3): 18–20.

Garrett, Geoffrey, and Peter Lange, 1995. "Internationalization, Institutions and Political Change." *International Organization* 49(4): 627–655.

Gelman, Vladimir, and Cameron Ross. 2010. *The Politics of Sub-National Authoritarianism in Russia*. Surrey: Ashgate.

2015. *Electoral Authoritarianism: Analyzing Post-Soviet Regime Change*. Pittsburgh: University of Pittsburgh Press.

George, Alexander, and Andrew Bennett. 2005. *Case Studies and Theory Development in the Social Sciences*. Cambridge: MIT Press.

Gereffi, Gary. 2001. "Shifting Governance Structures in Global Commodity Chains." *American Behavioral Scientist* 44(10): 1616–1636.

Gereffi, Gary, John Humphrey, and Timothy Sturgeon. 2005. "The Governance of Global Value Chains." *Review of International Political Economy* 12(1): 78–104.

Gerschenkron, Alexander. 1962. *Economic Backwardness in Historical Perspective*. Cambridge: Harvard University Press.

Gingrich, Jane. 2011. *Making Markets in the Welfare State: The Politics of Varying Market Reforms*. Cambridge: Cambridge University Press.

Gokhale, Nitin A. 2017. *Securing India The Modi Way: Pathankot, Surgical Strikes and More*. New Delhi: Bloomsbury Publishing.

Goldgeier, James M., and Michael McFaul. 2003. *Power and Purpose: U.S. Policy toward Russia After the Cold War*. Washington: Brookings Institution Press.

Goldman, Marshall. 1963. "From Sputniks to Panties: Is Economic Development Really That Easy." *The Business History Review* 37(1/2): 81–93.

Goswami, Omkar. 1990. "Sickness and Growth of India's Textile Industry: Analysis and Policy Options." *Economic and Political Weekly* 25(45): 2496–2506.

Gourevitch, Peter. 1978. "The Second Image Reversed: The International Sources of Domestic Politics." *International Organization* 32(4): 881–912.

1986. *Politics in Hard Times: Comparative Responses to International Economic Crises*. Ithaca: Cornell University Press.

Gourevitch, Peter, and James Shinn. 2005. *Political Power and Corporate Control*. Princeton: Princeton University Press.

Grande, Edgar, and Louis W. Pauly. 2005. *Complex Sovereignty: Reconstituting Political Authority in the Twenty-First Century*. Toronto: University of Toronto Press.

Great Northern Telegraph Company. 1969. *The Great Northern Telegraph Company: An Outline of The Company's History, 1869–1969*. Copenhagen: Kongens Nytorv.

Gregg, Amanda Grace. 2015. "Factory Productivity, Firm Organization, and Corporation Reform in the Russian Empire, 1894–1908." Doctoral Dissertation, Yale University.

Grigor'ev, L. and M. Aksentsova. 1960. "The Soviet Textile Industry and Foreign Trade in Textile Goods and Raw Materials." *Problems of Economics* 3(4): 16–21.

Group of Twenty. 2016. "China's Efforts to Phase Out and Rationalize Its Inefficient Fossil-Fuel Subsidies." *G20 Peer Review*.

Guillen, Mauro F. 2001. *The Limits of Convergence: Globalization and Organizational Change in Argentina, South Korea, and Spain*. Princeton: Princeton University Press.

Gunitsky, Seva. 2017. *Aftershocks: Great Powers and Domestic Reforms in the Twentieth Century*. Princeton: Princeton University Press.

Guthrie, Doug. 1999. *Dragon in a Three-Piece Suit*. Princeton: Princeton University Press.

Greene, Samuel A., and Graeme Robertson. 2019. *Putin v. the People: The Perilous Politics of a Divided Russia*. New Haven: Yale University Press.

Haggard, Stephan. 1990. *Pathway from the Periphery*. Ithaca: Cornell University Press.

———. 2018. *Developmental States (Elements in the Politics of Development)*. New York: Cambridge University Press.

Hall, Peter, ed. 1989. *The Political Power of Economic Ideas: Keynesianism Across Nations*. Princeton: Princeton University Press.

Hall, Peter, and David Soskice. 2001. *Varieties of Capitalism: The Institutional Foundations of Comparative Advantage*. Oxford: Oxford University Press.

Han, Jiyun. 2005. "Strengthening Arrangement and Utilization of Foreign Resource in China." *Intertrade* 285(9): 47–51. (In Chinese.)

Han, Rongbin. 2018. *Contesting Cyberspace in China: Online Expression and Authoritarian Resilience*. New York: Columbia University Press.

Hanzl, Doris and Peter Havlik. 2003. "Textiles in Central Eastern Europe and Russia: A Comparative Analysis in the European Context." *Journal of Economics and Business* 6(2): 63–88.

Harriss, John. 1982. *Rural Development: Theories of Peasant Economy and Agrarian Change*. London: Hutchinson.

Harrison, Ann, Benjamin Hyman, Leslie Martin, and Shanthi Nataraj. 2019. "When Do Firms Go Green? Comparing Command and Control Regulations with Price Incentives in India." NBER Working Paper No. 21763.

Harrison, Ann, and Andrés Rodríguez-Clare. 2010. "Trade, Foreign Investment, and Industrial Policy for Developing Countries." *Handbook of Development Economics* 1(5): 4039–4214.

Harwit, Eric. 2008. *China's Telecommunications Revolution*. Oxford: Oxford University Press.

Held, David, Anthony McGrew, David Goldblatt, and Jonathan Perraton. 1999. *Global Transformations: Politics, Economics, and Culture*. Stanford: Stanford University Press.

Henisz, Witold J., Bennet A. Zelner, and Mauro F. Guillén. 2005. "Market-Oriented Infrastructure Reforms, 1977–1999." *American Sociological Review* 70(6): 871–897.

Herrera, Yoshiko M. 2004. *Imagined Economies: The Sources of Russian Regionalism*. Cambridge: Cambridge University Press.

———. 2010. "Imagined Economies: Constructivist Political Economy, Nationalism, and Economic-Based Sovereignty Movements in Russia." In *Constructing the International Economy*, edited by Rawi Abdelal et al., 114–133. Ithaca: Cornell University Press.

Herring, Ronald. 1999. "Embedded Particularism: India's Failed Developmental State." In *The Developmental State*, edited by Meredith Woo-Cumings, 306–334. Ithaca: Cornell University Press.

Hirata, Koji. 2020. "Steel Metropolis: Industrial Manchuria and the Making of Chinese Socialism."*Enterprise & Society* 21(4): 875–885.

Hiscox, Michael J. 2001. "Inter-Industry Factor Mobility and the Politics of Trade." *International Organization* 55(1): 1–46.

Ho, Selina. 2019. *Thirsty Cities: Social Contracts and Public Goods Provision in China and India*. New York: Cambridge University Press.

Hollingsworth, J. Rogers, Philippe C. Schmitter, and Wolfgang Streeck. 1994. *Governing Capitalist Economies: Performance and Control of Economic Sectors*. New York: Oxford University Press.

Hou, Yue. 2019. *The Private Sector in Public Office: Selective Property Rights in China*. Cambridge: Cambridge University Press.

Hsueh, Lily. 2019. "Corporations at a Crossroads: How Multilevel Governance Interactions Shape Participation and Effort in Private Governance Regimes." *Governance* 32(4): 715–760.

Hsueh, Roselyn. 2011. *China's Regulatory State: A New Strategy for Globalization*. Ithaca: Cornell University Press.

    2012. "China and India in the Age of Globalization: Sectoral Variation in Postliberalization Reregulation." *Comparative Political Studies* 45(1): 32–61.

    2014. "Taiwan's Treaty Trouble: The Backlash Against Taipei's China Deal," Foreign Affairs (June 3).

    2015. "Nations or Sectors in the Age of Globalization: China's Policy Toward Foreign Direct Investment in Telecommunications." *Review of Policy Research* 32(6): 627–648.

    2016. "State Capitalism, Chinese-Style: Strategic Value of Sectors, Sectoral Characteristics, and Globalization." *Governance* 29(1): 85–102.

    2020. "Synergies of Comparative Area Studies: Theory Development, New Inquires, and Community," Symposium Comparative Area Studies: Methodological Rationales and Cross-Regional Applications (CAS). *Qualitative and Multi-Method Research Newsletter* 17–18: 1 (Spring).

    2021. "Why China May Not Bail Out Evergrande," *Foreign Policy* (November 1).

Hsueh, Roselyn, and Michael Nelson. 2018. "China and the Telecommunications Revolution in Africa: The Politics of Infrastructure Development for Resources and Markets." https://ssrn.com/abstract=3069863

Huang, Yasheng. 2003. "One Country, Two Systems: Foreign-Invested Enterprises and Domestic Firms in China." *China Economic Review* 14(4): 404–416.

    2008. *Capitalism with Chinese Characteristics*. Cambridge: Cambridge University Press.

Human Rights Watch. 2018. "No Support Russia's 'Gay Propaganda' Law Imperils LGBT Youth (December 11, 2018)."

Huntington, Samuel. 1968. *Political Order in Changing Societies*. New Haven: Yale University Press.

Hurst, William. 2009. *The Chinese Worker after Socialism*. Cambridge: Cambridge University Press.

    2018. *Ruling Before the Law: The Politics of Legal Regimes in China and Indonesia*. New York: Cambridge University Press.

Hyde, Susan, and Elizabeth Saunders. 2020. "Recapturing Regime Type in International Relations: Leaders, Institutions, and Agency Space." *International Organization* 74(2), 363–369

India Ministry of Statistics and Program Implementation. 2020. "Periodic Labor Force Survey Annual Report 2017–18," *Economic Survey 2019–2020*, Chapter 10, Volume 2.

India Ministry of Textiles. 2001. Annual Report (2000–2001).

India National Commission for Enterprises in the Unorganized Sector. 2008. *Report on Conditions of Work and Promotion of Livelihoods in the Unorganized Sector*. New Delhi: Academic Foundation.

Indukaev, Andrey. 2020. "The Political Roles of State-Promoted Venture Capital in Russia." Paper Presented at the Annual Meeting of the American Political Science Association, Virtual Presentation.

International Trade Commission. 2010. Russia Market Report. World Trade Organization and United Nations.

Iyer, Lakshmi, Tarun Kanna, and Ashutosh Varshney. 2012. "Caste and Entrepreneurship in India." Working Paper 12-028. Cambridge: Harvard Business School.

Jackson, Gregory, and Richard Deeg. 2008a. "Comparing Capitalisms: Understanding Institutional Diversity and its Implications for International Business." *Journal of International Business Studies* 39(4): 540–561.

2008b. "From Comparing Capitalisms to the Politics of Institutional Change." *Review of International Political Economy* 15(4): 680–709.

2019. "Comparing Capitalisms and Taking Institutional Context Seriously." *Journal of International Business Studies* 50(1): 4–19.

Jackson, Jason. 2016. "Varieties of Economic Nationalisms in Post-War Brazil and India." Paper Presented at the Annual Meeting of the American Political Science Association, Washington, DC.

Jacobson, Harold, and Michel Oksenberg. 1990. *China's Participation in the IMF, the World Bank, and GAAT*. Ann Arbor: University of Michigan Press.

Jamal, Amaney, and Nooruddin Irfan. 2010. "The Democratic Utility of Trust: A Cross-National Analysis." *The Journal of Politics* 72(1): 45–59.

Jenkins, Rob. 1999. *Democratic Politics and Economic Reform in India*. Cambridge: Cambridge University Press.

Johnson, Chalmers. 1962. *Peasant Nationalism and Communist Power: The Emergence of Revolutionary China, 1937–1945*. Stanford: Stanford University Press.

1982. *MITI and the Japanese Miracle*. Stanford: Stanford University Press.

1987. "Political Institutions and Economic Performance: The Government-Business Relationship in Japan, South Korea, and Taiwan." In *The Political Economy of the New East Asian Industrialization*, edited by Frederic C. Deyo, 136–164. Ithaca: Cornell University Press.

Jones, Eric L. 1981. *The European Miracle: Environments, Economies, and Geopolitics in the History of Europe and Asia*. Cambridge: Cambridge University Press.

Joshi, Vijay, and I. M. D Little. 1994. *India: Macroeconomics and Political Economy 1964–1991*. Washington: World Bank.

Kahler, Miles, and David Lake, eds. 2003. *Governance in a Global Economy: Political Authority in Transition*. Princeton: Princeton University Press.

Kaplan, Stephen. 2021. *Globalizing Patient Capital: The Political Economy of Chinese Finance in the Americas*. Cambridge: Cambridge University Press.

Kapur, Devesh. 2010. *Diaspora, Democracy and Development: The Impact of International Migration from India*. Princeton: Princeton University Press.

Katada, Saori, and Mireya Solís, eds. 2008. *Cross Regional Trade Agreements: Understanding Permeated Regionalism in East Asia*. London: Springer Science & Business Media.

Katzenstein, Mary F. 1979. *Ethnicity and Equality: The Shiv Sena Party and Preferential Policies in Bombay*. Ithaca: Cornell University Press.

Katzenstein, Peter J. 1978. *Between Power and Plenty: Foreign Economic Policies of Advanced Industrialized States*. Madison: University of Wisconsin Press.

  1996. *The Culture of National Security: Norms and Identity in World Politics*. New York: Columbia University Press.

  1998. *Cultural Norms and National Security: Police and Military in Postwar Japan*. Ithaca: Cornell University Press.

Katzenstein, Peter J., Robert O. Keohane, and Stephen D. Krasner. 1998. "International Organization and the Study of World Politics." *International Organization* 52(4): 645–685.

Kelly, Tim, Martin Salamon, and Hans-Peter Grassman. 1992. "Swords into Ploughshares, Tanks into Telephones." *OECD Observer* 1(177): 12–18.

Kelly, Sanja, Madeline Earp, Laura Reed, Adrian Shahbaz, and Mai Truong. 2014. "Tightening the Net: Governments Expand Online Controls." *Freedom on the Net*, 1–989. Freedom House.

Kennedy, Scott. 2005. *The Business of Lobbying in China*. Cambridge: Harvard University Press.

  2011, ed. *Beyond the Middle Kingdom: Comparative Perspective on China's Capitalist Transformation*. Stanford: Stanford University Press.

Kentikelenis, Alexander E., and Sarah Babb. 2019. "The Making of Neoliberal Globalization: Norm Substitution and the Politics of Clandestine Institutional Change." *American Journal of Sociology* 124(6): 1720–1762.

Keohane, Robert and Helen Milner, eds. 1996. *Internationalization and Domestic Politics*. Cambridge: Cambridge University Press.

Khemani, Stuti, Ernesto Dal Bó, Claudio Ferraz, Frederico Finan, Corinne Stephenson, Adesinaola Odugbemi, Dikshya Thapa, and Scott Abrahams. 2016. "Making Politics Work for Development: Harnessing Transparency & Citizen Engagement." Policy Research Reports. Washington: World Bank Group.

King, Gary, Jennifer Pan, and Margaret E. Roberts. 2013. "How Censorship in China Allows Government Criticism but Silences Collective Expression." *American Political Science Review* 107(2): 1–18.

Kinzley, Judd. 2018. *Natural Resources and the New Frontier: Constructing Modern China's Borderlands*. Chicago: University of Chicago Press.

Kitschelt, Herbert. 1991. "Industrial Governance Structures, Innovation Strategies, and the Case of Japan: Sectoral or Cross-National Comparative Analysis?" *International Organization* 45(4): 453–493.

Kitschelt, Herbert, Peter Lange, Gary Marks, and John D. Stephens, eds. 1999. *Continuity and Change in Contemporary Capitalism.* Cambridge: Cambridge University Press.

Knutsen, Carl Henrik, Asmund Rygh, and Helge Hveem. 2011. "Does State Ownership Matter? Institutions' Effect on Foreign Direct Investment Revisited." *Business and Politics* 13(1): 1–31.

Knutsen, Carl Henrik and Magnus Bergli Rasmussen. 2018a. "Electoral Rules, Labor Market Coordination and Macroeconomic Performance." *Scandinavian Political Studies* 43(1): 367–378.

2018b. "The Autocratic Welfare State: Old-Age Pensions, Credible Commitments, and Regime Survival." *Comparative Political Studies* 51(5): 659–694.

Koenker, Diane P. 1981. *Moscow Workers and the 1917 Revolution.* Princeton: Princeton University Press.

Kohli, Atul. 1987. *The State and Poverty in India.* Cambridge: Cambridge University Press.

1990. *Democracy and Discontent: India's Growing Crisis of Governability.* Cambridge: Cambridge University Press.

2004. *State-Directed Development: Political Power and Industrialization in the Global Periphery.* Cambridge: Cambridge University Press.

2012. *Poverty Amid Plenty in the New India.* Cambridge: Cambridge University Press.

2020. *Imperialism and the Developing World: How Britain and the United States Shaped Global Periphery.* New York: Oxford University Press.

Kornai, Janos. 2000. "What the Change of the System from Socialism to Capitalism Does or Does Not Mean." *Journal of Economic Perspectives* 14 (1): 27–42.

Kosack, Stephen. 2012. *The Education of Nations.* New York: Oxford University Press.

Kostka, Genia, and William Hobbs. 2012. "Local Energy Efficiency Policy Implementation in China: Bridging the Gap between National Priorities and Local Interests." *The China Quarterly* 211: 765–785.

2015. "Command without Control: The Case of China's Environmental Target System." *Regulation & Governance* 10(1): 58–74.

Kotkin, Stephen. 2001. *Armageddon Averted: The Soviet Collapse, 1970–2000.* New York: Oxford University Press.

Kurtz, Marcus J. and Brooks M. Sarah. 2008. "Embedding Neoliberal Reform in Latin America." *World Politics* 60(2): 231–280.

Kuchins, Andrew, Amy Beavin, and Anna Bryndza 2008. "Russia's 2020 Strategic Economic Goals and the Role of International Integration." In *Europe, Russia, and United States: Finding a New Balance*, 1–21 (July). Washington: Center for Strategic and International Studies.

Kuhonta, Erik. 2011. *The Institutional Imperative: The Politics of Equitable Development in Southeast Asia.* Stanford: Stanford University Press.

Kuromiya, Hiroaki. 1990. *Stalin's Industrial Revolution: Politics and Workers, 1928–1931.* Cambridge: Cambridge University Press.

Kurth, James. 1979. "The Political Consequences of the Product Cycle." *International Organization* 33(1): 1–34.

Lagunes, Paul, and Oscar Pocasangre. 2019. "Dynamic Transparency: An Audit of Mexico's Freedom of Information Act." *Public Administration* 97(1): 162–176.

Lake, David A. 2009a. *Hierarchy in International Relations*. Ithaca: Cornell University Press.

2009b. "Open Economy Politics: A Critical Review." *Review in International Political Economy* 4(3): 219–244.

Lake, David A., and Robert Powell. 1999. *Strategic Choice and International Relations*. Princeton: Princeton University Press.

Lampton, David M. 1987. *Policy Implementation in Post-Mao China*. Berkeley: University of California Press.

2001. *Same Bed, Different Dreams: Managing U.S.-China Relations 1999–2000*. Berkeley: University of California Press.

LaPorte, Jody, and Danielle Lussier. 2011. "What Is the Leninist Legacy? Assessing Twenty Years of Scholarship." *Slavic Review* 70(3): 637–654

Lardy, Nicholas R. 2002. *Integrating China in the Global Economy*. Washington: Brookings Institution.

2014. *Markets Over Mao: The Rise of Private Business in China*. New York: Columbia University Press.

Lau, Lawrence, Yingyi Qian, and Gerard Roland. 2000. "Reform Without Losers: An Interpretation of China's Dual-Track Approach to Transition." *Journal of Political Economy* 108(1): 120–143.

Leutert, Wendy. 2020. "State-Owned Enterprises in Contemporary China." In *Routledge Handbook of State-Owned Enterprises*, edited by Luc Bernier, Massimo Florio, and Philippe Bance, 201–212. New York: Routledge.

Levi-Faur, David. 2004. "Comparative Research Designs in the Study of Regulation: How to Increase the Number of Cases Without Compromising the Strengths of Case-Oriented Analysis." In *The Politics of Regulation: Institutions and Regulatory Reforms for the Age of Governance*, edited by Jacint Jordana and David Levi-Faur, 177–197. Cheltenham: Edward Elgar.

2013. "The Regulatory State and the Developmental State: Towards Polymorphic Comparative Capitalism." In *The Rise of the Regulatory State of the South*, edited by Navroz K. Dubash and Bronwen Morgan, 235–245. Oxford: Oxford University Press.

Levy, Jonah, ed. 2006. *The State After Statism: New State Activities in the Age of Liberalization*. Cambridge: Harvard University Press.

Lewis, J. Patrick. 1976. "Communications Output in the USSR: A Study of the Soviet Telephone Systems." *Soviet Studies* 28(3): 406–417.

Li, Ling. 2020. "The 'Organizational Weapon' of the Chinese Communist Party China's-Disciplinary Regime from Mao to Xi Jinping." In *Law and the Party in China: Ideology and Organization*, edited by Rogiers J. E. H. Creemers and Susan Trevaskes, 187–213. Cambridge: Cambridge University Press

Lieberthal, Kenneth, and Michel Oksenberg. 1988. *Policy Making in China*. Princeton: Princeton University Press.

Lieberthal, Kenneth, and David M. Lampton. 1992. *Bureaucracy, Politics and Decision Making in Post-Mao China*. Berkeley: California University Press.

Lin, Kun-Chin. 2018. "For Whom the Road Tolls Rise: The Politics of Financing the Highway Boom in China." *Asian Survey* 58(3): 511–534.

Lin, Yi-min. 2017. *Dancing with the Devil: The Political Economy of Privatization in China*. Oxford: Oxford University Press.

Lindblom, Charles. 1977. *Politics and Markets: The World's Political Economic Systems*. New York: Basic Books.

Little, Andrew. 2016. "Communication Technology and Protest." *The Journal of Politics* 78(1): 152–166.

Liu, Andrew. 2020. *Tea War: A History of Capitalism in China and India*. New Haven: Yale University Press.

Locke, Richard, and Kathleen Thelen. 1996. "Apples and Oranges: Contextualized Comparisons and the Study of Comparative Labor Politics." *Politics & Society* 23(3): 337–367.

Lomagin, Nikita. 2012. "Interest Groups in Russian Foreign Policy: The Invisible Hand of the Russian Orthodox Church." *International Politics* 49(4): 498–516.

Lorentzen, Peter L., and Xi Lu. 2018. "Personal Ties, Meritocracy, and China's Anti-Corruption Campaign." https://ssrn.com/abstract=283584

Luo, Zhaotian, and Adam Przeworski. 2019. "Why Are the Fastest Growing Economies Autocracies?" *The Journal of Politics* 81(2): 663–669.

Lustick, Ian S. 1996. "History, Historiography, and Political Science: Multiple Historical Records and the Problem of Selection Bias." *The American Political Science Review* 90(3): 605–618.

Lynch, Julia. 2013. "Aligning Sample Strategies with Analytical Goals." In *Interview Research in Political Science*, edited by Layna Mosley, 31–44. Ithaca: Cornell University Press.

Ma, Qiang. 2005. "A Long-Term Industrial Policy Called For: Problems Concerning Upgrading of Processing Trade in China." *Intertrade* 278(2): 15–18 (In Chinese.)

Magee, Stephen P. 1980. *International Trade*. Reading: Addison-Wesley Publishing Company.

Mahoney, James. 2000. "Strategies of Causal Inference in Small-N Analysis." *Sociological Methods & Research* 28(4): 387–424.

March, Luke. 2007. "Russian Nationalism under Putin: A Majority Faith?" In *Elusive Russia: Current Developments in Russian State Identity and Institutional Reform under President Putin*, edited by Katlijn Malfliet and Ria Laenen. Leuven: Leuven University Press.

Maréchal, Nathalie. 2017. "Networked Authoritarianism and the Geopolitics of Information: Understanding Russian Internet Policy." *Media and Communication* 5(1): 29–41.

McFaul, Michael. 2001. "Ten Years After the Soviet Breakup: A Mixed Record, An Uncertain Future." *Journal of Democracy* 12(4): 87–94.

McKinsey Fashion Scope. 2020. "The State of Fashion 2020." In *The Business of Fashion*, edited by Achim Berg and Imran Amed, 1–107. New York: McKinsey & Company.

Menaldo, Victor. 2016. *The Institutions Curse: Natural Resources, Politics, and Development*. Cambridge: Cambridge University Press.

Mengin, Françoise. 2015. *Fragments of an Unfinished War: Taiwanese Entrepreneurs and the Partition of China*. Oxford: Oxford University Press.

Mertha, Andrew. 2005a. "China's Soft Centralization." *The China Quarterly* 184: 792–810.

2005b. *The Politics of Piracy*. Ithaca: Cornell University Press.

2008. *China's Water Warriors: Citizen Action and Policy Change*. Ithaca: Cornell University Press.

2009. "'Fragmented Authoritarianism 2.0': Political Pluralization in the Chinese Policy Process." *The China Quarterly* 200: 995–1012.

Meyskens, Covell F. 2020. *Mao's Third Front: The Militarization of Cold War China*. Cambridge: Cambridge University Press.

Michael, Jon D. 2020. "We the Shareholders: Government Market Participation in the Postliberal U.S. Political Economy." *Columbia Law Review* 120(2): 465–547.

Midford, Paul. 1994. "International Trade and Domestic Politics: Improving on Rogowski's Model of Political Alignments." *International Organization* 47 (4): 535–564.

Miller, Manjari Chatterjee. 2014. *Wronged by Empire: Post-Imperial Ideology and Foreign Policy in India and China*. Stanford: Stanford University Press.

Milhaupt, Curtis J., and Wentong Zheng. 2015. "Beyond Ownership: State Capitalism and the Chinese Firm." *Georgetown Law Journal* 103(3): 665–717.

Minzner, Carl F. 2011. "China's Turn Against Law." *American Journal of Comparative Law* 59(4): 935–984.

Misra, Sanjiv. 2000. "India's Textile Policy and the Informal Sectors." In *India's Development and Public Policy*, edited by Stuart S. Nagel, 9–27. Burlington: Ashgate.

Mitter, Rana. 2000. *The Manchurian Myth: Nationalism, Resistance and Collaboration in Modern China*. Berkeley: University of California Press.

Montero, Alfred. 2002. *Shifting States in Global Markets: Subnational Industrial Policy in Contemporary Brazil and Spain*. University Park: The Pennsylvania State University Press.

Montinola, Gabriella, Yingyi Qian, and Barry R. Weingast. 1995. "Federalism, Chinese Style: The Political Basis for Economic Success in China." *World Politics* 48(1): 50–81.

Moore, Thomas G. 2002. *China in the World Market: Chinese Industry and International Sources of Reform in the Post-Mao Era*. Cambridge: Cambridge University Press.

Morrison, Claudio. 2005. *A Russian Factory Enters the Market Economy*. New York: Routledge.

Mosley, Layna. 2003. *Global Capital and National Governments*. Cambridge: Cambridge University Press.

2013. *Just Talk to People? Interviews in Contemporary Political Science*. Ithaca: Cornell University Press.

Mueller, Robert III. 2019. *Report on the Investigation into Russian Interference in the 2016 Election*, vol. 1. Washington: United States Department of Justice.

Mukherji, Rahul. 2008. "The Politics of Telecommunications Regulation: State-Industry Alliance Favoring Foreign Investment in India." *Journal of Development Studies* 44(10): 1405–1423.

2014. *Globalization and Deregulation: Ideas, Interests, and Institutional Change in India*. New Delhi: Oxford University Press.

Murillo, Maria Victoria. 2001. *Labor Unions, Partisan Coalitions, and Market Reforms in Latin America*. Cambridge: Cambridge University Press.

2009. *Policymaking in the Reform of Latin American Public Utilities*. New York: Cambridge University Press.

Nahm, Jonas, and Edward Steinfeld. 2014. "The Role of Innovative Manufacturing in High Tech. Product Development: Evidence from China's Renewable Energy Sector." In *Production in the Innovation Economy*, edited by Richard M. Locke et al, 139–167. Cambridge: MIT Press.

Naseemullah, Adnan. 2017. *Development after Statism: Industrial Firms and the Political Economy of South Asia*. Cambridge: Cambridge University Press.

Nayar, Baldev Raj. 1989. *India's Mixed Economy*. Bombay: Popular Prakashan.

2005. *The Geopolitics of Globalization: The Consequences for Development*. New Delhi: Oxford University Press.

Naughton, Barry 1995. *Growing Out of the Plan: Chinese Economic Reform, 1978–1993*. Cambridge: Cambridge University Press.

Naughton, Barry, and Kellee Tsai, ed. 2015. *State Capitalism, Institutional Adaptation, and The Chinese Miracle*. Cambridge: Cambridge University of Press.

Nesvetailova, Anastasia. 2005. "United in Debt: Towards a Global Crisis of Debt-Driven Finance." *Science & Society* 69(3): 396–419.

Noam, Eli M. 1992. *Telecommunications in Europe*. New York: Oxford University Press.

Nolan, Peter, and Fureng Dong. 1989. *Market Forces in China*. London: Zed Books.

Nooruddin, Irfan, and Nita Rudra. 2014. "Are Developing Countries Really Defying the Embedded Liberalism Compact?" *World Politics* 66(4): 603–640.

Oi, Jean. 1992. "Fiscal Reform and the Economic Foundations of Local State Corporatism in China." *World Politics* 45(1): 99–126.

1999. *Rural China Takes Off: Institutional Foundations of Economic Reform*. Berkeley: University of California Press.

Ong, Lynette. 2012. *Prosper or Perish: Credit and Fiscal Systems in Rural China*. Ithaca: Cornell University Press.

Ó Riain, Sean. 2000. "The Flexible Developmental State: Globalization, Information Technology, and the 'Celtic Tiger'." *Politics and Society* 28(2): 157–193.

Pallin, Carolina Vendil. 2017. "Internet Control Through Ownership: The Case of Russia." *Post-Soviet Affairs* 33(1): 16–33.

Parris, Kristen. 1993. "Local Initiative and National Reform: The Wenzhou Model of Development." *The China Quarterly* 134: 242–263.

Paul, Thazha V., G. John Ikenberry, and John Hall. 2003. *The Nation-State in Question*. Princeton: Princeton University Press.

Pearson, Margaret. 2005. "The Business of Governing Business in China: Institutions and Norms of the Emerging Regulatory State." *World Politics* 57(2): 296–322.

2015. "State-Owned Business and Party-State Regulation in China's Modern Political Economy." In *State Capitalism, Institutional Adaptation, and The Chinese Miracle*, edited by Barry Naughton and Kellee Tsai, 27–45. Cambridge: Cambridge University Press.

Pearson, Margaret, Meg Rithmire, and Kellee Tsai. 2020. "Party State Capitalism in China." Working Paper #21-065. Harvard Business School.

Peerenboom, Randall. 2001. "Globalization, Path Dependency, and the Limits of Law: Administrative Law Reform and Rule of Law in the People's Republic of China." *Berkeley Journal of International Law* 19(2): 161–264.

Pennar, Karen. 1992. "In Russia, a Journey Back to the Future." *Business Weekly* 48–49.

Perkins, Dwight. 1966. *Market Control and Planning in Communist China*. Cambridge: Harvard University Press.

1986. *China: Asia's Next Economic Giant?* Seattle: University of Washington Press.

Pierson, Paul. 1994. *Dismantling the Welfare State? Reagan, Thatcher, and the Politics of Retrenchment*. Cambridge: Cambridge University Press.

2004. *Politics in Time: History, Institutions, and Social Analysis*. Princeton: Princeton University Press.

Polanyi, Karl. 1944. *The Great Transformation*. Boston: Beacon Press.

Pomeranz, Kenneth. 2000. *The Great Divergence: China, Europe and the Making of the Modern World Economy*. Princeton: Princeton University Press.

Pop-Eleches, Gigore. 2008. *From Economic Crisis to Reform: IMF Programs in Latin America and Eastern Europe*. Princeton: Princeton University Press.

Pop-Eleches, Grigore, and Joshua Tucker. 2017. *Communism's Shadow: Historical Legacies and Contemporary Political Attitudes*. Princeton: Princeton University Press.

Post, Alison. 2014. *Foreign and Domestic Investment in Argentina: The Politics of Privatized Infrastructure*. Cambridge: Cambridge University Press.

Przeworski, Adam, and Fernando Limongi. 1993. "Political Regimes and Economic Growth." *Journal of Economic Perspectives* 7(3): 51–69.

Przeworski, Adam, Michael E. Alvarez, José Antonio Cheibub, and Fernando Limongi. 2000. *Democracy and Development: Political Institutions and Well-Being in the World, 1950–1990*. New York: Cambridge University Press.

Qian, Yingyi, and Barry R. Weingast. 1997. "Federalism as a Commitment to Reserving Market Incentives." *Journal of Economic Perspectives* 11(4): 83–92.

Rado, Mei Mei. 2016. "When Modernity and Nationalism Intersect: Textiles for Dress in Republican China." *Perspective* 1(0): 180–187.

Reich, Simon. 1989. "Roads to Follow: Regulating Direct Foreign Investment." *International Organization* 43(4): 543–584.

Remington, Thomas. 2001. "Putin and the Duma." *Post-Soviet Affairs* 17(4): 285–308.

Repnikova, Maria. 2018. *Media Politics in China: Improvising Power Under Authoritarianism*. Cambridge: Cambridge University Press.

Roberts, Margaret. 2018. *Censored: Distraction and Diversion Inside Chin's Great Firewall*. Princeton: Princeton University Press.

Robertson, Graeme. 2010. *The Politics of Protest in Hybrid Regimes: Managing Dissent in Post-Communist Russia*. Cambridge: Cambridge University Press.

Rodrik, Dani. 1998. "Why Do More Open Economies Have Bigger Governments?" *Journal of Political Economy* 106(5): 997–1032.

1999. *Making Openness Work: The New Global Economy and the Developing Countries.* Washington: Overseas Development Council.

2007. *One Economics, Many Recipes: Globalization, Institutions, and Economic Growth.* Princeton: Princeton University Press.

Rosen, George. 1992. *Contrasting Styles of Industrial Reform.* Chicago: The University of Chicago Press.

Rosenbluth, Frances, and Michael F. Thies. 2010. *Japan Transformed: Political Change and Economic Restructuring.* Princeton: Princeton University Press.

Ross, Michael L. 2015. "What Have We Learned About the Resource Curse?" *Annual Review of Political Science* 18(1): 239–259.

Roy, Tirthankar. 1998. "Development or Distortion? 'Powerlooms' in India, 1950–1997." *Economic and Political Weekly* 33(16): 897–911.

Rozelle, Scott, Jikun Huang, Ruifa Hu, Cuihui Fan, and Carl E. Pray. 2002. "Bt Cotton Benefits, Costs, and Impacts in China." *AgBioForum* 5(4): 153–166.

Rutland, Peter. 2010. "The Oligarchs and Economic Development." In *After Putin's Russia: Past Imperfect, Future Uncertain*, edited by Dale R. Herspring and Stephen K. Wegren, 159–182. Lanham: Rowman & Littlefield Publishers.

Sachs, Jeffrey D. 2005. "The Development Challenge." *Council on Foreign Relations* 84(2): 78–90.

Samuels, Richard J. 1994. *Rich Nation, Strong Army: National Security and the Technological Transformation of Japan.* Ithaca: Cornell University Press.

Sang, Baichuan. 2005. "Focusing on High Employment: FDI Implications on Employment in China." *Intertrade* 278(2): 49–52. (In Chinese.)

2006. "The Situation and Impacts of Transnational Corporation M&A Leading Companies in China's Equipment Industry." *Intertrade* 291(3): 13–16. (In Chinese.)

Saxena, S.D. 2008. *Connecting India: Indian Telecom Story.* New Delhi: Konark Publishers.

Saylor, Ryan. 2014. *State Building in Boom Times: Commodities and Coalitions in Latin America and Africa.* New York: Oxford University Press.

2020. "Why Causal Mechanisms and Process Tracing Should Alter Case Selection Guidance." *Sociological Methods & Research* 49(4): 982–1017.

Schneider, Ben Ross. 2004. *Business Politics and the State in 20th Century Latin America.* Cambridge: Cambridge University Press.

2013. *Hierarchical Capitalism in Latin America: Business, Labor, and the Challenges of Equitable Development.* Cambridge: Cambridge University Press.

Schneider, Martin R., and Mihai Paunescu. 2012. "Changing Varieties of Capitalism and Revealed Comparative Advantages from 1990 to 2005: A Test of the Hall and Soskice Claims." *Socio-Economic Review* 10(4): 731–753.

Scheppele, Kim Lane. 2003. "Cultures of Facts." *Perspectives on Politics* 1(2): 363–368.

2017. "The Social Lives of Constitutions." In *Sociological Constitutionalism*, edited by Paul Blokker and Chris Thornhill, 35–66. Cambridge: Cambridge University Press.

Seawright, Jason, and John Gerring. 2008. "Case Selection Techniques in Case Study Research: A Menu of Qualitative and Quantitative Options." *Political Research Quarterly* 61(2): 294–308.

Segal, Adam, and Eric Thun. 2001. "Thinking Globally, Acting Locally: Local Governments, Industrial Sectors, and Development in China." *Politics and Society* 29(4): 557–588.

2006. "Globalization is a Double-Edged Sword: Globalization and Chinese National Security." In *Globalization and National Security*, edited by Jonathan Kirshner, 293–316. New York: Routledge.

Sethi, Vishal. 2006. *Communication Services in India: 1947–2007*. New Delhi: New Century.

Shadlen, Kenneth. 2017. *Coalitions and Compliance: The Political Economy of Pharmaceutical Patents in Latin America*. Oxford: Oxford University Press.

Shafer, Michael. 1994. *Winners and Losers: How Sectors Shape the Developmental Prospects of States*. Ithaca: Cornell University Press.

Shambaugh, David. 2002. *China's Military Modernization*. Berkeley: University of California Press.

Sharafutdinova, Gulnaz. 2010. *Political Consequences of Crony Capitalism Inside Russia*. Notre Dame: University of Notre Dame Press.

Sheng, Yumin. 2007. "Global Market Integration and Central Political Control: Foreign Trade and Intergovernmental Relations in China." *Comparative Political Studies* 40(4): 405–434.

Shih, Victor. 2008. *Factions and Finance in China: Elite Conflict and Inflation*. Cambridge: Cambridge University Press.

ed. 2020. *Economic Shocks and Authoritarian Stability: Duration, Financial Control, and Institutions*. Ann Arbor: University of Michigan.

Shirk, Susan L. 1993. *The Political Logic of Economic Reform in China*. Berkeley: University of California Press.

Shleifer, Andrei, and Daniel Treisman. 2000. *Without a Map: Political Tactics and Economic Reform in Russia*. Cambridge: MIT Press.

Shonfield, Andrew. 1969. *Modern Capitalism: The Changing Balance of Public and Private Power*. Oxford: Oxford University Press.

Sigeman, Tore. 1995. "Individual Employment Relations." In *International Labor Law Reports* Volume 13, edited by Benjamin Aaron, Felice Morgenstern, Jean-Maurice Verdier, Lord Wedderburn of Charlton, Thilo Ramm, Tore Sigeman, and Zvi H. Bar-Niv, 164–342. London: Martinus Nijhoff Publishers.

Sil, Rudra. 2018. "Triangulating Area Studies, Not Just Methods: How Cross-Regional Comparison Aids Qualitative and Mixed-Method Research." In *Comparative Area Studies: Methodological Rationales and Cross-Regional Applications*, edited by Ariel I. Ahram, Patrick Köllner, and Rudra Sil, 225–246. New York: Oxford University Press.

Sil, Rudra and Peter Katzenstein. 2010. *Beyond Paradigms: Analytic Eclecticism in the Study of World Politics*. New York: Palgrave McMillan.

Simon, Herbert A. 1985. "Human Nature in Politics: The Dialogue of Psychology within Political Science." *American Political Science Review* 79(2): 2093–2304.

Simmons, Beth, and Zachary Elkins. 2004. "The Globalization of Liberalization: Policy Diffusion in the International Political Economy." *American Political Science Review* 98(1): 171–189.

Simpser, Alberto, Dan Slater, and Jason Wittenberg. 2018. "Dead but Not Gone: Contemporary Legacies of Communism, Imperialism, and Authoritarianism." *Annual Review of Political Science* 21(1), 419–439.

Singh, J.P. 1999. *Leapfrogging Development: The Political Economy of Telecommunications Restructuring.* Albany: State University of New York Press.

    2000. "The Institutional Environment and the Effects of Telecommunication Privatization and Market Liberalization in Asia." *Telecommunications Policy* 24(10–11): 885–906.

    2005. "FDI Variations in Emerging Markets: The Role of Credible Commitments." *Information Technologies and International Development* 2(4): 75–87.

Sinha, Aseema. 2004. "Ideas, Interests, and Institutions in Policy Change: A Comparison of West Bengal and Gujarat." In *Regional Reflections: Comparing Politics Across India's States,* edited by Rob Jenkins, 66–108. New Delhi: Oxford University Press.

    2005. *The Regional Roots of Developmental Politics in India: A Divided Leviathan.* Bloomington: Indiana University Press.

    2016. *Globalizing India: How Global Rules and Markets are Shaping India's Rise to Power.* New York: Cambridge University Press.

Sinha, Nikhil. 1996. "The Political Economy of India's Telecommunication Reforms." *Telecommunications Policy* 20(1): 23–38.

Skocpol, Theda, and Margaret Somers. 1980. "The Uses of Comparative History in Macrosocial History." *Comparative Studies in Society and History* 22(2): 174–197.

Slater, Dan and Daniel Ziblatt. 2013. "The Enduring Indispensability of the Controlled Comparison." *Comparative Political Studies* 46(10): 1301–1327.

Smith, Benjamin. 2007. *Hard Times in the Lands of Plenty: Oil Politics in Iran and Indonesia.* Ithaca: Cornell University Press.

Snyder, Richard. 2001. *Politics After Neoliberalism: Reregulation After Mexico.* Cambridge: Cambridge University Press.

Soederberg, Susanne, Georg Menz, and Philip Cerny, eds. 2005. *Internalizing Globalization: The Rise of Neoliberalism and the Decline of National Varieties of Capitalism.* Basingstoke: Macmillan.

Soldatov, Andrei, and Irina Borogan. 2015. *The Red Web: The Struggle Between Russia's Digital Dictators and the New Online Revolutionaries.* New York: Public Affairs.

Solinger, Dorothy. 1991. *From Lathes to Looms: China's Industrial Policy in Comparative Perspective, 1979–1982.* Stanford: Stanford University Press.

    2009. *States' Gains, Labor's Losses: China, France and Mexico Choose Global Liaisons, 1980–2000.* Ithaca: Cornell University Press.

Sood, Atul, and Bimal Arora. 2006. "The Political Economy of Corporate Responsibility in India." Technology, Business and Society Program Paper Number 18. United Nations Research. Institute for Social Development.

Sood, Atul, Paaritosh Nath, and Sangeeta Ghosh. 2014. "Deregulating Capital, Regulating Labor. The Dynamics in the Manufacturing Sector in India." *Economic & Political Weekly* 49(26–27): 58–68.

Streeck, Wolfgang, and Kathleen Thelen, eds. 2005. *Beyond Continuity: Institutional Change in Advanced Political Economies*. Oxford: Oxford University Press.

Steinfeld, Edward. 2004. "China's Shallow Integration: Networked Production and the New Challenges of Late Industrialization." *World Development* 32 (1): 1971–1987.

2010. *Playing Our Game: Why China's Rise Doesn't Threaten the West*. Oxford: Oxford University Press.

Stern, Rachel E. 2013. *Environmental Litigation in China: A Study in Political Ambivalence*. Cambridge: Cambridge University Press.

Stiglitz, Joseph. 2001. *Globalization and Its Discontents*. London: W.W. Norton.

Stockmann, Daniela, and Mary E. Gallagher. 2011. "Remote Control: How the Media Sustain Authoritarian Rule in China." *Comparative Political Studies* 44(4): 436–467.

Stoner-Weiss, Kathryn. 2006. *Resisting the State: Reform and Retrenchment in Post-Soviet Russia*. New York: Cambridge University Press.

Strange, Susan. 1996. *The Retreat of the State: The Diffusion of Power in the World Economy*. Cambridge: Cambridge University Press.

Stubbs, Richard. 1999. "War and Economic Development: Export-Oriented Industrialization in East and Southeast Asia." *Comparative Politics* 31(3): 337–355.

2005. *Rethinking Asia's Economic Miracle: The Political Economy of War, Prosperity and Crisis*. Basingstoke: Macmillan.

Su, Fubing, Ran Tao, and Dali L. Yang. 2018. "Rethinking the Institutional Foundations of China's Hypergrowth: Official Incentives, Institutional Constraints, and Local Developmentalism." In *Handbook on the Politics of Development*, edited by Carol Lancaster and Nicholas van de Walle, 1–36. Oxford: Oxford University Press.

Subramanian, Arvind. 2008. *India's Turn: Understanding the Economic Transformation*. New Delhi: Oxford University Press.

Sugihara, Kaoru. 2009. "The Resurgence of Intra-Asian Trade, 1800–1850." In *How India Clothed the World: The World of South Asian Textiles, 1500–1850*, edited by Giorgio Riello and Tirthankar Roy, 139–169. Leide and Boston: Brill.

Sun, Jianjun, and Xiu'er Zhang. 2005. "Overseeing the Chinese Industries Upgrading from Trade Conflicts." *Intertrade* 288(12): 13–15. (In Chinese.)

Suttmeier, Richard. 2005. "A New Technonationalism?: China and the Development of Technical Standard." *Communications of the ACM* 48(4): 35–37.

Szakonyi, David. 2020. *Politics for Profit: Business, Elections, and Policymaking in Russia*. Cambridge: Cambridge University Press.

Tan, Yeling. 2020. "Disaggregating China, Inc.: The Hierarchical Politics of WTO Entry," *Comparative Political Studies* 53(13): 2118–2152

Tavares, Jose, and Romain Wacziarg. 2001. "How Democracy Affects Growth." *European Economic Review* 45(8): 1341–1378.

Taylor, Mark Zachary. 2012. "Toward an International Relations Theory of International Innovation Rates." *Security Studies* 21(1): 113–153.

2016. *Politics of Innovation: Why Some Countries are Better than Others at Science and Technology.* New York: Oxford University Press.

Teitelbaum, Emmanuel. 2007. "In the Grip of a Green Giant How the Rural Sector Tamed Organized Labor in India." *Comparative Political Studies* 40 (6): 638–664.

Ten Brink, Tobias. 2019. *China's Capitalism: A Paradoxical Route to Economic Prosperity.* Philadelphia: University of Pennsylvania Press.

Terebova, S. V. 2017. "Cooperation between Russia and the European Union: From Importing to Exporting Technology." *Studies on Russian Economic Development* 28(3): 327–337.

Tewari, Meenu. 2006. "Most-MFA Adjustments in India's Textile and Apparel Industry: Emerging Issues and Trends." Working Paper No. 167. New Delhi: Indian Council for Research on International Economic Relations.

Thachil, Tariq. 2014. *Elite Parties, Poor Voters: How Social Services Win Votes in India.* Cambridge: Cambridge University Press (Studies in Comparative Politics Series).

Thelen, Kathleen. 2004. *How Institutions Evolve: The Political Economy of Skills in Germany, Britain, the United States and Japan.* New York: Cambridge University Press.

2014. *Varieties of Liberalization and the New Politics of Social Solidarity.* Cambridge: Cambridge University Press.

Thiruvengadam, Arun K., and Piyush Joshi. 2013. "Judiciaries as Crucial Actors in Regulatory Systems of the Global South: The Indian Judiciary and Telecom Regulation (1991–2012)." In *The Rise of the Regulatory State of the South*, edited by Navroz K. Dubash and Bronwen Morgan, 136–162. Oxford: Oxford University Press.

Thun, Eric. 2006. *Changing Lanes in China: Foreign Direct Investment, Local Governments, and Auto Sector Development.* Cambridge: Cambridge University Press.

Thun, Eric and Timothy Sturgeon. 2019. "When Global Technology Meets Local Standards Reassessing China's Communications Policy in the Age of Platform Innovation." In *Policy, Regulation and Innovation in China's Electricity and Telecom Industries,* edited by Loren Brandt and Thomas Rawski, 177–220. Cambridge: Cambridge University Press.

Titov, N., and D. Galanin. 1960. "The Soviet Chemical Industry and Foreign Trade in Chemical Products." *Problems of Economics* 3(4):10–16.

Trachtenberg, Marc. 2009. *The Craft of International History: A Guide to Method.* Princeton: Princeton University Press.

Tsai, Kellee. 2002. *Back-Alley Banking: Private Entrepreneurs in China.* Ithaca: Cornell University Press.

2006. "Adaptive Informal Institutions and Endogenous Institutional Change in China." *World Politics* 59(1): 116–141.

2007. *Capitalism without Democracy: The Private Sector in Contemporary China.* Ithaca: Cornell University Press.

2016. "Adaptive Informal Institutions." In *The Oxford Handbook of Historical Institutionalism*, edited by Orfeo Fioretos, Tulia G. Falleti, and Adam Sheingate, 1–20. Oxford: Oxford University Press.

Tsai, Lily. 2007. *Accountability without Democracy: Solidary Groups and Public Goods Provision in Rural China*. Cambridge: Cambridge University Press.

Tudor, Maya. 2013. *The Promise of Power: The Origins of Democracy in India and Autocracy in Pakistan*. Cambridge: Cambridge University Press.

Vail, Mark. 2018. *Liberalism in Illiberal States: Ideas and Economic Adjustment in Contemporary Europe*. New York: Oxford University Press.

Van Wersch, Hubert W.M. 1992. *The Bombay Textile Strike, 1982–83*. Bombay: Oxford University Press.

Van der Kamp, Denise. 2020. "Blunt Force Regulation and Bureaucratic Control: Understanding China's War on Pollution." *Governance* (Early View: March 2020): 1–19.

Van Rooij, Benjamin, Rachel E. Stern, and Kathinka Fürst. 2014. "The Authoritarian Logic of Regulatory Pluralism: Understanding China's New Environmental Actors." *Regulation & Governance* 10(1): 3–13.

Varshney, Ashutosh. 1998. "Mass Politics or Elite Politics? India's Economic Reforms in Comparative Perspective." *The Journal of Policy Reform* 2(4): 301–335.

Verma, Samar. 2002. "Export Competitiveness of India Textile and Garment Industry." Working Paper No. 94. New Delhi: Indian Council for Research on International Economic Relations.

Vogel, Ezra F. 1991. *The Four Little Dragons: The Spread of Industrialization in East Asia*. Cambridge: Harvard University Press.

Vogel, Steven K. 1996. *Freer Markets, More Rules: Regulatory Reform in Advanced Industrialized Countries*. Ithaca: Cornell University Press.

2006. *Japan Remodeled: How Government and Industry Are Reforming Japanese Capitalism*. Ithaca: Cornell University Press.

2018. *Marketcraft: How Governments Make Markets Work*. New York: Oxford University Press.

Vu, Tuong. 2010. *Paths to Development in Asia: South Korea, Vietnam, China, and Indonesia*. Cambridge: Cambridge University Press.

Wade, Robert. 1990. *Governing the Market: Economic Theory and the Role of Government in East Asian Industrialization*. Princeton: Princeton University Press.

2000. "Wheels Within Wheels: Rethinking the Asian Crisis and the Asian Model." *Annual Review of Political Science* 3(1): 85–115.

Wakeman, Frederic E. 1991. "Models of Historical Change: The Chinese State and Society, 1939–1989." In *Perspectives on Modern China: Four Anniversaries*, edited by Thomas Bernstein et al., 68–102. Armonk: M. E. Sharpe.

Wang, Alex. 2013. "The Search for Sustainable Legitimacy: Environmental Law and Bureaucracy in China." *Harvard Environmental Law Review* 37(2): 365–440.

Wang, Xiaohong. 2005. "Policy Suggestion on How to Use Foreign Funds to Reorganize State-Owned Enterprises." *Macroeconomics* February: 43–46. (In Chinese).

Wang, Yuhua. 2016. "Beyond Local Protectionism: China's State–Business Relations in the Last Two Decades." *The China Quarterly* 226: 319–341.

Wang, Yuhua, and Carl Minzner. 2015. "The Rise of the Chinese Security State." *The China Quarterly* 222: 339–359.

Ward, Chris. 1990. *Russia's Cotton Workers and the New Economic Policy: Shop-Floor Culture and State Policy 1921–1929*. New York: Cambridge University Press.

Wedeman, Andrew. 2012. *Double Paradox: Rapid Growth and Rising Corruption in China*. Ithaca: Cornell University Press.

2018. "The Rise of Kleptocracy: Does China Fit the Model?" *Journal of Democracy* 29(1): 86–95.

Weinberg, Robert. 1993. *The Revolution in 1905 in Odessa: Blood on the Steps*. Bloomington: Indiana University Press.

Weiss, Jessica Chen. 2014. *Powerful Patriots: Nationalist Protest in China's Foreign Relations*. Oxford: Oxford University Press.

Weiss, Linda. 2003. *States in the Global Economy: Bringing Domestic Institutions Back In*. Cambridge: Cambridge University Press.

Wengle, Susanne. 2012. "Post-Soviet Developmentalism and the Political Economy of Russia's Electricity Sector Liberalization." *Studies in Comparative International Development* 47(1): 75–114.

2015. *Post-Soviet Power: State-Led Development and Russia's Marketization*. Cambridge: Cambridge University Press.

Weyland, Kurt. 2006. *Bounded Rationality and Policy Diffusion*. Princeton: Princeton University Press.

2007. "Toward a New Theory of Institutional Change." *World Politics* 60: 281–314.

White House. 2019. Executive Order on Securing the Information and Communications Technology and Services Supply Chain.

Whiting, Susan. 1999. *Power and Wealth in Rural China: The Political Economy of Institutional Change*. Cambridge: Cambridge University Press.

Wilbur, C. Martin. 1984. *The Nationalist Revolution in China, 1923–1928*. Cambridge: Cambridge University Press.

Wilensky, Harold L. 2002. *Rich Democracies: Political Economy, Public Policy, and Performance*. Berkeley: University of California Press.

Woo-Cumings, Meredith. 1991. *Race to the Swift: State and Finance in Korean Industrialization*. New York: Columbia University Press.

1999. *The Developmental State*. Ithaca: Cornell University Press.

Woodruff, David. 1999. *Money Unmade: Barter and the Fate of Russian Capitalism*. Ithaca: Cornell University Press.

2004. "Property Rights in Context: Privatization's Legacy for Corporate Legality in Poland and Russia." *Studies in Comparative International Development* 38(4): 82–108.

World Bank. Various Years. Statistical Datasets and Reports.

Wright, Teresa. 2001. *The Perils of Protest: State Repression and Student Activism in China and Taiwan*. Honolulu: University of Hawaii Press.

2018. *Popular Protest in China*. Cambridge: Polity Press.

Wu, Yu-Shan. 1995. *Comparative Economic Transformations: Mainland China, Hungary, the Soviet Union, and Taiwan*. Stanford: Stanford University Press.

Xu, Zhangrun. 2018. "Imminent Fears, Imminent Hopes." Online Critique Beijing. Unirule Institute of Economics. July 24.

Yakubovich, Valery, and Stanislav Shekshnia. 2012. "The Emergence of the Russian Mobile Telecom Market." In *The Emergence of Organizations and Markets*, edited by John F. Padgett and Walter W. Powell, 334–346. Princeton: Princeton University Press.

Yang, Guobin. 2009. *The Power of the Internet in China: Citizen Activism Online*. New York: Columbia University Press.

  ed. 2015. *China's Contested Internet*. Copenhagen: NiAS Press.

Yang, Dali L. 2004. *Remaking the Chinese Leviathan*. Stanford: Stanford University Press.

Yasuda, John. 2017. *On Feeding the Masses: An Anatomy of Regulatory Failure in China*. Cambridge: Cambridge University Press.

Ye, Min. 2014. *Diasporas and Foreign Direct Investment in China and India*. New York: Cambridge University Press.

  2020. *The Belt Road and Beyond: State-Mobilized Globalization in China: 1998–2018*. Cambridge: Cambridge University Press.

Yeh, Wen-hsin. 1996. *Provincial Passages: Culture, Space, and the Origins of Chinese Communism*. Berkeley: University of California Press.

Yeo, Yukyung. 2020. *Varieties of State Regulation: How China Regulates Its Socialist Market Economy*. Cambridge: Harvard University Press.

Yeung, Henry Wai-Chung. 2016. *Strategic Coupling: East Asian Industrial Transformation in the New Global Economy*. Ithaca: Cornell University Press.

Zhao, Guoqing (2006). "In Search of China's Optimum Degree of Dependence of GDP upon FDI and in the Hunt for the Best Scale of FDI." *Management World* 1(0): 57–66.

Zheng, Wentong. 2017. "Untangling the Market and the State." *Emory Law Journal* 243(0): 243–291.

Zheng, Yongnian, and Yanjie Huang. 2018. *Market in State: The Political Economy of Domination in China*. Cambridge: Cambridge University Press.

Zhou, Bin. 2005. "Balance and Harmony: Principles for Adjusting Chinese FDI Utilization Policy." *Intertrade* 286(10): 51–55.

Ziegfeld, Adam. 2016. *Why Regional Parties? Clientelism, Elites, and the Indian Party System*. Cambridge: Cambridge University Press.

Zimin, Dmitry. 2007. From 2 to 72: An Illustrated Book. *Dynasty Foundation*. Available at www.dynastyfdn.com/english/zimin/book.

Zweig, David. 2002. *Internationalizing China*. Ithaca: Cornell University Press.

Zysman, John. 1983. *Governments, Markets, and Growth: Finance and the Politics of Industrial Change*. Ithaca: Cornell University Press.

  1994. "How Institutions Create Historically Rooted Trajectories of Growth." *Industrial and Corporate Change* 3(1): 244–283.

Index

For EU product safety concerns, contact us at Calle de José Abascal, 56–1°, 28003 Madrid, Spain or eugpsr@cambridge.org.

www.ingramcontent.com/pod-product-compliance
Ingram Content Group UK Ltd.
Pitfield, Milton Keynes, MK11 3LW, UK
UKHW042140130625
459647UK00011B/1116